PACIFIC
STARS AND STRIPES

THE FIRST
40 YEARS 1945 – 1985

PRESIDIO

Library of Congress Cataloging-in-Publication Data
Main entry under title:

Pacific stars and stripes.

    Includes index.
    1. United States--History, Military--
20th Century--Addresses, essays, lectures.
1. Pacific stars and stripes.
E745.P23   1985   973.92   85-9600
ISBN 0-89141-249-2 (paper)
ISBN 0-89141-255-7 (hardbound)

DEDICATION

These are the helmsmen who, as Editor-in-Chief, steered Pacific Stars and Stripes through peace and war, calm and stormy times. This book is respectfully dedicated to...

Maj. J.C. Parks (A)	Oct. 3, 1945—Jan. 27, 1946
Lt. J.P. Chamberlain (A)	Jan. 27, 1946—Feb. 3, 1946
Maj. K.L. Halverson (A)	Feb. 3, 1946—July 7, 1946
Capt. J.V. Field (A)	July 7, 1946—Dec. 22, 1946
Capt. C.B. Taylor (A)	Dec. 22, 1946—Dec. 14, 1948
Maj. F.W. May (A)	Dec. 14, 1948—May 15, 1950
Lt. Col. G.B. Schuyler (A)	May 15, 1950—June 14, 1951
Capt. S.B. Cardozo (A)	June 14, 1951—April 2, 1952
Lt. Col. J.E. Morgan (A)	April 2, 1952—Sept. 12, 1954
Lt. Col. E.E. Ewing (AF)	Sept. 13, 1954—Jan. 10, 1955
	July 10, 1955—March 10, 1956
Lt. Col. J.A. Klein (A)	Jan. 10, 1955—July 10, 1955
Lt. Col. W.H. Witt (A)	March 10, 1956—July 22, 1958
Maj. P.C. Rapp (A)	July 23, 1958—May 9, 1960
Lt. Col. J.P. Kelly (A)	May 10, 1960—July 24, 1963
Lt. Col. W.V. Schmitt (A)	July 25, 1963—July 24, 1967
Col. P.C. Sweers, Jr. (A)	July 24, 1967—July 22, 1969
Lt. Col. J.F. Townshend (AF)	July 22, 1969—Dec. 14, 1969
Col. W.V. Koch (A)	Dec. 14, 1969—June 30, 1972
Col. P.L. Mason (A)	July 1, 1973—Sept. 16, 1975
Lt. Col. J.W. Kinkele (AF)	Sept. 17, 1975—Dec. 23, 1975
Capt. H.E. Darton (N)	Dec. 24, 1975—Jan. 24, 1979
Col. R.F. Delaney (A)	Jan. 25, 1979—July 27, 1981
Col. J.E. Burlas (A)	July 18, 1981—July 27, 1984
Col. D.M. Mehigan (A)	July 27, 1984—June 27, 1985
Col. R.E. Stevenson (AF)	June 28, 1985—

(A) Army   (N) Navy   (AF) Airforce

...To the dedicated military and civilian staff members, some of whose names are printed on the inside covers...and to our devoted, beyond-count readers, all of them.

CONTENTS

FOREWORD

"These proceedings are closed," General of the Army Douglas MacArthur intoned on the deck of the battleship Missouri, saving for himself the curtain line on World War Two.

The signatures of Japanese Foreign Minister Mamoru Shigemitsu and General Yoshijiro Umezu were drying on freshly signed surrender documents. Thousands of Americans moved ashore to begin a temporary but meaningful occupation of defeated Japan — almost seven years to dismantle an aggressive military machine and restore the Japanese economy from feeble pulsebeat to full roar — to transform a vanquished enemy into a close friend.

Americans in Tokyo and points far beyond — all over troubled or tranquil Asia — would always have an informative friend.

Pacific Stars and Stripes.

Their own daily newspaper was one of the first American traditions imported ashore and one that would hang in for four decades. The right to know would be constant and reaffirmed, at any displaced American's fingertips.

This was a descendant of the daily soldier's newspaper founded in Paris in 1918, reborn in London in 1942. There were shortlived editions published in Honolulu and Shanghai in the last days of the Pacific War and one other newspaper, the Daily Pacifican, printed briefly in Manila. All were remotely related to single-page newssheets that followed troops on both sides of the Civil War.

Pacific Stars and Stripes reports to Oct. 3, 1945, as its founding date — a first edition printed in the face of formidable difficulties.

The occupation was but a few hours old when a two-man search team got into a jeep and drove through the streets of Tokyo — a devastated civic cemetery, full of ruins that were like broken headstones. The two explorers had most of the road to themselves — there was no other traffic except for olive drab military vehicles and charcoal-powered buses and taxicabs that left a bluish wake of blinding fume.

They easily found what they were looking for — the English-language Japan Times, which only days before had been publishing virulent anti-American propaganda. Requisitioning cramped but suitable office space, the team then traveled several blocks to the Asahi newspaper and took over the largest printing press in Asia.

At the Times, an editorial staff of 19 soldier newsmen wedged into working space so narrow that typewriter carriages regularly crashed into elbows. Two floors down, a few American printers moved among Japanese compositors.

The workday began as it would 40 years later: under an immense pile of news stories and features. These went from typewriter and teletype to editor before they were lowered on a jerry-built dumbwaiter, a bucket on a string, to printers — most of them the Japanese who read no English but could "sight-copy" it on a Linotype keyboard. Printers carried the newly set type in long trays as it was locked into "forms" that would become the printed pages. They moved cautiously, making carefully sure they didn't jostle anybody as they threaded through their limited workspace; it was too fearfully easy to collide with a co-worker and send a tray of loose type crashing to the floor.

The forms were moved to matting machines and five tons of pressure impressed the type, and every grain and detail of the zinc plates on which photographs had been engraved, onto a sheet of fibrous composition called a mat. On most papers, there would have been only a short walk to a foundry, where the mats would have been used to cast circular metal plates that would have then been attached to nearby presses to print the paper.

Not on Pacific Stars and Stripes — not in those hectic days. The mats were scooped up and rushed outside to a waiting jeep or motorcycle that sped long blocks to the Asahi — where the plates were cast and the newspaper finally printed. It was a hell of a way to run a daily newspaper but it had to do.

Once printed, that first edition moved — to points as close as MacArthur's headquarters at the Dai Ichi Insurance Building and on to all of Japan and Okinawa, the Philippines, Guam and the garrison that occupied the southern half of Korea, divided by drastic political surgery between the United States and the Soviet Union.

That first edition was hardly a collector's item; only four pages thick, it was an ungainly sheet that would have made a professor of journalism gasp. A kind of makeshift makeup jammed 28 stories on the front page, the largest and most important bringing the welcome news that readers with 60 or more rotation points — awarded for length of time overseas — of being home for Christmas.

Another story might have been taken as an ominous kind of prophecy. It told of an impending clash between French troops and Annamese rebels in Indochina.

As stodgy and unimpressive as that first edition looked, it was the cornerstone of a tradition. For forty years, it would dispassionately report as Japan became a soaring economic phoenix. It would chronicle wars, sweeping gains in science and technology, decades of explosive crisis and kaleidoscopic changes on the face of the globe.

Pacific Stars and Stripes has twice mastered the most drastic test of a newspaper's mettle — covering a war.

Its newsmen were also soldiers, and had to take a soldier's chances to do a newsman's job. This was not done without risk or cost. Cpl. Ernie Peeler and Pvt. Hal Gamble were dispatched to the Korean battlefront, right behind the first American infantry ordered in to fight a fingerhold delaying action. Peeler and Gamble lived as hard as the riflemen, foraging for fact and food, knowledgeably quoting Clauswitz as they wrote of a new war that was only five years behind the last.

As the flood of invading North Koreans reached the flashpoint and threatened to spill all the way down the peninsula, Peeler vanished — drove out of besieged Taejon with another correspondent into a grimly anonymous limbo: missing in action.

Years later, Peeler would be declared officially dead.

For the rest of a war that moved from promise of victory to paralytic stalemate, outstanding Stripes correspondents like John Sack, Bill Fitzgerald and Murray Fromson ducked shellfire, quarreled with censors and used the hoods of jeeps as worktables as they hammered out stories. Newsmen wearing the Stripes shield patch walked neutral ground at Kaesong and Panmunjom, watching Communist negotiators fire invective across a green felt-covered table at patient American negotiators. When a truce stilled the shooting, Stripes had its own stirring, distant-trumpet story to tell of that.

Years later, a Stripes correspondent would say he found the final episode of the TV series, "MASH," to be dramatically fine, but with one large flaw.

"They made it look as though after the Armistice was signed, the war was over and everybody went home," he complained. "That sure as hell didn't happen."

He was speaking in a restaurant in Seoul, making an early-to-bed pledge to himself because a Stripes news team had to be up early to cover Exercise Team Spirit, a massive annual readiness exercise that pairs an American division — still in place close to a silent battlefront — with South Koreans and other Americans airlifted from Hawaii and California.

A truce frequently flawed by gunfire is still in force, and the two sides have never moved. close to settlement or treaty. Stripes is still there.

In the late 1950s, Stripes sent its photo chief, Sandy Colton, in a trip around Southeast Asia — Laos, Cambodia and Vietnam, regarded by most Americans as benign and scenic.

Colton didn't see it that way, turning in a telling picture story of American advisers training South Vietnamese — priming them for a backcountry bush war that was growing in velocity and size.

By 1963, Stripes had a fulltime bureau there, manned by an enterprising Marine sergeant, Steve Stibbens, and staffers on loan from Tokyo. When controversial President Ngo Dinh Diem and his brother, Ngo Dinh Nhu, were overthrown and killed by their own army, communications were shut down and on-the-spot newsmen had no way to get their story out. Al Kramer, on the Stripes desk in Tokyo, managed to pry through with a long-distance call and got an Asia-wide scoop.

Stibbens, a man seldom seen in Saigon, was often first out of a helicopter on an assault — one of the very few of the very first to cover the conflict as it expanded and thousands of Americans swarmed in. The bureau, first on Troung Tan Buu and then Vo Tanh in the capital, was full of light and life at all hours, for this was a war that never went to sleep. Kim Ki Sam, pulled out of South Korea to help out in South Vietnam, had men killed on both sides of him as he covered a battle near the edge of North Vietnam.

Gary Cooper, a Navy man stained with infantry mud, walked with a squad that ran into a large force of Viet Cong and was inches away from being annihilated — saved by a map Cooper took from a wounded man and gave to a sergeant. A radio message brought an approaching rifle company in for a just-in-time rescue.

On April 18, 1969, the worst thing happened — another man lost. Spec. 5 Paul D. Savanuck, on the newspaper for only a few weeks, was slain in a firefight in Quang Tri province.

Stripes people were there — all the way.

The world turned in ceaseless change and Stripes readers, through their newspaper, saw it all.

The face and surroundings of Stripes would change, too — from that commandeered, closet-sized working space into a rambling wooden bungalow that put typewriters and presses under the same roof. In 1962, staff and newspaper moved a few feet from that site into a $2 million, four-story building — built and leased to them by the Japanese government, now a provider and treaty partner.

In future years, the newspaper would close down its composing room, doing away with the noisy and noxious Linotype machines that used molten lead to cast lines of type. Coldtype computers were installed, able to set stories in print immediately after they were typed and edited. At this writing, Pacific Stars and Stripes is one of the few American newspapers with full pagination — the ability to assemble news pages entirely by computer.

And bureaus in Japan, Korea, Okinawa, the Philippines and Guam still get the daily story from flightline or foxhole, cockpit or four-star executive suite.

It's all changed at Pacific Stars and Stripes — and yet hasn't changed at all.

Read on now, and know us better — from that stained and dusty first front page to now.

FIRST STRIPES HOME, from 1945 until 1953, was the third floor of the Japan Times, where the staff covered the Occupation and the Korean War in cramped but adequate space. One large minus in that operation was that the newspaper had to be written at the Times and printed several blocks down at the Asahi Shimbun.

WITH TYPEWRITERS AND PRESSES under one roof, Pacific Stars and Stripes used this building — a kind of bungalow on stilts — for nine years. It was on a corner of Hardy Barracks, which had once been an Imperial Army headquarters.

STRIPES TODAY prints in this four-story building that is full of space and light and would have been unimaginable to the soldier newsmen who put out that first front page. The paper is written, edited and set into type on automated computers and is one of the very few with full pagination — pages composed and assembled on a computer screen. Stripes is old but growing young and modern.

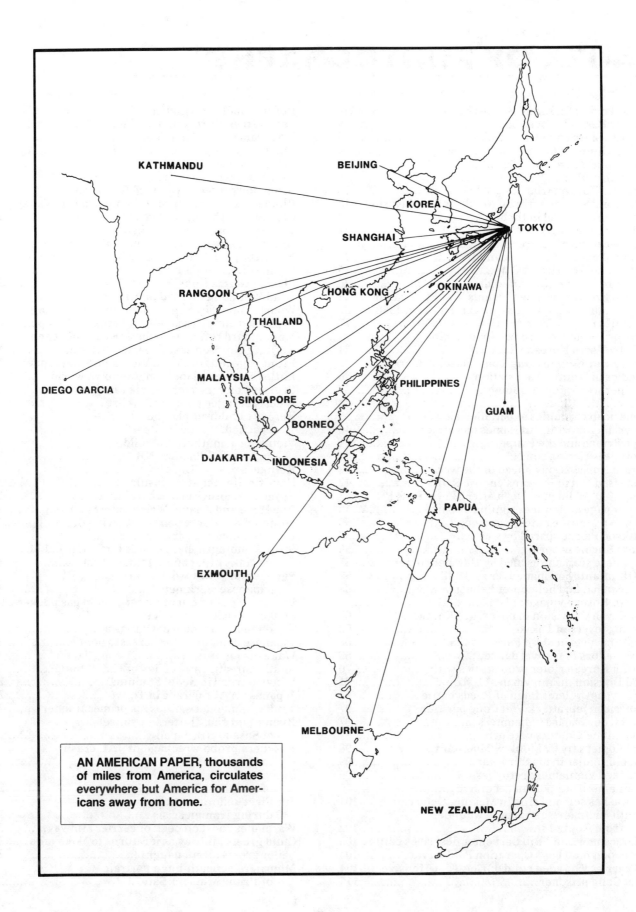

KATHMANDU

BEIJING

KOREA

TOKYO

SHANGHAI

RANGOON

HONG KONG

OKINAWA

THAILAND

DIEGO GARCIA

MALAYSIA

PHILIPPINES

SINGAPORE

GUAM

BORNEO

DJAKARTA

INDONESIA

PAPUA

EXMOUTH

MELBOURNE

AN AMERICAN PAPER, thousands of miles from America, circulates everywhere but America for Americans away from home.

NEW ZEALAND

INDEX OF PHOTOGRAPHS

THE OCCUPATION YEARS

1945-1950

STARS AND *Pacific* STRIPES

PUBLISHED DAILY IN TOKYO   **FOR U.S. FORCES**   **IN JAPAN AND KOREA**

VOLUME 1, NUMBER 1   DISTRIBUTION: FREE   WEDNESDAY, OCTOBER 3, 1945

ANNAMESE GIRD FOR BATTLE IN INDO-CHINA

Casualties Mount as Rebellion Continues; Java Is New Hot Spot

SAIGON (ANS-AP)—As rebellious Indo-China natives appeared Tuesday to be gathering on the outskirts of Saigon for a concerted attack on 1,000 French reinforcements who were to land Wednesday, late totalling of casualties for last week's sporadic fighting rose to 319 dead and 234 wounded, of whom at least 100 were French civilians.

Th Annamese are reported to have a force of 20,000 men, of whom three-fourths are said to be armed.

Meanwhile, an unestimated number of armed natives are said to be massing in the southern sector.

The Associated Press reported that the British commander of the Saigon Control Commission had ordered active participation of Japanese troops in an effort to quell the Annamese.

Chinese Ask Questions

In Chungking it was reported that the Chinese foreign office had instructed the embassy in Washington to ask the Siamese minister to the United States for an explanation of the recent clashes in Bangkok between the Chinese and Siamese.

The Chinese asked what steps were being taken to prevent a recurrence and what compensation was being arranged for the victims. The influential newspaper, Takungpao, Demanded that Siam be completely disarmed and put under Allied control. It urged punishment for all Siamese war criminals, pro-Japanese and fascist perpetrators of

(Continued on Page 4)

'MAGIC CARPET' TO TAKE VETS HOME

2,000,000 Pacific Troops Due Boat Ride

(By Combined Press Service)

A Naval 'magic carpet' that will take home 2,000,000 Pacific servicemen within the next 12 months began operating Tuesday when the aircraft carrier, Ticonderoga, left Honolulu carrying 2,500 service personnel.

Code name for the operation is 'magic carpet,' the Navy announced. Barring unforseen changes in the Japanese occupation plan, it will be using 40 escort carriers and 200 attack transports by the end of the year.

Some 400,000 men from the Pacific are to reach Stateside ports within the next three months, the army revealed. Tentative plans will send 75,000 home in October, 141,000 in November, and 180,000 in December. Planes were due for an increasing role. A Tokyo announcement said US troops in China within about 10 days will start flying to Shanghai to board ships. Two hundred fifty planes will shuttle men to the No. 1 Chinese port from Chungking, Liuchow, Chengtau and Chinking. The overall demobilization picture was clarified in statistics released

(Continued on Page 4)

London Train Wreck —Kills 28; Injures 94

LONDON (ANS)—Twenty-eight persons were killed and 94 injured when the Scottish Express locomotive and six front coaches of the London-bound train plunged over an embankment 30 miles from London Monday night as it neared the end of its 450-mile journey from Perth Scotland.

The train ground itself into a heap of steel 30 feet high after hitting an open switch.

Home-Bound Yanks Set Speed Record in B-29s

Sacramento, Calif. (ANS)—Completing a 2,900 mile hop from Hawaii 25 minutes ahead of schedule, 14 B-29s of the global 20th Air Force landed at Mather field this morning. They brought home the first of a large group of Superfortress airmen set for demobilization.

The Weather

Japan north of Tokyo—Cloudy with drizzles Wednesday, cloudy with rain Thursday; little change in temperatures.

Japan south of Tokyo—Cloudy with showers Wednesday, cloudy and colder Thursday.

Korea—Rain Wednesday, cloudy and colder Thursday.

Truman Looks In

WASHINGTON—President Truman paid an unprecedented visit to the opening session of the Supreme Court and saw his first nominee to a high bench, Harold H. Burton of Ohio, sworn in as an associate justice. Court attaches said the visit was the first made by a president in the 125-year history of the high tribunal.

FRESH FOODSTUFFS ARRIVING SOON

Thirty Days' Supply Due in at Yokohama

YOKOHAMA—Hungry GIs in Japan soon will polish their biscuspids on fresh pork chops and potatoes. An 8th Army source said that a refrigerator ship, hauling fresh foodstuffs and steaming north from Okinawa, was due in Yokohama shortly.

The ship is jam-packed with meat, stuffs. It is carrying a 30 days' stuffs. It is carrying a 30 days' supply of fresh food for all units drawing rations from the 8t Army, which occupies the Tokyo area and Northern Honshu. There is everything aboard except fresh eggs, which will be shipped up at a later date.

The refrigerator ship will anchor off Yokohama and barges will bring the foodstuff ashore. When the refrigerator ship's supplies run low, other boats carrying food from the States and from Manila will replenish its larder. This will make it unnecessary to erect extensive reefer facilities at the Quartermaster depots.

To further appease the GI palate, Army agencies are looking for facilities for making icecream. PX supplies are expected to arrive in the near future. Army officials predict that life in Japan soon will be even more cushy than it was in Manila.

Current plans call for the Army to feed its men without drawing upon Japanese food foodstuffs, since the civilian food shortage here would become even more critical. Diet staples now are canned B-rations. But an Army official states that chow in Japan soon will be equivalent to GI meals in the States.

Six Corregidor Vets Given Purple Hearts To Go With Freedom

TOKYO (INS)—General MacArthur has announced the award of the Purple Heart for wounds received three and a half years ago on Corregidor to the following recently-liberated war prisoners:

Pvts, Estil J. Cohorn, Covington, Ky; Leland Crumett, Vale, Ore; George W. Middleton, Wichita, Kan; Willie Templin, Coleman, Tex.; Joseph Viterna, Lackawanna, N.Y.; and Franklin L. Wiggs, Augusta, Ark.

'Democracy' Heard In Chinese Confabs

CHUNGKING, (AP)—A program designed to erase the difference between the Chinese communists and Kuomintang has emerged from current conferences, it was announced Tuesday. Final decision hinges on whether the communists yield in their demand for virtual autonomy. Danger of failure still is prevalent but prospects are brighter.

The program includes formation of a political council of all parties; peaceful reconstruction; recognition of the equal status of different political parties; punishment of traitors; disbanding of puppets; democratization of politics; nationalization of armies; release of political prisoners; and abolition of laws at variance with freedoms enjoyed by other democratic countries.

Japanese Air Force Demobilized by GHQ

TOKYO (UP)—General MacArthur's headquarters announced yesterday the complete demobilization of the Imperial Japanese general air force.

All Japanese matters pertaining to the air are now handled by the U.S. Army aeronautical headquarters.

308th At Seoul

FIFTH AIR FORCE, Korea—Headquarters of the 308th Bomb Wing of the Fifth Air Force, air arm occupying Korea, has been established at Keijo University in Seoul, capital city of Korea.

ANOTHER FIRST FOR THE FIRST

YOU ARE NOW ENTERING **TOKYO** *Courtesy of* **1st CAVALRY DIVISION** *The First Team* **FIRST IN MANILA   FIRST IN TOKYO**

The First Cavalry Division rang up another record and is telling the world about it. First in Manila, the First Cav has been selected as honor guards of Tokyo.

Pacific Stars & Stripes Photo

World Government For Atomic Power Control Recommended By Roberts

(By Combined Press Services)

WASHINGTON—With the U.S. and the world awaiting a message this week from President Truman baring his recommendations for control of the atomic bomb, former Supreme Court Justice Owen D. Roberts and 38 other prominent Americans recommended establishment of a world government to control the bombs.

"Let us be done with 'Big Threes,' Big Fours and Big Fives," said the group in a direct appeal to the President. "Let us have the Big One."

A world government, the recommendation stated, would prevent battles over atomic power.

Meanwhile, the President has conferred with Prime Minister Mackenzie King of Canada. It was understood the two leaders discussed problems of atomic power, since Canada is one of the countries now sharing the secret.

The President characterized the conversation as "interesting and important" and said they were satisfactory.

House Says "Keep Secret"

The House appropriations subcommittee, meanwhile, recommended to President Truman Tuesday that the secret of atomic energy be kept by the United States pending a study of its development by a commission of scientists.

One scientist, Larry Crosby, head of the Crosby Research Foundation, said that a defense technique had been devised against the atomic bomb, so simple that bombs can be detonated without knowing their exact location. No details were announced, but Crosby said the

(Continued on Page 4)

Red Light Off

TOKYO—Military Police have placed more than a hundred houses of prostitution off-limits to soldiers and sailors by order of Brig. Gen Hugh Hoffman, Provost Marshal of Tokyo. The action by the MPs was taken on Monday and Tuesday after a medical survey showed that most of the women had at least one venereal disease. In one area, almost 100% of the women were contaminated.

In another order by the Provost Marshal of Tokyo, most Military Police, with the exception of those guarding prisoners, money and occupied buildings, were prohibited from carrying sidearms.

DEGAULLISTS WIN IN LOCAL VOTING

National Victory Seen At Oct. 21 Elections

PARIS (ANS)—Nearly complete results of the run-off balloting for local French government offices apparently assured victory for the DeGaulle policies in the national elections October 21.

Returns covering nearly 2,400 of 3,028 councillors general to administer French departments give the DeGaulle Socialists and affiliate groups 844 seats. Leon Blum's Radical Socialists followed with 693. The Rightist parties won 530 seats Communists, 321.

Passenger Sky Giant Reaches Calcutta In Globe Hopping Trip

CALCUTTA, (ANS)—Five minutes ahead of schedule the globe encircling Globster, giant C-54, arrived in Calcutta yesterday and then hopped off for Dufiang, China.

Nineteen passengers picked up in Cairo increased the passenger list to 28, all air corps crewmen bound for China and India. The C-54, which left Washington Friday afternoon and is expected back late tomorrow, picked up two hours lost in rain and fog over the Azores in the Atlantic crossing and passed into the "hot" phase of its flight.

The trip from Tripoli to Cairo measuring 1,097 miles, was made in five hours and 13 minutes.

World News Coverage Now On Daily GI Menu

This is the first issue of Pacific Stars and Stripes, the daily newspaper for U.S. occupational forces in Japan and Korea.

In addition to its coverage of events and activities among members of the armed services in the occupational zones of Japan and Korea, Pacific Stars and Stripes will furnish a complete relay of news from the United States and other parts of the world. This is the first issue of the news provided through Army News Service, Associated Press, United Press and International News Service.

The newspaper is published in Tokyo by the Information and Education Detachment, GHQ AFPAC. Editorial offices are on the third floor of the Nippon Times plant; circulation and business offices on the fourth floor of Radio Tokyo.

Free distribution by truck, train and plane will be made to members of the U.S. armed services in all parts of Japan and Korea. Units are invited to appoint news correspondents for Pacific Stars and Stripes. Individual contributions of news items, feature stories and pictures will be welcomed. All correspondence should be signed, and should be addressed to Pacific Stars and Stripes, Tokyo, APO 500.

Allies To Relinquish Large Portion of Italy

WASHINGTON (AP)—All of Italy with the exception of small areas on the Yugoslav border will be turned back to Italian control late this fall, the Allied commission announced today.

At the same time, the political section commission abolished the political advice being given Italians by the British and American embassies. The commission's report disclosed that Italian naval, air and land forces gave the Allied forces heavy support as co-belligerents with the Army in combat against the Germans as early as March, 1944.

Korean Occupation Ousting Japanese

SEOUL (AP)—Latest reports in Korea indicate that American occupation of this peninsula is progressing smoothly.

Following early criticism that American forces were relying too heavily on Japanese officials in establishing a temporary control for the liberated country, indications now are that the policy of weeding out all Japanese is being strictly adhered to, with a steady increase in number of Koreans in the government.

Halsey Ready to Bow Out

Honolulu (AP)—Admiral Halsey has announced that he was asked to be retired. "I am an old man," he said. "Let the young fellows take over."

Christmas at Home Possible for 60s

By Cpl. PETER GRODSKY
Pacific Stars and Stripes Staff Writer

YOKOHAMA—Enlisted men with as low as 60 points have "a fair chance" of being home for Christmas, Col. L. B. Shaw, the Eighth Army's G-1 executive officer, predicted yesterday, emphasizing that only a shortage of shipping facilities will prevent completion of that goal.

"There's not an empty bunk on any sort of vessel or plane bound for the States which is not being used to return men for discharge," Colonel Shaw declared.

The Eighth Army expects to have shipping available to send back 34,000 officers and enlisted men during October, and 38,000 during November.

Thousands of enlisted men became eligible for discharge on October 1, when the War Department lowered the score to 70 points. Additional thousands will become eligible November 1, when points drop to 60.

However, having points in the 60s and 70s does not mean that on October 2 or November 2 all men within those groups will board Stateside-bound vessels. Men will be called from their units as soon as shipping is available, with the highest-point men getting first call.

Once a man is called out of his outfit, he knows that shipping is available for him and that he won't be in the replacement depot for more than an average of 48 hours.

He will be "processed" at the depot, meaning that his personal records—pay, allotment, clothing, service record, etc.—are brought up to date.

"Processing" will not delay a man's departure, said Colonel Shaw. He told of an instance where a Navy ship radioed it would have room for 112 men, but could stop for just a few hours. The men were hastily summoned to the depot, processed and on their way home the same day. Though the replacement depot in Yokohama has just been set up and can handle about 50 men a day, by October 15 it will be able to accommodate 10,000 men. As the need grows, the depot will be expanded.

There have been instances—and there are probably cases now—the colonel asserted, where high point men are in Japan, while lower point men are on their way home. He explained that these men who should have been on their way earlier are now being given priority on discharge.

Those men haven't left yet due to the fact that they or their records were probably in transit when the lower point men were sent back to the States. "It's strictly a transitional problem and is being rectified," Colonel Shaw declared.

Army headquarters is keeping a close tab on units to assure their prompt compliance with demobilization, officials reported.

No C. O. can hold any enlisted man eligible for discharge—with very few enumerated exceptions—until a replacement comes. The C. O. has no alternative but to let the man go home. He may keep an officer, for 60 days beyond the time he becomes eligible.

Any man who feels he is being retained unjustly may report it to his local Inspector General's office and expect to receive satisfaction. The War Departments regulations on the duties of the C. O. with regard to discharge are very clear, experts agree.

UNION CLAIMS AUTO MAKERS STIR STRIKES

R. J. Thomas Charges Companies Not Ready For Reconversion

CHICAGO (ANS)—R. J. Thomas, international president of the United Automobile Workers, CIO, Tuesday charged automobile manufacturers with being "on strike," and declared they were seeking to provoke labor troubles now because they were not ready for reconversion.

"The automotive industry, and not the union, is on strike," Thomas said at a meeting of 150 UAW regional representatives. "Cutting of wages and provoking of grievances are aimed at getting unions to strike at this time."

Thomas said the Ford Company's dismissal of workers because of a strike at Kelsey Hayes Company, manufacturers of Ford wheels, was unjustified.

"Kelsey Hayes Company was not the only source of supply for wheels of the Ford Motor Company," he said. "No firm as large as Ford has only one source of supply. If we settled the Kelsey Hayes strike tonight, Ford still would not open tomorrow."

Nation's Strike Idle Cut As Workers Return

CHICAGO (ANS)—Strike idleness throughout the country fell to approximately 352,000 Tuesday, in the first major reduction in more than a week.

The total was whittled down as 38,000 white collar workers of Westinghouse Electric Company, who struck September 9 in demand for bonus or incentive pay plans, voted to return to work. This strike had spread to 14 plants in Pennsylvania, Ohio, New Jersey, Massachusetts, Maryland and New York.

Lee F. Bollens, president of the Federation of Westinghouse Salaried Unions, said members had voted to go back pending outcome of negotiations.

(Continued on Page 4)

Argentine Government Frees Revolutionists

BUENOS AIRES (ANS)—Tension appeared to be relaxing in Argentina today following the release of hundreds of persons detained last week under a state of siege proclaimed by the military government.

Gen. Arturo Rawson, who led the abortive revolt by the Cordoba garrison which helped precipitate the state of siege, had been flown to Buenos Aires for questioning by Vice President Juan Peron.

ODs by Oct. 10, Army Promises

TOKYO—The U.S. Army soon will take action against the bers and chills of the Japanese climate. A GHQ spokesman revealed Tuesday that men will be issued winter OD uniforms by Oct. 10.

Men stationed in northern Japan and in the mountainous areas where the cold becomes most bitter will be first on the priority list for the issue. In the meantime, to make sure that there are britches and shirts and jackets for everyone, the Army is maintaining a continuous shipment of cold weather garments.

Tokyo to Have Face Washed

TOKYO (INS)—Needled by caustic comments of Allied correspondents, the Japanese have proclaimed a cleanup drive during which every effort will be made to brighten the face of Tokyo. Face-lifting began Monday, will extend through the 10th.

8 MILLION IDLE BY NEXT SPRING

Jobs, Demobilization Fail to Keep Pace

WASHINGTON (ANS)—Reconversion Director John W. Snyder said Tuesday there might be 8,000,000 unemployed by next spring with "high unemployment" persisting through 1946.

He made this prediction in a 40-page report to the President and Congress.

Snyder's forecast was based on the contention that job-giving will be unable to keep pace with a prospective million-a-month demobilization.

He said 4,700,000 men would be released from the Army and 3,000,000 from the Navy by next July.

But he was "firmly optimistic" about the future, provided the nation works as a team. He asserted:

1. Prompt peaceful settlement of labor-management differences is a reconversion must.

2. Congress should act promptly on those four points in the presidents program calling for full employment, transitional tax adjustments, broadening and raising unemployment compensation and raising minimum wages.

The tax steps recommended were repeal of the three per cent normal tax on individuals, repeal of excess profits tax effective Jan. 1, 1946, and setting a definite date for reducing excises.

3. The executive branch "must and will be as vigorous in its policies and programs to solve peacetime problems as it was in solving wartime problems."

"Cooperation and teamwork among management and labor; business and farmer; federal, state, and local governments, is indispensable if there is to be rapid expansion of peacetime production, jobs for all those willing and able to work and stable markets for business.

Pointing to prospects of about 8,000,000 unemployed by spring, Snyder said the country must face the fact that substantial unemployment lies ahead.

"That in itself will not stamp reconversion successful or unsuccessful. It takes time for industry to turn around to stop work on munitions and retool for work on peacetime products," he said.

Shakeup in Japanese Cabinet Rumored In Capitol This Week

TOKYO (INS)—Tokyo buzzed today with undercurrent rumors of an imminent major shakeup in the Japanese cabinet under premiership of Prince Naruhiko Higashikuni.

With Nippon public newspapers called for retirement of Japanese war leaders from political, economic and other fields to "make way for men of ability to assume leadership in the new Japan," observers said the Japanese was "not to stick out necks" for fear that they would land on MacArthur's war criminal list when their names are checked against wartime records.

However, they also pointed out that if potential leaders all crawl into shells for fear of allied action, occupation forces will face a tough time administering the country without Japanese leads to lead their own country along democratic lines as outlined by the allies.

The main upheaval expected by many high ranking Japanese will come after Oct. 15 when complete disarmament of all Japanese services is scheduled to be completed.

One of the most serious hurdles facing Higashikuni appears to be the intense popular dislike of some men mentioned for cabinet posts despite their asserted non-affiliation with wartime machines.

Urges Carefulness

NEWTON, Mass. (UP)—To remind motorists that the end of gasoline rationing does not mean the start of a new era of speed, the Newton Police Department has posted signs reading: "Motorists be careful. Remember—death is permanent."

Raw Rubber Hits U.S. From Pacific

SAN FRANCISCO (ANS)—The Goodyear Tire and Rubber company Tuesday announced receipt of the nation's first shipment of crude rubber from the Pacific since Pearl Harbor.

Forty-two tons of crude—produced under the noses of the Japanese in the Philippines—were landed in San Francisco by the steamer Thomas Nelson.

"HE FEARED FOR JAPAN"

DEC. 17, 1945 BY SGT. PETER GRODSKY
OGIKUBO, Japan — Prince Fumimaro Konoye, three-time premier of Japan and close adviser to the emperor, committed suicide by swallowing poison Sunday, the day he was to have submitted to arrest on war criminal charges. He declared he could not "stand the humiliation of being apprehended and tried by the American court."

In a note which he hastily penciled in Japanese at 1 a.m. in the bedroom of his suburban Tokyo home, the aristocratic political leader declared: "It is indeed a matter of great regret to have been named as a war criminal by the United States, with whom I wanted and tried to work together for a peaceful solution of Pacific affairs."

General MacArthur on Dec. 6 ordered the arrest of the prince and other prominent political figures in Japan, giving the Japanese government 10 days in which to deliver them to Sugamo prison in Tokyo.

Tomohiko Ushiba, long-time secretary to the 54-year-old Konoye, reported that the prince's wife, Princess Chiyoko, found the body. She noticed the light was on in his adjoining room at about 6 a.m. and upon investigation found the prince stretched out on the Japanese-style bed on the floor, clad only in pajamas, with a small empty bottle beside him.

The prince had an informal party of about 10 intimate friends and a few members of the family the night before and Ushiba said he appeared in good spirits but looked a bit tired. Though he gave no indication of his intentions, Ushiba said the conversations indicated, in hindsight, he may have had suicide in mind.

"He was very pessimistic about the future of Japan," asserted the sad-faced secretary who had worked with the prince for 10 years. "He was greatly concerned about the emperor and was also concerned about the extreme attitude the press had taken since it had become free."

Writing his impressions of things discussed, his second son, Michitaka, disclosed that his father had prepared some memoranda on the process of conversations between Japan and America during his second and third cabinet and the other on the tripartite alliance.

"He put down all he wanted to say about those matters in the documents," said the 22-year-old son, "and wants to be judged by these documents."

Michitaka did not immediately reveal that his father had given him the early-morning note. It was found only after he had been questioned by investigators under Lt. Col. B.E. Sackett, former New York FBI chief and chief investigator for War Crimes Prosecutor Joseph B. Keenan.

Though the prince was dressed in pajamas when he swallowed the fatal drug, reporters were not allowed to view his body until he had been clad in the white ceremonial kimono.

Meanwhile, procesutor Keenan asserted there was not "the slightest justification for any innocent man taking his own life."

"No person confined as a suspect need fear unless his own conscience insists on or emphasizes his guilt," declared the American prosecutor.

The last chapter in the Konoye tragedy was written on Dec. 8, 1967, when a story in Pacific Stars and Stripes told of the discovery of Konoye's diary on the eve of the 26th anniversary of the Pearl Harbor attack. It recounted his role in the "coup of senior statesmen" who forced the resignation of militarist premier Hideki Tojo. Written in the last days of the Pacific War, the diary told of Konoye's desire for peace — and his fears that an Allied invasion might bring exiled Communist leader Sanzo Nosaka back to seize power.

USA

GINZA AND Z, the Times Square of Tokyo and a landmark thousands of Americans would know, looked like this on Oct. 3, 1945 — the day Pacific Stars and Stripes first printed in a conquered enemy capital. The Wako Department Store, with its cathedral-like clock tower, was one of the very few downtown buildings that came out of the fire raids whole and unhollowed by flame. At right, the smudged shell of the Mitsukoshi Department Store would be torn down and a new facade built over its steel bones. The rubble heap across the street would make way for the Lion Beer Hall — today the site of an auto agency.

The atomic bomb had made a barren wilderness of two cities and seemed more than a match for a mere battleship — even one of the largest and most powerful ever built. The Nagato, once the grey and princely pride of the Japanese Imperial Fleet, had barely survived the costly Philippine Sea battle. Now she was the only surviving capital warship of defeated Japan. Her demise, under the atomic mushroom off Kwajalein, was to be ignoble and symbolic. Sgt. John Hancock did a fine feature on the Nagato's proud past and impending doom.

EXECUTION BY A-BOMB

FEB. 17, 1946 BY SGT. JOHN HANCOCK
    YOKOSUKA, Japan — Riding at anchor here is the once-mighty Nagato, sole surviving battle-wagon of the Japanese Imperial Navy. And soon even this dubious distinction will be denied her. In remote waters off the Marshall Islands this May, the Nagato has a rendezvous with the A-Bomb.

Daily the Navy grooms her for her date with destruction. Technicians poke around her vast innards, readying her engines, boilers, and electrical system for her historic one-way voyage.

This 25-year-old sea fortress is rusty, bomb-twisted, plastered with barnacles. Sitting near the queenly Iowa, flagship of Vice Adm. Sherman's Fifth Fleet, the Nagato looks like a tramp. The contrast is symbolic.

In her heyday, however, the 35,000-ton battle-ship was the toast of the Nipponese navy with her eight 16-inch guns, her roomy turrets, her heavy armor plate, and her sturdy engines copied mainly from American and British marine models.

Commenting on the Nagato's protective armor, Lt. Cmdr. E.S. Gilfillan, executive officer, says, "She has a center section like a big steel box." Gilfillan mentions the accent on roominess and says, "If we had built her, I think we'd have jammed her in tighter here and there."

Evidently the U.S. Navy took care of that item during the Battle of the Philippine Sea, for she's jammed in plenty.

"The Nagato is a contemporary of our Maryland," remarks Capt. W.J. Whipple, com-manding officer. "Originally she was faster than the Maryland, cruising at 25 knots."
Construction costs touched $25 million, the captain estimates, pointing out that in Japan labor was comparatively cheap.

In 1922, the year of the Washington Disarma-ment Conference, a clever tonnage juggling act saved the Nagato from the scrap heap. Re-portedly, through a smooth job of sentimental-ity salesmanship, her sister ship, the Mutsu, also sneaked by the quota. The Mutsu was built with funds contributed by loving little school-children, pleaded the Japanese, and thus the Imperial navy tucked an extra ace up its blue sleeve.

Destroyed by internal explosions, the Mutsu was "one we didn't have to sink," says the captain.

Four days before Japan's surrender, the Nagato carried a skeleton crew. When the Americans boarded her, she was a lifeless hulk, a ghost ship. Although no sabotage was in evidence, looters had stripped her like a ripe banana. "It was so bad," says a naval officer sadly, "I couldn't even get a souvenir for myself."

Mystery still clouds certain details concerning the Nagato, the Navy hints, and information is sketchy. Numbering an estimated 2,000 officers and men, the original crew conveniently took off and scattered. Japanese naval sources claim to have only a foggy idea of the ship's accomplishments. An American now aboard her declares the Japanese had "written her off" a year before the war ended.

Air attacks created most damage, spokesmen indicated. In the admiral's conference cabin, however, is double-holed proof of a small surface shell bouncing off the water and ripping through opposite bulkheads. Fascinating is the fact that directly in the obvious path of the projectile is a long polished conference table around which the gold-braid boys hatched their mischief.

A U.S. Navy crew will sail the doomed battlewagon to the Marshalls. When asked if the Nagato fills the bill for accurate atomic bomb experiments, Whipple declared, "She's a good example of a battleship and the results should be conclusive."

A burly seaman in charge of a gang of Japanese swabbing down the splinter-proof teakwood decks later snorted: "I ain't gonna stick around to see."

But the Nagato fooled the doomsayers. On July 1, 1946, she was moored off Kwajalein with the Nevada, the Arkansas, the German Prinz Eugen and other grey giants. Maced by one of the mightiest explosions in history, the Nagato did not bow her head and quickly sink. Aflame and badly damaged, she stayed afloat for 28 days after the atomic thunderclap.

TOJO SLAPPED

MAY 4, 1946 BY CPL. AMERICO PAREDES

TOKYO — War crimes defendant Hideki Tojo was slapped smartly on his bald pate twice during his arraignment and that of 27 co-defendants before the Military Tribunal for the Far East at the War Ministry building in Tokyo Friday.

The slapper was Shumei Okawa, one of the defendants and self-appointed star performer of the proceedings.

The arraignments began at 11:30 a.m., one hour late because of the expected arrival of defendants Seishiro Itagaki and Heitaro Kimura, who were brought to Tokyo from Bangkok. They arrived at Atsugi airdrome Friday morning but did not appear in court until after the noon recess.

Tribunal President Sir William F. Webb, representing Australia, opened the proceedings with a statement in which he said that the coming trial was as important as any criminal trial in all history.

"To our great task we bring open minds both on the acts and on the law," Sir William's statement said. "The onus will be on the prosecution to establish guilt beyond a reasonable doubt."

The day was taken up with the reading of the indictments, 47 counts of which were gone through Friday. The remaining two of the 49 counts included in the indictment presumably were to be read Saturday.

The defense interrupted the reading of the indictment counts on two occasions. Prof. Kenzo Takayanagi of the Tokyo Imperial College, special defense counsel, interrupted the reading in the early afternoon to object that "there were substantial errors" in the Japanese translation.

Prosecution chief Joseph B. Keenan defended the indictment and the court ruled that the reading should proceed.

After a 3:30 p.m. recess, during which Shumei Okawa caused a mild disturbance with the antics, one of Okawa's lawyers tried to introduce a speech into the record in which he made an appeal for his client. The court ruled the speech was out of order.

Court adjourned at 4:45 p.m., with resumption of proceedings set for 9:30 a.m. Saturday. During the Friday morning session Lt. Gen. Robert L. Eichelberger, Eighth Army commander, Chinese General Chu Shi-ming, representative to the Allied four-power council, were among those present.

Chu returned in the afternoon and read a copy of Pacific Stars and Stripes during lulls in the proceedings.

Five hundred spectators and 100 Allied and Japanese newspaper, movie and radio men were present at court Friday.

Chief of the Allied-appointed defense counsel is Capt. Beverly M. Coleman, USNR, with Maj. Franklin E.N. Warren as his assistant.

Shumei Okawa, who added color to an otherwise routine proceeding, showed considerable signs of nervousness after the noon recess. He twisted and squirmed in his chair like a schoolboy and wiped his eyes as if he were weeping.

Finally he took off his coat, revealing gray pajama tops. He unbuttoned these, and Lt. Col. Aubrey S. Kenworthy, chief of military security for the war crimes trials, reached around Okawa's neck and buttoned his pajamas from behind.

Suddenly he half rose from his seat and slapped Tojo, who was seated in front of him, on the head. Tojo half turned and smiled embarrassedly as MPs restrained Okawa, who grinned delightedly at his little joke.

At 3:30 p.m. a short recess was called and photographers were given a chance at the prisoners. When a newsreel cameraman started to photograph Okawa, he rose, slapped Tojo's shining dome again. Tribunal President Sir William F. Webb had to call the court to order. The prisoners were taken out for a recess, Okawa babbling gibberish as he was led out. When the court convened again at 4 p.m., Okawa was seated out of reach of Tojo's gleaming cranium. He wept through most of the last part of the proceedings.

Shumei Okawa was considered a brilliant man and a creative writer before the war. He was an officer of the South Manchurian Railway and is alleged to have been the organizer of the Mukden Incident in 1931, which provoked Japanese attacks against China. Okawa was a propagandist for the expulsion of the white races from Asia by aggressive war. Court officials said he had been acting strangely the morning before the indictments.

Justice was slow, ponderous and thorough. It was not until Nov. 12, 1948, that the defendants stood for the verdict — minus Okawa, who had been declared insane, and two other defendants who had died. All were found guilty. On Dec. 23, Tojo and six others were hanged in gloomy, fortress-like Sugamo Prison.

Long before there was a Berlin Wall, there was the 38th Parallel — the latitudinal line that halved tiny, remote Korea.

A land of tough, aloof agrarians, Korea had perhaps the saddest history of any country in Asia. It had been ravaged or subjugated by every conqueror from Genghis Khan to the ambitious Japanese, who began to engulf Korea in the last days of the last century and finally fastened a brutal and rigid dictatorship on it. In mid-1945, as the Pacific War swayed against Japan, the Soviets pondered what their role as neutrals in that struggle had brought them — an unenviable postwar tactical position. On Aug. 8, 1945, they made an 11th hour declaration of war on Japan. Crack Mongol troops swarmed into Korea and easily swept aside the flabby Kwantung Army garrison. Korea was to be occupied half by Americans, half by Soviets. The agreed-upon dividing line was randomly chosen by a U.S. Army major — one Dean Rusk.

Russian and U.S. delegates met in Seoul as they had at Yalta, for what Americans and Korean onlookers hoped would be the first steps toward an independent and unified Korea, free of foreign influence. Sgt. Robert Cornwall was there for Pacific Stars and Stripes. While he did a vivid and incisive reporting job, Cornwall could hardly be called an uninvolved spectator. He obviously shared the high hopes of the Americans and Koreans.

"I GREET THE KOREAN PEOPLE ..."

JAN. 18, 1946, BY SGT. ROBERT CORNWALL

SEOUL, Korea — What is expected to become the most important and significant series of meetings held on the soil of modern Korea began here Wednesday. Surrounded by the pomp and fanfare of a great state occasion and watched by the eyes of the world, high Soviet Russian and American military leaders gathered to plan the steps this nation will take along the road to freedom.

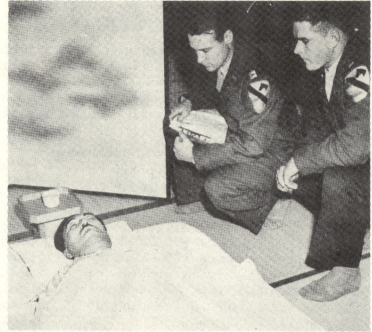

CHOOSING SUICIDE over being charged as a war criminal, Prince Fumimaro Konoye took poison and left only a note for the Americans who were to have arrested him. Below, Gen. Hideki Tojo — who had succeeded Konoye as wartime premier and was himself a failed suicide — is sworn in before testifying on his own behalf before the International War Crimes Tribunal. Tojo, convicted of plotting aggressive war, was sentenced to hang by those who defeated him.

USA

8

In his welcoming address to the Russians, Lt. Gen. John R. Hodge, U.S. commander in Korea, said: "It is my great privilege to open this important series of international conferences and to welcome to Seoul Col. Gen. Shtikov and the other distinguished officers.

"It is my hope and that of my government as well," Hodge continued, "that these present conversations will result in an agreement which will, in administrative and economic spheres, bring to an end the trials and difficulties of the Korean nation brought about by over 35 years of Japanese oppression and misrule."

Col. Gen. Teremtyi Shtikov, head of the Russian delegation replied:

"Allow me to thank you with all sincerity for the warm and courteous reception given me and the officers who accompanied me. I greet the Korean people, freed by the valiant forces of the Red Army and the army of our allies, the USA, from long years of oppression by Japanese militarists."

The Russian general continued: "I hope our conference convoked in accordance with the decision taken at the conference of the three foreign ministers in Moscow, will, by common and friendly efforts, successfully fulfill the task entrusted to it. This will be our first joint step for establishment in the administrative-economic realm of lasting coordination between the American command in southern Korea and the Soviet command in northern Korea, so essential to the restoration of the normal economic life of Korea."

Meeting in the magnificent Throne Room of the Government Building, Hodge and Shtikov shook hands warmly before sitting down to the conference that plans to erase the artificial division of Korea at the 38th parallel and seeks a formula enabling the Korean people to unite in a common cause of forming a democratic provisional government.

Flood lights were trained on the leading officials at the huge conference table while Korean and foreign newsmen and photographers swarmed around the seated conferees. American, Korean and Russian flags were draped behind the speaker and interpreters of the three nations labored at the microphone to translate the speeches to the audience.

Persons at the table included several officers of both armies, civilian diplomatic representatives and a battery of interpreters that included two attractive Russian women. A third Soviet woman is here in uniform.

In his address Hodge designated Maj. Gen. A.V. Arnold as his representative in the forthcoming discussions with H.M. Benninghoff also present as political adviser for the U.S. State Department.

As the world well knows, the high hopes were to be false ones. Artificial or not, the boundary remained — until the Soviet-oriented leaders of the North Korean Communist regime decided themselves to erase it.

Some of the best reading in Pacific Stars and Stripes in those early years could be found in Comment and Query — a fearlessly independent column of opinions and gripes. Letters on any subject or problem were printed — including this classic, which had an unintentional humor and poignancy Ring Lardner couldn't have matched.

VALUE, $0.25???

NOV. 20, 1946, BY PFC ORVILLE WOMACK

Well I think it is time I put my to bits Worth in the Stars and Strips. I thought the Army Was getting Prettie bad, but now I am beginning to believe it is the Guys thats in the Army. This morning I got off of Guard duty and sat down to listen to the Radio. When I turned the Radio on the first think I heard was some man With a Rough voice say (I hope you liked our Records this Morning, but if you didin there is Nothen you can do about it). I dont no Maby that man was trying to be funny and make some body laugh, but I would like for him to know that he broke my buddy heart. My buddy Cryied for 2 hours. I tryed to get him to stop, but he said the Radio announcers are getting just like the MPs. I can't stand it any longer, and he grabbed a club and swung at the Radio. It was luckey he Missed the Radio and knocked a Wall down. I finaly got him to his bed and made him lay down and I faned him while he cooled off. My buddy than said that damn Radio has gone to talking just like the 25th Division MPs. We are just new over here I don't guess we have learned how to act yet. My buddy has been overseas since the first of May in 1945 and I have been over since February 1945. Yes my friend you guessed it We are RA. and We are glad of it. Just think a stateside furlough, Who would every think of turning a Furlough down even if you Was going to hell when your furlough was over. We even get to stand in the front of the pay line each month, I think We Will be eating with the officers before long take it easy men don't do nothen I woulden.

There was turmoil in Trieste, Communist partisans had inundated the Greek countryside and the Russians were making bold and pushy moves against the American presence in Berlin. Those were the stories getting the headlines, but Asia was hardly a sleeper as far as war and politics were concerned. As Andrew Headland Jr. discovered, there were all kinds of remote and dangerous places where a man could get killed. A nervy and enterprising reporter, Headland took a chance to get a story — and got a good one.

"DID YOU HEAR ANY RIFLE FIRE?"

APRIL 10, 1947, BY ANDREW HEADLAND JR.

PEKING — To say the three-party truce teams that operated in China and Manchuria to stop the civil war didn't have a chance to succeed is putting it too strongly.

The odds were against their succeeding, but while they operated they accomplished some good amid terrific difficulties. Actually, the teams were neither a success or a failure, and probably will be remembered as a brave but futile gesture to bring about the internal unity that some day must be China's.

There were, last winter, eight of these truce teams operating out of Changchun, Manchuria, under direction of main headquarters at Peking and Nanking. Each team, composed of American, Chinese Nationalist and Chinese Communist representatives was located either in an actual trouble spot or in a spot likely to become, without mediation, an active battleground.

The team selected for our visit was No. 33, deep in Communist territory at a village called La Fa Chan, scene of large battle that summer, and some 150 miles from the Nationalist-controlled city of Changchun. Since our visit, the entire area has become a general battle area.

For purposes of making the trip I went along assigned as an "assistant courier" on a two man supply team. The other courier was Sgt. John Fox, an old China hand whose native state is Montana. Supply teams acted as "lifelines" to the men in the field, carrying provisions, mail from home and official communications.

John and I spent nearly a full day getting cargo ready for the trip. We filled crates full of articles such as canned foods, flour, sugar, salt, candy, winter clothing, and even tossed in a ping pong set for diversion. Entertainment is scarce in the Manchurian wilderness.

At four the following morning we were loading up the two vehicles that were to make the trip — a jeep for the team, and a weapons carrier for ourselves — on a flat car. It was necessary to travel most of the way by rail, for highways were either impassable or unsafe because of guerrillas.

The 150-mile trip by flat car to La Fa Chan by way of Kirin (where the second largest dam in Asia is located) was slow and cold.

At Kirin we crossed the beautiful Sungari

River, the "Mississippi of Manchuria," on a wobbly wooden bridge replacing another dynamited by the Communists, who by now are probably the most expert bridge blowers in the world.

Four members from Team 33 — an American Army sergeant and a captain, accompanied by two Chinese Nationalist and Chinese Communist interpreters — were waiting to meet us at a neutral station near La Fa Chan when we arrived a day and a half after leaving Changchun.

All of the men were tense and quiet. There wasn't a loading platform, so we shoved the jeep and weapons carrier off the flat car on to a slope, and a few minutes later were ready to take off for La Fa Chan.

"Keep up with the escort," called the sergeant as we started. "We weren't flying a white flag on the way in and almost got a hand grenade."

"We've got to make La Fa before dark, or we'll never get there," the captain added.

I looked at the winter sun. It was low in the western sky, and there was a mountain to cross. The tunnel through the mountain, constructed when Japanese controlled Manchuria, was dynamited. At the foot of the mountain we were stopped by guards from a Communist outpost, while during much conversation, officials examined our credentials.

"What do they say?" I asked John, looking again toward the sinking sun.

"They say," John replied, "that there were only four going out but six coming back. They say that's not good."

Meanwhile one of the soldiers started practicing bayonet lunges in front of the weapons carrier, while others loosened hand grenades. Still another fingered the fabric of my woolen trousers as I sat fixedly in the front seat of the weapons carrier trying to look unconcerned.

Fox spoke Chinese like a native and between him and the two team interpreters, they talked our way free. Credentials in any language out there meant little, because few people could read.

We were stopped twice again before reaching La Fa Chan just at dusk. At team headquarters supplies were hurriedly unloaded before Communist guards who marched stiffly up and down. Headquarters didn't amount to much more than an oversized shanty, but it was the most welcome sanctuary I had ever stepped foot in.

John and I were warned not to start back too early in the morning, as at that time Communist patrols would still be stiff with cold from night duty, and therefore doubly hard to approach — or pass. We left in the weapons carrier about 8:30, earlier than the team wished to see us go.

At the first Red outpost, our Communist interpreter jumped off the truck to talk to the guards, who, as always, acted as though they would refuse passage. When the go ahead signal was finally given, as it always was, I looked back to see the interpreter ominously was missing from the truck.

A mile down the trail it happened. Communists hiding in ambush in fields and from hillsides started firing on us. The escort jeep in front immediately picked up like a wild hare and literally flew off across the fields, while we lumbered slowly behind. "Ping, ping," went the bullets as they nipped the landscape around us. John pressed the throttle to the floorboard and could hardly hold the truck to the trail.

If the Communists were just trying to frighten us, they succeeded.

If they were poor shots, they missed.

We caught up with the jeep, which had been stopped by another patrol, two miles down the road. This patrol, it seems, wanted to know about the firing, and why we were in such a hurry.

"Did you fellows hear any rifle fire?" the Nationalist interpreter cried, suddenly leaving the Communist soldiers to run back toward us.

"No!" I shouted. "We didn't hear a thing."

More words passed between the patrol leaders and interpreter, who without waiting to dissolve a matter which might never have been settled in our favor, jumped into the jeep, and by mutual, unspoken consent, we all took off simultaneously. The move was successful. No gunfire followed from the surprised patrol and in a few minutes we were out of sight behind trees and hills.

Almost immediately, however, the jeep left us behind, and John started cursing in two vocabularies. We rolled into a small village. I stood up and started tossing out salutes like a robot.

"That's right," said John grimly. "Salute every damned one!" It wasn't brave on my part and it wasn't impressive. No one returned a single salute. "Well," I thought, "this is where we get it."

What we got, however, was heart's relief — just around the next corner. There stood the jeep, flags flapping jauntily in the breeze. "You!" shouted John to the driver. "Why in the hell do you keep running off and leaving us behind?"

"You're all right now," said the sergeant, grinning. "This is Nationalist territory. That last stretch back there was no man's land."

Years later, Headland would be Pacific Stars and Stripes Bureau Chief on Taiwan — the island outpost of the Nationalist Chinese after the Communists drove them from one of the most populous and important areas in the world. He was still there, long retired, when the United States recognized the Peking Government and severed relations with what would now be defined only as Taiwan.

In late World War II, the Nazis hurled the V-1 and V-2 rockets across the English Channel at London — fluttering, flame-spitting horrors that flattened whole city blocks. The Japanese had earlier wanted to hit the American West Coast, but were badly hampered by two things: the Germans would not share their long strides in rocketry with their allies, and there was far more distance than 20 miles of channel to contend with. What the Japanese came up with was a laughable non-solution — a fantastic scheme to launch explosive-laden balloons that the winds would carry across the Pacific. Almost two years after the war, a 1st Cav. Div. reconnaissance patrol stumbled across the launching site for the balloons — perhaps the first cumbersome attempt at an ICBM. Capt. S. Ambrose Freedman, who was along with the party, may never have attacked a typewriter before in his life — but wrote a finely detailed yarn that shed a revealing light on one of the most heavily censored stories of the war.

THE $200 MILLION BALLOON BUST

MAY 11, 1947, BY CAPT. S. AMBROSE FREEDMAN

OTSU, Japan — In the isolated ravines of the remote Otsu Peninsula, a 1st Cav. Div. reconnaissance party today found a score of concrete-lined sites from which the Japanese Army launched bombing balloons with intent to blast the United States with high explosives.

Amazing revelations of the vast extent of Japan's novel aerial bombing project were disclosed by what the cavalrymen found scattered over hundreds of acres in northern Ibaraki Prefecture approximately 125 miles north of Tokyo. The area lies within the occupation zone of the division's 2nd Brigade, commanded by Brig. Gen. Hugh Hoffman of San Antonio, Texas.

Led by Lt. Col. C.C. Clendenen, the cavalrymen found in half a dozen green-clad canyons hydrogen generating plants, inflating platforms and other facilities.

It was from this region of scenic magnificence that thousands of silken, gas-filled balloons, carrying deadly loads of explosives, soared high above the clouds and were wafted toward North America. Borne by the steadily blowing eastward gales of the upper reaches, the balloons remained aloft for days, but most of them never found their targets and are presumed to have gone down in the sea.

It is known, however, that a few balloons spanned the Pacific.

Only a mile from one of the most beautiful surflands in the world, Nagahama Beach, the reconnaissance party found what once were among the most elaborate and highly scientific installations of wartime Japan.

The explorers found rusted boilers and distilling apparatus of the hydrogen generating plants which produced the gases for inflating the balloons. These generating plants were located in several adjoining canyons, and next to the plants were great launching platforms, set into sunken concrete circular walls. The hydrogen pipelines from the generating plants extended into them.

It was on the concrete emplacements that the bags were filled and the bundles of explosives were fastened to the balloons with ingenious timing devices for automatic release of the destructive loads.

Whole installations, with barracks that housed thousands, were constructed in the vicinity. The Japanese worked feverishly day and night to send a maximum number of balloons floating toward the United States during the estimated eight months of fantastic effort.

So much faith did the Japanese have in the novel method of striking at the far-away enemy that vast sums were poured into the project. It is estimated the equivalent of $200 million was spent on the bombing balloon attempt.

Thousands of Japanese fishermen and farmers were evacuated from the area. Great winding roads were constructed into the installations. Even special railroads were built to carry the mass of balloon silks, chemicals, mulberry paper, rope, explosives, and other paraphernalia from the main rail trunks leading from the factories in Tokyo and other industrial regions.

All these were found by Clendenen's reconnaissance party.

Utmost secrecy was employed by the Japanese in all the bombing balloon activities. Every road was closely guarded. The countryside was honeycombed with caves in which well-armed troops were stationed day and night.

Although the inhabitants of the countryside for miles around could see the balloons ascending daily, their purpose remained a secret.

The theory is held in some quarters that the Japanese hoped continually for the news that an important city in the United States had been mysteriously bombed. The propaganda effect would have been of inestimable value, especially after the sensation created in Japan by the Doolittle air raid.

It was not until after the Doolittle raid, in fact, that the balloon bombing project was launched. Apparently it was the desperate desire for retaliation in kind that led to the effort which resulted in the expenditure of vast sums and the employment of tens of thousands of Japanese in the manufacture of the equipment.

Despite the fact that some balloons reached North American shores, not the slightest information reached the Japanese to give any hint of the results of their intensive effort.

Most of the crime news printed in Pacific Stars and Stripes in those days was of a routine and benign sort. There was seldom anything worth a large headline or a follow-up story. But in early 1948, a lone bandit walked into a Tokyo bank and committed one of the most brazen and shocking mass murders in criminal history. He didn't use a knife or a gun — only a cool, pretentious manner and a ruthless knowledge of the Japanese psychology. He knew his countrymen seldom questioned an official or an order. This sketchy, under-pressure account of the crime began a story that would still be news 40 years later.

"DRINK THIS. IT'S MEDICINE"

JAN. 28, 1948

TOKYO — Twelve persons are dead and 4 are in critical condition today following a mass poisoning by a bank robber who yesterday tricked them into taking an "anti-dysentery" medicine as a preliminary to "fumigating" a bank branch office in Shinamachi, Toshima Ward.

Posing as a health officer, the robber entered the building, a branch of Teikoku Bank, at about 3 p.m. He said he was about to fumigate the premises and ordered the employees to drink a colorless and odorless liquid.

Within a few minutes, the bank employees were writhing in agony in the bank office and halls. When police arrived they found 10 bodies strewn about the floors. This morning at 9 a.m. the death toll had risen to 12, with four survivors in critical condition.

The Teikoku Bank head office, it was learned, had delivered ¥1 million to the branch near St. Paul's University. Whether this money was stored in the bank's safe was not learned. Surviving employees were in a comatose condition when interviewed.

Warning the employees that a mass outbreak of dysentery was raging in the neighborhood, the visitor handed the assistant manager a vial of colorless liquid and urged that all the workers take rapid doses before locking the safe.

The patient and methodical Japanese police went to work, questioning no fewer than 8,000 persons before they arrested a 57-year-old artist named Sadamichi Hirazawa on Aug. 21, 1948. On Sept. 28, Pvt. Larry Sakamoto stood with other newsmen and heard Hirazawa say, "I have nothing to say in my defense and I am sorry that I did it." A lengthy investigation and long trial ended on July 24, 1950, when Hirazawa was convicted in Tokyo District Court and sentenced to death. At this writing, Hirazawa was past 90 and still dodging the hangman through legal ploys and protestations of innocence. His case had become a torchlight cause for those who oppose capital punishment.

"You, Joe, and all of you out there on Leyte. It's too bad your kids are going to be orphans...." This chilling threat would be followed by a blare of popular music. Wherever American troops went in the Pacific, it seemed, the voice of the soft-spoken doomsayer called Tokyo Rose followed them — assuring them in a low but vehemently passionate voice that fighting for their country was a foolish way to die. Some of her listeners might have been unnerved, but most were merely curious. Who was she? Very obviously, she was of Japanese ancestry — but with her command of English and the American idiom, she could have only been an American. So she was; and when Allied occupation forces came into Tokyo, Mrs. Iva Toguri D'Aquino, the daughter of a California grocer, was locked up in Sugamo Prison. Released after a year, she became secluded and unapproachable — and it took a good reporter's initiative and tact to get an interview. Pacific Stars and Stripes staff writer Yo Tajiri had both.

"THIS IS BEGINNING TO SOUND LIKE AN INTERVIEW"

JULY 29, 1948 BY YO TAJIRI

TOKYO — "Tokyo Rose" yesterday denied that she had ever been officially approached by anyone from the U.S. Department of Justice in what was obviously a reluctant interview with this Stars and Stripes reporter.

In answer to what she thought about recent reports that U.S. Attorney General Tom Clark may prosecute her on treason charges, Mrs. Iva Toguri D'Aquino said, "I don't know what new evidence they could have uncovered, if they couldn't find it before. This has been going on for three long years, it will probably go on for three more years. The Department of Justice hasn't even sent me a postcard. The only way I have of learning about my case is what I read in the newspapers."

Mrs. D'Aquino was released from Sugamo Prison, October 1946, after a year's imprisonment. At that time, Army intelligence officers could not find sufficient evidence for a grand jury treason case.

"I have never signed a statement that I was Tokyo Rose," she said firmly. "There were several other girls who broadcast on those programs. They were put on all over the Far East; in Hongkong, Shanghai, Manila besides Tokyo," she added.

Newspaper accounts once described this 32-year old American-born former broadcaster as buxom and comely. We found her to be neat and attractive but quite thin and not more than 5' 4" in height. She met us in the foyer of a shabby Japanese-style house in Setagaya ward in a one-room upstairs flat.

She was dressed for the hot weather in a pink cotton sports blouse over a plain blue cotton petticoat and blue bobby socks. Her hair was neatly put up in one tight roll around her head and set off with a white ribbon.

The woman, who once talked freely and pleasantly to newsmen, told us that she has decided against any more interviews. "Anything I have to say will come out in court," she said.

To most questions, she would answer, "This is beginning to sound like an interview."

She appeared embittered and has developed a defense mechanism of countering most leading questions with a question of her own or answering them curtly or sarcastically.

Asked if she is working on a book about her wartime activities, clearing up her much-publi-cized story, she answered, "No, I've given up that project. But if the book is written, I will do it myself. It will not be ghostwritten."

She says she has no plans for the future. "What would you do if you were in my position?" she asked. "Why, I can't even buy a plate for the house or take a job because I might be arrested tomorrow.

"I'm not doing anything right now — just sitting around waiting for the newspaper men who always come around when something comes up in my case," she said.

"We heard that you do a lot of reading," we said.

"Where would I get anything to read?" she answered.

The only time "Rose" ever relaxed and seemed natural was when we thanked her and said goodbye. Then she smiled for the first time since the conversation began and said, "I'm sorry I couldn't say any more. Once I was willing to talk, but that was a long time ago. You should have come to see me then."

Inevitably, Mrs. D'Aquino, was flown back to the U.S. and tried in a federal court in San Francisco. Convicted in 1949 of treason, she was fined $10,000 and sentenced to 10 years in prison, serving seven before she was paroled in 1956.

One of the greatest advantages of being a newspaperman is to have a front row seat at the pageant of history. Americo Paredes saw war criminals brought before the bar of international justice. Andrew Headland Jr. witnessed the strife that was an overture to decades of turmoil and tragedy in Asia. And H.H. Hathaway saw the birth of the Republic of Korea. The newspaper's first civilian managing editor, Hathaway wrote of a nation and a man. His story, while hardly a piece of dispassionate reporting, echoed the hopes of millions of Koreans and the man who would once more be a symbol of determined strength to them.

"AS YOU EMBARK ON YOUR DESTINY"

AUG. 16, 1948 BY H.H. HATHAWAY

SEOUL, Korea — The "Cap" came to Korea and work-gnarled hands of thousands gave it salute as the symbol of an effort that had made them free, had given them a republic.

The thousands who lined the streets from Kimpo airport to the gray capitol building where the speech-making took place, saw in the Cap — in General of the Army Douglas MacArthur's presence — fresh assurance to their hopes.

They were getting a republic and they would be free men and women in it. And there was the Cap, frayed and stained by the weather and sweat of island battle campaigns to prove that they were.

The Cap was worn by MacArthur — and that

was as it should have been; but as he wore it today it stood not for him alone. It stood for the millions of freedom-loving Americans who wished well for this new Republic of Korea. It stood for millions of Koreans who were at last taking their place as a nation in a family of nations made of a synthesis of blood, tears and labor, sacrifice and death.

One could look at the faces staring up at figures of Dr. Syngman Rhee, first president of the republic, at MacArthur and at Lt. Gen. Hodge who has discharged an arduous mission with honor and credit. In the faces one read of a section of humanity facing a new direction and new problems, of hope that what they here were told would turn out the way it was told them.

Fans stirred the air in the blazing sun beating down on the capitol grounds — steadily and rhythmically — as though a tempo was being set in their resolves for the future; steadily and rhythmically toward a nation working its destiny under the sign of freedom.

"As you embark upon your destiny as a free and independent republic, the measure of the wisdom of your chosen leaders will do much to provide the measure of your strength as a nation," MacArthur spoke on:

"Well-being of the individual.

"Progress limited only by nature and degree of industry.

"Personal dignity with opportunity of progress."

Words; but words which had behind them the stern realities of duty to the democratic ideal — an ideal here primarily proved. It was up to them now to work for the things for which the great guns of World War II roared. The guns had done their work. Men in the troubled peace had done theirs. It is now up to them.

America wore its "Cap" proudly today.

Hathaway had no way of knowing that his references to "blood, tears and labor, sacrifice and death" were grimly fitting. Less than two years later, the young republic was fighting for its life.

THE
KOREAN
WAR

1950-1953

PACIFIC STARS AND STRIPES

EXTRA!

VOLUME 6, NUMBER 149 — SHARE THIS PAPER — SUNDAY, June 25, 1950 — SHARE THIS PAPER — AP, UP, INS WIRE SERVICES

KOREA AT WAR

Northern Government Declares State of Hostilities; 60,000 Red Troops Attack Along 200-Mile Front; Rhee Telephones Appeal for U.S. Help to Tokyo

TOKYO (INS)—The long-feared civil war in Korea began with bloody fighting Sunday morning.

The Communist troops of the north hit the 38th parallel with tremendous power at 5 a.m.

Six hours later, at 11 a.m., the Pyongyang Radio announced a declaration of war by the Communist regime of the north against the anti-Communist government of the south.

BY NOON the Communist regulars, 60,000 crack troops trained by Russian military experts, had established a line averaging three kilometers in depth south of the border across the whole peninsula on a 200-mile front.

President Syngman Rhee in Seoul telephoned an appeal for American aid to Tokyo.

Specifically he wants bullets for the rifles of his 95,000 infantrymen, each of whom has been issued only 50 rounds of rifle ammunition.

THE CABINET went into an emergency session in Seoul at 2 p.m. to formulate strategy and to frame a plea for American aid.

A plane-load of American officers already was en route to Seoul when the cabinet session began. The Americans left Haneda at 1 p.m.

Northern Communists appeared to have heavy military advantages over the South.

IN APRIL the Defense Ministry in Seoul issued the following analysis of Northern strength:

195,000 first-line troops, crack units trained and armed by the Russians.

195 aircraft of all types, including bombers.

16 steel-clad warships.

Good supply of bazookas and mortars and some tanks.

350,000 second line troops, organized as a constabulary.

LARGE NUMBERS of Russian "Yak" machine guns.

"Enormous" numbers of American "Eddystone" rifles, used in the first world war and given to the Chinese to use against the Japanese before Pearl Harbor.

The Defense Ministry pointed out the Communist mortars are 120mm guns that shoot 2,000 yards further than the 81mm mortars of the Southern Army.

South Korean government spokesman Clarence Ryee said there were 4,000 dead on both sides in the first few hours of fighting in which the Communists captured a number of important South Korean towns.

He said that the government of President Syngman Rhee will appeal directly to General Douglas MacArthur for immediate aid, particularly in rifle ammunition which is critically in short supply and aircraft for observation purposes.

THE APPEAL to SCAP will stress that the situation is desperate.

So far, Ryee said in a telephone conversation there have been no uprisings, but police throughout the south of the peninsula has been alerted for possible trouble such as the bloody revolt in 1948.

The war, Ryee reported, opened with sporadic attacks at 5 a.m. Sunday along the entire 200-mile length of the 38th parallel.

KAESON, he said, fell at 10 a.m., Ongjin was surrounded at 9:45 after the important nearby town of Paik Caom had been captured.

Po Chun, a few miles from Kangnum along the 38th parallel cutting across the peninsula, also was captured.

The Seoul government, Ryee declared, would make a formal declaration at 2 p.m. Sunday.

• • •

SEOUL (UP) — American Ambassador John J. Muccio broadcast the following statement to the 2,000 Americans in Korea, including the military mission, over the English-language radio station WVTP Sunday:

"At 4 o'clock this morning North Korean armed forces began unprovoked attacks against defense positions of the Republic of Korea at several points along the 38th parallel.

"Korean defense forces are taking up prepared positions to resist the northern aggression. Both Korean officials and security forces are handling the situation calmly and with ability. There is no reason for alarm.

"As yet it cannot be determined whether the northern Communists intend to precipitate all-out warfare.

"New developments will be reported regularly over WVTP.

"Mission personnel are advised to travel about as little as necessary. The ambassador requests American mission personnel (State Department, ECA, military advisory group employes and dependents) to remain at home or at their posts as the situation may dictate."

Airliner Missing With 58 Aboard

MINNEAPOLIS, Minn. (INS)—A Northwest Airlines DC-4 transport plane, carrying 58 persons, disappeared early Saturday over stormy Lake Michigan in what may be the worst disaster in the history of American commercial aviation.

Shortly after noon (3 a.m. Sunday, Tokyo DST) two search ships reported by radio that they had sighted "unmistakable signs" of some wreckage approximately 8½ miles east of South Milwaukee, Wis.

THE MESSAGE was sent by ship-to-shore radio to Milwaukee Fire Chief Edward Wischer. He said it came from a Milwaukee fireboat and the Coast Guard cutter "Joy."

The area where the ships reported sighting the wreckage is the same vicinity where a National Guard plane crashed about two months ago.

There were no further details from the fireboat and the cutter.

NORTHWEST AIRLINES earlier issued a statement which said:

"It is presumed the plane is down."

Hours after all contact with the plane was lost, search planes sighted three oil slicks and what appeared to be some wreckage in the area where the plane was last reported. However, further search failed to locate the reported wreckage.

THE PLANE, carrying 55 passengers and a crew of three, took off from New York at 7:25 p.m. EST Friday night on a non-stop flight to Minneapolis. It was due to arrive at 1:23 a.m. CST.

The last report from pilot Robert G. Lind came at 11:13 p.m. CST, 22 minutes after he had reported flying over Battle Creek, Mich. He asked for permission to change altitude, presumably to avoid a thunderstorm that swept over the lake from Milwaukee about that time.

IF THE PLANE crashed, killing all aboard, it was the worst disaster in U.S. airline history. The worst previous one was on Nov. 1, 1949, when a fighter plane crashed into an Eastern Airlines plane near the Washington National Airport, killing 55 persons.

9 from Ditched B-29 Picked Up in Pacific

HONOLULU (AP)—A brief message out of the Pacific Saturday said nine of 11 crewmen of an ill-fated Superfortress were safe.

And the Navy tug Munsee, directing a wide surface search, said it was steaming toward a tenth survivor who had been located on a lifeboat.

The Superfortress was ditched in the tossing Pacific late Thursday about 140 miles southeast of Guam. It was returning to its home base after a simulated bombing run on Okinawa, 1,200 miles to the west.

An Air Force spokesman on Guam said the first eight men picked up all were in good condition.

Smuggling Ring Broken by U.S.

WASHINGTON (INS)—The government has broken wide open a huge alien smuggling ring and arrested 80 persons including two members of the Sicilian "Guiliano gang."

Most of the persons involved in the smuggling were arrested in recent months in Detroit, New York and Cleveland.

William F. Kelly, chief enforcement officer of the U.S. Immigration Service, said the crackdown netted the capture of Gaetano Badalmente and another Italian, identified only as Messale.

Both men were said to be alleged leaders of the Sicilian gang headed by Guiliano, an almost legendary bandit who for years has defied the efforts of Italian police to arrest him.

Badalmente was among 50 persons held in Detroit. Messale was caught in the New York raids.

Immigration service officials said during the 12 months ended last April 1 the government picked up about 200 stowaways arriving from Mediterranean countries.

U.S. To Hold Russia Responsible for War

WASHINGTON (UP)—State Department officials said Sunday that the United States will hold Russia responsible for the Communist North Korean attack against the independent South Korean republic which this country and the United Nations brought into being and have supported.

But there was no indication that the United States intends to take direct military action of its own in defense of South Korea.

North Korea is a nominally independent "people's republic" backed by Russia.

While officials here did not say it for quotation, there was a general feeling that if the North Koreans have Russian support from Manchuria and elsewhere they could overrun the south with comparative ease. That would bring Communist forces to within 100 miles from the American flank in Japan and raise grave new problems in connection with the precarious Western position in Asia.

The Korean Embassy said that North Korea's declaration of war is "probably the next step of Soviet Russia to dominate Korea, Japan and probably the whole Far East."

SCAP Rejects Purge Protest

TOKYO (INS)—General Douglas MacArthur rejected the Soviet protest against the purge of 41 Japanese Communist party leaders Sunday as "shameful misuse of diplomatic privilege."

The general once again used strong language to attack the Soviet concepts and actions and charged the Soviet note was designed "to support and encourage those few irresponsible Japanese bent upon creating mass confusion and social unrest."

HE SAID he had carefully examined the Soviet note "in vain search for some semblance of merit and validity" and concluded that "rarely indeed have I perused such a conglomeration of misstatement, misrepresentation and prevarication of fact."

The general's answer was made with unusual speed. The Soviet note, written by Col. S. Polyashenko, acting chief of the Soviet mission in Japan, was delivered Saturday evening and the answer was distributed shortly after 11 a.m. Sunday.

POLYASHENKO had demanded the immediate rescension of the order which purged 41 Communist party leaders. The Soviet officer charged "police club" law was established in Japan by the occupation and the Japanese government.

General MacArthur answered that:

"So complete is the unrealism of its (the note's) premise, that it offers no basis for rational discussion."

THE FULL TEXT of General MacArthur's answer, contained in a "memorandum for the Soviet Member, Allied Council for Japan, follows:

"I have received your note of June 24 and have carefully considered its context in vain search for some semblance of merit and validity.

"Rarely indeed have I perused such a conglomeration of misstatement, misrepresentation and prevarication of fact.

"WITHOUT NEW or constructive thought, it is but a labored repitition of the line of fantastic propaganda which for some time has been emanating from centers within the orbit of Communist totalitarian imperialism.

"So complete is the unrealism of its premise that it offers no basis for rational discussion.

"Its plain purpose to support and encourage those few irresponsible Japanese bent upon creating mass confusion and social unrest leading to violence and disorder is a shameful misuse of diplomatic privilege which ill becomes the representative of a nation charged with a measure of responsibility in the democratic reorientation of Japan.

"I AM accordingly left no other alternative than to disapprove its intemperate proposals, and indeed to reject the complete context of the document itself."

Accord Periled By Aggression, Sebald Asserts

YOKOHAMA (UP)—SCAP diplomatic chief William J. Sebald Sunday said that international cooperation was being threatened by "rampant imperialistic aggression which disregards the common interest of all for the sake of immediate advantage on the part of one nation or group."

Sebald spoke at graduating exercises of St. Joseph's College, an international school. He warned the graduates that when they went out into the world they could not ignore international problems or "escape some responsibility for the fate of your country and that of the world."

"YOU HAVE worked, studied and played shoulder-to-shoulder with fellow students of different race and nationality," Sebald said. "You have demonstrated in your school life that national, racial and traditional differences can be overcome in the pursuit of a common purpose.

"You have also had the advantage of growing up in a country whose culture in many respects differs from the atmosphere of your own family circles. With your own eyes you have seen the terrible destruction which war can bring to a nation.

"YOU HAVE before you living proof that 'isms' and lack of international responsibility are mankind's worst investment."

Stressing the interdependence of peoples in the world economically and technically, Sebald said:

"Yet for all these very encouraging signs of international coperation in a common world cause, there still hangs over us the threat of rampant imperialistic aggression which disregards the common interest of all for the sake of immediate advantage on the part of the one nation or group."

Assembly Ousts Bidault Cabinet

PARIS (INS) — France's middle-road government was ousted by the National Assembly Saturday night despite the warning of defeated Premier Georges Bidault that the action might have "grave consequences" on the French plan to pool European industries.

Socialists, Communists, De Gaullists and others united for their own varying reasons to topple the government by a 352-230 vote—the first time since the war that such a heavy majority of 122 votes has been cast against a cabinet.

THE VOTE was on a domestic issue. Bidault had refused Socialist demands to increase civil servants' salaries.

Dulles To Talk to SCAP On Korean War Situation

By Cpl. Ernie Peeler

TOKYO—John Foster Dulles, State Department adviser, will confer with General of the Army Douglas MacArthur concerning the Korean war Sunday evening as soon as he arrives by plane from Kyoto.

Dulles did not indicate whether he would ask General MacArthur to rush immediate aid to the free Korean forces.

The State Department adviser, in an exclusive telephone conversation with Pacific Stars and Stripes said he had heard only scattered reports of the war in Korea, and had no comment to make.

UPON BEING informed by Pacific Stars and Stripes that the conflict was being waged on a major war scale, he expressed surprise.

He told Stars and Stripes that during his visit to Korea a week ago he visited Kaesong, the first town to fall to the North Korean Reds.

AT THAT TIME he had inspected South Korean installations along the 38th Parallel with military leaders of the free republic and American military advisers.

Dulles asked a Stars and Stripes reporter how much resistance the free Korean government was putting up against the attack.

"I am surprised," he said, "that war has broken out," but he added he had "no comment" to make until after he had talked with General MacArthur.

DULLES PLAYED a major role in establishing the free Korean government with his resolution before the United Nations.

Last week he paid a visit to the free Korean President, Syngman Rhee and upon Dulles' return to Tokyo said he "was encouraged by the free will of the people in the free portion of Korea to maintain its independence and economic existence."

HE TOLD newsmen at that time that he was convinced the independent government of Korea had done a better job of combating the rising tide of communism of the Red influence in Asia than any other threatened nation.

• • •

SAW AREA OF ATTACK—A week ago John Foster Dulles (in black suit), State Department adviser, paid a visit to the area shown above along the 38th parallel in Korea and inspected installations of the South Korean government. This was one of the first sectors to fall to the Reds Sunday morning. Shown above (left to right) Colonel Ham, of the Korean Army; General Yu Jae Heung, Korean division commander; Dulles; Maj. J. W. Bilello, KMAG senior adviser to the Korean Division and Col. W. H. S. Wright, chief of KMAG, is shown to the left and behind Dulles. (KMAG Photo)

President Foresees Continued Prosperity

BALTIMORE (UP) — President Truman Saturday confidently predicted that the American economy will continue to expand as long as the American people are willing to plan for expansion.

Speaking at the dedication of Baltimore's new Friendship International Airport, the President derided the "mossbacks" who, he said, would hold back the progress of the nation.

"THIS AIRPORT has been planned on the sound assumption that our economy will continue to grow and expand," Mr. Truman said. "I believe this assumption is correct. I am confident that our economy will continue to grow and expand.

"Of course, this will not happen automatically. Our economy will expand only if we plan for expansion. All of us make some plans for the future."

HE SAID that if these plans are based "on the belief that our output will remain static, on the expectation that incomes will fall, on the assumption that changes in the present situation will be injurious to existing interests—then we may expect the economy to decline and contract.

"If on the other hand we base our plans on the assumption of increasing output, growing efficiency and higher real incomes, we can make continued economic progress."

STARS AND STRIPES

An official Army newspaper published by and for military personnel six times weekly in Tokyo, Japan, APO 500 by the Troop Information and Education Section, GHQ, FEC for free distribution to U.S Armed Forces in Japan, Korea, Marianas Bonins Islands, the Ryukyus and the Philippines. Local news may not be republished without obtaining official clearance, except that AFPS material may be reprinted by civilian papers without specific AFPS clearance. Editorial views and opinions expressed in the paper are not necessarily those of the Department of the Army. Address all communications to Officer-in-Charge, Pacific Stars and Stripes, APO 500.

"Thank you," Gen. Douglas MacArthur said calmly as he was told in Tokyo that the Soviet-sponsored North Koreans had invaded South Korea. "Please keep me informed as the situation develops." A few days later, American troops were ordered into the fight. Stripes dispatched Cpl. Ernie Peeler and Pvt. Hal Gamble, enterprising, chance-taking professionals who watched a gutsy few try to do too much.

Fighting like groggy, back-pedaling boxers, savagely outnumbered American troops could do only one thing — bleed the enemy dearly as they gave ground. Reporting the most dangerous and unpredictable kind of war story — a delaying action — Peeler, Gamble and a few other correspondents took a soldier's chances to do a newsman's job. In his best and last story, Peeler told of how beardless novices discovered instant manhood.

"THEY ARE WAR VETERANS ... MEN OVERNIGHT"

JULY 9, 1950 BY CPL. ERNIE PEELER

SOMEWHERE IN KOREA — American soldiers — until recently most of the kids on dates and burning up the roads in hot rod cars — turned into men Friday and Saturday in a gallant stand at a South Korean town approximately 40 miles north of Taejon.

When they first went into action they reacted as normal kids facing danger for the first time. They were scared and their faces turned white when the enemy started peppering the town with small arms fire. However, it didn't take them long to grit their teeth and start pouring out streams of deadly lead into the faces of the Communist invaders.

During the action, those kids huddled behind weather-beaten, mud-thatched buildings, gripping their rifles with trembling hands.

They had read of war, and they had seen war movies, but out here they were faced with a grim game of killing for the first time in their lives.

Veteran officers and noncoms told them to hold their positions. They broke twice in face of the enemy fire, but spurred on by their leaders, they responded as American kids have always done in past wars.

By night they fought off the attacks by the Communists, and Saturday morning, when the enemy moved in again, the kids fired with more confidence, took the offensive and drove North Koreans out of town.

Even when the enemy slashed the defenses of the city with tanks, those men, with fighting hearts, lashed back and knocked out three tanks and forced the rest of the armored column to withdraw from the battle-scarred South Korean city.

Those kids, dead tired, battle-fatigued — and some of them wounded — drove the Communists out of the railway station on their left flank and proceeded to hammer against the invaders at every point.

They are no longer battle-shy kids.

They are war veterans. They are men who grew up overnight. They are now eager for battle and they are eager to meet the Communist invaders and kick the HELL out of them.

They may lose other battles before this conflict is over. Other American veterans have too, but before the final gong is sounded in this Korean scrap, these kids will have hit victory lane.

On July 28, a brief, dispassionate story on the last page of Pacific Stars and Stripes reported that Peeler was missing in action. He, International News Service correspondent Ray Richards and a jeep driver had last been seen heading toward a frontline infantry battalion — and believable reports later had it that they had run into a North Korean tank. They were never seen again.

The invading North Koreans, trained for a quick knockout, were forced by American and South Korean stubbornness to fight past the tenth round. MacArthur saw their guard drop at Inchon, a shabby, tin-roofed port town on the west coast of southern Korea, and countered with a masterstroke amphibious landing. Capt. Tom Baird, chief of the Pacific Stars and Stripes Korea Bureau, saw the landing in cycloramic splendor and perilous close-up, pounding out this colorful account.

A DREAM OF CONQUEST DIES

SEPT. 19, 1950, BY CAPT. TOM BAIRD

INCHON FRONT — The Red dream of conquest in Korea literally began to go up in smoke at about 4:30 p.m. last Friday when blazing naval guns opened with all-out fire preparatory to the assault on two beaches here.

The word beaches should be in quotation marks, for each consisted not of sand but of a seawall. Reading from north to south they were Red and Blue and were about fives miles apart measuring along the shore.

Midway between the beaches and out to sea the fighting ships were anchored in an irregular line. Farther inshore hundreds of small craft, amphibious tanks, personnel carriers and other types of vehicle-boats as well as LSTs, LCVPs and others, circled in orderly confusion waiting for H-hour, which was 5 p.m.

No one could see the whole operation from the small boats. Each man saw only a small part of it, once the attack began.

Here is a conducted tour of the battle, as seen by one observer:

Guns had been firing intermittently during the afternoon at specific objectives or simply to harass the enemy. At H minus 30 the tempo stepped up, and up, and up to an unbelievable high.

The tremendous booming of broadsides from cruisers mingled with the rapid firing of lighter naval arms which sounded like gigantic hammers driving home nails of monstrous weight.

The rocket ships opened up and their fire defies imagination and vocabulary, so far as adequate description is concerned. Imagine one hundred Roman candles of diameters measured in many inches with a sound like dozens of concrete mixers amplified a thousand times. The rockets detonated in bunches of dozens along the sea walls and in their blazing glare, rocks, dirt and other debris leaped briefly into the air.

Through all this hell of noise, flame and smoke, planes dived continuously, firing rock-

ets and dropping bombs along the assault area. They continued to dive, firing rockets and dropping bombs along the assault area. They continued to dive, fire, pull out, turn, and return.

These sights were not intermittent, like a July Fourth fireworks display. It was continuous, swelling — the smoke constantly rising and spreading from the increasing shell bursts, and the great fires in the town.

Off on the northern flank enemy fire began to come from the forward slope of a small island hill. A fighting ship traversed its guns and at point blank range loosed one broadside. The hill was silent.

The boats circling nearest the shore — all amphibians — straightened out into one long line and began their drive for the beach. Another followed at an interval of four minutes; and another and another. Soon the foot troops were moving in the LCPs. And with them the reporters and photographers.

We had been told that boats of the preceding waves would divide and swing to the flanks. Through the murky air we could not see them.

Wih agonizing slowness, the high, steeply-sloping seawall was mounting; no chance here to drop off the front end of our assault craft. The boats swung broadside to the wall and each man jumped, scrambled upward, clutched desperately for the top and tumbled into a deep enemy-dug trench.

Two things were apparent almost immediately.

First, no one preceded us over the seawall. There was none of the gear — lifejackets and the like — commonly discarded immediately after the beach is hit.

Second, lack of visibility brought us far to the left to blue beach, and about 50 yards from the wall there began another, and unexpected, expanse of water. It could be seen, in the light of the great fires farther inland, that this was an unfinished tidal basin more than a thousand yards long and about half as wide.

There were two platoons of Marines in this force and instead of forming to move inland as skirmishers, they formed two columns of file well-extended and moved to the left, or north, around the perimeter of the basin. The change was made without undue trouble and the march began as a cold rain started to fall. Men moved cautiously, hitting the ground, as the surprisingly light fire — mostly automatic weapons — came our way. The basin's northern limit was reached and the files turned to the east along a narrow way. Up on the point protecting our advance, a movement was detected. The column halted. We heard loud voices. Soon five men in white — North Korean Reds — shambled to the rear under guard. The Marines on this beach had taken their first prisoners.

The end of the march was reached and the platoons were at the edge of the city of Inchon when again there was fire forward — enemy fire. It was impossible for so small a force to risk capture by a larger one here. The traditional Marine assault tactic of fire and rapid movement wouldn't serve us, since we knew we had no supporting elements coming to this beach. Darkness fell and the fires from the guns was slackening sharply. Only one plane was visible. We began the hike back. Again North Koreans were detected. There was a sharp exchange of small arms fire. A Marine threw a grenade. A swift rush caught nine Reds. Seven were docile enough, but two stubbornly resisted capture as prisoners of war. Three of the enemy fell, two killed by the grenade and one by rifle fire.

The Marines had yet to suffer a casualty.

The march was resumed. We turned on a road running south of the tidal basin. There was a shack near the road in black silhouette against the light of a burning warehouse beyond. Suddenly, a flag appeared. Shrill Oriental voices called, as the flag waved: "We are friends. We are friends."

Marines went forward, tense, with rifles ready.

"C'mon outta there."

Nothing happened. They tried again, and again. Still nothing.

On order of his squad leader, one Marine fired two rounds through the roof of the shack. That got action — seven or eight women, two with babies too young to walk, and two men shuffled out.

Then there was discussion: Shall we leave them, or take them along? We took them; refuse to accept the possibility of a trap and you've had it. They moved with us to the end of the road.

Again, there was small arms fire to the front. No casualties, but the second of our two getaway roads was obviously blocked.

It was decided that we must return to the seawall area. Guards were posted quickly on our arrival. Everything that began three hours before with such noise and tumult was ending. Machine guns in the city raved intermittently. The ships' fire slowed down. The only glowing thing was the flames rising from Inchon buildings, with occasional great clouds of fire puffing skyward as gasoline and oil supply points suddenly ignited.

The Marines were weary, not so much from physical effort as from the inevitable letdown after nervous excitement.

We stumbled into the trenches behind the seawall for a night of uneasy sleep. The rain all but stopped, but a cold wind rose to torment us.

A triumphant sweep north was thrown back by a massive intervention of Chinese "people's volunteers" and thousands of refugees joined a southward exodus. They were a tiresomely tragic sight, dispossessed innocents who plodded down the roads like figures in a never-ending pageant and bore their plight with a terrible stoicism. With a compassionate eye and a few words, Cpl. John Bowers fashioned a vivid and telling picture.

"MANY CHINESE, ONLY FEW AMERICANS"

DEC. 19, 1950 BY CPL. JOHN BOWERS
WITH 25TH INF. DIV. IN KOREA — Thousands upon thousands of North Korean refugees crowding roads, rail lines and winding river trails, marching south between Hanju and Kaesong, make up a parade of pathos.

A short time ago, they were liberated. Now they are fleeing from Chinese and North Korean troops.

A 25th Division civil assistance officer claims they were either driven out by the advancing enemy armies, or left for fear of being killed.

The migrants carry their worldly possessions on their backs, or balanced precariously on their heads.

They destroyed everything else when they burned their houses and villages to prevent the enemy from using them. Going over the route of their march, I saw the scorched earth policy the Russian made famous in the Ukraine.

An accurate count of their number is impossible. It is estimated at about 1,350,000 in northeast Korea alone.

Without the Oriental garb, this parade of pathos could have been Poles, Belgians or Frenchmen fleeing the Huns in World War II.

There was a bearded centenarian wearing the white robe and hair hat plodding along with the aid of a hand-carved cane.

A toothless, wrinkled old woman who was paralyzed from the waist down, rode in an oxcart. There were crying children and expectant mothers. I saw one woman in an advanced state of pregnancy, carrying an infant on her back, leading two others, and balancing a huge crock on her head. She was fording a freezing stream.

One pallid youth in GI attire left a hospital bed in Pyongyang to join the exodus. Asked why his people fled, he answered in a mixture of broken Japanese and English, "Many Chinese, only few Americans."

Tiny, obscure, locked in by mountains and totally insignificant — all these things made the village of Chipyong an ideal place for a classic battle in which men became heroes in anger or by chance. Cpl. Bruce Williams skillfully combined the big picture with the mud-level view of the rifleman. Here is his report.

THE BATTLE OF CHIPYONG

MARCH 11, 1951, BY CPL. BRUCE L. WILLIAMS

WITH 2ND DIV., KOREA — If the Korean War has produced a name to match those of Bunker Hill, the Alamo, Anzio and Guadalcanal, it is that of Chipyong.

The four-day siege of this South Korean village started Feb. 13.

It become a military classic when an American regimental combat team and a French volunteer battalion stood up and outfought four Chinese divisions, although cut off and isolated from neighboring units.

There was no attempt to withdraw or break out of the encirclement. The Chipyong garrison held fast until help came to them. By doing this they inflicted the first major ground defeat on enemy masses since the battle for Wonju.

Chipyong is not a large place. At best it would compare to an American town of 3,000 population. Before the war it was a prosperous village with a railroad, a flourishing mill, a school house and an Oriental shrine.

The main street runs along a fair sized stream, which never froze over. To the north fans a wide valley of well-kept rice paddies. Mountains close in to the edge of the village from the east and west.

It was on these mountains that Col. Paul L. Freeman Jr., commander of the 23rd Inf. Regt., built an impenetrable line of defense. From the center of the village it was possible to walk to any unit, even those on the highest ridge lines and mountain tops, in a half hour.

Actually, Chipyong was a neatly welded fortress long before the Chinese struck. Elements of the regiment, with the French, broke into the town from the south on Feb. 4, following their victory at the Twin Tunnels. They set up their perimeter and waited. Until the night of the 13th there was little shifting around, except for patrol actions and light feints of the Chinese.

When the fight for Chipyong came it was

A FOUNDLING OF WAR, a lost little girl cries on a street in Inchon after Marines and Army troops, landed in MacArthur's master-stroke invasion, drove Red forces from the port. Scenes like this were sadly common.

USING A "CHURCH" to store ammunition, the North Koreans discovered, didn't work. A B-26 Invader, foraging over Wonsan, singled it out with a 500-pound bomb in this picture (L), taken by a Far East Air Forces photographer despite a bolt of impact that severely shook the plane. The North Korean Air Force, trained by Soviet military advisers, was hardly in the war — shot out of the sky in a few days by Fifth Air Force pilots who then bombed enemy targets with impunity — although ground defenses were sometimes as deadly as they would be at Thanh Hoa in another war. In those early and desperate days, Americans fighting for time often joined dispossessed refugees in a melacholy exodus south — people without village or home, owning only what they carried or wore. Many parentless children would be picked up and "adopted" by GIs who passed murals of misery like this every day.

USAF

USA

24

BOUND AND SHOT, a soldier who trustfully surrendered to the North Koreans was dealt murder instead of mercy — one of four 21st Infantry Regiment GIs executed this way after their position was overrun in July, 1950. All had been shot through the head. The United Nations Command formed a War Crimes Commission but no captured North Koreans held responsible for such incidents were ever tried because the Korean War Armistice forced the UNC to return captives to the Communist side. even those suspected of multiple instances of torture and murder. Sgt. 1st Class Richard Drozdowski (with walking stick) was far luckier — liberated alive from Chinese Communists who had taken him prisoner. An allied hand helped him along — that of Australian Pvt. Roy Ingle, whose country was one of 16 that joined a unified effort in Korea. In the background is a place Drozdowski, an upstate New Yorker, probably never wanted to see again — the village in which he was held before friendly troops broke through the enemy line.

EMBARRASSED BUT ALIVE, a forlorn North Korean is marched to the rear — forced to keep his hands on his head as his loose trousers suddenly become leggings. Enemy prisoners were often marched naked because, too often, they attempted to kill their captors with grenades and small weapons hidden in their clothes. Once out of the war, many found that the routine of a prisoner was little different than that of a soldier, including the discomfiting but necessary ritual of being "dusted" — sprayed with choking clouds of DDT. Typhus was prevalent and dangerous in a devastated war zone. As the war neither side had wanted to be a long one dragged on, thousands more were captured and sent to offshore islands like Cheju and Koje-do. At Panmunjom, Red negotiators demanded that all prisoners held by the UNC be turned over — although many made it clear they didn't want to go back. The issue stalled the truce talks and prolonged the fighting for several months. The UNC successfully insisted that all Red captives be brought to Panmunjom to be given an either-door, north-or-south choice. Of the 22,000 processed, some 600 chose repatriation. The others — many of them masked to prevent reprisals against relatives in their abandoned homeland — turned south.

USA, Enrique Marques

USA

26

BROTHERS IN MISERY, sailors and Marines both felt the stinging force of the Siberian current when the brutal Korean winter closed in. None of the aged but still useful Corsair fighters on the deck of the carrier Leyte flew in December, 1950 until seamen cleared the flight deck of snow. The "bent-wing bastards" were then launched to support Leathernecks marching out of the "crucible of ice," battering a Chinese army group on the way.

individuals who waged it and won it. This is their story.

This individual is a Frenchman whose name became obscure in the melee of battle. Yet at a critical hour when enemy penetration came dangerously close to the command post, he led a charge of his French comrades with one arm in a sling and in his stocking feet because medics refused to release him.

Sgt. Junior Crayton of Shinston, W.Va., is an infantryman. He walked alone after seven Chinese hiding among some rocks a short distance from his company's position. As he turned the corner of a large boulder, the muzzle of an automatic rifle pressed against his stomach. Crayton did not bargain with the enemy. He shouted for them to surrender and they did.

Out of ammunition, a 17-year-old corporal clubbed two Chinese to death with the butt of his carbine. He broke one carbine stock, picked up another weapon and broke that. In the end he was wielding a steel pole from a reel of barb wire. He was Curtis Rhodes, of Korbyville, Texas.

Angered by the death of a longtime friend, Cpl. Billy Turner, Brownfield, Texas, picked up a pair of field glasses and his rifle and went hunting Chinese. He spent a full day on a rocky hilltop and by nightfall had killed 12 enemy.

Sgt. Orville Hughes of Denver, Colo., was once a chaplain's assistant. He had less than a month in a line company. He was a quiet soldier. When his company was pushed off a hill and lost its machine gun, he quietly went after it. He searched the enemy held hill on his hands and knees in the dark and brought the gun back.

There were other individuals, many others — the whole regiment and their French allies — who fought long and hard to win, and did.

Obscure mountains and long ridgelines continued to become briefly revered monuments — places of horror and honor to men who walked, limped or were carried off them barely alive. There were no eulogies or inscriptions — except in the memories of young men who lost their boyhood or their best friends. Hill 479 was a place that deserved a larger tribute. And Cpl. Murray Fromson gave it something more than a nod and a few words.

SCRATCH ONE MARINE COMPANY — ONE RED REGIMENT

JAN. 28, 1952 BY CPL. MURRAY FROMSON

WITH 1ST MARINE DIV. — Hill 749 is just another Korean ridge to Marine replacements who have arrived here during the last few weeks.

As you drive up the bumpy roads leading to the frontline, the frozen snow capping 749 is deceiving. Its white, clean looking blanket has covered pockmarks which tell the real story of what took place only four short months ago.

It started on the evening of Sept. 15 and ended in the early dawn of the 16th, but to members of F Co., 1st Marine Regt., who have survived, it seemed like a lifetime.

This is the story of one company of Marines who fought off and annihilated an entire North Korean regiment.

More, it is the story of the second platoon of F which started out with a reinforced unit of 68 men. When the battle finally ended all were either killed or wounded in action.

Few of its surviving members are still in Korea to retell the story of the heroic effort turned in by these Marines, who in the face of the most adverse conditions imaginable, refused to yield ground and withstood a fanatical banzai attack by the 91st Regt. of the 45th North Korean Army.

Second Lt. Birney Adams, Tacoma, Wash., winner of the Silver Star and three Purple Hearts for his actions in this fight and the preceeding day's encounter, is one who lived to tell about it. And although he was carried from the hill before the actual banzai started, he can unfold the story in its most minute detail.

Designated to replace the first platoon in the assault, Adams aided personally in coordinating the supporting weapons fire, artillery, mortars and air strike preparatory to the jumpoff.

The attack was delayed all afternoon of the 15th. But finally at 5:10 in the evening, the second platoon moved out. The objective however was changed at the last minute and the Leathernecks had to advance without support. It was done with the aid of one machine gun and an air strike which went after the original target.

The new objective was a knob situated around a bend on the ridgeline spine which commanded the way to Hill 812.

"We got to the bend without resistance," Adams said, "and when two of our men were shot all hell broke loose — and I mean all hell."

This was Adams' first opportunity to lead a platoon in the assault and he admitted later, "You're so damn scared you don't want to move, but you know the men are counting on you so you move."

The Reds had high ground, excellent cover and concealment, fields of fire, fortified bunkers "at least six feet thick" and connecting trenches from the forward to reverse slope.

Two machine guns pinned down the platoon, in addition to a bevy of burp guns. Adams went for one himself (for which he received the Silver Star) and Pvt. Tom Ricardi, Brooklyn, got the other.

Ricardi, a young reservist, passed Adams on the hill, threw him his carbine and said, "I'm goin' after the other gun." Armed with one grenade, he crawled up the forward slope and lobbed the "pineapple" into the Communist position. But nothing happened. It was a dud.

With bullets whizzing overhead he rushed to the rear, grabbed a machine gun and set it up on open ground fronting the Red gun mount. A tremendous stream of fire followed to KO the Communists.

Adams describes Ricardi as "the only man I ever saw who was unafraid at all times." Originally attached to the first platoon, he volunteered to go along on the assault. Now in the States, Ricardi has been recommended for the Navy Cross.

A few minutes after knocking out the two Red machine guns, the Marines assaulted the hill. As the small force got to within five yards of the top, the Reds started rolling grenades down the slope. Within ten seconds, more than 25 exploded in the midst of the assaulting element. Adams was hit in the left leg, but didn't realize

the seriousness of his wounds until he tried to walk. His leg buckled from under him and he was carried from the scene.

Cpl. Bob Morgan, then a Pfc., Oklahoma City, was appointed platoon leader as Adams left on a litter. Morgan and Cpl. Joe Vittori, Beverly, Mass., another volunteer, covered the withdrawal of the platoon which fell back to the point of its original jumpoff.

Morgan has been recommended for the Silver Star, while Vittori, an automatic rifleman later killed in the banzai attack, has been recommended for the Medal of Honor.

When the withdrawal had been completed, Morgan, acting with all the cool efficiency of an experienced platoon leader, reorganized the men, aided in the evacuation of wounded and helped run up a supply of ammunition.

Shortly after midnight Morgan was relieved of his extra burden and Lt. Edward B. Boyd, Pierce, Neb., stepped in.

It was comparatively quiet at midnight with only a few probing attacks breaking the still air.

Then at 1 a.m., they came.

The first wave of fanatical Reds yelling "Marines die, we die, all die!" hit the entire company line, with the second platoon bearing the frontal assault. They were short on ammo. Artillery and mortar fire from the "Four Deuces" was called in and the enemy retired to his position.

They came again about 2:30 and were repulsed only after almost all ammunition and grenades had been expended.

The final banzai hit F at 3:55, preceded by a heavy artillery barrage. The attack lasted one hour, but the Reds were whipped.

As daylight broke on 749, 187 North Korean dead were counted in front of the company lines and an additional 400 to 500 were estimated killed.

Only 11 Marines were still in their holes when A Co. marched through to secure Hill 812 ahead as well as 749 — and they were all wounded. Those wounded could probably thank Navy Hospitalman Tony La Monica, Chicago, whose "selfless devotion to fellow men" gained him recommendation for the Navy Cross. La Monica himself was killed during the banzai.

The survivors have either been rotated or dispersed to other units, but it is doubtful that any will ever forget the nightmarish night on Hill 749.

What makes a hero? Bravery? Impulse? This story doesn't pretend to tell; it merely relates how a sailor thrust only a finger between 250 pounds of steel-jacketed explosive, his ship and the lives of his friends — not to mention his own.

HOLD IT, RALPH ... HOLD IT

MAY 1, 1952

ABOARD USS BOXER IN KOREAN WATERS — The boy who plugged the leak in the dike with his finger has nothing on Ralph V. O'Dell, an aviation ordnanceman first class, who used his finger to keep an armed bomb from exploding.

O'Dell, whose wife and two children live in La Jolla, Calif., was on the flight deck of the carrier Boxer when an F-6F Panther jet plane came from over North Korea with a 250-pound bomb the pilot had been unable to release.

The plane hit the arresting gear and snapped to a halt. The bomb, finally loosened, thundered on up the deck with the little arming propeller on the nose fuse spinning.

Tumbling end over end, the bomb thudded to a halt 500 feet up the deck with its side jammed against the wheel of a parked jet.

It was fully armed and exceptionally sensitive after its rough landing. A tap or pressure on the nose could explode it.

With other planes circling to land and the deck needing clearing, two flight deck crewmen seized the bomb by the tail fin and started to drag it out of the way, not realizing its dangerous condition.

Before they could do any harm, O'Dell, an expert on bombs and fuses, jabbed his finger into the space between the striking pin and the fuse body. This made sure that the plunger couldn't be pushed in accidentally and set off the bomb.

He held his finger in place while Robert R. Baker, aviation ordnanceman first class, Reseda, Calif., and Robert C. Combs, chief aviation ordnanceman, Chula Vista, Calif., carried the bomb to one side of the deck.

By the time, Lt. Frank D. Roberts, Seattle, Wash., air ordnance and bomb disposal officer, could reach the spot, O'Dell had slipped a piece of wood into the mechanism in place of his finger and was calmly removing the fuse.

The still touchy bomb and fuse were both quickly thrown over the side and the circling planes resumed their landing.

One frequently-trumpeted Communist propaganda charge had it that the United States and her 16 allies slaughtered all their North Korean and Chinese captives in a ruthless no-prisoner policy. Hardly true; thousands of docile or defiant prisoners were hauled away from the battleline and interned in coastal areas or offshore islands — and the most well-remembered was to be Koje-do, a green, spacious island a few miles southeast of Pusan. For weeks into months, it would be identified with tragedy and riot. After one American and almost 100 internees died in two riots at troublesome Camp No. 1, the United Nations Command sent 8th U.S. Army Deputy Chief of Staff Brig. Gen. Francis T. Dodd to take over. On May 7, 1952, Dodd trustfully walked to the gate of notorious Compound 76 to talk with prisoners who had asked for him. Before bewildered guards knew what was happening, Dodd was engulfed by prisoners and spirited into the compound.

Dodd was held for a propaganda ransom. He would be released only if the UNC admitted alleged maltreatment.

THE CASE OF THE KIDNAPPED GENERAL

MAY 10, 1952, BY M.SGT. BILL FITZGERALD

HQ. EIGHTH ARMY — Brig. Gen. Francis T. Dodd, a prisoner of his own Red prisoners on Koje-do since Wednesday afternoon, got word out of his compound Friday morning that he "is being treated fine."

The genial commander of the United Nations Prisoner of War Camp No. 1 was dragged inside the compound with another officer who later managed to escape. Friday morning Eighth Army said messages from within the compound are being transmitted by field telephone from Dodd to a telephone in the sentry box just outside the enclosure.

"American cooked meals are being passed through the gate to the general," the announcement said.

Thursday night the Communist prisoners of war had demanded 1,000 sheets of paper. These were at the compound gates Friday morning but had not been delivered.

Dodd had asked that the paper and a hospital representative be allowed to come through the gate.

Friday morning Brig. Gen. Charles F. Colson, Charleston, S.C., who is now the Koje-do commandant, made a new demand for Dodd's release.

Gen. Matthew B. Ridgway, at a planeside press conference Friday morning, told newsmen that the situation on Koje-do was "too tense" to permit their presence on the island immediately. But he said he had no objection to their going to a Fifth Air Force base on the South Korean coast. Many reporters made plans for a morning flight to "sweat out" entry to the island, among them Stars and Stripes staffer Sgt. Murray Fromson.

Dodd and the other officer were in conference with Communist prisoner bigwigs at the gate of one of the compounds on the bleak island of Koje off southern Korea just after 3 p.m. Wednesday.

The Reds pounced on Dodd and his fellow officer and dragged him inside the enclosure, an official release said.

Eighth Army information on Dodd's dramatic seizure was meager at first. It said a note in his handwriting had been received "indicating that he is unharmed."

The official statement also said "efforts are being made to effect the release of General Dodd."

Dodd, who is 53 years old, was graduated from West Point in 1923. Before coming to Korea he was 4th Army Chief of Staff at Fort Sam Houston in San Antonio.

Dodd became deputy chief of staff early in February of this year. He was given command of the UN Prisoner of War Camp No. 1 following the bloody uprising on February 18, when 78 Communist civilian internees were killed and 136 wounded and one American soldier was killed.

In another incident on March 13. South Korean army guards fired on demonstrating North Korean prisoners, killing 12 and wounding 26.

There was only one way to assure Dodd's safe return — agree to a watered-down version of the Red demands. Once out of the compound, Dodd was flown to Tokyo and later demoted to colonel. Brig. Gen. Haydon L. Boatner, a leathery veteran of Heartbreak Ridge, was told to lance the boil in Compound 76. One month and three days after Dodd had been kidnapped, gas-masked troops with bayoneted rifles moved behind a screen of tear gas into 76 and other compounds. Forty-three prisoners were killed and 135 wounded; but many of the dead and injured had fallen under the homemade knives and spears of their comrades when they tried to flee. Corpses that had been buried or otherwise concealed were found in other parts of Compound 76 — the bodies of backsliders who had tried to change ideologies. All of this was seen and well reported by Cpl. Murray Fromson.

Stories of friends, cousins and long-lost brothers finding each other in the vastness of the Army are endless — but seldom has it occurred in the tragic circumstances that Pfc. Jim Morrissey related in one of the most gripping stories of the war.

MEDIC FINDS TWIN MORTALLY WOUNDED

WITH U.S. 40TH DIVISION — A 21-year-old Army medic, called to treat his first combat casualty recently, found his twin brother lying mortally wounded in a shallow trench, just one year to the day from the time the twins entered the service.

The medic, Pvt. Irwin Rietz, Rock Island, Ill., said he was so busy treating the wounded man that he did not recognize his brother, Edwin, until he lifted him into a litter jeep.

"You do not have time to worry about who you are treating at a time like that," Rietz said. "I rolled him over, ripped open his shirt, and exposed a small wound in his chest."

As he started to apply a bandage, his wounded brother raised his head and moaned. Without looking up from his work, Rietz said, "Take it easy, buddy, you are going to be all right."

It was only when he and two other men lifted the wounded man into an evacuation jeep that he got a look at his patient's face and realized that it was his twin.

"I knew that I had done everything possible for him on the hill, so I followed him down in another jeep. I thought he was wounded only slightly. When I arrived at the collecting station, the doctor told me he was dead."

First Lt. James M. Lawson, Rochester, N.Y., who treated Rietz, said that a small sliver of shrapnel from a mortar severed an artery, causing severe internal bleeding. Lawson said it was only a pinpoint wound, but that Rietz was bleeding so badly that there was no chance of saving him.

The twins had been in the service exactly one year and had never been separated. They were assigned, at their own request, to the same company when they arrived in Korea about two months ago.

A third brother, Ronald, recently rotated to the States after serving with a combat engineer outfit in another division. He made a surprise visit to the twins on the frontlines just before leaving for home.

The surviving twin was immediately taken off line and will accompany his twin's body back to the States.

Pfc. John Sack came to Pacific Stars and Stripes with a reputation of sorts. Before entering the Army, he had written a book about a deadly Peruvian mountain called Yerupaja, claiming his work was "the worst selling book on the best seller list." Be that as it may, he was one of the finest reporters the newspaper ever had. These three pieces, written in about a month's time, beat out heavy competition to be Sack's best.

.45 SILENCES MACHINE GUN

FEB. 22, 1953, SPOTTER PILOT, OBSERVER SILENCE 'NEST' WITH .45

ON THE WESTERN FRONT — First Lt. Edward G. Polanski dove his observation plane at a Chinese machine gun Friday morning while his observer knocked it out with a .45 pistol.

Then 1st Lt. Walter Moran, his observer, put his lethal .45 back in the holster, and the pair put-putted back home in their light plane. Polanski didn't think it was very strange.

"You get pretty frustrated up there," he said. "You adjust artillery, of course, but you can't shoot anything yourself."

Polanski, who comes from Wallingford, Conn., had flown over 140 observation missions in his L-19 before he tried some shooting on his own. Moran, a regular "passenger," is from Atlanta, Ga.

"We were up early this morning looking for targets for the tanks. Then this machine gun started firing at us. That's happened a lot of times, but this guy persisted. We got pretty "teed off" — me and Moran.

"So I said to Moran, 'Let's make a pass at them' and he pulls out his .45 and fires a clip.

"Then I made another pass and Moran fired another clip. So the machine gun stopped firing — it didn't fire again — and we figured a possible kill."

WHO'S ON BALDY?

MARCH 27, 1953

AT AN OBSERVATION POST NEAR BALDY — A man walked in here Tuesday afternoon and said, "Who's on Baldy? Regiment wants to know."

Sgt. Samuel Hamilton, Philadelphia, had been staring at the dusty knob all day through powerful binoculars. "I don't know," he said. "You can't tell."

For two days Old Baldy had been a no-man's-land — with men on it. The hill is not a tall one. Its top is flat and its sides fall off gently.

On the slope lies the wreckage of bunkers, and shells kick up nothing but dust, as if they had fallen into a flour keg.

On the sides of Old Baldy the trenches are still intact. Every now and then you can see men in them, running uphill in a low stoop, ducking to the ground as the black puff of a mortar appears nearby, running back when the fire gets too heavy.

Once or twice a man turned the corner in a trench. A shell exploded behind him, and you hold your breath. Is he hurt? Nobody goes to get him, and you know he is safe.

You can't see any Chinese. They are hiding in trenches at the top of the hill or on the slope behind it. Now and then they toss a grenade over the top, and now and then our men see someone to fire at.

These are the men that division is talking about when they speak of "our furthest line of advance," or "the U.N. position."

But here is the best OP near Baldy; it isn't so easy to tell. A colonel and a lieutenant colonel stood at the binoculars yesterday morning and tried to figure out where our soldiers were, so our artillery would hit the right people.

"Give me the furthest limits of their advance," said the colonel into a field phone. "Have they passed the saddle there on the other side of the lumber pile?"

"No definite answer on that," said the voice on the other end. He was on Baldy itself and he wasn't sure where the lines were. "I'll try and tell you in just a moment."

"You see that round that just came in?" asked the colonel. "Where are you in reference to that?"

At the base of Baldy we could see the smoke of dropping artillery, sometimes three or four in a second. Then we heard the sound over the phone, and a few seconds later the sound itself. By then a dozen more shells had fallen.

The door of the bunker opened, and Lt. Gen. Maxwell D. Taylor walked in. The Eighth Army commander had just flown up from Seoul.

"See that bunker with the large aperture?" the colonel said to him. "We think that's as far as our troops have gotten."

"Put the scope where you think our frontlines to be — our advanced troops," said Taylor. The colonel did. For 15 minutes the men looked over the hill.

"I'm not up here to tell you how to run this," Taylor explained. "But I've . . ." As he gave his suggestion a personnel carrier covered with dead Chinese made its way slowly down the slope.

That's what has been happening on Baldy for the last two days. And it may keep happening for a few more.

UN MERRY-GO-ROUND

MARCH 29, 1953, BY PFC JOHN SACK

SEOUL — By the sacred white elephant, zis United Nations army she makes dizzy ze mind, niet waar?

You could drive along the battle-front last week and here's what you'd see; a battalion of Americans, a battalion of Dutchmen, a battalion of French, and a battalion of Siamese — all of them side by side.

You could drive it on a gallon of gas, and what's worse, I did.

It's the United Nations-ingest line in Korea. "How are you getting along with the Dutch?" I asked at the American battalion.

"Brother, you mean how could we get along without them," said a sergeant from Texas. "We were on a patrol last night and we ran into a whole slew of Chinese. They had us backed up against our minefield, and we had to fight it out.

"The Dutch heard the shooting and came running to help us. Except for them, we'd of never gotten out."

"OK," I said, "now I'll ask the Dutch about it." And I started down the road in the jeep, and got lost.

"Is this the Dutch Battaion?" I asked a soldier who looked sort of Dutch.

"Me ne talkie Inglis so bun," he said.

"All right, I'll say it slower, is this the — holy cow, what language was that?" It sounded like English and Dutch and French, and by gosh, it was.

"It's talkie-talkie," said the soldier.

USA, Winslow

DEATH BY SUFFOCATION was the sentence retreating North Koreans passed on political dissidents as United Nations Forces closed in on Hamhung. A weeping townswoman finds faces she knew among prisoners who were herded into caves, then sealed off to die. This war was full of frightful images.

BREATHING THUNDER, 155mm Long Toms light up mountain and paddy as they send crate-sized shells soaring toward Chinese and North Koreans opposing the early 1951 UNC counteroffensive that would seize back miles of ground lost in the Red assault late the year before. The long guns were just south of the Imjin River, the moat that failed to stop Lt. Gen. Matthew Ridgway as he launched Operations Killer and Ripper, deflating the Chinese theory that in numbers, there was invincibility. The "human sea" attacks sank under the shattering firepower of field artillery and naval guns.

LIFE OR DEATH battle is fought by unarmed medics behind a broken wall, close to a rifle-to-rifle brawl in a gutted Korean town. Any clearing or clump of trees could become an outdoor hospital heaped with moaning wounded — dispatched there by the urgent cry: "Medic!" One medic, having done all he can for a casualty, appears to clasp his hands in an appeal beyond mortal effort or medicine — a gesture seen often seen in crowded frontline aid stations.

USA, Albert Chang

WEEPING FOR A LIFELONG FRIEND, a soldier is comforted by a medic in one of the most widely seen and best-remembered pictures of the Korean War. The GI's lifelong buddy had been hit by mortar fire on Subok Mountain, close to Masan, and died as he looked on and another medic marked off a life on a casualty tag. Sgt. Ist Class Al Chang, an Army photographer, happened by and hurriedly snapped a classic photograph — later picked by Edward Steichen for his Family of Man display, seen by millions all over the world.

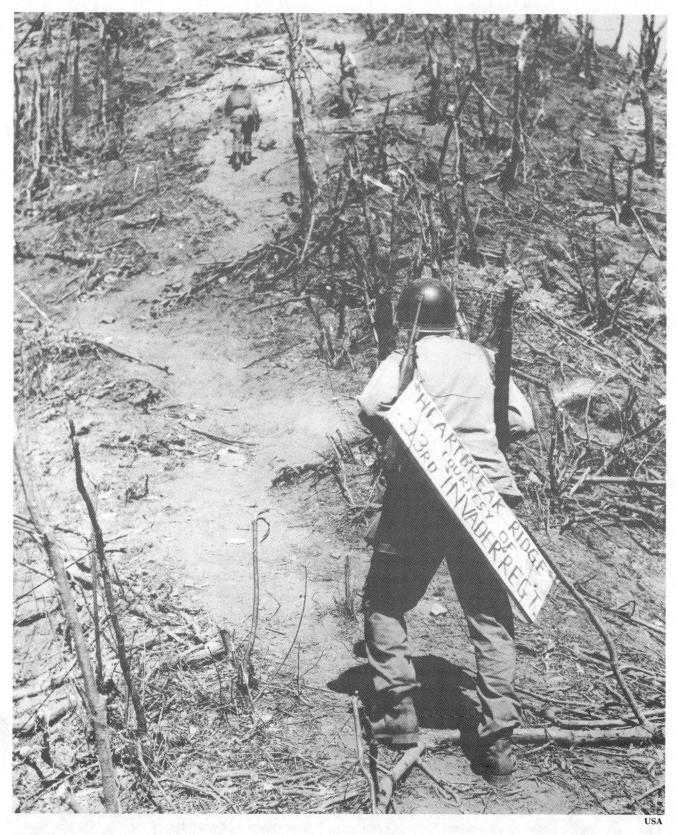

USA

HEARTBREAK RIDGE was so named because of the lives lost on its slope and crest — 597 Americans and soldiers from the French Battalion attached to the 2nd Infantry Division. Survivors earned the right to post this sign.

SAVING ONE LIFE, a frontline medic with too few hands will soon have another to fight for as GIs pull a wounded buddy onto a plateau pressed into service as a dispensary. In this "hospital," a patient's helmet was his pillow and his bed a canvas litter on hard ground. Trees served as plasma racks and sunlight illuminated an operating room. A casualty often clung to his rifle as if it were the comforting hand of a good friend and an anchor on life.

CRASHING IN FLAMES, an old Skyraider drafted as a Korean War workhorse comes apart in a spectacular series of photographs on the deck of the carrier Philippine Sea. Hit by anti-aircraft fire over northeast Korea, it limped back to home deck and first shed its engine, then was blanketed in a bright roll of flame, coming to rest as a hollow hulk. To everybody's prayerful relief, the pilot walked away with minor bruises and burns. The Skyraider would also do yeoman work in Vietnam.

USN Photos

PRINCE AND THE PAUPER was a tragic but touching vignette in a small village trampled to death by war. Cpl. James R. Areys of the 27th Infantry (Wolfhound) Regiment hardly looked princely in field jacket and grenade harness, but he was nobilty to a blind and abandoned little Korean girl he found squalling with hunger. The war was just ahead, but Areys found time to open a can of rations. What happened to the little girl? Was she taken in hand to join one of the refugee columns that streamed ceaselessly southward?

USA, Eugene Fox

USA, Peter Ruplenas

WHERE TO GO? Refugees dispossessed from home ground had no real idea, following only the instinct to flee the sound of guns. North Koreans released from POW camps disdained their homeland and sought a new life.

USA

WORN AND HAGGARD, Maj. Gen. William F. Dean shows the effects of a 3½-year ordeal as a North Korean prisoner. Dean commanded the 24th Infantry Division and led the first finger-in-the-dike force against the North Koreans.

"Sure," he said. "Mama, papa, me — where I come from, everybody talk talkie-talkie."

"Where do you come from?" I asked.

"Dutch Guiana. In South America."

At least this is the Dutch battalion I figured. Maybe.

"Our language is kind of mixed up," said the soldier.

"Quite," I agreed. "Do you know where S-2 is?"

"We also have five Hindus. They speak Hindu," he said.

When I found S-2, 15 minutes later, an officer from Rotterdam told me about the patrol.

"The American patrol, and he has troubles," said the officer. "We send advance out so man to help thems — give them stand by.

"And the sergeant shoot a light flare and someone say, 'Hey some man already shoot — pfft, pfft.' So we save American!"

"Well," I said, "I guess that clears that up."

The door to S-2 had a sign in Dutch on the outside and a sign in English on the inside. The one on the outside said: "Wees militair groet en meld je." (Be a good soldier and report)

The one on the inside, under a rather nude pin-up said, "Say big boy, I know you are hot to go! But . . . sign out."

"Do you folks get much Dutch food?" I asked the officer.

"Sure," he said. "We get rice twice a week."

"Is that Dutch food?"

"Well, he said, "many of us fought in Indonesia. It comes now, we like rice." He offered me a beer mug carved like a barrel.

"Heinekens?" I asked.

"Lemonade," he said.

"Now one more question. How do you get along with the French, on your other flank?"

"Often," said the officer, "we do five Dutch soldiers and five French soldiers to make a screening patrol. And here is a man" — he pointed at a man — "who shoots mortar flares when the French ask them."

I asked the man: "Where are you from in Holland?"

"Poland," he said.

"His Polish name is Obuch," said the officer. "We call him Opoe, because that's Dutch for grandmother." They both laughed, but not very hard.

"I see," I said. "Now I go to the French

Battalion, and ask them about the screening patrol."

But I had other things to tell the French. "Did you know," I told them, "they have men from South America and Poland in the Dutch Battalion?"

"No no," said a captain, "We have no men here from ze South America."

"No," I said, "Dutch Battalion."

"We have a man here from ze Africa."

"An ARAB?" I asked.

"Most certainly, ze Arab." He whistled, and along came an Arab. "This is Monsieur Medda," the captain said. "He is from ze Algeria. We have 100 of him in the battalion."

What language does he speak?" I asked.

"Kabyle, of course."

"Please say something in Kabyle," I asked Medda. He seemed to gargle for a few seconds. "What did he say?"

"Ah, I may not tell you," said the captain. "He says bad things about your mother."

"When you pray to Mecca," I asked Medda, "do you face east or west?"

"We face east," he said. "Moslems always face east to Mecca."

"But Mecca is west," I said.

"Nevertheless we face east," said Medda. "We face around the world and there it is again."

"What I really want to know," I told the captain, "is how you folks get along with the Dutch."

"Ah, with ze Hollanders we are great friends. On patrols we — hey!" He whirled to a Korean houseboy who was walking by. "Jimmy!" he said, putting the accent at the end, "I've been looking for you." And he rattled off something in French.

The Korean, who was about 14 or 15 years old, replied, "Non, mon capitaine. Je ne l'ai pas fait. Ce sont mes camarades."

"He says he didn't do it, it was his friends," said the captain disgustedly.

"Now about these Dutchmen . . .?"

"Also," said the captain, "we are great friends with ze Thailanders. Often we invite them for wine."

"You have wine here?" I asked.

"But of course!" he said. "Ze men at ze front have ze wine in ze jerrycan. Or in ze canteen."

"I think I'll check with the Thailanders," I said.

"I maybe know about the French on one

44

night," said a Thailander, three miles and ten minutes down the road. "My patrol go out to the front and see about the three men.

"So we call our S-2 and our S-2 check to the French. 'Is that the French send your soldiers on patrol?,' My S-2 asks the French.

"Okay, I send my soldiers," says the French. "So my S-2 tells me don't shoot, it is the French."

"You mean," I asked, "you saw three soldiers in the night? You thought they were Chinese? But they weren't, they were French?"

"That's right," said the Thailander. "But of course we help the French too. Our French soldier and our Thai soldier don't know each other to the language, but we are good friends."

"How about the Americans on your other flank?"

"I tell you funny story," said the Thailander. "My soldier he drives truck yesterday, he sees some GIs hitchhiking. He stops truck. 'Get in my truck,' he says."

"When he gets out of truck, GI says to my soldier," 'Wish you luck!' "

"So my soldier says, 'Oh, never mind, today hava yes, tomorrow hava no!'"

"Why did he say that?" I asked.

'He thought the GI wanted a Lucky Strike," said the Thailander.

"Oh," I said, "Now tell me how come golden umbrellas are sacred in Thailand?"

"Because the king and the queen, wherever they go, they have golden umbrellas above them."

"If the king came to Korea, would he have to have a golden umbrella?"

The Thailander stroked his chin. "In the front, maybe not use."

"I guess that does it," I said. "Thanks a lot." And I started the jeep. "Say, incidentally — which of you is firing the artillery? The Thailanders, the French, the Dutch, or the Americans?"

"The artillery?" said the Thailander. "That is from the Scotsmen."

So I drove away, and picked up a hitchhiker about a mile down the road. He looked sort of Oriental, but he wore Canadian clothes, a chartreuse scarf, and a beret.

On the beret was a pin with the words, "Ubique quo fas et ducunt gloria."

That's Latin.
"Are you a Thailander?" I asked.
"No," he said.
"Are you a Korean?"
"No."
"What outfit are you from?"
"No."
"Nihongo-wa wakarimasuka?"
"No."

He got off at the 2nd Division. I don't know. Maybe he was a Communist.

And then a long, indecisive shooting war transformed into a truce — one that was to be the longest armistice in history. It ended with the bang of the last shots, the whimper of the wounded and dying and the scratching of fountain pens. There wasn't much for SSgt. Bob McNeill to tell — just a careful recitation of wooden formalities.

THEY SIGNED QUICKLY, QUIETLY AND SOLEMNLY

JULY 27, 1953 BY SSGT. BOB McNEILL

PANMUNJOM — Truce delegates this morning quietly wound up their two years of peace-waging and rang down the curtain on the 37-month shooting war in Korea.

The formal end of the war was wrapped up in 10 minutes of document signing. Chief United Nations Truce Delegate Lt. Gen. William K. Harrison and North Korean General Nam II sat down at 10 o'clock this morning and in a business-like manner wrote the Korean war into history.

The first document of the imposing pile was signed by the opposing sides at 10:01. It took the generals 10 minutes to work their way through the war-ending papers.

At 10 o'clock tonight soldiers will turn over the problems of Korea to powers of the governments concerned. The shooting phase of the bloody war will then be over.

The copies of the armistice agreement were delivered to General Mark Clark at Munsan-ni and to the Communists at Pyongyang. General Clark signed his copies today at 1 p.m. The North Korean commander at the time of his signing was still unknown this morning.

There were 18 copies of the agreement. The U.N. prepared nine and the Reds nine. General Clark and the Communist commanders signed their respective copies earlier this morning before they were brought to Panmunjom.

When they signed the documents prepared by the opposing sides today the armistice was complete.

The armistice was prepared in three languages, English, Korean, and Chinese. Each got three copies of each, making a total of 18 copies that were signed this morning.

The ceremony was staged in the tar-papered, straw-matted building built by the Communists last week especially for the occasion.

The delegates arrived simultaneously at 10 a.m. They immediately sat down and began the actual signing.

The signatures were applied on a row of three tables that were stretched for about 30 feet. The Reds sat on the north end and the U.N. delegates on the south. In front of each senior delegate was his flag — a U.N. flag for Harrison and a North Korean one for Nam II.

The U.N. group included Rear Adm. John C. Daniel, Brig. Gen. Ralph N. Osbourne, and Maj. Gen. George F. Finch.

They sat silently at the south end of the U.N. table while Harrison put his name on the truce agreement.

As Harrison signed the papers, Col. James C. Murray, senior U.N. liaison officer, picked up each copy and arranged them for presentation to the Reds.

High ranking officials from both sides watched the ceremony. The Communists sat on the north side of the building and U.N. personnel were seated on the south side.

The Communists split into two groups — North Korean and Chinese. The North Koreans were dressed in red-striped blue trousers and olive drab jackets, the Chinese "volunteers" sat opposite them wearing dull olive drab trousers and tunic, minus rank insignia.

The U.N. copies were bound in blue-backed volumes. The copies prepared by the Reds came in red leather folders.

U.N. correspondents almost filled the area alloted for visiting officials. Only about a dozen Red reporters were on hand.

The Communist reporters, not as lucky as U.N. ones, were jammed between the right of the camera battery and the wall.

Neither the flash bulbs nor the noises made by the photographers seemed to disturb Harrison and Nam II. They signed quickly, quietly and solemnly.

AFTER KOREA

1953-1970

Truce Signed

STARS AND STRIPES
PACIFIC

UNOFFICIAL PUBLICATION OF UNITED STATES FORCES, FAR EAST

Vol. 9, No. 207   Entered as third class matter in the Tokyo Central Post Office   Monday, July 27, 1953

Fighting Ends Tonight

Ike Declares Challenge Met by U.N.

WASHINGTON, July 27 (AP)—President Eisenhower declared today that in the Korean war just halted by an armistice the U.N. had met the challenge of aggression "with deeds of decision."

But the chief executive warned the American people in an extraordinary radio-TV broadcast from the White House that "we must not relax our guard."

During the coming times of screening prisoners of war and exchanging them, and of the political conference "looking toward the unification of Korea," he said, the U.S. and its allies must be "vigilant against untoward" events.

MR. EISENHOWER began the brief but historic broadcast a little less than one hour after the armistice agreement was signed at Panmunjom.

He sat at his desk in the White House broadcast room.

"Tonight," he began, "we greet with thanksgiving the signing of an armistice."

"The cost of repelling aggression has been high. . .incalculable. , it has been paid in terms of tragedy."

The President expressed "solemn gratitude for those who gave up their lives in a foreign land."

Mr. Eisenhower said the Korean war had proved that "only courage and sacrifice can keep freedom alive upon this earth."

"**IT IS PROPER** that we salute particularly the valor of the armies of South Korea," Mr. Eisenhower said.

He said that men of the West and men of the East can fight
(Continued on Page 16, Col. 4)

By S/Sgt. Bob McNeill

PANMUNJOM, July 27 (Pac. S&S)—Truce delegates this morning quietly wound up their two years of peace-waging and rang down the curtain on the 37-month-old shooting war in Korea.

THE FORMAL END to the war was wrapped up in 10 minutes of document-signing. Chief United Nations Truce Delegate Lt. Gen. William K.

Harrison and North Korean General Nam II sat down at 10 o'clock this morning and in a business-like manner wrote the Korean war into history.

THE FIRST DOCUMENT of the imposing pile was signed by the opposing sides at 10:01. It took the generals 10 minutes to work their way through the war-ending papers.

At 10 o'clock tonight sol-
(Continued on Page 16, Col. 4)

Clark Says Difficulties Not Ended

SEOUL, July 27 (Pac. S&S)—General Mark W. Clark today told the troops in his command that "we cannot turn our backs on the conflict and go home" after an armistice is signed.

The U. N. commander described this morning's armistice as a possible step toward peace but not the end of the war until the opposing governments work out a firm political settlement.

The leader of the 21 nations arrayed against the Communists in Korea told Allied forces their responsibilities and duties would now be heightened and intensified rather than diminished.

"**THIS IS WHY,**" the general said. "An armistice is a military agreement between opposing commanders to cease fire and to permit opposing sides to attempt a solution of the conflict by a political conference."

The military leaders of each side have agreed to recommend to their governments that a political conference be held within three months.

General Clark said flatly the armistice does not mean an immediate or even an early withdrawal from Korea. He stated the U. N. would not lower its guard or dissipate its strength after the signing of the truce.

HIS COMPLETE MESSAGE follows:

"Three years of agonizing conflict, accompanied during the past two years by determined and frustrating negotiations, have at last brought an armistice to the valiant people of South Korea and her allies.

"This armistice is of vital im-
(Continued on Page 16, Col. 2)

SOLEMN SIGNING—Lt. Gen. William K. Harrison, chief U.N. truce delegate, autographs copies of the truce document he helped hammer out in two years of sometimes bitter negotiations while two aides look on in Panmunjom. (AP Photo)

Korea was still a land divided when the 1953 Armistice was signed; the Demilitarized Zone slashed jaggedly across the 151-mile front, with 4,000 meters of wilderness between the Communist and UNC lines. It was full of thick forests, dead farmland and deserted villages — with one flicker of life on the United Nations side. Tae Song Dung has often been compared to the Mediterranean principality of Monaco. Its citizens live in a strange political limbo, well described by Pvt. Al Ternes.

STRANGERS WHEN THEY MET — AND MARRIED

DEC. 13, 1955, BY PVT. AL TERNES

TAE SONG DUNG IN THE DMZ, Korea — Miss Pak Yung Soon bowed deeply Monday to a man she had never seen before and became the first bride in five years in this isolated village between North and South Korea.

Her marriage to Chung Il Tong was performed with ancient rites and symbols, but an unusual modern influence was present.

Parked outside was a U.S. Army 2½-ton truck. It carried the bridegroom and relatives to the wedding.

The only way the bridegroom could come to the wedding was in the Army truck. He also had to have special permission and be escorted by Maj. Francis Birnley, civil affairs officer of the 24th Infantry Division.

Tae Song Dung is shut off from all other villages. Only with a special pass and under escort of a U.S. officer can a Korean enter or leave the cluster of huts that makes up the village.

Swiss and Swedish officers from the Neutral Nations Supervisory Commission at Panmunjom joined Birnley and other Americans at the wedding. This village is one of the few places the Neutral Nations members can visit freely.

Tae Song Dung became a village without a country July 27, 1953, when the U.N. and Communists agreed to a truce and each pulled back two kilometers to form a buffer zone.

The village was inside the buffer zone and was given to U.S. Forces for administration. Its residents now lead a strangely peaceful, happy and prosperous life between the ready guns of two big forces.

But neither bride nor bridegroom seemed aware of the international aspects as they nervously went through the wedding ceremony before a well-laid table.

The bridegroom, wearing a black hat, maroon decorated robe and black felt shoes, entered the wedding area first and walked to the table. Then the bride, escorted by two older women, emerged from her room and walked to the table, holding a veil over her face.

After both bride and bridegroom bowed and drank from a brass cup, she lowered the veil. For the first time she saw her husband. The marriage was arranged by a matchmaker and the two families.

Then the couple went into an adjacent room, and like everybody else, ate a wedding meal.

"This is the first wedding in Tae Song Dung since 1950," Kim Nam Soo, the village chief, said. He was especially pleased with the proceeding, he said.

The entire village waited to see if the wedding would come off and somehow the chief's reputation depended upon its success. The exact date was arranged through ancient sacred Korean books and if the wedding had not taken place Monday, it would have had to wait an entire year.

Pfc. Mel Derrick was out of his bailiwick on this story. Ordinarily a sports writer and a good one, he was in Korea interviewing football coaches of military teams when Gene Donner, the Korea Bureau chief, noticed a stir of activity near UNC headquarters in Seoul. Donner asked bystanders the right questions and got a valuable tip. The next morning, Derrick walked into enemy territory and got a stirring feature.

THE FLOWERS ON HILL 139

AUG. 24, 1956, BY PFC MEL DERRICK

IN THE DMZ, Korea — Atop Hill 139 in the North Korea sector of the Demilitarized Zone is a small bush. Its tiny purple flowers look strangely out of place in the rusted clutter of a once-bloody battlefield.

It was here, 16 miles northeast of Munsan-ni and 1,000 yards on the North Korean side of the DMZ, that UNC/MAC Joint Observer Team No. 2 Wednesday reclaimed portions of the remains of two U.S. servicemen believed killed in February 1953. Five other bodies were returned last week.

Wednesday's vehicle caravan to the DMZ was led by Lt. Col. Allen R. Lawrence, senior member of the UNC/MAC team, and escorted by 24th Div. military police to the jointly patrolled military demarcation line.

After a brief meeting with the Reds requesting safe conduct to the spot where the bodies were located. The U.N. group walked single file to a battle-scarred hill designated Hill No. 139.

Battered, dusty remains of the fight cluttered the hill and its ridges. A half-destroyed machine gun stood crazily on two legs. A U.S. flamethrower with the name June Christy neatly lettered on its tanks lay to one side. Ammunition and hand grenades and rusted parts of other weapons, both U.S. and Communist, littered the hill.

The lower slopes were covered with waist-high grass and small shrubs. On the west side, a huge bunker had collapsed and on the east a bomb or ammunition dump explosion had carved out a 25-foot crater. The top was bare, except for the small bush.

Armed Communist guards slouched nearby as the American graves registration team began its search for the remains.

Picking away at the loose dirt in bunkers, team members uncovered parts of rifles, many bones, helmets and buttons from Marine Corps clothing. A water can with markings of the 3rd Bn., 7th Regt., 1st Marine Div., was found during an earlier expedition. A Marine Corps dog tag was also uncovered.

The U.S. soldiers dug gingerly. You dig that way when three-year-old unexploded hand grenades lie just under the surface. "We hit one with the pin rusted about three-fourths of the way through," Cpl. Dick Garfield, of Jacksonville, Ill., said during a smoke break. "The handle was bent and we weren't sure the pin would hold until we could get it out of the way. It was pretty touchy but we knew remains were there so we removed it."

Being in Communist territory didn't worry the graves registration men nearly as much as the grenades.

"I was a little shook about coming over the first time," said Pfc. 3 Joe Meley of Lancaster, Pa., "but this is my second trip across the line and I feel OK now."

"It's a job," added Sgt. 1 C. Russell Adams, of Lawrence, Kan., non-commissioned officer in charge of the graves registration. "No matter where, it's got to be done."

There was little attempt at fraternization between the working Americans and the ever-watchful North Koreans.

One American officer had a small portable radio. The North Koreans were fascinated when he flipped it on during the lunch break. They grinned as he tuned in Radio Pyongyang and turned pokerfaced when he switched to an AFKN disc jockey program out of Seoul. But then they moved closer to listen.

The North Korean uniforms varied, apparently according to personal choice. Most of the privates wore tennis sneakers and faded, baggy cotton khaki uniforms, reinforced in the seat with a large circular patch.

The top officers, a pair of lieutenant colonels, had on black, knee-high boots, black riding pants and white cotton shirts buttoned to the neck.

Flashiest dresser of all was a cocky young

Communist in khakis trimmed with a small red shoulder patch and tremendous red epaulets.

U.S. interpreter Samuel Kim explained he was a private in the North Korean Military Police.

By 2 p.m., the Americans had finished their search of Hill 139 and had started back to free territory, bearing their finds on stretchers. Halfway back, the only thing that distinguished 139 from the rest of the North Korean hills was a small bush with tiny purple flowers.

They didn't look much alike, the old philosopher in an African jungle and a young former Navy lieutenant who walked into a remote corner of Laos. But Albert Schweitzer and Thomas A. Dooley both dedicated themselves to a life of compassionate sacrifice. Dooley was to die tragically young — but not before he accomplished part of a noble purpose. He was on his way to Laos when City Editor Pat Carroll caught him for a brief but vibrant interview.

A DREAM AND $29,000

AUG. 25, 1956, BY TECH. SGT. PAT CARROLL
TOKYO — A young ex-Navy doctor with a dream in his heart and $29,000 in his bank account breezed through Tokyo Friday heading for the Kingdom of Laos to spend the money for medical care.

Dr. Thomas A. Dooley, author of the best seller, "Deliver Us From Evil," arrived from the U.S. enroute to Vientiane, the capital of Laos, where he will set up a medical headquarters. There, with his team of three ex-Navy corpsmen, he will travel from village to village and tribe to tribe dispensing medical care.

The cost of the operation will be paid from the profits of his book and donations received from other Americans and supplies from business firms to help him with his work.

"All the wealth I have came from Asia," he said Friday, "and I intend to go back there."

Dooley, a former enlisted man in the Navy during World War II, resigned his commission earlier this year to return to Indo-China.

After the fall of Dien Bien Phu, Dooley was placed in charge of a small Navy medical unit in Haiphong, North Vietnam, to assist refugees fleeing Communism.

The unit built huge refugee camps for the thousands of escapees who sought freedom in the south. In his time there, he processed and treated some 600,000 people. It was this story that made his best seller.

Now he is returning to the same area where he may again treat many of the 600,000 who passed through the camps. He will be one of only two doctors among the two million people.

"We want to be on the offensive for America, not just denying what the Communists say about us, but getting there and doing something about it," he said. "We shall try to translate the democratic ideals we do possess into Asian realities that they can possess. Our instrument shall be medicine."

"While we (the U.S.) are preaching God's precepts," Dooley explained, "and the Voice of America proclaims our good intentions, the Communists are moving in among the naked masses of humanity who never saw a missionary, nor heard a radio; and they appear to practice exactly what we preach.

"I want to get down among them, I want to show them four young Americans who are willing to come to them, to treat them and help them, for no other reason than because they want to. That's the kind of American democracy I want them to know." The doctor explained that they are associated with no church, missionary group or State Department organization. "We are strictly on our own," he said.

Al Ricketts was for years the first name many daily readers turned to — a wise and witty critic who chronicled show business and interviewed the famous.

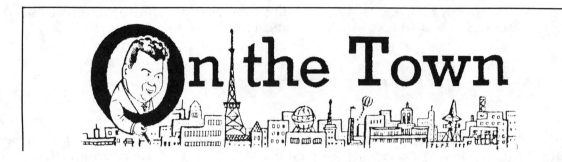

On the Town

FEB. 2 1957, BY AL RICKETTS

Everybody asks us the same question about Marlon Brando "What's he like?"

The answer isn't simple. To say what Brando is "like" would be harder than re-winding an unraveled golf ball.

In the first place, we don't know him. We've met him and we've talked to him for a while. But we don't know him. We'll wager that few people do.

We only can give our impressions — impressions formed after three comparatively brief meetings. To begin with, he makes you nervous. You get the feeling he may explode and splash all over you without warning.

He suggests violence without committing it. Violence of the table-clearing variety depicted in "Streetcar Named Desire." It's probably this one characteristic that makes him the great actor he is.

Brando is not interested in small talk. He can make polite conversation but obviously doesn't enjoy it. Yet he becomes very talkative when a subject strikes his fancy.

The camera you're carrying might interest him — and if it does, he'll ask a lot of questions. When he has learned all he wants to know, he settles back in his chair and waits for you to carry the ball.

Marlon never answers a question without giving it a lot of thought. His answers are long and tedious and he sometimes gets lost in the middle. When this happens, he smiles and starts over again.

Our most recent meeting with Marlon took place in Kyoto where he is starring in Warner Bros. "Sayonara."

While we were talking, he summoned a room boy and placed an order for three fried eggs, bacon, toast and coffee. This was a big mistake. Any Japan veteran who has ordered a "piece of pie" and wound up with a "pizza pie" could predict what would happen next.

Counting three of us in the room (a Stripes photographer was the third party), the boy summed it up and came back with three orders of two fried eggs instead of one order of three fried eggs.

Marlon didn't say a word. He fixed the boy with his best "On the Waterfront" stare, signed the tab and said in an almost inaudible voice, "Thank you." The boy bowed out of the room, happy that he had pleased Marlon Brando.

Marlon was silent for a moment or two before sighing. "You can't win . . . Would you fellows like some eggs?"

While Marlon ate we talked about a lot of things. He repeated that he wasn't happy with his performance in "Teahouse of the August Moon" and dismissed his part in "Sayonara" with, "You can't really tell yet."

He seemed quite enthused over his independent motion picture company (called Pennypacker). When he returns to the States he'll produce, direct and star in a Western, tentatively titled, "Beast of Vermillion."

At the end of our talk, Marlon apologized because he didn't feel it had gone too well. "I'm sorry," he said. "I had something on my mind."

We learned later that photographer Hank Simons, who was shooting during the interview, had distracted him. This puzzled us no end. We felt quite sure that the Brando we had heard about would speak up if something was bothering him.

What's Marlon Brando like?

We honestly don't know.

Meet you . . . On the Town

Anyone who has ever read Edgar Allan Poe's "The Premature Burial" or "The Cask of Amontillado" can find the same horror in the real-life ordeal of Sgt. I.C. Asa Lewis, who spent a terrifying hour in an undersea air trap. Jim Wilson, a veteran newsman who had worked for the International News Service Washington Bureau, talked to the white and shaken Lewis just after he was rescued — and got a raw and chilling first-person story.

"IT WAS DARK AND WE WERE SINKING"

AUG. 27, 1958, BY SGT. I.C. ASA LEWIS AS TOLD TO JIM WILSON

TOKYO — "I heard a terrific 'bang.' The next thing I knew, Summers (M. Sgt. Floyd Summers, 32, Hazelton, W.Va.) was yelling, 'Hey, Lew, let's get out of here.'

"Then we were upside down. I was knocked out a few minutes. When I came to, the compartment was dark. We were sinking.

"Water in the compartment was up to our shoulders and mattresses were floating around. I found the Japanese cook and mess boy but I could not find Summers. There was a small air pocket near one corner of the compartment, so I told the two Japanese to stay there.

"The compartment was dark, black, so I had the Japanese rub each other's back so the phosphorus in the salt water would glow and give us a little light, just enough to work with.

"Then I tried to find the escape hatch. I had to dive through four or five feet of water in the compartment. When I found the hatch, it was covered by a mattress but I was able to pull it away and open the hatch.

"I told the mess boy to find me a life preserver. Then I told the cook to tear up a sheet. I tied the sheet to the life preserver, tied one end inside the tug and sent the preserver through the escape hatch. Then I told the mess boy to follow the sheet and he'd probably get out and be able to get help before we drowned like rats. If he got out, he was to give me a signal. He went out. But we didn't hear from him again.

"We didn't know we were in 40 feet of water. We knew there was pressure because our lungs were hurting. Then the water began to rise to the very top of the compartment.

"I told the cook to follow the sheet. He said he couldn't because he was too old. I asked him to try but he wouldn't go.

"Then I told him 'goodbye.' I said if I could make it, I'd send a diver down for him." Both the cook and the mess boy were saved.

"I got through the hatch but became tangled in wire and fire hoses on the deck. Finally, I kicked myself free and shot upward. But I couldn't make it. I had to take one, then two, big gulps of water before reaching the surface.

"I looked around and was picked up by a rescue boat. Then I was taken to the Yokohama dispensary and later transferred to the Army hospital at Camp Zama.

"They treated me for shock and a lot of cuts and bruises. I got banged up a bit when the bunks and other gear fell on me when the tug overturned.

"I never saw Summers again. He may still be in the engine room or under the bunks that fell on us.

"The hardest thing will be to face his wife. I don't know how to do it. That's going to be rough on me."

The Communist artilley offensive on Quemoy was a "flash fire" crisis of 1958 and a difficult and dangerous story to cover. Sgt. Larry Miller and Pfc. Al Kramer sailed with a small fleet of newsmen toward the battered Nationalist Chinese island, which is just a few miles from the mainland, and were among the handful who got onto Quemoy after an exploding wall of water turned other correspondents back. Besides their timely and exciting news stories, the two combined efforts on an entertaining personal account remindful of "Don't Go Near The Water."

"TURN BACK OR MY BOSS WILL BUY YOUR NAVY!"

SEPT. 28. 1958, BY SGT LARRY MILLER AND PFC AL KRAMER

QUEMOY — The signal bridge of an LSM (landing ship medium) is just about large enough for two sailors. But for eight frustrating, fearful and funny 6 hours early this month it became an overcrowded, albeit historic, press box for 30 correspondents making the first press tour of the "Formosa Strait War" to Quemoy.

The pencil-camera-notebook invasion was the last leg of an off-again on-again trip that had been cancelled so many times that, even aboard the ancient World War II vintage troop ship, newsmen were still betting they would never reach the island.

Arrangements for the trip were made by the Nationalist Information Office in an effort to quiet the clamor of foreign newsmen.

Correspondents from all over the world were arriving on Taiwan daily with orders from their editors to "get to Quemoy."

Each newsman had a scheme to beat his competitors to the island and get an "exclusive" first story on the situation. But all worked collectively pressuring the Chinese information office.

Suddenly the dam broke under the pressure.

On Sunday afternoon, Aug. 31, a group of 30 correspondents — Chinese, American, English and French — boarded the "Flying Elephant," a "creaphant," a creaking old C-46 that flew us to Makung, capital city of the Pescadores and jumping-off point for Quemoy.

For Stars and Stripes reporters the trip was a new experience. We were the "new China hands." Most of the other foreign correspondents were "old China hands." Many covered news on the mainland before the Reds took over.

We also soon learned why the "old China hands" looked so well groomed, particularly in the Pescadores. Most of the pretty girls on the islands are lady barbers. If our stay had been more than one day, two Stars and Stripes reporters would have been sporting Yul Brynner hairdos.

Once aboard ship we jockeyed for a niche for ourselves in the tiny open-air "stateroom." This was like a bull seal marking off his corner of the beach. By crawling over Wade Bingham and Pete Kalischer of CBS News, the proud owners of inflatable pillows, stepping carefully around John Dominis, Time-Life, and ducking under AP photographer Fred Water's feet, you arrived at Stars and Stripes' Quemoy (we hoped) News Bureau afloat. The furnishings consisted of two camera cases and a bunch of bananas.

No sooner had our ship passed through the antisubmarine net around the harbor that it began to circle back toward port.

The voices of the 30 newsmen rose as one in angry screams of protest. Jim Bell, Time-Life bureau chief, who had journeyed from Hong Kong for the trip, shouted, "Turn the ship toward Quemoy or I'll have Henry Luce buy the whole Chinese navy."

It was only after Lt. Cmdr. Liu, our Chinese naval officer escort, explained that we were circling while we waited for our convoy to form that things quieted down to what passed for normal.

While the camera and newsreelmen took pictures, we decided to get some interviews with the 400 soldiers aboard. It turned out to be quite a feat since we spoke no Chinese.

We got our interviews after a fashion, learning that these guys were just like any other soldiers. They had girl friends, hangovers and pay problems.

Afterward a British correspondent asked how we had managed to get interviews if we didn't speak Chinese and they didn't speak English. We explained as simply as we could.

A lot of soldiers spoke a kind of Japanese, we told him. "Then you chaps speak Japanese" he asked. Not really, maybe about 10 words between us, we replied.

"I see," he lied. As further explanation we told him there was Chinese officer with the troops who spoke French. "Ah," he grinned, "you speak French."

No, we answered, but French is pretty close to Spanish and we learned a little of that in high school. Our British friend left us looking ill. Maybe he was seasick.

Pete Kalischer came up with the idea of recording some "battle song." The troops were more inclined to sleep.

For a while it looked as though Pete was going to do all the singing. Only after a lot of arm waving, pantomime and a little yodeling, did he get his point across.

The troops finally obliged by singing for the tape recorder.

Shortly after midnight our vessel stopped engines and we prepared to climb down landing nets to the small craft that appeared out of the gloom of Quemoy harbor.

It seemed like a good time for some brave comments, but no one had much to say. The S&S bureau was first over our side of the ship.

A REAL SWINGER, Marilyn Monroe swivels off the Air Force transport that brought her to Seoul just after the truce — giving waiting fans a heatwave thrill before she boarded a chopper that took her to 7th Infantry Division troops along a silent frontline. Armistice or not, a lot of entertainers and showmen came in to soften the monotony of policing the Demilitarized Zone — Bob Hope, Danny Kaye, Red Skelton and Johnny Grant. The war had thankfully bypassed ornate landmarks like the 450-year-old Duksoo Palace — an ideal backdrop for a GI to take a snapshot of his date.

USA

PS&S, Bob Wickley

SCENIC MONUMENT to Japan's greatest ruler of modern times, Meiji Shrine, brings out early strollers who want to beat the crowd crush as winter passes and spring temperatures rise. All that was old and traditional — bridges, lanterns and temples — was erected within the shrine grounds to honor the emperor whose 40 years on the throne brought Japan out of feudalism and into the world as it was. Towering Formosan cedars rival the redwoods of Sequoia.

HIS LIFE HANGING on a cable lowered by a U.S. Air Force helicopter, a Japanese seaman is lifted off the stricken freighter Tanda Maru in late 1955. He was safe and so were 13 other sailors pulled to safety after roaring winds ran the ship aground. In Korea, readiness was still the stand-down watchword and South Korean riflemen took up down-to-earth defensive positions in a rice paddy close to the DMZ. It was a maneuver, but North Koreans on the other side of the truce line frequently made things real with shooting incidents.

Father Charles L. Meeus

HORSEHAIR HAT of a Korean *yangban*-(land-owning aristocrat) stands high in stark cultural collision with a flight helmet worn by an Army helicopter pilot, but both were light and practical. The pilot never strayed close to this alleged village (below) on the edge of the war-years wound called the DMZ. North Koreans built it as a model community to be seen by UNC patrols and observation posts, but picky critics said it was a shabby facade, pointing out that nobody lived in a movie-set town.

PS&S, Fred Braitsch Jr.

On the other side five correspondents made the treacherous transfer and assisted their friends by catching thrown camera and lowered tape recorders.

Fran Robertson, London Daily Telegraph, was hanging on the net when the first squirt of tracers came in.

One disconcerting fact was bitterly obvious — we were under fire. The Communists had evidently sent out a half dozen or more torpedo boats to break up the landing. They were doing a fine job of it as far as we were concerned.

The three landing boats headed for the beach, leaving the sea war to be fought between the Nationalist gunboats and the Red torpedo boats.

Like a fire hose spraying molten lead, the .50 caliber tracers splashed above and around us.

Our coxswain shoved off for the beach leaving Robertson hanging in the net, letting the night know what he thought of the whole show.

Alfred Smoular of Paris-Match and Bruce Russel, Reuters, also had made it into our boat. A handful of Chinese correspondents and a few troops comprised the rest of the landing party.

We watched the fight between our convoy and racing Red torpedo boats with as much detachment as it's possible to muster at a time like that.

The tracers were coming at us and some 3-inch shells burst overhead to light up the scene like Times Square on New Year's Eve.

Fortunately the escort vessels of our convoy got into the brawl soon enough to beat the PT boat off our tail. We were very happy to feel the landing craft crunch onto the beach.

There was a certain amount of confusion on the beach, then a hair-raising ride in the blacked-out jeep and a reunion with the others who "made it."

Our group was down to nine. It included Jom Bell and John Dominis of Time-Life; Greg McGregor, New York Times; Charles Smith, UPI; Bruce Russel, Reuters; Alfred Smoular, Paris-Match, and Loren Chang, NBC-TV; and two Stars and Stripes.

Left aboard the landing ship were 10 "lucky" or unlucky" correspondents, their relative fortune depending on your interest at visiting a tiny island that serves as an impact area for Communist artillery.

Most of these men not only missed going ashore but had lowered their cameras, clothes and other gear into the boats ahead of them.

As there was no Associated Press men on Quemoy, Charlie Smith had a ball posing with Forest (Woody) Edwards' typewriter and smoking the rival newsman's cigars. Edwards said later that the cigars were sorely missed. He had to make it all the way back to Makung without a smoke.

Now that the press junket was on Quemoy the problem reversed itself. How would we get off? Stepped-up blockade action and bad weather conspired to keep us on this red-hot rock.

We worried, but not half as much as our escort officers. A couple of days with this group of newsmen was plenty for him. The prospect of having us around for the duration was more than he could stand.

Indicative of the things that our escort put up with was Dominis' attempts to get night shelling pictures.

When the firing started, usually around midnight, Dominis would leap out of bed and gallop through the blacked-out streets to a building offering a good view.

From the roof he would try to get his pictures. The fact that it was forbidden to go out at night without an escort meant that our Chinese friends had to go with us. They did not get much sleep.

Most of the shelling while we were there was directed at Little Quemoy. From our location in Kinmen city on Quemoy proper we could get a very clear view.

Most of the shells passed overhead near us, but sometimes a short round would rock the city. Our last night there a big shell slammed into a field near where we were watching.

Communications-wise the group made quite an impact on Quemoy. The cable office there is designed to handle the normal flow of traffic from a city of perhaps 6,000 people. It probably seldom handled more than two or three messages a day. Under the press of stories filed by the correspondents, the two operators worked their fingers off on an antiquated hand key.

A lot of copy was still waiting in Quemoy to be sent when we got a break and were flown out.

The last moments on Quemoy were climaxed by a foot race. Because the Communists have a habit of shelling the airfield while planes are arriving and taking off, the waiting room is a line of foxholes.

These are located about a quarter of a mile from the strip. The game is to wait until the plane is turned around and warmed up, then dash out and pile in.

In our case something went wrong. we loped out at a signal, only to be waved frantically back to our holes. Considering that we were carrying all the extra gear our friends had left in our boats, it was a chore to race back and forth across broken ground.

We no more than made it to the holes than the signals were called again and away we went on a mad dash. Sweating, swearing and gasping for breath, we piled into the C-47 that growled down the runway even before the door was closed.

We were all happy to have made the trip and come out in one piece. Liu was the happiest man in town when we hit Taipei.

For the first time in a long time he could smile and mean it.

"Perhaps," he confided, "I will get real lucky and get sent back to sea duty before the next press tour is scheduled."

This story was sheer luck for the reporter who wrote it. He went to a special showing of silent films expecting to get a routine, labored feature on the return of the nickelodeon. Then he heard the voice of a human sound system and got a story that was an offbeat natural

MOVIE VOICE CRACKS SOUND BARRIER

NOV. 24, 1958, BY HAL DRAKE

TOKYO — A forgotten man in Japanese movie houses relived his days of cinematic glory in Tokyo Friday.

Ichiro Yamano, a famous benshi of silent film days, sat beside a screen in Tokyo's Yamaha Hall and revived the lost art of movie narration for a packed house of modern-day movie fans.

Benshi — who narrated silent pictures in Japan before a fatal novelty called "talkies" came along — were big men in the old days.

Most early films shown here were foreign-made and the benshi's job was to tell the story that the English, German or French titles couldn't put across to Japanese movie audiences.

Benshi became revered figures to Japanese moviegoers. In his heyday, Yamano was as well known as any famous movie star or director.

Then came sound. And Yamano, along with John Gilbert and other famous silent film figures in the U.S., became an antique personality.

But for an hour and a half Friday, during a showing of four old films by the American Cultural Center and the Japanese Ministry of Education, Yamano was in his former glory.

He was again a human sound system as he narrated "Broken Blossoms," a 1919 film about love in the London slums. The audience was with him, whistling, clapping and cheering as he unfolded the story on the screen. A small cinema orchestra — a standard prop in Japanese silent movie houses — thumped out a spirited accompaniment.

Yamano's voice trembled as the hero took a heavy blow. It dripped verbal acid on the villain. It sweetly imitated the distressed cries of the heroine.

When the films were over, Yamano stood up, took his bow, and walked back into obscurity.

"It was a little hard," he said after he finished the seven-reel film. "But it was fun and I'm sure they liked it."

But it would have been all in an easy night's work some 30 years ago, he added.

The hardest cinema narration job he can remember was "The Ten Commandments," Cecil B. DeMille's 1925 Biblical drama.

This ran 12 long, emotional reels, he recalls and was such a wearisome weeping and shouting job that three benshi had to take it on in shifts. His career was hard, short and famous. He started as a benshi in 1920 and by the middle of the decade was a topflight moneymaker.

Then, in 1929, a sound film called "The Alibi" opened in Tokyo and the handwriting was on the wall. But unlike silent screen workers in other parts of the world, the benshi was reprieved for a few years longer.

"Luckily, the sound systems were crude and sometimes failed," Yamano said. "And some of the pictures were only part talkie. There was still a limited need for narration."

But in 1931, the blow fell. "Morocco," an all-talking picture, appeared with the new innovation of Japanese subtitles. It caught permanent fancy with the public and the day of the benshi was done.

In an effort to protect their dying trade, many benshi demonstrated before the theaters, brought whole blocks of tickets to keep the public out, and even smashed sound equipment and tried to narrate the pictures.

But Yamano, who is now a moderately well-to-do stage actor and comedian, says he wasn't bitter about it then and isn't now.

"Actually, I think sound pictures are a lot better," he said

Millard Alexander, today the successful owner-publisher of the Tokyo Weekender, was an editor's dream of a reporter — a writer who could tell a moving story in very few words. This is his airport interview with two men who had been fugitives from reality for 16 years. Bunzo Minagawa and Masashi Ito might have flown in a time machine instead of an aircraft — because they stepped back into a modern world they had once erased from their minds. The two men, stationed in a Japanese Army garrison on Guam after it fell to Japanese forces early in World War II, fled into the jungle when the Americans came back in 1944. They became holdouts — defiant loners who held to the Japanese Imperial Army's "no surrender" doctrine. One was finally spotted and captured by chance and talked the other into giving himself up. Alexander recalls getting this story under terrifc difficulties — an onrush of relatives and bystanders as the two men stepped off the plane and questions shouted in two languages. But he got it and here it is.

"BECAUSE OF ONE ANOTHER, WE LIVED"

MAY 29, 1960, BY MILLARD ALEXANDER

TACHIKAWA AB, Japan — Two Japanese soldiers came home Saturday after 16 years of fear, hunger, loneliness and uncertainty in the jungles of Guam to be greeted — and thrown into confusion — by friends, relatives and well-wishers.

Bunzo Minagawa, 40, and Masashi Ito, 39, flew here aboard a regularly-scheduled contract airliner and stepped down the ramp onto their home soil still uncertain of their fate.

Ito confessed soon after landing that he wasn't sure until he saw farmers in rice paddies and tiny, patchwork fields of grain that he was actually coming to Japan. Both still felt they were being flown to America or to a prison camp.

Ito's 75-year-old mother, Yasu, traveled from Yamanashi Prefecture to be in the crush of people at planeside after she had finally been convinced that her son was still alive and returning home.

She had refused to believe the story of the two soldiers being found in the wilds of a Guamanian jungle until Friday night.

A crowd of about 2,500 Japanese lined the fences and gates surrounding Tachikawa AB in hopes of getting a glimpse of the two former members of the 8th Unit, 63rd Bn.

Relatives were buffeted about and old Mrs. Ito was nearly pushed down as the mass of newsmen converged on the aircraft's ramp. One boyhood chum of Ito's jumped onto the ramp to seize his coat, shouting "Oi, Ito! Oi!"

Both men looked trim, tanned and in good health. Both were dressed in natty sports clothes, provided by the American Red Cross.

In a press conference held before a phalanx of television cameramen and newspapermen, the two holdouts fidgeted nervously, wiped their faces and told of their 16-year adventure of hiding.

"Because of one another, we lived," Ito said in an emotion-charged voice. "If Minagawa had died, I would surely have killed myself. We cared for one another and kept one another alive.''

What was their biggest problem? ''Food,'' Minagawa replied promptly. ''We were always hungry, but we couldn't go too far from the jungle to look for anything to eat. American bombers hit a pig pen in 1944 and lots of pigs escaped in the jungle. Three times in 16 years we caught a pig in a native trap.''

''We caught river eels sometimes and coconuts were very good for us,'' Ito continued. ''But by the time we were found out, all the food was gone. There was no fruit, we could find no game or fish and the grass roots we ate were causing weakness and worms.''

Minagawa weighed 165 pounds when he left for the Army, his sister Kimiko said. He now weighs 99 pounds.

Ito insists he was never captured. He says he looked two days for Minagawa and finally heard him calling to give himself up. Both felt they would be killed by the Americans if they were caught.

They both recalled how a third holdout, Tetsuo Uno, died of malnutrition in 1948 — they think. Both were confused about actual dates. They brought Uno's remains back to Japan, keeping a pledge they made to their dying companion.

They said they were sure there are no other holdouts on Guam.

Both found it hard to believe Japan had lost the war, but Minagawa said he had also given up caring. They had no thoughts of active resistance but lived in fear of the natives of Guam. Ito was once shot in the hip by hunters but Minagawa pulled him through.

Minagawa said, ''I feel my entire life has been wasted. My health is very poor now. I don't know what I will do. It's good to be home.''

"I hate to dash away," Press Secretary James C. Hagerty told newsmen at Kadena AB, Okinawa, "but I don't want to disappoint all those people who are waiting for me in Tokyo."

What Hagerty met at Tokyo International Airport was a raging mob of leftists who surrounded his car and briefly besieged him and U.S. Ambassador to Japan Douglas MacArthur II. They had to be rescued by helicopter. The aim of the leftists was clear — they wanted President Eisenhower to call off his impending visit to Japan. They succeeded. The visit was permanently "postponed." Reporter Jim Shaw stood in the midst of the crowd and saw it all — and rushed back to pound out this under-pressure account for an extra.

"IF YOU WANT IKE TO LIVE, TELL HIM NOT TO COME!"

JUNE 10, 1960 BY JIM SHAW

TOKYO — Thousands of screaming, fanatical leftist demonstrators smashed and jumped on the car of White House Press Secretary James C. Hagerty at Tokyo International Airport Friday before he was whisked away from the crowd by helicopter.

Hagerty was unhurt. He and U.S. Ambassador Douglas MacArthur II sat calmly in the car while mobs danced around the car shouting anti-American slogans.

One of the demonstrators said, "We'd like to turn the car over, but we've been ordered not to."

A veteran Japanese newspaperman said, "This is one of the wildest demonstrations I have ever seen in Japan."

Demonstrators began gathering at the airport terminal about noon, when a group of ultra-rightists marched out to the observation platform.

A few minutes later, a group of about 150 leftist demonstrators joined them and it appeared they would clash.

When the leftists attempted to march against the rightists, there was a brief fight, but it was quickly broken up by police.

By the time Hagerty's plane, an Air Force C121, arrived at the airport, there were thousands of pro-American demonstrators waving flags and banners, greatly outnumbering the anti-American group.

Thousands of leftist demonstrators jammed the roads leading into the airport, however, and when Hagerty's plane touched down, they pushed through police lines and started running the half-mile to the terminal.

Two U.S. helicopters were waiting on the

airport apron when Hagerty's plane arrived, but officials decided to attempt to drive to Tokyo instead.

The trouble started when Hagerty's limousine was blocked by mobs near the airport gate. American plainclothes security guards surrounded the car, but demonstrators jumped on the hood and roof and smashed windows.

Hagerty and MacArthur appeared tense, but remained inside, talking and smiling. Hagerty even snapped a picture of the mob.

One of the demonstrators pushed a petition into the car and Hagerty took it and read it. Apparently it was a petition urging that President Eisenhower postpone or cancel his scheduled June 19 visit to Japan.

A Marine Corps helicopter attempted to land near the ambassador's limousine minutes after it was stalled, but hundreds of demonstrators stood in its way and refused to budge.

Several times police attempted to clear a path through the crowd so the helicopter could edge toward the car, but demonstrators defied them and the whirling blades and stood underneath, waving signs and banners.

Police reinforcements finally arrived, however, and a double cordon was formed so that the ambassador and Hagerty could get to the helicopter. They finally made it at 4:50 p.m., nearly one and a half hours after leaving the terminal.

As the helicopter zoomed off, however, demonstrators clung to the landing gear and dropped off only after it had risen 10 or 15 feet. Others hurled rocks and signs at the fuselage and blades.

Scores of persons were injured, including 30 policemen, but no Americans are known to be hurt.

Although the crowd was angry and the frenzy was nearly at the boiling point, Americans in the crowd were not threatened. Several American newsmen and many tourists were caught in the mobs.

One middle-aged Japanese man approached a group of Americans and shouted, "Hey, Americans, let this be a warning! If you want to save Eisenhower's life, you better tell him not to come!"

Long lines of chanting left-wing students, Socialists and Communists marched past Americans but didn't attack them.

Hagerty and MacArthur landed at the Stars and Stripes heliport in Tokyo and rushed to waiting cars which took them to the Embassy, where thousands of more demonstrators waited.

A helicopter circled overhead to distract the crowd, while the car bearing the ambassador and Hagerty drove in a back gate.

Hagerty scheduled a press conference for 8 p.m.

An estimated 8,000 demonstrators and police jammed the roads leading into Haneda airport and another 6,000 were waiting outside the American Embassy.

Some of the signs seen in the crowd said, "Against Ike for Peace," "Take Your Bases and U-2, Too," "To Hell With Ike," "Be Filled with Hate for the New Pact," and "Go Home U.S. Army."

Police seemed reluctant to engage in a pitched battle with the mobs, which greatly outnumbered them, but fought back when the crowd threatened to storm Hagerty's car.

Although there were all the elements for a disaster, actual violence was relatively small.

Demonstrators threatened to wait outside the American Embassy until they saw Hagerty and crowds were still milling around and chanting at 7:30 p.m.

Leftwing elements hailed the demonstration as a great victory for the factions which oppose the revision of the U.S.-Japan security pact.

By any standards, it was one of the greatest anti-American displays staged in Japan since the war.

There was no immediate announcement by Embassy officials as to whether or not the President's visit would come off as planned.

Eisenhower's decision to forestall his visit — which never came off — caused shock and national shame in Japan. "We have won, we have won," leftist demonstrators chanted in the streets, but police got tougher with them and Stripes newsmen — covering demonstrations in later years — got well used to the sight of club-swinging, blue-helmeted riot police and the stinging stench of tear gas.

Marine Sgt. Ed Grantham, chief of the Pacific Stars and Stripes Philippines Bureau, saw a different kind of mass hysteria — the face of superstition and panic. The end-of-the-world scare that swept Manila looked all too much like the panic that followed the Orson Welles Halloween broadcast of 1938. In the street, on the phone and at his typewriter, Grantham skillfully combined facts with impressions and came up with a taut story that showed the truth in Thomas Jefferson's contention that the most frightening thing to behold is ignorance in action.

P.I. PANIC ENDS; WORLD SURVIVES

JULY 15, 1960, BY SGT. ED GRANTHAM

MANILA — The end-of-the-world scare fizzled here Thursday in the wake of a wildfire exodus of thousands of Filipinos from this capital city to their country homes.

Youthful gangsters took advantage of the panic to loot deserted areas and strongarm citizens but most of the populace remained calm, skeptical and apprehensive.

Those stricken with the malady of panic left their homes and jobs in this city to be with their loved ones in the outlying farmlands, where rumors of the doomsday began and were rampant for days.

In Cavite City across the bay, many residents were frightened by press and radio reports quoting Italian mystics on the predicted end. The scare was intensified by a local press report that the U.S. Navy at Sangley Point NS was issuing gas masks to its civilian employees there. A Navy spokesman said the issuing of protective gear was "a ground defense exercise that is held once a month."

"These drills have been held every month for the past few years," he added.

Bus and rail lines in Manila were jammed with workers and students trying to get out of the city and reach home before the "end."

One Filipina hanged herself last week after reading "end-of-the-world" reports.

"Canto boys," the youthful gangsters and thieves from Manila's waterfront slums, moved through Manila on a projected campaign of looting and violence.

They were reported to have spread and enlarged on the rumors themselves on buses, street corners, in stores and even government office buildings in order to empty possible rich looting grounds.

The 12 to 20-year-old boys, most of whom cannot read or write, moved in with their loot bags as the easily-swayed minority fled.

Besides looting, the waterfront toughs were reportedly robbing women, children, policemen and even priests.

Scattered reports reaching the Philippine Constabulary headquarters at Camp Crame in Quezon City indicated many rural residents flocked to nightly prayer meetings and settled their affairs before the forecast doomsday.

In Malolos, Bulacan, north of here and only a few miles from Clark AB, a press report that was unconfirmed by the constabulary said: "Local inhabitants are becoming hysterical over news that the world will come to a violent end on Thursday."

Many associated the prediction with the unrevealed third secret of the Fatima miracle of 1917, when three Portuguese shepherd children saw a vision of the Virgin Mary.

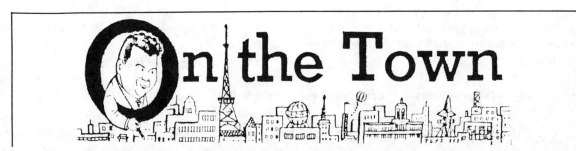

JULY 1, 1960, BY AL RICKETTS

We entered her small Roppongi, Tokyo, apartment (wearing a Frank Buck helmet and a sheath knife) and tried to appear nonchalant.

There was a copy of "The Snake Pit" on an end table and a little rubber snake (red) dangled from her bed lamp.

"A gift from one of the neighborhood children," explained Rosita.

After exchanging a few pleasantries and commenting on the big ad posters — showing Rosita and a snake in a basket — on the wall, we asked, "Where are they?"

"They?" said Rosita.

"You know. THE SNAKES," we shrieked, finally cracking under the strain.

"Oh, THEM," said Rosita, just as though she was referring to dogs or cats — or children.

It turned out that Pedro (14 feet long) was soaking in the sink. "He's shedding," explained Rosita. Diamond, another 14-footer, was in a wooden box on the top of the pantry and Carlos (only 12 feet long) was under the bed.

"Diamond," said Rosita, "is female. So is Carlos."

"Carlos is a female?" we said. It seemed to us that a female snake called Carlos could wind up with one whale of a complex. Biting people, for instance, might be one way of showing impatience with such a situation. But Rosita assured us this wasn't true.

"Carlos doesn't mind," she laughed. "She doesn't even know the difference." (We started to suggest that Carlos might have a few things to say about that last statement but Diamond, who was now curled up kitten-like at our feet, stopped us with a room-sized yawn.)

Rosita, a tiny girl who has no business being so calm around things that crawl, is of Spanish ancestry and hails from Australia, where she spends her spare time "milking" snakes, i.e., removing the venom from their fangs (she has the scars on her legs to prove it).

Boa constrictors and pythons, such as those used in her dancing act, have human-like emotions, she told us.

Also, if a python ever wraps itself around your neck ("They always go for the neck"), it will let go if you just tickle it under the chin, (we suggest tickling it from stem to stern — just to be sure).

As we were leaving we noticed a fish tank containing a couple of small Japanese snakes (Bill and Lulu). "For my hair," explained Rosita. "When I get two more I'll train the four of them to stay in my hair while I'm dancing."

Halfway out the door, Rosita made us a dandy offer. "Would you like to curl Carlos around your neck?" she asked. "No. Thank you," we giggled, backing down the steps and loosening our tie.

Meet you . . . On the Town

(Lionel Hampton, one of the most exciting musicians on the jazz scene today, will kick off a tour of Japan in April. Fact or fiction, the following vignette involving the legendary Lionel remains one of our all time favorites.)

MARCH 9, 1963, BY AL RICKETTS

There's a story musicians tell when they gather for an after-hours session and a couple of drinks before calling it a night.

The story, if told by an experienced hand, is one that invariably leaves the listeners in a state of respectful meditation as they mourn the loss of a potentially great jazz musician.

It all happened years ago when bandleader Lionel Hampton discovered a young pianist-organist playing in a Cleveland church.

Hampton was amazed at what he heard. With eyes closed and just a slight trace of a smile on his thin lips the boy was playing well-known hymns with subtle jazz undertones.

Burning with enthusiasm, Hampton approached the boy and offered him a job with his band. But the talented youngster was only interested in hymns and the church. So Hampton left without him.

For more than a year, Hamp traveled and played and told fellow musicians about his amazing find. Then, just before the band's big opening at a Harlem theater, Hamp received a telegram. The boy had changed his mind and would join the band in Harlem.

Opening day found the theater jammed to the rafters. The wailing Hampton group had played the same spot just a year before and literally brought down the house. Their wild version of "Flying Home" had put the patrons in such a frantic mood that they tore up the seats and danced in the aisles.

"Flying Home," by special request of the management, would not be played this year.

As the curtain rose, Hamp introduced his young discovery. The boy sat down at the organ, paused and then attacked the keyboard. People who were there say it was some of the greatest jazz they had ever heard.

His eyes were shut tight and the boy's fragile frame seemed to quiver from head to toe as he strained, grimaced and hunched his shoulders in tortured, blissful agony.

Music that seemed to be torn from the soul poured from his racing fingers and held the audience entranced. Then, with tears streaming down his face, the boy rose from the keyboard, walked out of the theater and returned for good to his church in Cleveland.

He sacrificed the music he loved so much, for the hymns he loved even more.

It's a story musicians tell when they gather for an after-hours session and a couple of drinks.

Meet you . . . On the Town

The assassination of President John F. Kennedy is well remembered at Pacific Stars and Stripes for two things — the tragedy of the event and the hectic pace of the day. The day before, much of the newspaper's staff had been moved out of billets in Tokyo and transferred to quarters that were on the outskirts of town and miles from the office. Toshikazu Motohashi, night teletype man, saw the stark bulletin "KENNEDY SHOT" at about 4 a.m. Tokyo time, Nov. 23, 1963. There may have been noon sunshine in Dallas, but it was still dark in Tokyo. Phone calls from Motohashi jolted some staffers awake; others got it by radio, television, calls from co-workers. Everyone — editors, reporters, printers — made it in. Everyone was hard-pressed, including the faraway news bureaus, but everybody delivered. Okinawa Bureau Chief Matt Matheson, a Marine gunnery sergeant, told of how the shocking event fell on an American community thousands of miles from America.

"I SAW A HERO CRY"

NOV. 24, 1963, BY GUNNERY SGT. MATT MATHESON

FORT BUCKNER, Okinawa — "Stunned shock" was the reaction of U.S. military personnel and Ryukyuan citizens on Okinawa Saturday as news of President Kennedy's death spread throughout the island.

Marines of the 3rd Marine Div. were told of the president's death during reveille while others were awakened in their barracks by radio news broadcasts which carried the news.

"Today I saw a grown man cry unashamedly," said SSgt. Frank R. Candelario, Yucca Valley, Calif., Hq. Co., Hq. Bn., Camp Hauge. "I woke up hearing the terrible news on the radio. I felt I had to tell someone so I woke him up. He was a holder of the Silver Star for bravery in Korea.

"I told him the President had been assassinated. He stared at me in complete disbelief. Tears welled in his eyes. He cried without shame for the loss of so great a man."

Official word hit the island from the United States at about 5 a.m. Telephones hummed as word of the President's death passed from unit to unit.

All U.S. flags were hoisted to half-staff at all military installations. Troops, most of whom had heard the news on radios in their barracks, were officially informed at troop formations Saturday morning.

Rear Adm. Robert A. MacPherson, commander of the U.S. Taiwan Patrol Force and Patrol Forces, Seventh Fleet told Pacific Stars and Stripes in a direct telephone call Saturday morning that, "I am terribly distressed about the death of President Kennedy.

"This is a great loss to the U.S. Navy and to the whole nation," MacPherson said.

Lt. Gen. Paul W. Caraway, representative of the Commander-in-Chief, Pacific in the Ryukyu Islands, said here Saturday:

"I was shocked to learn this morning of the death of the President of the United States.

"A great leader has died. His death is a terrible tragedy for the United States and the entire Free World.

"The soldiers, sailors, airmen and Marines stationed in the Ryukyu Islands extend their sympathy to the President's family. We here in the Ryukyu Islands have lost our Commander-in-Chief."

Seitoku Shinzo, director general of the Okina-

PONDEROUS WAR MACHINES roll down a country road in South Korea in 1962, past scrubby spruce trees struggling for life in soil that was poisoned by shellfire during a 3½-year war silenced by signatures on an Armistice Agreement. A Korean farmer watches friendly outlanders in the convoy, perhaps wondering if renewed warfare might move over his battered acres again. The Americans, wearing the 1st Cavalry Division patch later seen in Vietnam, were conducting a maneuver — a rehearsal for what they hoped would never come.

IT'S SPRING IN TOKYO and young lovers put aside their inhibitions, cuddling in the park and whispering of a happy lifetime together. Cherry blossoms, squealing traffic on a nearby road, the noise and worry of the world's largest city — it's all lost on lovers who want to talk of love. Where is all of the supposed Japanese reserve and inhibition? Not in any Tokyo park when spring makes a warm and soft arrival and young lovers come out.

PS&S photos, Katsuhiro Yokomura

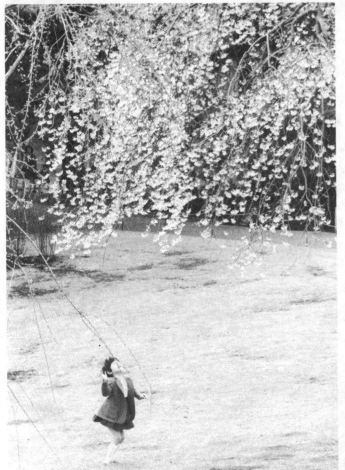

WONDERS OF NATURE are often most beautiful through the eyes of a child, and the pink and white canopy of cherry blossoms that burst open in Meiji Park are a sight to make this moppet skip for joy. Later, thousands will turn a long, blossom-shaded mall into a playground and picnic area, for only the most hard-hearted employers would refuse to give everybody from janitors to executives a day off to view the blossoms.

68

PS&S, Morodomi

IN THE SWING of a Japanese festival, sailors off the carrier Shangri-la perform in the step-turn-clap processional that is traditional during Obon — the annual autumn tribute to the spirits of the departed. It's a time for family gatherings, soothing sips of sake — and very often, for Americans to discover the fun of a rhythmic ritual many have compared to square dancing.

PS&S, Burge

RIOTS FLARE when protest rises in South Korea, and this raging demonstrator tries symbolic suicide with a small knife to protest his government's close ties with Japan, the country that colonized Korea for 40 years. Later, a stinging drift of tear gas would dissolve the demonstration.

RIFLE AT THE READY, a soldier of the 2nd Infantry Division prepares for a hard day along the Berlin Wall of the East — the Demilitarized Zone set up as an arms-length buffer between the armed frontiers of North and South Korea. Unborn when the truce was signed, he worked as a DMZ policeman as the longest unresolved armistice in history moved past its third decade, with no solid sign that political wounds between the two Koreas would heal.

wa Liberal Democratic Party said:

"I was greatly shocked to hear the news early this morning.

"President Kennedy was truly a progressive democratic president and he bravely put his ideas into action in a strong way. He was a great statesman and showed his greatness in solving many national and international problems, such as a nuclear test ban, racial feuds and many others.

"The OLDP expresses a deep condolence for his death.

"President Kennedy had a deep understanding for Okinawa problems and we had expected a great deal of him. His death is a great loss for the U.S., to the world and needless to say, for the Ryukyus. His new policy announced in March gave us great hopes."

It was a Saturday afternoon. Much of the staff of the Pacific Stars and Stripes editorial room was in the club one floor above their desks, talking about that day's biggest story — the crash of a Canadian Pacific Airlines plane at Tokyo International Airport the night before. The phone at the end of the bar rang and a staff member was called to it — to be asked by a friend if he knew anything about an airliner going down over Mount Fuji. The caller had half-heard a bulletin over Japanese television. Half-finished drinks were left as the club emptied out. Downstairs, teletypes were checked and phone calls made. A hastily formed task force was headed by Joe Schneider. Four men drove to the scene of the disaster and spent a chilly and sleepless night getting the story and pictures. They sped back to Tokyo and Schneider groggily made that morning's deadline. This is his report.

JET CRASHES INTO FUJI — 124 DIE

MARCH 7, 1966, BY JOE SCHNEIDER

GOTEMBA, Japan — A British jetliner, spewing smoke, plummeted from the skies Saturday afternoon and crashed into the rugged slopes of Mount Fuji, killing all 124 persons aboard, including 89 Americans.

The crash, which took place minutes after the plane left Tokyo International Airport, was Japan's third major air disaster in a month. A total of 321 persons have been killed in the crashes.

A scene of horror and destruction was reported by members of the Japanese Ground Self-Defense Force who arrived at the crash site about 22 minutes after the British Overseas Airways Corp. Boeing 707 plunged to the Earth.

A victim's shattered watch fixed the crash time at 2:10 p.m.

Most of the bodies, with seat belts still fastened, were found inside the shattered fuselage. About 15 others had been thrown clear of the rubble and were mutilated.

Wreckage was scattered over two acres. Bits of debris hung from bare trees. Clothing, luggage, magazines and other personal belongings of the passengers lay in a mountain of rubble.

The Japanese military men said they found no sign of life when they arrived.

There was no fire in the fuselage section and all of the victims appeared to have been killed by the impact.

Flaming sections of the wings and engines, torn from the fuselage, started a small brush fire which was extinguished by local firemen.

Seventy-five of the American victims were reported to be traveling on a 17-day tour of the Orient. The trip was sponsored by the Thermo King Corp., refrigeration manufacturer in Minneapolis, Minn.

Strong winds buffeted the Fuji area Saturday afternoon. Steady winds ranged from 70 to 90 mph, and weathermen said gusts could have gone much higher.

Although nearby Atsugi NAS reported scattered clouds at 2 p.m., 10 minutes before the crash, the weathermen said the possibility of visual obstruction was very remote.

The weather reports said it was very possible that there was severe air turbulence in the area at the time.

Eyewitness accounts of the crash varied:

—Maj. Eisuke Matsumoto, duty officer of the nearby Fuji Combined Armed School, Japan Ground Self-Defense Force, said:

"I heard a big explosion. I looked up and saw the inside right engine smoking, and then the plane fell straight down and burst into flames just before it hit the ground."

—Col. Takashi Moriyama, commanding officer, 1st Inf. Regt. JGSDF, said:

"I first noticed the plane at 2:07 p.m. It was straight overhead — near Koyama village. It was headed for Mount Fuji at an altitude of about 9,000 feet.

"The plane was flying slowly and belching smoke from the right side of the fuselage — in the after portion of the plane. About a minute later the tail section disintegrated. There was no sound.

"The plane flew for about two or three seconds more in a straight path and then nosedived. It didn't spin at all — just fell straight into the ground. I also saw two small flaming objects fall from the nose of the plane. When the plane hit the ground there was a loud explosion."

A series of pictures of the crash was taken by photographers Hideo Kitagawa and Eiichi Yoshida of Toei Movie Studio, both shooting practice scenes three-quarters of the way up the 12,397-foot mountain when the jet fell.

The four photos showed: 1) Smoke pouring from the rear of the plane, 2) The tail section exploding, 3) The plane falling in a horizontal position, 4) Explosion on impact.

The photos appeared in a Japanese newspaper Sunday and reportedly will be used in an investigation of the crash.

The crash site was about 100 yards southeast of Tarobo Peak, which is about a thousand yards southwest of the summit of the snow-capped Mount Fuji. The area is 70 miles southwest of Tokyo and is regarded as one of the leading vacation spots in Japan.

At last report early Sunday, 10 of the bodies were still missing, believed to be buried under the rubble of the fuselage.

Truckloads of the pine-encased bodies were seen passing on the deeply pock-marked road to Gotemba. The bodies will later be taken to Tokyo.

In the other two major air disasters, an All-Nippon Airways Boeing 727 plunged into Tokyo Bay Feb. 4 killing all 133 aboard. It was the world's worst single plane disaster.

On Friday, a Canadian Pacific DC-8 smashed into a retaining wall at Haneda International Airport, Tokyo, killing 64 of the 72 persons aboard.

This is the stuff of which fictional dreams and spy thrillers are made — and it all began with what promised to be a routine and tiresome story. The United Nations Command called a meeting of the Military Armistice Commission at Panmunjom, set up after the 1953 truce to supervise the armistice and resolve violations. The Communists looked upon it as something else — a propaganda sounding board. Delegates sat themselves on the north and south side of a long, green felt-covered table — with a microphone cord marking the exact boundary left by the truce. This MAC meeting was little different from the 241 others that had preceded it; the North Koreans charged that United Nations Command soldiers had fired into their territory. The UNC senior member, Maj. Gen. Richard G. Ciccolella, charged the Reds with dispatching armed agents into the south. The meeting broke up as indecisively as always and the newsmen from the UNC side were hustled aboard a bus and driven away — a little too speedily, some thought suspiciously. They were right. The real story broke a few minutes later.

"KIM IL SUNG WON'T SLEEP TONIGHT"

MARCH 24, 1967

PANMUNJOM, KOREA — A North Korean newsman jumped into a United Nations Command sedan at the Panmunjom truce site Wednesday and escaped to freedom in a hail of bullets.

"I was starved for freedom," said Lee Soon Keun, 43, vice chief of the official North Korean

Central News Agency, who voluntarily entered a vehicle occupied by an American officer at the end of the 242nd meeting of the Joint Military Armistice Committee.

"Kim Il Sung (the North Korean premier) will not be able to sleep tonight when he finds out the news of my defection," Lee added. "He will be enraged."

Two North Korean guards tried to force their way into the sedan, whose other passenger was Lt. Col. Donald E. Thomson, commander of the Joint Security Area Support Group. Failing this, several Red guards drew their 7.62mm pistols and pumped a fusillade of shots at and over the vehicle as it sped down a winding road.

The North Koreans dropped a wooden pole barrier in another attempt to halt the vehicle. The driver, whom UNC officials refused to identify, plowed through it with a crash that shattered the sedan's windshield. The car paused for a second, then sped past the last Communist checkpoint in the truce zone to the Joint Security Area Base Camp that lies just outside of it. No one in the car was injured.

After a brief rest at the officers' club, Lee was taken to Seoul via U.S. Army helicopter. He landed at Yongsan helipad, near UNC headquarters, to be greeted by Republic of Korea Vice Defense Minister Sue Ryong Kang and a swarm of newsmen. This was at 7:10 p.m., one hour and 50 minutes after they entered the sedan at Panmunjom and fled south.

Lee told reporters he left his wife and three small children in Pyongyang, the North Korean capital. He had worked as a newsman at Panmunjom for three years.

The newsman, who is the third North Korean journalist to defect to the ROK, said he had learned of progress there through classified news films shown only to top Communist officials.

Lee reportedly was taken to Seoul Military Hospital, a U.S. facility, for a physical examination before he was released to ROK officials, who permitted no further interviews.

The other two defectors were Tong Lee, former correspondent for the official Soviet newspaper Pravda who defected in 1959, and Jae Duk Hahn, one-time North Korean Central News Agency editor who fled to the ROK from Japan.

KCNA charged in a broadcast from Pyongyang that Lee had been "kidnapped" by UNC guards and demanded his return.

The meeting had been called by the UNC. Maj. Gen. Richard G. Ciccolella charged the Communists with attacking a UNC guard post in the Demilitarized Zone Monday night.

Shortly after Lee fled, the Communists called a meeting of the Military Armistice Commission secretaries for 2 p.m. Thursday. No reason was given, but Col. George F. Charlton, UNC secretary, planned to protest shooting by the North Koreans in the Joint Security Area.

But this was only the first chapter in a story that would have taxed the imagination of Len Deighton or Ian Fleming. Contrary to what Lee said about Kim Il Sung's insomnia, the North Korean premier probably slept very well that night, smugly satisfied that one of the boldest intelligence ploys in history was a huge success. Lee Soon Keun was a false defector — a counterfeit traitor. Trustfully accepted by the ROKs as a man who had seen the ideological light, he was given a grand tour of the republic's defenses and industries — and was often the hero of stadium-sized rallies, giving fiery speeches about the failure of communism and the miserable lot of his countrymen in the north. Yet, in conversations away from the speaker's stand, he said things that made listeners doubt that he had really abandoned Marxism. The ROK Central Intelligence Agency was already suspicious of Lee when he disguised himself and fled the country with a stolen passport. He was later tracked to Hong Kong, where he fought off kidnap attempts by ROK consular officials. Then he brazenly boarded a plane that was destined for Phnom Penh but stopped in Saigon — a fatal mistake. Vietnamese police pulled Lee and another man off the aircraft and turned them over to South Korean agents. Flown to Seoul, Lee was convicted of espionage and hanged on July 3, 1969.

These are two of the better crime stories of recent years — one light and poignant, the other shocking and unbelievable.

$200,000 BEQUEST A HOAX

APRIL 10, 1966

OTSU, Japan — A former U.S. serviceman confessed to Japanese police Friday that he had lied when he claimed he was seeking a one-time bar hostess to give her $200,000.

"I'm sorry I caused you so much trouble," said 29-year-old Gordon Bobell, a Los Angeles policeman who Japanese police said came to their station in this western Japan resort city Thursday and told them he was trying to locate a girl known only as "Chizuko."

Shiga Prefectural Police Inspector Toshimatsu Imai said Bobell told them he had been sent by the Rev. Leon Kennedy, father of Harold Kennedy. Bobell said the younger Kennedy had died from injuries suffered in a traffic accident, and had willed $200,000 to a girl who had befriended him when he was stationed with the 7th Cav. Regt. at Camp Otsu with Bobell in 1955.

Imai confirmed to Pacific Stars and Stripes that Bobell confessed he had concocted the story only to find the girl, with whom he was in love, as quickly as possible. He said Kennedy was alive and there was no $200,000 willed to anybody.

Meanwhile, Chizuko — whose real name was Tsuruko Ono before she married an American — angrily called police to "set the record straight." She said she had known Kennedy well and Bobell very slightly when she worked as a hostess at the Bar Shamrock, outside the camp's main gate, and had never been Bobell's girlfriend as some press reports had claimed.

"I will be in trouble with my husband if he hears of this," said the woman, who now lives in Iowa and was visiting relatives in Osaka.

Imai told Pacific Stars and Stripes Bobell, whom he confirmed was a member of the Los Angeles Metropolitan Police Dept., could be prosecuted under Japan's Minor Offenses Law, but likely will not be.

"It's a love story," Imai said, "and besides, he apologized."

DOCTOR ADMITS SPREADING TYPHOID

APRIL 16, 1966

TOKYO — A 33-year-old doctor reportedly confessed Thursday, that he deliberately had spread typhoid and dysentery germs to get human guinea pigs for medical research and also to spite a small hospital which worked him long hours with no pay.

Police said Mitsuru Suzuki broke down and sobbed, "I did it," after days of questioning.

Police said they had discovered 11 different outbreaks at three hospitals in which "well over" 100 persons had been infected. Four, including a former teacher of Suzuki's, died.

Police emphasized that Suzuki had not admitted causing all of the outbreaks and that they had not proved he was responsible for the deaths.

Suzuki first admitted giving sponge cake contaminated with dysentery germs to four co-workers at Chiba University Hospital where he was an unpaid medical researcher, police said. They came down with dysentery the same day.

Suzuki later confessed, police said, giving bananas infected with typhoid germs to 13 others at the university hospital last September, and infecting 13 employees of the Kawasaki Steel Co. by implanting typhoid germs in their soft drinks.

Police said Suzuki told them that he resented being worked long hours as a researcher with no pay. That practice is common in Japan for undergraduates or those working on a medical thesis, they said.

Suzuki also said, police reported, that he had infected patients "to establish an entirely new medical theory."

Police said they were continuing to question Suzuki.

Panmunjom, a name long absent from world headlines, had its hour on the stage again — as one of the final settings of the long Pueblo drama. Spec. 4 Craig Garner of the Pacific Stars and Stripes Korea Bureau watched as Cmdr. Lloyd M. Bucher led his crew to freedom at the truce site, leaving months of horror and misery behind them.

PUEBLO CREW COMES BACK

DEC. 24, 1968, BY SPEC 4 CRAIG GARNER

PANMUNJOM — The 82 crewmen of the Pueblo began their trek to freedom Monday at 11:30 a.m. Korean standard time across a small foot-bridge nicknamed "the bridge of no return" leading from North Korea to the truce site at Panmunjom.

The march from Communist captivity came exactly 11 months after North Korean patrol boats seized the U.S. Navy intelligence ship off the port of Wonsan last Jan. 23.

Cmdr. Lloyd M. Bucher, the captain of the Pueblo who came under much fire for not putting up a struggle at the time of the seizure, was first across the bridge as a steady snow fell. He identified the six officers, 74 enlisted men and two civilians who filed into the Panmunjom Joint Security Area after him.

The body of Seaman Duane D. Hodges, of Creswell, Ore., who was seriously injured when the ship was captured and died later, was also returned.

The formal signing of the document which handed the crew over to the U.S. was conducted at Panmunjom at 9 a.m. Monday between senior United Nations command delegate Maj. Gen. Gilbert H. Woodward and North Korean spokesman Maj. Gen. Pak Chung Kook.

The document prepared by the North Korean and read by Woodward said that the Pueblo had illegally intruded into North Korean territorial waters and conducted espionage activities.

Immediately after reading the statement, Woodward followed up with a repudiation in which he said U.S. authorities have found "no convincing evidence that the ship at any time intruded into the territorial waters claimed by North Korea."

Woodward made it expressly clear that he signed the Communist document "to free the crew and only to free the crew."

He explained at a press conference after the signing that he did not think it meant "a humiliation" for the U.S. government.

The U.S. never did "apologize" for the alleged intrusion as the North Koreans had insisted in countless propaganda broadcasts.

However, a U.S. Defense Department spokesman said the U.S. concurred to sign the "purported agreement" since the North Koreans had taken a firm stance in the 28 secret meetings held at Panmunjom since the seizure that "the crew would be held indefinitely if the statement was not signed."

In Woodward's repudiation he firmly asserted that "the ship was not engaged in illegal activities" and that "he could not apologize for action which he did not believe took place."

At the brief 9 a.m. meeting across the Panmunjom conference table North Korea's Gen. Pak told Woodward that "the crew was in normal condition." Woodward said in Pak's terms this means the 82 crewmen were in good health.

Pak during the meeting threatened to delay the release since he said the U.S. State Department had violated the agreement between the two nations about publicizing the time of the release. However, he later reneged and delayed the return only a half hour.

Woodward said he was certain there was no compensation paid to the North Koreans by the U.S. for the men's freedom.

After the Pueblo crew was exchanged at Panmunjom's Joint Security Area they were scheduled to be taken to the UNC advance camp, four miles south of the truce area.

At the advance camp they were to clean up and be given a meal in private. Then they were to be transported to the 121st Evacuation Hospital at ASCOM near Seoul where each crew member was to receive a physical examination.

A Defense Department spokesman said plans called for the crew members to be taken to a U.S. naval hospital in San Diego upon leaving Korea.

Their scheduled departure time from Korea is still tentative, but the spokesman said naturally everyone hoped the crew would be able to be home for Christmas.

The Pueblo was seized last January and precipitated a crisis in the U.S. which saw

President Lyndon Johnson activate over 14,000 Air Force reservists and dispatch the nuclear aircraft carrier Enterprise off the coast of North Korea.

Many U.S. congressmen branded it an act of war as a speedy military buildup in South Korea was carried out.

Since then the U.S. and North Korean negotiators have been locked in verbal combat over how and when the surviving crew members would be returned. It appears that the major breakthrough took place at the 26th Pueblo meeting at Panmunjom on Dec. 17.

Staff Sgt. Russ Anderson, Pacific Stars and Stripes Thailand Bureau Chief, went to the Bridge on the River Kwai, the romanticized subject of a novel and film, but found it to be more of a shrine than a setting of high adventure.

A BRIDGE OF SORROWS

AUG. 3, 1969, BY STAFF SGT. RUSS ANDERSON

BANGKOK — There is 24 years of water under the famous bridge on the River Kwai.

But at Kanchanaburi, Thailand, the memory lingers on.

It was on this western Thai river near the Burmese border that Allied prisoners during World War II built the railway bridge that was popularized by the American movie — "Bridge on the River Kwai."

The memory lingers because the bridge remains today much as it was in 1945 — scarred and shellpocked. Memories linger because of two nearby Allied military cemeteries which are manicured daily.

But most people in Thailand remember because the bridge has become one of the country's most popular tourist attractions. It became that way after Pierre Boulle's book became a movie and the world heard what happened on the Kwai.

Or got a fairly good idea, at least. The movie stretched a scene or two, according to local Thai guides who are familiar with the facts. The story is brief and brutal.

In 1942 the Japanese wanted to build a railway through Thailand into Burma. It had to be done in 18 months — 250 miles and the bridge.

Imperial troops brought British and Australian prisoners of war from Malaya, Burma, Hong Kong, Singapore and other points into Thailand. They also conscripted over 100,000 Chinese, Burmese, Malays, Javanese and anyone else they could find for the job. Some Dutch and American POWs wound up at Kwai, too.

Things were easy at first for the POWs. They were fed fairly well and could shop from the Thais. But work fell behind and the Japanese imposed their "speedo" policy. Things changed.

Food and medicine became scarce. Disease became epidemic. The death toll rose.

The job was finished but in the end 16,000 allied POWs had died. Between 80,000 and 100,000 of the other conscripts also died.

There is no sign of bitterness among the plaques and memorials at the River Kwai or the nearby cemeteries. Alongside the Allied remembrances is a Japanese memorial to both sides.

Today one of the strongest messages conveyed from the site is that the dead are not forgotten.

Each stone at the Kanchanaburi War Cemetery carries the name, rank and unit of the soldier along with a short inscription from his loved ones.

The stones impart messages of love, honor, pride, understanding and misunderstanding.

"Able Seaman C.C. O'Neal. Our darling 'Chicka' died for peace. Now in peace with God."

"W. Kemp," who was 51 when he died, "His spirit lives on. My Black Watchman fought bravely in two wars."

"Pvt. A. Proctor. Far away beneath foreign skies, in a hero's grave he lies."

"Cpl. B. Mitchell. Someday, Tom, I will understand," from his wife.

And "Cpl. John Dryer. Rest with Australia's brave, my beloved."

There are almost 7,000 of these at the Kanchanaburi cemetery.

It is visited daily by hundreds of persons — strangers, old comrades and relatives.

The land for the two cemeteries was donated by Thais in Kanchanaburi who had become close to the POWs during the war. They are maintained by the Commonwealth War Grave Commission headquartered in London.

American servicemen on rest and relaxation breaks from Vietnam are frequent visitors to the River Kwai and the war cemeteries.

At one of the grave sites, an American infantryman in his late teens was reading a stone marker.

"What do you think?" another soldier asked.

"I feel like I know some of these guys," he said.

He went down the line of grave sites — reading. Somewhere along the line he must have seen the inscription on an Australian private's grave: "He did not waver when his country called."

And that's the kind of memory that lingers on around the River Kwai.

It was a story that belonged to classic Japanese literature or theater — ronin, rogue samurai, held terrified travelers at swordpoint and demanded that a high-ranking hostage accompany them to a rival kingdom. But the time was early 1970 and the setting was an airliner that sped at a high altitude. And there was nothing romantic about the villains — they were hijackers, young leftists who wanted to go to North Korea to practice their beliefs and attitudes about revolution. That was the beginning of the story — this was the end, as written by Korea Bureau Chief Bob Cutts. Cutts' careful attention to suspenseful detail was worthy of the finale in an Alfred Hitchcock film.

THE LONGEST HIJACKING

APR. 5, 1970, BY BOB CUTTS

SEOUL — Nine young Japanese students, perpetrators of history's longest aerial hijacking, Friday smiled, waved, shook hands with their former hostages and exchanged them for a Japanese cabinet vice minister.

Then they were flown to Pyongyang, the capital of North Korea, in the Japan Air lines jetliner they seized over Japan early Tuesday and held at Seoul International Airport for 3½ days.

One hundred three persons aboard the Japanese aircraft walked to freedom. Japanese Parliamentary Transportation Vice Minister Shinjiro Yamamura boarded the plane as a volunteer hostage. All but three of the repatriates were flown in a Japan Air lines DC8 to Fukuoka in southern Japan and Tokyo.

The Rev. Daniel S. MacDonald, a 35-year-old Maryknoll priest, stayed in Seoul to rest. Herbert Brill, a 50-year-old executive for Pepsi-Cola and the only other foreigner aboard, made the return trip to Japan.

A crowd of harried newsmen stood 200 yards away from the captive Boeing 727 jetliner Friday afternoon and watched a tense tableau break days of hard and dangerous bargaining. They watched as several of the students, who seized the plane over Japan at swordpoint and brandished what appeared to be explosives, softened their hostility and suspicion and got out of the plane for several minutes of informal conversations with their former "deceivers."

South Korean officers and soldiers had disguised the airport to resemble the one in Pyongyang and had dressed some men in North Korean uniforms in an effort to lure the students out of the plane just after it landed.

The release began at 2:59 p.m. Friday after refueling, engine maintenance, removal of baggage and other details had been seen to.

A passenger ramp was pushed up to the plane and the front door finally swung open, three days after it had been sealed shut in Fukuoka with 115 persons aboard — including the pilot and crewmen who were kept aboard to fly the craft to Pyongyang.

A stream of passengers, half of those aboard, was led down the ramp by one of four blue-clad JAL hostesses — the first part of the release bargain made with the young hijackers.

Some of the passengers smiled. Some shook hands with waiting officials on the ground and all walked in an orderly, unhurried fashion to waiting buses.

Three young hijackers, nervous and jittery at first but later relaxed, appeared in the doorway after the first half of the passengers had left. One hijacker was clad in a dark suit and light shirt, one in a pink shirt and sport coat, and another in shirtsleeves. They kept their hands on sheathed Japanese swords, each about 18 inches long, but never visibly threatened anyone.

They waited 12 minutes for Yamamura to keep his part of the bargain and come aboard, then ordered a crewman to shut the door when the volunteer hostage failed to appear.

After a brief telephone conversation with the plane, Yamamura could be seen shaking hands near the aircraft with Japanese Ambassador to Korea Masahide Kanayama. He walked to the ramp and the door swung open again. As Yamamura ascended, the dark-suited hijacker, weaponless, came down and left the ramp.

Once on the ground, the hijacker shook hands with an unidentified official and began discussions with them at planeside. The other hijackers and Yamamura greeted each other and stepped back to let the rest of the passengers flow out uninterrupted, except for the last man.

Brill and MacDonald were among the last to leave. Both men shook hands with their captors and smiled as they said goodbye. They descended the ramp to waiting buses.

Then Yamamura reappeared, smiling and waving to the crowd below and talking laughingly with the hijackers in the doorway. One student loosely held his arm halfway around the vice minister as if to keep him from bolting but soon dropped it. As the hijacker on the ground continued talking with officials there, Yamamura went back inside the plane and the last passenger — who looked a great deal like the vice minister — appeared at the door and stopped to talk with the hijackers. They smiled and waved to the crowds below.

Then the last hijacker picked up the vice minister's luggage and started to go back aboard. As he did so, the passenger above him started down. They stopped, shook hands and went their ways, the beaming passenger into the hands of waiting officials.

The door slammed shut on three crewmen, nine hijackers and the vice minister, not to open again in the Republic of Korea.

VIETNAM

1963-1973

Blast Wrecks Indiana Plant—10 Die

TERRE HAUTE, Ind. (AP) — An explosion ripped the Wabash River plant of the Home Packing Co. here Wednesday morning, killing at least 10 workers and injuring 55, four of them seriously.

One hundred rescue workers, wearing gas masks, dug into a mountain of rubble, hunting for victims.

Ten bodies were recovered by late Wednesday and at least five more were believed buried under tons of brick.

About 1,200 day workers had just reported for duty when the blast demolished a third of the two-story meat packing plant about 7:30 a.m.

The plant had been closed for the Christmas holidays. Some firemen thought a gas leak may have caused the blast, but a fire department official said, "I just don't know. No one smelled anything—it just went whoomp."

Ammonia fumes gushed from broken refrigeration lines after the explosion.

Among the dead was Donald W. Scott, a salesman and brother of the firm's president, Robert Scott. George Obenchain, secretary-treasurer, estimated damage to the plant at close to $2 million.

(Continued on Back Page Col. 1)

PACIFIC STAR AND STRIPES

AN AUTHORIZED PUBLICATION OF THE U.S. ARMED FORCES IN THE FAR EAST

10¢ DAILY
15¢ WITH SUPPLEMENTS

Vol. 19, No. 3 FIVE-STAR EDITION

昭和三十四年一月二十二日国鉄局特別承認新聞紙第175号（日刊）
（昭和34年4月22日第3種郵便物認可）

Friday, January 4, 1963

BIG VIET BATTLE; 3 AMERICANS DIE

SAIGON (UPI)—A U.S. Army captain and two sergeants were killed Wednesday during a furious battle in which communist gunners shot down five American helicopters in the Plain of Reeds south of Saigon.

Their deaths raised to 30 the number of Americans killed in action since the United States began aiding the Republic of Vietnam in its war with communist rebels.

The Army captain was hit while serving as an adviser to a Vietnamese Army battalion taking

Vietnam's Deadly Waiting Game—Page 5

part in an assault. He was hit in the chest and neck by a burst of automatic weapons fire while helping lead the attack.

He was flown back to the airfield here by helicopters but died while undergoing emergency treatment.

"He was one of the best we had," said one comrade of the unidentified captain. "Like most battalion advisers he was out front trying to help move them on when he got it."

(Continued on Back Page Col. 1)

Philadelphia's Worst Fire

Smoke continues to rise from a fire described as the worst in Philadelphia's history. It destroyed a 9-story factory building, at least 25 homes and 3 other buildings and caused the evacuation of 2,000 persons in 29-degree weather. The 11-alarm fire in north Philadelphia started in the factory building (center) and spread to a row of houses. For a time it threatened a 9-square block area near Temple University but firemen controlled it after more than three hours. No serious injuries were reported. (AP Radiophoto)

Guns Reply To Tshombe

LEOPOLDVILLE, The Congo (UPI)—The United Nations Command, in the face of the heaviest fighting thus far in the current action, pushed an advance assault force across the Lufira River Wednesday in its drive on reported Katangese strongholds at Jadotville and Kolwezi.

A United Nations spokesman

(Continued on Back Page, Col. 1)

Weather

Tokyo Area Forecast
Friday: Fair; High 50, Low 23.
Saturday: Fair; High 47, Low 28.
Wednesday's Temperatures: High 40, Low 22.
(USAF Weather Central, Fuchu Air Station)

Cancer Kills Jack Carson

ENCINO, Cal. (UPI)—Comedian Jack Carson, 52, died at his home Wednesday of cancer.

The heavy-set comedian was stricken with the disease two months ago and failed to respond to treatment. The malignancy was in his liver.

Norstad Gives NATO Reins to Lemnitzer

PARIS (UPI) — General L. L. Lemnitzer took over as supreme commander of NATO forces in Europe Wednesday with a pledge to carry on the Alliance's collective defense "for the preservation of peace and security."

Lemnitzer, 63, assumed his post in impressive change-of-command ceremonies from General Lauris Norstad, 55-year-old U.S. Air Force officer who is retiring to civilian life after six crisis-filled years as chief of the North Atlantic Treaty Organization. He has had 36 years of service in the American armed forces.

Norstad said at the changeover at Allied Headquarters just outside Paris that Western strength at present provides "confidence and hope" for the future.

Lemnitzer, former chairman of the U.S. Joint Chiefs of Staff, said he would seek to justify the "confidence and trust" placed in him by the 15 NATO member nations. He will command more than 1 million Allied fighting men.

Norstad later took off by jet for Lisbon and Ottawa for short farewell visits to Portugal and Canada, both members of the Atlantic Alliance, on his way home to Washington and retirement.

(Continued on Back Page, Col. 1)

Five years after the fall of the French fortress at Dienbienphu, two Americans advising the non-Communist South Vietnamese were slain by a bomb thrower who sympathized with the Communist North. American involvement in a war against Marxist-led insurgents was steady and gradual, and Marine Staff Sgt. Steve Stibbens got a gripping and unforgetable feature about a tragic exodus in the face of terror.

NO ROOM FOR AN OLD WOMAN

SEPT. 27, 1963 BY STAFF SGT. STEVE STIBBENS

BA DONG, Republic of Vietnam — They came in droves, running across the field, crying women clutching babies in their arms, old men half-carrying their young boys. Some had managed to grab up a few family belongings in tattered blankets or cloths.

A hundred yards away, across a canal, were the guerrilla-held swamps. In between were smoldering ashes that had been simple peasant homes.

We took as many as possible aboard our helicopter and had to leave the rest. One old man begged us, with his wrinkled hands clasped in front, to take just one more passenger — his wife.

As the copter lifted off the ground, he tried to hang on a steel landing strut.

Old-timers in this "dirty little war" say that you soon get used to the tragedy and pathos of the years-old battle against Communism here.

But I hope I never forget what I saw at Ba Dong, a tiny coastal hamlet in the Ca Mau Peninsula, about 75 miles south of Saigon.

It all began as a somewhat routine mercy mission for helicopter crewmen of the 114th Air Mobile Co., based at Vinh Long. Just before dusk, a call came in for eight UH-1B helicopters to evacuate villagers from Ba Dong, which was about to be overrun by the Viet Cong.

The Viet Cong guerrillas, estimated to be a reinforced company, had appealed to villagers the night before to give up their arms and come over to the Communist side. They were answered with gunfire.

All night the villagers, supported by a handful of Civil Guardmen, withheld the overwhelming fire as Vietnamese Air Force planes kept the enemy ground lit with flares.

In the morning, bodies were counted — one civil guard dead, 14 wounded. Just outside the village gate lay the bodies of 11 Viet Cong.

The guerrillas waited across the canal, like vultures, until nightfall when they would go in, this time for the kill.

A half hour after leaving Vinh Long, Sgt. I.C. Royce Linch, the copter's gunner, from Hico, Texas, pointed ahead where T-28s were strafing and bombing a clump of brush alongside the canal. The "Huey" ahead of us reported he was receiving fire and we swooped down to cover him.

Suddenly there was an ear-shattering blast as two rockets fell out in front of us and spiraled lazily toward the ground.

Linch leaned out the door and emptied a magazine from his M-14 automatic rifle as we passed over.

The Viet Cong had dug foxholes in the swampy brush and paddy fields. A Viet Cong flag was flying brazenly from the middle of a blown-out bridge leading to the hamlet.

While the fighters and other choppers covered us, we broke out of the "daisy chain" formation and landed behind the hamlet to pick up 14 men, women and blank-faced children. Each helicopter followed in succession until each was filled.

Five Hueys, designed to hold only 10 persons, each managed to pick up 102. They could hold no more.

The last ship to land must have had it the roughest. Some 23 villagers, mostly children, climbed aboard before the crew chief was forced to leave the remaining 60 behind to await their fate in the night.

Longtime Stripes reporter Al Kramer was at his under-fire best when boxed in by a tight deadline. The downfall of Republic of Vietnam President Ngo Dinh Diem was one of the most uncooperative stories in years. Communications out of Saigon were shut down when dissident troops attacked the presidential palace; everything that was significant or decisive broke on the wrong side of the clock. With minutes crumbling away, Kramer grasped at a straw — he picked up the phone on his desk in Tokyo and prayerfully chanced a call to U.S. military headquarters in Saigon. It paid off in a good story and a clean beat — Pacific Stars and Stripes was the first newspaper in Asia to tell of Diem's overthrow.

DEATH OF A GOVERNMENT

NOV. 2, 1963, BY AL KRAMER

TOKYO — A military revolt toppled the government of President Ngo Dinh Diem Saturday after bitter fighting in the streets of the Republic of Vietnam's capital city.

In a direct telephone call to Saigon, a U.S. military spokesman told Pacific Stars and Stripes the Diem government had surrendered to the rebel forces after artillery and mortar fire demolished the presidential palace.

The spokesman said there were no American casualties in the fighting, but the toll among Vietnamese troops was believed high.

The Vietnamese government was being run Saturday morning by a council of generals who led the revolt, the spokesman said.

He said the council had named former Vice President Nguyen Ngoc Tho to head a new government under the title of prime minister.

Rebel forces were in control of the city Saturday morning, the spokesman said.

But he added that scattered gunfire was still heard in the capital as rebel soldiers hunted down disorganized bands of Vietnamese special forces troops who supported Diem.

The bulk of the fighting in the revolt centered around the presidential palace, guarded by Diem's elite palace guard brigade.

The spokesman said that as rebel units were leveling the palace with artillery and mortar fire, two planes zoomed low over the city and fired rockets at the palace, apparently missing it.

All Americans were being warned to remain off the streets and stay in their quarters Saturday unless on urgent business.

The Vietnamese ambassador to Japan was not available for comment in Tokyo Saturday morning, but Press Secretary Tran Viet Chau told Pacific Stars & Stripes that it was his personal opinion that there would be "no major changes in Vietnam's policies toward the West" under the new government.

He added that he hoped the new government would take stronger anti-Communist measures in order to cope with the "exceptional situation."

The following additional information was provided by the Associated Press and the United Press International.

(Insurgent radio broadcasts monitored in Singapore and Tokyo identified the leader of the uprising as Maj. Gen. Duong Van Minh, 40, a former member of the Vietnamese General Staff. The reports said 14 generals and 10 colonels have announced support of the rebellion, which Radio Saigon said was prompted by the Diem regime's "treatment of the Buddhists and the students" and his alleged plans to "make a deal with Communist North Vietnam."

(The broadcasts added that U.S. Ambassador Henry Cabot Lodge conferred with Diem shortly after the uprising started. They added that Duong broadcast an appeal to the people to support the rebels, who have imposed an 8 p.m. to 7 a.m. — 7 a.m. to 6 p.m. EST — curfew on Saigon and the adjacent Chinese-populated suburb of Cholon.

(Duong declared in a brief communique that he and his committee of generals had "no political ambitions." He said that military governors and regional commanders from various provinces have sent messages of support to the insurgents, and that 70 per cent of the armed forces were on the rebels' side.)

The armed forces rebels announced over captured Radio Saigon, which they rechristened "Voice of the Armed Forces," that they had acted "to save the country from a Communist takeover."

Diem and his brother, Ngo Dinh Nhu, surrendered in their palace bunker-basement after the building was bombarded by rocket-firing aircraft and shelled by tanks.

Reports reaching Bangkok said the Air Force had gone over to the side of the insurgents but that the position of the Navy was not known. Navy ships fired on some of the planes and several senior Vietnamese naval officers were reported assassinated.

The reports reaching Bangkok said there were no reports of attacks on or injuries to American diplomatic or military personnel or their dependents.

As the war worsened for the South Vietnamese government, the Viet Cong upped the stakes by striking directly at American installations — not just the advisers who went to the field with government troops. A horrendous explosion demolished an American billet in the coastal city of Qui Nhon — and Pfc. Mike Mealey was on the scene to get a story of horror and courage.

"COME ON ... YOU CAN MAKE IT"

FEB. 15, 1965, BY PFC MIKE MEALEY

QUI NHON — "Come on, man, come on. Don't stop now. You can make it . . . you're almost there."

The Army enlisted man was only a few feet from freedom now, crawling the best he could for someone who just had part of his leg amputated.

A rescuer, hunched down in the tunnel running through the debris, was doing what he could to help. Finally the wounded man's hand protruded from the hole.

The rest came easy, and for the first time in 18½ hours, the young soldier took his first breath of fresh air.

He had only one foot now, though. The other one was buried under a wall.

This was the ruins of Viet Cong Hotel in downtown Qui Nhon, blasted into a pile of broken concrete by two Viet Cong bombs. So far, one dead American had been found, and 19 wounded had been dug from the rubble. Twenty two were still missing. Rescuers had voice contact with four men still trapped. Fate of the others was unknown.

The hotel had been four stories high, with a sun deck built on its roof.

A Korean doctor, an American doctor and an Army medic performed the amputation on this latest man to be rescued after all attempts to free his foot failed. Capt. Un Sup Kim of the Republic of Korea gave a local anesthetic, then used what medical instruments he had, including an electric saw, to take the foot off above the ankle.

The soldier was told of the operation, and agreed it was the only way he could be freed.

The operation was performed while dust fell as workers attempted to free another man on the far side of the demolished building. It took 30 minutes.

"We're supposed to be advisers here. This was a deliberate attack on buildings where people live who repair airplanes. They aren't here for combat . . ." These were the words of a bitter Col. Theodore Mataxis, senior adviser to II Corps, in which Qui Nhon is located.

Capt. Charles A. Brassert, an adviser in Qui Nhon, was two blocks from the hotel when he heard gunfire in the area. "After the shots, I heard an explosion then more shots, then a second explosion.

"When the second explosion went off, the top of the hotel vanished from view."

One rescuer said, "We joke with them when we tunnel in to take them out. We got one out after 14 hours. . . . I was looking, asking him if he had a girl, just anything to keep them from thinking about the explosion."

Some of the men who were later rescued were singing to each other, laughing and joking among themselves, another rescuer reported.

Capt. Steven W. Henault, commanding officer of the 140th Transporation Det. which occupied the hotel, looked older than his 37 years as he stood grim-faced before the rubble, watching rescuers tunnel toward the trapped men.

When asked what he had felt when he first reached the scene, he said simply, "I can't describe a feeling like that."

He added, "I've been with them since Jan. 3 ..."

His voice broke, and he turned away.

As U.S. involvement in Vietnam increased, American wounded began to flood hospitals in Southeast Asia. Joe Schneider, bureau chief in the Philippines, got one man's wide-awake nightmare in an interview that had to be an exchange of notes and gestures.

"THEY USED MY CHEST FOR A GUN REST"

MAY 30, 1965 BY JOE SCHNEIDER

CLARK AB, P.I. — "The Viet Cong used my chest for a gun rest. Each time he fired he took hunks of meat out of my arm."

Sgt. Richard Bartlett, Det. B, 1st Special Forces Group, was describing his experience in the grim battle of Song Be, Republic of Vietnam, as he lay recovering from wounds at U.S. Air Force Hospital, Clark AB, P.I.

Viet Cong guerrillas attacked Song Be, capital of mountainous Phuoc Long Province, 73 miles northeast of Saigon, May 11. The guerrillas took and held the town for more than eight hours before being ousted in one of the bitterest Vietnam battles in months.

Bartlett, still deaf from the concussion of grenades, told his story by jotting it down on a pad.

"I was in a foxhole with a machine gun. The weapon malfunctioned and I was trying to fix it when my buddy, Staff Sgt. Horace Young, yelled that the Viet Cong were throwing grenades.

"I heard one thud in the trench with us and Young was blown on top of me. I thought he was killed and kept trying to get the machine gun to fire.

"Another thud — I looked down to see a Viet Cong grenade sputtering at my feet. I tried to jump out of the hole but I didn't make it. My legs went numb.

"I crawled back to the next trench and loaded magazines for Sgt. Maj. Robert Frander and S. Sgt. Aldridge Martin.

"Then I decided to try to get back to my room and get my rifle and ammunition — once inside I started looking around. Then there was an explosion. It knocked me down, cut my neck and I was deaf.

"I yelled for a medic. But no one came, I staggered out of the room and fell in a hole where I thought I'd die. . . . I was bleeding badly from neck and leg wounds.

"I was in the hole about two hours when Capt. Miller (he couldn't remember the captain's first name) carried me to the mess hall which was being used as an aid station.

"I was in there about an hour. There was much small arms and mortar fire outside — I remember seeing Viet Cong all over the mess hall — they thought I was dead. They stepped on me and kicked me — I played dead — there was no way to defend myself.

"Pretty soon daylight came and part of a patrol came into the mess hall and got me out. While in the mess hall, I think Viet Cong had control of the camp.

"When they were taking me to an air evac helicopter, I remember a lot of sniper fire.

Bartlett said that as he was playing dead, a Viet Cong used his body as a support to steady the aim of his carbine and that each time the Red fired, bullets grazed his arm.

Bartless was literally sprayed with deadly fragments. He said he was grateful for the care he received in Vietnam and at the Clark hospital which has become the medical center of Southeast Asia.

Bartlett was especially grateful to Capt. Miller — "He saved my life," the soldier said.

Light moments in the Vietnam War were rare and golden — such at this one.

CHAPLAIN HAS 'KEY' TO MORALE

JULY 26, 1965 BY AL KRAMER

BIEN HOA, Republic of Vietnam — It may seem strange to hand out church keys during an open-air religious service — stranger still if you know "church key" is the slang expression for beer can opener.

But that's what happened at Sunday services here as the chaplains of the 173rd Airbone Brigade (Separate) passed out some 400 openers to paratroopers.

"I had just told the men I had something for them — church keys," said Chaplain (Lt. Col.) James W. Morrill with a twinkle in his eye.

Chaplain (Capt.) James W. Kennedy dished out the hefty load of church keys during services.

It all came about because of a story on the front page of the Tulsa, Okla., World and a sympathetic Tulsa woman, Mrs. R. L. Hood Jr.

The story in the Tulsa World told of how there was serious shortage of openers for U.S. troops in Vietnam and how they were selling for as much as $1.50 each in Saigon stores.

Mrs. Hood got three Tulsa merchants to add to her own donation and bought a case of 500 openers.

She addressed the case and a letter to the chaplain of the 173d and handed them over to the Oklahoma Air National Guard, which saw that they were put on a plane for Vietnam.

"I handed out the church keys at the end of services when we usually pass out religious literature," Chaplain Morrill said.

"Of course I didn't tell the men they were beer can openers . . . I just said they were openers for soft drinks or whatever you like."

Mrs. Hood also sent the chaplain a box of clothes and toys for needy Vietnamese.

"I'm going to write Mrs. Hood a letter of thanks, and so are some of the men," Chaplain Morrill said.

Viet Cong attacks on Americans at Pleiku, Qui Nhon and other places brought a firm response from President Lyndon B. Johnson — air strikes into North Vietnam that were gradually stepped up until jet screams sounded at all hours. A Pacific Stars and Stripes reporter went to Yankee Station in the Tonkin Gulf to watch tired but selfless young Americans drop a sledge of air power on an aggressive enemy.

"DON'T KNOW ABOUT YOU, PEE WEE"

AUG. 25, 1965 BY HAL DRAKE

WITH THE U.S. SEVENTH FLEET — The two flickering specks might have been the lights of a distant ship.

But there was suddenly a soaring flash and a pulsing glow; and the faraway specks winked out like sparks in a fireplace.

"That's the coastline," someone said. For an instant the mountainous profile of North Vietnam was etched against the flaring explosion.

"Ammo dump," another shadowy figure added matter-of-factly. He rustled up to the flying bridge's railing for a closer look and listened expectantly for the sound of the cracking explosion that had to roll across miles of Tonkin Gulf that separated the hostile coast from the 80,000-ton U.S. attack carrier Independence.

The diamond-shaped echelon of jet fighter-bombers that demolished the ammunition dump had rushed off the carrier's fanlike flight deck a few minutes before.

Below the bridge, there was a thundering symphony of flash and sound. There was a wail and roar as an A4E Skyhawk, a white-hot streak of blistering heat pouring from her jet exhaust, poised on the catapult and waited to be launched. Waves of stifling heat washed over the flight crews behind the jet but they went right on working, trundling another aircraft up to the catapult as soon as the first had flashed away.

Three catapults worked in unison as the jets were flung into the air like bolts from a giant crossbow.

It was 1:30 a.m. Sleepers below decks were jarred awake by the volley of jet blasts and the trolley-like rumble of the catapults as they slid back into position after a launch. The more seasoned carrier sailors slept peacefully, and were not disturbed by the scraping and twanging noise the jets made as they returned to the flight deck and caught the arresting cable.

A night launch is noisy, terrifying and impressive. By day, the spectacle is etched in detail. The green-jacketed maintenance men, the red-vested bomb and fuel handlers and the yellow-shirted flight crews scatter among the silvery flock of jets like specks in a kaleidoscope. It is as if they were clambering around some gigantic movie set, and the voice that booms over the ship's bullhorn was that of a film director preparing to shoot a big scene in a super-spectacle.

Everyone does everything just right, with precision and elan.

The Independence is the flagship of Task Force 77, the apex of the prowling gray force that is ceaselessly and methodically erasing North Vietnam's war-making potential.

North Vietnam has declared itself the aggressive enemy of America's friend. She must not be allowed to mass troops, stockpile ammunition or maintain air fields. Life must be made sleepless and unbearable for her.

But denying strength and rest to the enemy means losing sleep yourself.

The crews you see working in the morning sunlight are the same that labored in the midnight darkness. At the end of 18 hours, they are spreading themselves thin — but they still appear alert and tireless.

And some have been up longer than that.

"Thirty hours," drawls Aviation Boatswain's Mate 2.C. Wayne Ian Gibson, a 37-year-old veteran from Cash, Ark., who was as young as most of his fellow catapult crewmen when he enlisted 17 years ago. There's a startling contrast between veteran and youngster as he stands beside 20-year-old Ray Clough, a short,

diminutive New Hampshireman who is unwillingly known as "Pee Wee."

"I don't know what my bunk looks like anymore," says Gibson. "I haven't seen it in three or four nights. We just flop up against a bulkhead. This shift has been hard. We had our three regular strikes and planned to knock off. Then this special sortie came up.

"We were up before that," breaks in Clough. "Remember? We had to shoot that one no-load (test firing of the catapult) so we'd be sure the . . . would work."

"Don't know about you, Pee Wee," says Gibson, sighing and shaking his head. "All this cussing, smoking and gum chewing. What would your Ma say?"

The others laugh and Pee Wee shrugs it off. He is prodded constantly because of his youth and size — but he doesn't have to apologize to anybody for the way he performs a man's job.

While Gibson is seated below decks at a console board, controlling powerful tons of steam pressure. Clough is on deck attaching cables between the jet aircraft and the sled — a heavy block of solid steel that pulls the plane forward for the launch.

Clough must stay beneath the plane and make certain the cables are secure and tense, jumping aside at the last moment before 12 tons of aircraft are hurled off the deck. He often has only two seconds to spare. It takes agility, timing — and nerve.

He does it — again. So do the others. The jets are hurled into the air like silvery javelins. Some crewmen now plod down ladders and flop thankfully into their racks. The ship's business goes on around them. As the last of the jets thunder off, a calm and modulated voice breaks into the public address system.

"Protestant services will be held. . . ."

Reporter Drake, assigned as fleet correspondent in the opening weeks of the Rolling Thunder air offensive, was flown by helicopter and high-lined from ship to ship. Aboard one carrier, he saw the name Tchudy decaled below the cockpit of one parked plane — the name of a man who had gone down over North Vietnam and was behind enemy wire. Eight years later, as Drake covered the return of POWs at Clark AB, Philippines, he saw Tchudy get off the plane that had flown him from Hanoi — a pinnacle moment for both the reporter and the returnee.

On June 11, 1966, Gunnery Sgt. Jack Baird tracked the spoor of a battle in the Central Vietnam Highlands and got one of the best stories of the war — an interview with Capt. Bill Carpenter, the onetime West Point football star who called down clouds of napalm on his own position as North

Vietnamese troops threatened to engulf it. Four days later, on a routine sweep of news sources, Baird found another hero — Staff Sgt. Jimmy E. Howard, who told of a fierce and desperate struggle that got down to rock throwing. Here is Baird's report.

"MY WIFE WANTS ME HOME"

JUNE 18, 1966 BY GUNNERY SGT. JACK BAIRD

CHU LAI, Vietnam — Sixteen U.S. Marines and two Navy Corpsmen held off a North Vietnamese battalion early Thursday for about five hours and when they ran low on rifle ammunition threw rocks at the enemy.

The savage fighting took place twelve miles northwest of Chu Lai.

A U.S. spokesman said the Marine reconnaissance team killed at least 40 Communists and more wounded and friendly casualties were heavy.

Just after dawn, a company-size relief force was heli-lifted in and gave pursuit. The company knocked out one machine gun and killed three Reds who had been left as snipers.

SSgt. Jimmie E. Howard, 36, the reconnaissance platoon leader, described the action late Thursday from his bed in the intensive care ward of the 1st Marine Div.'s medical battalion here.

Howard said, "My wife she didn't want me to get any more Purple Hearts. She just wants me to get home."

Howard is in good condition with a machine gun wound in his upper right thigh.

"We were on a routine reconnaissance mission," he said.

"Wednesday night we received word about a hardcore battalion in our area. We had no way to get out. I got my team leaders together and we formed defensive positions on a hill.

"We were about three feet below the crest of the hill. Marine pilots were bombing the top of the hill. We hid under large rocks.

"About 10 p.m. Wednesday we started hearing whistles and the enemy signalling by hitting pieces of sticks together. The noises from the sticks and whistles came from several directions.

"They had come out of their positions to see us. From then on it was just 'Katie bar the door.' Then they were hammered by Marine jets and Huey gunships.

"We had no opportunity to dig foxholes. We made like gophers. We had two M79 grenade launchers, 14 rifles, grenades and two AFR15's.

"My M79 man was just standing to fire when automatic weapons fire hit him. They had us completely surrounded. But the air support was beautiful.

"They (the enemy) were lobbing grenades at us. You could see black objects being hurled at us. Then they got smart. They could see the grenades were not hitting us, so they started lobbing in mortars.

"I called my CO, requesting more helicopter air support, I thought we might get our injured out.

"They charged us in waves. The choppers and the jets put their rounds in the back rockets. The ground shook and we could feel the heat of the bomb bursts."

Air Force "Providers" which dropped flares during action had the code name of "Clubfoot."

But "there was nothing clubfoot about the way they were dropping those flares," Howard said.

He said he could not ask the helicopters to come in for them because if they did "we would have lost more aircraft and good men."

One Marine helicopter was downed during the action. Two of the three men aboard were casualties.

"I told the pilots," Howard said, "just keep them off our back."

There was hand-to-hand combat, said Howard, and he pointed to the corpsman in the bed next to him. He was Hospitalman 3.C. Billie Holmes.

"Doc was just like a rifleman. A grenade landed between us. Doc was momentarly blinded."

Howard said the corpsman fought hand-to-hand and did what he could firing at them.

"We ran out of grenades and M79 rounds not long afterwards.

"It was rifles and rocks against machine guns, mortars and grenades. You can't describe it. They (the platoon) were outstanding — the greatest. They did one helluva job and I'm proud to be their platoon leader.

"There were 12 rounds with seven of us still able to pull the trigger when relief got here.

"The longest movie is just a blinking of the eye compared to last night," the stocky Marine said.

Col. W. G. Johnson, commander of Marine Air Group 36, and his helicopter took several hits during the early morning action but he managed to bring the crippled ship home to Chu Lai.

Capt. Jim Perryman, who was flying an armed Huey escort for other H34 helicopters during the action, said, "They were pinned down real bad and there was no suitable spot for a landing zone."

Throughout the darkness, Perryman alternated with Capt. John M. Shields to cover the Marines. While one was firing his rockets and M60 machine guns the other was back at the base rearming.

About a dozen Marine A4 Skyhawk jets scrambled from Da Nang to assist the beleaguered marines.

The French used to call it a "spitting rain" — the spiteful, ceaseless downpours that made the Mekong Delta canals flow faster and bogged cursing troops in glue-like, ankle-deep mud. In another war, the monsoon was just as constant — and just as miserable. Airman 2.C. Bob Cutts, later a civilian newsman on Pacific Stars and Stripes, walked into the grey, slanting torrent with the troops and drew this mosaic of misery.

RAIN — TODAY, YESTERDAY, TOMORROW

MAY 25, 1966, BY AIRMAN 2.C. BOB CUTTS

THE MEKONG DELTA, Vietnam — Rain. Big fat drops plummeted out of the pearl-gray sky, splattering against the soldier's helmet and splotching his shaggy brown fatigues.

The Vietnamese rifleman took his eyes off the nearest tree line and looked up to see the black mass of clouds blotting out the sun.

The grape-size drops fell faster and faster. The sheets of rain partially hid the Viet Cong hiding place in the tangled trees.

Lying in mud near a paddy dike, the soldier could do nothing to shield himself from the torrent. If he moved, he'd make a good target for the snipers. He tried to shield his weapon and failed.

The mud beneath him began to turn into oozing slime.

It was late afternoon, and the daily monsoon was at work again.

The soldier and his buddies spaced along the dike were all miserably soaked, but it wasn't anything new.

It rained yesterday, and the day before that. It would rain again tomorrow, and the next day. At least two inches a day.

Starting late in May and lasting until mid-November, the massive wet torrents will drift across the Cambodian border to assault the delta plains and fill canals, rivers, streams, and swamps to overflowing.

It's also Charley season.

The VC take advantage of both the excess water and the slackened maneuverability of truck-borne troops to launch what they call "a monsoon offensive."

"The Cong can move more troops and supplies by sampan and junk much faster over a much wider area in the wet season, and it's easier for them to get food," said a U.S. intelligence adviser to IV Corps.

"But the main difference is that Charley can get drinking water much easier in the field. The water is brackish and slimy in the dry season but it runs deep, clear and fresh during monsoons.

"We counter these advantages by relying on an airmobile support to keep up the number of government operations or actually increase them in the wet season."

It was on one of these operations that the Vietnamese soldier now found himself facing the enemy.

The VC were trapped there, without any exit. The fields on the other side of the tree line were also ringed with government soldiers.

Normally, air strikes, both U.S. and Vietnamese, would be called in to finish the job, but the rain canceled the chance of air support.

So the ARVN unit had to take the VC company alone.

Mortar rounds, grenades and machine gun fire pelted the trees, as the attack began but no answering fire blasted back. The tree line was still.

Afraid of a trick, the Vietnamese commander sent scouts to flank and see why Charley wasn't firing.

Charley wasn't there. A small stream, unmarked on the map and normally dry, flowed through the center of the tree line. Filled by the monsoon rains, it is behind dense foliage as it wound towards open country.

A kilometer away, they found two of the camouflaged sampans used to escape, more were undoubtedly using the big canals and rivers of the Delta as escape highways, carrying boatloads of innocent looking "fishermen" and their hidden weapons.

It isn't unusual. What is unusual is that this year, for the first time in the war, the VC haven't made boastful threats, or scattered loud propaganda about a promised "monsoon offensive."

"We've hit them so hard this year they're really hurting for men and ammo," said the intelligence man. "We don't think they could launch any offensive now no matter how bad the weather.

"But of course, we don't know for sure. We've got to play it safe. We have to treat it as an 'ominous silence' until the monsoon is over."

He glanced out of the window, where it was beginning to rain again. "If it ever ends."

Just after he joined the Pacific Stars and Stripes Vietnam Bureau, Navy journalist Gary Cooper got off a helicopter with other newsmen and introduced himself to a brigade commander. The officer's eyes went up at Cooper's name. When the next man said, "I'm Winston Churchill," there was an urgent pause for quick explanations. Cooper was not related to the film actor; Winston Churchill IV was a grandson of the late prime minister. And Cooper's readers were to know him by more than just a distinctive name. He was a reporter willing to share their chances and dangers. Here is a story Cooper might have never lived to write.

"STARS AND STRIPES ... I'M HIT ... HELP ME"

JULY 10, 1966, BY PO 3.C. GARY COOPER

WITH THE 3RD BRIGADE, 25TH INF. DIV, Vietnam — Dawn, less than half a mile from the Cambodian border.

A 12-man squad is winding its way to home base through thick, dark jungle after spending a long restless night at Outpost Cord No. 4 watching for Viet Cong.

Fifteen minutes from now, five of the 12 men will be wounded. Two will be near death.

Moving along a creek bed, the men try to stay as quiet as possible.

The squad leader, Sgt. John Smith, throws one hand up over his head. Everyone freezes.

One, two, three breathless seconds pass as Smith searches the mass of jungle to his left.

Slowly, he raises three fingers, one by one, and whispers, "I've spotted three of 'em over there."

The tense silence erupts as the Viet Cong open up with automatic weapons.

We dive for the sand and scramble madly for a tree trunk near the creek.

A soldier at the end of the trunk cries out as a slug tears into his chest. It doesn't take long to realize there are more than three. Many more.

"You, you and you," Smith says. "Get across the creek before we're surrounded." By twos and threes the men splash across the creek, staying so low their chins nearly hit the water.

The radio operator has made a frantic call to company base camp, telling them of our situation. The company is 2,000 meters from us across the same rugged, nearly impenetrable terrain. They are roughly 30 miles southwest of Pleiku.

Running, stumbling, firing to the left and right, carrying the wounded man, gasping for breath, we look around us for any kind of cover.

There is none, only elephant grass four feet high.

Two men in front of you drop, partially hidden in the grass. You do the same. Fifty thoughts race through your mind as you hug the ground. If only you had a rifle, a pistol, a grenade — anything.

It's not quiet now. You can't distinguish the sound of one bullet, or even a burst from a machine gun. It's all one terrible nightmare, sounding like a million rounds going off at once.

"Hey . . . you . . . help me . . ." You look around. "Stars and Stripes . . . I'm hit . . . help me . . ." It's Smith. He's about five feet away.

You start crawling to him. You don't really want to, but you do. What you really want to do is bury yourself as deeply as you can into the ground.

"Smitty, where are you hit?" His eyes stare skyward, looking at something you hope to never see. He drops his hand from his chest. Blood spurts into the air.

You find a bandage and tie it around him, telling him everything is going to be OK, thinking to yourself, wondering, will it?

Ahead of Smith, Pfc. Milton Vaughan is slumped against a tree, that same stare in his eyes. Gray matter is oozing out of the wound in his head.

You find another bandage and cover the holes as he mumbles, "My God . . . My God . . . My God."

All around you men seem to be shouting, yet trying to keep their voices at a muffled whisper. The Viet Cong, now maybe 50 or 60, have you surrounded.

They are screaming and yelling, hoping to panic the squad. It sounds like a Western movie with Indians whooping. But it's real.

The air is filled with the smell of cordite, leaving a dense haze, engulfing the seven men still able to fire.

Pfc. Gabriel Diaz, firing his M-60 machine gun into the grass, yells, "They're right there. I can see the bastards . . . They're right there, ten meters away."

The M-16 you found by Smith's side is ripping into the grass in front of you. There's nothing to see but grass and smoke. But they're there, ten meters away.

The rifle stops firing. You find another clip and slam it into the gun.

Viet Cong are screaming all around you.

Suddenly it hits you. You're fighting for your life.

The rifle jams.

The jungle turns dead quiet. Everything you've ever heard about an M-16 rifle races through your mind. It won't fire. No matter what you do it won't fire.

Another M-16 is laying close by. You grab it. Shove a fresh clip in and wait.

The jungle explodes in another wild burst of fire, cries and smoke. You level the rifle and squeeze the trigger. Nothing happens — nothing.

You drop the useless weapon and squirm closer to the ground.

One thought races very clearly through your mind:

"What in the hell are you doing here?"

"The map, I've got to have the map." It's Sgt. Richard C. Austin, who has taken command of the squad.

"Where is it?"

Austin says that Smith has it. You reach Smith again. "The map, Smitty, we've got to have the map." He's deep in shock. He says nothing.

Without the map we haven't got a chance. The company, now on its way to us, has to know exactly where we are.

You reach down Smith's bloodied chest and find the map. It's warm and sticky, covered with blood.

You crawl back to Austin and give him the map. He talks into the radio, telling the company where we are.

The area off to the right is wide open. You grab another rifle and make your way to the open spot.

A deafening blast sends your face deeper into the ground.

A grenade or mortar has landed where you had been only seconds before.

It's white phosporous. Little holes start smoldering on your back and legs from flesh-burns. You slap at the holes quickly then turn and look back down the barrel of the M-16.

Then the 30 minutes that has taken a lifetime to pass, is over. C. Co., 1st Bn., 35th Inf., has spotted the squad. You can hear them talking and shouting orders.

One of the first persons to reach us is Spec. 5 Glenn R. Bowers, senior medic for Charlie Co. He bandages the wounded, tries to calm them, and calls for makeshift stretchers to be made from tree branches and ponchos.

Forty-five minutes after Smith spotted the first three Viet Cong, he and the other four wounded are in a chopper, on their way to the field hospital in Pleiku.

Capt. Alvino Cortez, C. Co. commander, says his company has found four VC bodies, plus some ammo and automatic weapons. But there has to be more than that dead. You know there are.

That was the morning of July 7th. That night, Austin, Diaz and the other five who survived the fight unwounded were back at Outpost Cord No. 4.

They'll probably be there tonight. And every other night.

———————————

Brassy, enterprising Bob Cutts got one of the greatest scoops of the war — he was the first American correspondent to fly over North Vietnam during the devastating American aerial offensive. Here is a story full of sound, fury and authenticity.

"WE LOST ONE HERE THREE DAYS AGO"

JULY 15, 1966, BY AIRMAN 1C BOB CUTTS

NORTH VIETNAM — There it was below me as I sat, cramped and hot, in the Skyraider's cockpit — the first correspondent ever to fly in an air strike over that well-known yet unknown land above the 17th Parallel.

With the engine throbbing around me and the crackle of radio voices in my earphones, I was physically as detached from that shrouded land as if I were watching a movie in a theater.

But I know no American could fly over North Vietnam as an enemy and not feel affected by it in some way — even though it could have been a raid anywhere in this war.

I had casually asked the pilot, a World War II fighter veteran, if I could go on his next raid north.

Lt. Col. Dick Willsie stared at me. "Are you sure you really want to?"

"Well, if you've taken chances all these years, I guess I can take one," I said.

Now I wondered.

As we circled over North Vietnam, Willsie was tight-lipped, drawn-faced and grim, and I wondered why I was here.

But, nearing our target, I began to realize that just by my presence, by my being an American, I was here to kill or be killed. I was part of the war.

North Vietnam, a huge, glistening green map, was curtained with big thunderclouds, small pyramids of white fleece and slender shafts of sunlight filtering through gray rain clouds that lent a cathedral dignity to the scene.

Jagged, saw-toothed mountains swirled up at us, falling away into narrow gorges where mountain streams washed against rice paddies carved from rock.

The country's western half was in cloud shadow, and as we flew east at 6,000 feet, the golden band of coast, still sunlit, came into focus.

The clean, unmarred beaches were peaceful, and the rolling lowlands that reached for the mountains had the same patchwork farms I have seen in South Vietnam.

But the peaceful scene did not steady my nerves.

Off on the coast slouched Dong Hoi, where SAM sites and huge flak batteries glowered, waiting like spiders in their webs for the American flies.

I could see tiny specks of black all around, swooping, weaving in and out of valley and hills — and towers of dust and smoke reaching up toward them. The Thunderchiefs were at work again.

It was no longer hot, but sweat soaked my clothes and slid to the end of my nose. I saw Willsie's face beaded with the same nervous perspiration.

"We lost a Thud (F-105) here about three days ago," he said. I didn't answer.

As we searched for a target for napalm and

rockets, my throat itched dry. But somehow I felt it would be too casual for me to drink from the canteen we had.

Willsie never took his hawk eyes off the ground, except to scan quickly for nearby F-105s or MiGs.

He was looking for a new road that was supposed to wind south through the hills below us to the 17th Parallel.

On the ground, nothing moved. There were a number of roads and paths and tiny clusters of farm huts — but no movement.

"They're down there," Willsie told me. "If we get low enough, there'll be lots of action."

"Let's get rid of our napalm on that truck park down there," Willsie pointed to a road overgrown with jungle. I saw nothing. "It's camouflaged," he assured me.

From 8,000 feet we flung ourselves at the ground. At 3,000, we released the canisters and pulled up over a hilltop. Below, our wingman, Lt. Col. Jerry Ransom, dropped his on the same target. Smoke billowed up. Then we swooped in again, this time with eight 5-inch rockets.

The sky before the canopy filled with flame as they fired off in succession, then again that gut-grinding gravity as the engine's 18 big cylinders strained to pull her away from the ground.

When we circled back, the area was still aflame. "Must've got something in there — she's still burning. Hope it was a truck."

The air speed indicator read 150 knots and the altimeter 4,000 feet as we kept circling the hills, looking for the road. I held my breath each time one of the mountain peaks reached out for us. If a gunner was sitting up there . . .

I kept telling myself what an interesting experience it was, but my subconscious kept hoping we'd turn west and get out of here.

After an hour we headed out, then Willsie banked south again and flew almost to the DMZ. In desperation, I asked weakly, "When we headin' back?"

"Oh, I thought we'd stick around for a few more hours," he said. "Maybe fly up north and scare up some ground fire — that all right with you?"

He grinned. I grinned back, half-heartedly.

As we neared the valleys again, Willsie thought he saw something and dropped down low — real low for North Vietnam. About 2,000 feet.

We trimmed mountainsides, and I thought about the .50-caliber sites that may be hidden among those trees.

Nothing happened.

Climbing to 9,000, we headed home. As we neared the border, I settled back for a nap.

Willsie shook me awake. "Stay alert," he said. "If the flak's hot I want you to be ready to bail out. There's no place to land in the hills. And this is flak alley. They wait here for the Yanks on their way home. They've got some real accurate stuff down there," he said.

I stayed awake.

When at last the concrete ribbon of the runway poured under us again, three long hours after takeoff, I let out a long sigh. A real long one.

The general stared in astonishment at the slight figure who disembarked with the rest of the 25th Inf. Div. troops — he looked like a young stowaway who had stolen a uniform. But Pfc. Richard Hill had turned 18 on the boat that brought him back to Vietnam — the only reason he hadn't been left behind in Hawaii. Vietnam Bureau Chief Wally Beene watched as General William C. Westmoreland talked with Hill, a brash but likable kid who seemed very happy that he hadn't been left out of the war. A number of weeks later, Beene traveled to Hill's outfit to see how he was doing — and learned that the young soldier had grown up the hard way. He was in a hospital in Japan. A note to Tokyo sent another reporter to talk to Hill — a young man Beene probably wouldn't have known . . .

FAREWELL TO BOYHOOD

DEC. 11, 1966, BY HAL DRAKE

TOKYO — If I GO, I GO. If I don't go, I don't."

Pfc. Richard K. Hill said it lightly with a shrug — but with a terrible maturity that belied a grave, boyish face faintly spotted with freckles. Hill is 18. He celebrated that birthday quietly last January in the cramped, stuffy troop bay of a transport that took him from a dock near Schofield Barracks, Hawaii, to Vung Tau, Vietnam.

Hill is a man. Never mind the youthful face or the slight build that sparely distributes 120 pounds over a five-foot, six-inch frame. Ignore the traces of teen-age slang that linger in his speech. Forget about the nickname "Babysan," pinned on him by buddies while he was temporarily stationed in Japan.

Forged into manhood in the furnace of hardship, Hill left the roadsign marked "Boyhood" forever last Aug. 7, when he and several fellow soldiers in Reconnaissance Platoon Hq. and Hq., 2nd Bn., 27th Inf., 25th Inf. Div., swept a jungle-smothered flatland near Cu Chi for Viet Cong.

First, Hill was to recall during an interview, there was a warning whine from the scout dog held on a leash by the man in front of him — then the piercing snap of a sniper's bullet and the shattering crash of an automatic weapon.

Hill felt a fiery, stabbing pain on the inside of his right thigh and a gushing warmth down his leg. He fell into the clammy vegetation on the jungle floor, and recalls feebly crying, "Get the medic over here, I'm losing blood" before he passed out.

The bullet had gone through a vein and grazed a nerve. The wound healed slowly. Hill, fully recovered, faced the prospect of returning to "the Nam" or the more pleasant possibility of remaining in Japan — still a dream post for the single young serviceman.

Hill was neither afraid of returning nor anxious to. Whatever happened would be, he told himself and others. He had acquired a natural and healthy fatalism — the kind that turns a boy into a man and a man into a soldier.

But Hill, of Covington, Ky., is still in many ways a kid who should be tinkering with cars or raising rowdy hell in drive-ins back home. He still wears the sharp-toed kid leather cowboy boots which, along with his maddening fondness for a popular song, tagged him with the nickname "Boots" back in Hawaii.

"You know that Nancy Sinatra record, 'These Boots Are Made for Walkin'?' Man, I played that thing day and night. Everyone in the barracks was going crazy. Finally on the day we left, someone picked up the record and broke it across his knee. Man, I almost cried."

Hill had put aside his first childish thing, if not willingly. Regarded by his older barracks mates as something between a mascot and a nuisance, he learned that small things can irritate men when they're about to go to war. He had slogged with them as they climbed steep trails, struggled those dense, swampy forests in the Hawaii tourists never saw. Now he walked up the ramp of a troopship with them. Hill was on his way to being rough-thumbed into manhood.

Neither Hill's age nor his birthday meant much to his best friend, Johnny. Johnny was an Old Breed regular, the kind who could take a young recruit in hand and keep him in line. But after duty hours, he could cross the line and be friends.

"He was the only one who treated me like I was a man. There was never any of this Boots, kid or Babysan stuff. He took me to his home and I got to know his family. He was a great guy."

Was is tragically literal. Johnny is dead.

He was still a friendly voice and a hand on Hill's shoulder when the brigade debarked at Vung Tau, a resort town specked with palms and ringed by towering mountains. Up the peninsula lay the guerrilla-infested Central Vietnam Highlands, which were being slowly, and not cheaply, wrested from tough, seasoned Viet Cong regulars who had controlled them for years.

Hill's welcome was something he would never forget. His helmeted head barely came to General William C. Westmoreland's chin, but the general — perhaps struck by his obvious and startling youth — singled Hill out for a warm handshake and a personal welcome.

"He asked me about the food on the ship. I told him it was lousy. He asked me if we had exercised while we were sailing. I lied, sticking up for my platoon sergeant, and said we had. Then he asked me all kinds of questions about my home, where I had come from and all. He seemed like a patient and fatherly kind of guy, real sharp and cool — the kind you really need to run a show like that one.

"I kept telling myself, gee, this can't be me talking to a four-star general."

"Hey, Hill," a voice behind him ordered sharply, "get up on this truck." Westmoreland said, "good luck or best of luck," and the general and the private stopped holding up the war. Hill joined the rest of his outfit as they threw their gear into trucks, climbed in after it, and moved on.

However the general's good wishes were worded, they were soon needed. Hill and his buddies dug a deep, well-fortified perimeter around an artillery outfit that dropped explosive bludgeons on infiltrating Viet Cong. Mail came during a smoke break. Johnny got a letter from his wife and handed Hill a small, personally addressed note that had been enclosed with it.

"She told me, 'take care of Johnny' and I never got a chance to write back that I would." That same night, mortar fire blasted the perimeter. Johnny and another sergeant, caught outside their foxholes, were both killed.

Hill grieved briefly, then shook it off. There is not much else that can be done in war. He learned there were other friends, such as the one who saved him from drowning the night his squad forded a river on their way to take up positions as an ambush patrol.

"Going across, it was really up to my chest. I stepped in a hole and the water was over my head before I knew what was happening. My buddy grabbed me just in time."

There was another good friend, a Mexican, who was wounded and lost in a long night's battle with the Viet Cong. Hill and others heard him crying, "Don't leave me here" — and found his mutilated, headless body the next morning.

Another friend was captured alive — and was discovered with his head buried in a mound of dirt, dead.

Hill himself survived by learning that certain things were not done in war — such as swan-diving wildly into the brush when a sniper's rifle cracked. That time he was raked across the chest with a sharp bamboo stake which would have been fatal if it had pierced him. On another day, he was dispatched into a deep, narrow Viet Cong tunnel because of his spare build — and deafened himself for an hour afterward by firing his .45 at a noise that turned out to be a scampering rat.

Hill speaks knowledgeably and respectfully of "Charley," the shadowy enemy he has a deep hatred for. He tells of a peasant soldier "too tough to die" — who had half of his head shot away, but whose twitching hand still grasped for a weapon a few feet away.

There were many, many markers on the road to manhood. Hill passed them all. He'll be 19 in a few more weeks — and not old enough to vote or drink for two more years.

Col. Robin Olds was a flamboyant throw back to the days of Guynemer, Richthofen and Rickenbacker — to a time there was a dash of knighthood in plane-to-plane aerial combat. There was no better man to lead American pilots in the biggest air battle of the Vietnam War — and certainly no one more qualified to tell about it. In this report, Andrew Headland Jr. colorfully described both the battle and the personality and vigor of the man who led it.

"SEVEN MiGS MADE MISTAKES"

JAN. 5, 1967 BY ANDREW HEADLAND JR.

SAIGON — "To make a long story extremely short, they lost."

With this sentence Col. Robin Olds, a Seventh Air Force fighter wing commander, summed up the swirling air battle in which Air Force Phantom jets knocked seven MiG-21s out of the sky Monday northwest of Hanoi.

Olds, 44, gave details of the war's biggest aerial battle at Tan Son Nhut AB.

The battle raised to 34 the total of MiGs downed by U.S. pilots in the Vietnam War.

No U.S. planes were lost to the MiGs' missile and cannon fire.

Olds said his flight was attacked "very aggressively" by an unknown number of MiGs while making the sweep over North Vietnam.

The seven downed MiG-21s were shot down by air-to-air missiles.

Olds downed his first MiG during the battle. The kill brings his total of enemy planes to 25. He flew P-38s and P-51s in World War II.

Olds said one MiG got up behind him. "It wasn't the first time I have had someone behind

FLASHING ROCKETS rip from a jet to blast Viet Cong positions, softening up a tough objective as troops trudge to helicopters, the battle coaches that lift off to carry them in for the deadly piecework with rifles and grenades. This was the endless routine of assault against an enemy who might resist as a solid force or break up like quicksilver to retreat.

BOUND FOR MONKEY MOUNTAIN, a height that stands near Da Nang and was under ceaseless guerrilla siege, assault helicopters are about to clean the slopes and flatlands of infiltrators — again. American troops often held only the crest of the mountain, an important observation and communications post in the I Corps area — itself the slippery wedge against North Vietnam.

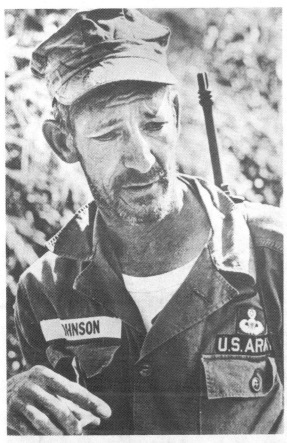

NOT WILLIE OR JOE, this is Master Sgt. Evans M. Johnson, an old soldier who was fighting his third war when Stripes correspondent Steve Stibbens took this masterful, Mauldin-like portrait of him in the Mekong Delta. President Johnson picked the shot for a pictorial record of the war. Besides being a fighter, many Vietnamese discovered, the GI was frequently a provider — the concerned hand that fed endless lines of hungry refugees, often paying out of his own pocket.

USA

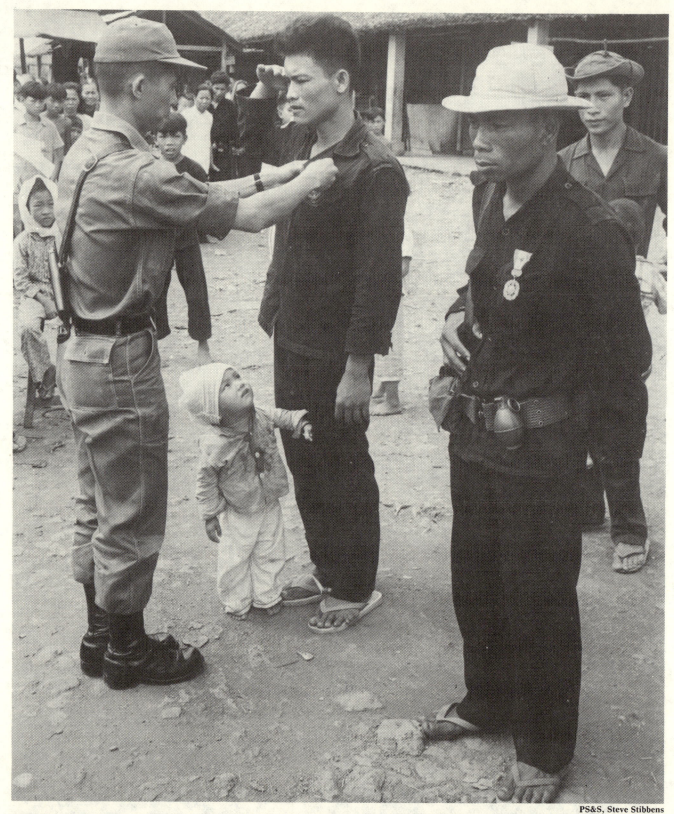

DADDY'S BUSY getting a medal but this toddler tugs at his pantleg and demands attention — a lighter moment in a war in which fathers and mothers frequently fought at their own front door for the life of their families. This militiaman and 18 others fought off Viet Cong for two nights, with their kinfolk crowding shelters during a desperate siege.

RIFLE AND RIFLEMAN both get a bath in a Mekong Delta canal as Pfc. Jesse Liddell engulfs himself in cool comfort to clean his fatigues and cleanse his M16 of muck that could cause a jam at a critical moment.

SOUTH VIETNAMESE WOUNDED are carried on old vehicle frames, abandoned grain carts, anything that can be pressed into service as a stretcher and speed casualties to lifesaving help. On Route 13 — called Thunder Road by Americans — there was a constant exodus of corpses and cripples.

SPOOKED EYES of Capt. Bill Carpenter, the famed "Lonesome End" during his West Point football days, tell of a grim game that was played with his life on the line. Wedged by a crushing force of Viet Cong, he called napalm strikes on his own command post as the enemy rushed in and threatened to overrun him. They died in clouds of flame and Carpenter was awarded the Medal of Honor.

103

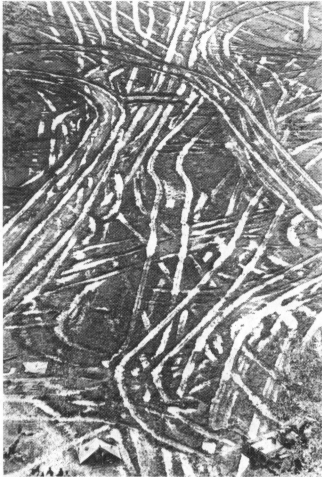

PS&S, Gary Cooper

MUD, deep and thick, was underfoot everywhere during the downpours of the monsoon season and was often the worst enemy of the ponderous portable firepower the United States Army carried to the field. Patton tanks made these deep impressions during Operation Paul Revere. The 1968 Tet Offensive was full of horrendous but sometimes compassionate images, such as this Marine who took time out to carry a wounded child to lifesaving help and safety.

PS&S, John Olson

me who was angry," he said. "I didn't worry too much, though, knowing that my flight was there providing protection."

At one point he had two MiGs in front and another on his left. He rolled up behind the MiG on his left, flying upside down until he lined up the enemy jet.

He fired a missile and saw a tremendous orange flash. One wing of the MiG flew out. The plane went out of control and plunged to earth.

Olds said, "I was elated. I was glad they tangled with us. It was what we'd been hoping for."

Asked if any of the MiG pilots made tactical mistakes, Olds replied, "Seven made mistakes."

He said the battle lasted between 12 and 14 minutes — "long for an air battle."

It was not known how many MiGs were in the battle or where they came from. "Some pilots saw only two MiGs, some saw five or six," he said.

Lt. Gen. William W. Momyer, Seventh AF commander, said the Air Force jets were sent up specially to attack any MiGs that came up. The Phantom crews took a day off from tactical bombing missions to take on the MiGs which had been attacking U.S. planes in the Red River Valley.

Momyer said the mission was similar to World War II and the Korean War — "to engage and destroy enemy fighters."

He said the Seventh AF was trying to do a "day-to-day job" and to destroy as many MiGs as time and fuel permitted.

A total of 14 flights of Air Force Phantoms and six flights of F-105s participated, Momyer said.

Olds said "Every single man present contributed to the battle by virtue of being there." No pilot shot down more than one MiG.

Olds, a former West Point football All-American, is married to former Hollywood actress Ella Raines.

Olds' father, Maj. Gen. Robert Olds, formerly commanded the Second Army Air Force.

One of the flight leaders, Capt. John B. Stone, of Coffeeville, Miss., said it is "hard to explain the feeling of finding and destroying your first MiG."

Other men with confirmed kills in Monday's sweep are 1st Lt. Ralph R. Wetterhahn, Aircraft Commander (AC), and 1st Lt. Jerry K. Sharp, of Corpus Christi, Texas; pilot; Capt. Walter S. Redeker, home town not reported, AC and 1st Lt. James W. Murray, McKeesport, Pa., pilot; 1st Lt. Lawrence J. Glynn Jr., of Arlington, Mass, AC, and 1st Lt. Lawrence E. Cary, of Pawnee City, Neb., pilot; Maj. Philip P. Combines, of Norwich, Conn., AC, and 1st Lt. Ree R. Dutton, Wyoming, Ill., pilot.

Olds' pilot was 1st Lt. Charles C. Clifton, of Fort Wayne, Ind. Flying with Stone was 1st lt. Clifiton P. Dunnegan, of Winston Salem, N.C.

There are two ways to write a war story; it can read drably, like a communique, or it can put the reader right into the battle. There is no place for depth, subtlety or expansive writing. Like a marksman who never wastes a shot, a good reporter makes every word count — the way Spec. 5 Gerard Forken did in this short, fast-moving gem.

INTO THE VOLLEY OF DEATH

MARCH 22, 1967 BY SPEC. 5 GERARD FORKEN

LAI KHE, Vietnam — Viet Cong troops wearing checkered scarves of the 273rd VC Regt., charged across a field into a volley of death here Monday.

When it was over, at least 227 Viet Cong lay dead. Bloody trails indicated many more bodies were hauled away by the VC.

The Operation Junction City battle began when the Cong launched a mortar barrage against a troop of the 3rd Sq., 5th Cav., and a battery of the 7th Bn., 9th Arty., both 9th Inf. Div. units.

The two U.S. outfits were camped at Bau Bang off Highway 13 just north of Lai Khe when the first enemy rounds hit at 40 minutes past midnight.

There was a brief lull when the mortars stopped. Then massed troops of the 273rd VC Regt. began pouring from the rubber tree forest across an open field.

Heavy U.S. fire cut down the Cong attackers.

Another lull, and the VC charged again, getting within 15 yards of the U.S. troops before they were stopped again.

The American forces, part of the 9th Inf. Div., but under 1st Inf. Div. control, called in artillery and air strikes before the VC could regroup.

Near 3,000 artillery rounds hit Cong positions, and Air Force pilots flew 26 strikes.

At the height of the battle, a platoon leader of A Troop, 3rd Cav. Sq., was firing from his armored personnel carrier when it was hit by recoilless rifle fire.

"My driver was wounded," and Lt. Roger Festa, of New Haven, Conn., "If the round had hit head-on it would have killed us right then." Festa carried the wounded driver — a sergeant — to a tent and called for a medic.

"Just as we got inside the tent a mortar hit right on top of us. I was blown out of the tent, but the sergeant was killed."

Troops of the 1st Sq., 4th Cav. joined the fight before dawn. By 9 a.m. the Cong had been pushed back.

U.S. losses were reported as five killed and 53 wounded.

"That's the way the ball bounces" — "Death is so permanent." These grim proverbs were part of an infantryman's lexicon in the Korean War and there were probably similar sayings in every war ever fought. Marine Sgt. Gene Young, a Pacific Stars and Stripes correspondent, recalled an old Vietnamese fatalism as he moved out with soldiers of the 1st Inf. Div. — and found it to be a starkly appropriate prelude to a fight in which Young was wounded and another man died.

NIGHT OF THE PHANTOM

MAY 14, 1967 BY SGT. GENE YOUNG

LAI KHE, Vietnam — There is an old saying in Vietnam — "If you go too many times into the night, you will meet the phantom." This was true for Lonnie Skaggs and almost true for me.

It was the last week of April when I arrived at the 3rd Brigade Hq. of the 1st Inf. Div. and asked to join the 2nd Bn. of the 28th Inf. operating just north of the Iron Triangle.

The next morning, I flew out to Alpha Co. on a resupply chopper. There I met Capt. Donald Sawtelle, who said his company was searching for a supply center in the area.

We got only about 1,000 yards into the brush before we started finding trench networks, small bunkers, spiderholes and tunnels. Then we got into the big stuff — reinforced concrete bunkers sunk into the ground with a trench system.

A FAC pilot reported two men running away nearby, so we knew there must be others about. Suddenly our point man, John Turner, spotted three VC at the entrance of a bunker, but they didn't see him.

Turner jumped back and pulled the pin on a grenade that he started to throw, but his arm tripped a booby trap — the VC put them up in trees to snag radio antennas.

Turner was hurt pretty bad, but he managed to throw the grenade in front of him. Some of the shrapnel from the grenade hit him and the VC opened up on him with small arms. He was shot in the shoulder, along with his other wounds.

Johnson, the medic, rushed up despite the fire coming from three directions and started working on Turner. That's when Skaggs opened up with his machine gun and pinned them down for a few seconds.

Sawtelle was trying to get somebody into the open where they could get a grenade into the trench with the three VC. More fire was coming from a hooch behind the bunker where Skaggs was firing.

Somebody jumped up over the bunker and

took a grenade that he rammed right down their throats. He was standing on top of the trench and I could hear Johnson yelling "You got them. You got them."

After the grenade went off, Turner started to crawl out and Johnson said he would give him protective fire. Turner was in shock and I was getting fire from only one side, so I went over to help him back to the big bunker where the chief medic was, Spec. 5 Avillz.

We could hear Sawtelle yelling "Move back, move back, clear the area" to his platoon leaders and we knew artillery was going to be called in.

We started back after getting some bandages on Turner and Skaggs told the captain to move everybody out — Skaggs said he had plenty of ammo to hold them off.

Avillz and I grabbed Turner, but he had to walk out — it was just too thick to carry a man. We kept him doped up, talked to him, and kept him moving on his feet while we tried to break a trail for him.

The whole company was moving back by this time and everybody thought Skaggs was with us, shooting on the run.

But he was still standing on the bunker, playing a song with his M-60. It was a surprise for the VC too, because they started coming down on both flanks without realizing Skaggs was right behind them.

When we got to the perimeter, everybody was looking for Skaggs. I could still hear his gun and suddenly he broke out of the brush. He ran out of ammo and out of jungle about the same time.

We pulled together and a chopper landed to take Turner out. I got to talking with Skaggs and asked him if he was going back in.

He said yes — he didn't like the idea of being chased out of a place.

We decided to go around and come into the area from behind. Just inside the jungle we found more bunkers and a cooking fire still burning. We were trying to flank the trail, but the VC spotted us. They let the pointman go by, because they spotted Skaggs with his gun and ammo. They opened up with an automatic burst that stitched Skaggs right up the back, but he didn't realize he was dead.

Skaggs started firing his gun and sank slowly to his knees and he held up his chin as his life and his bullets ran out at the same time.

Those few seconds let the company get set and they opened up from both sides. I was about 15 feet away from Skaggs when he went down. Sawtelle and Lt. Foote, the forward observer, were by me and they said we would have to move back and bring in more artillery.

Again Johnson ran up through the fire and got to Skaggs because he thought Skaggs was still alive. He started pulling him back and dragged him about 20 yards, where he started trying to dress his wounds.

But Johnson got his arm up too high and they shot him in the arm. The bullet tore the bone from his shoulder to elbow.

They moved him out and discovered Skaggs was dead. A platoon sergeant came up 100 yards through a minefield and picked up Skagg's body. Then he carried him right back through the booby traps.

We started moving out and it was an orderly withdrawal — no panic. The lieutenant picked up a rifle and I found a helmet.

The captain was calling on the artillery to follow us out. He gave me a .45 and said "you might need this."

We came to a small trail and the captain said, "Is that a VC down there?"

We both started firing at him and drew fire. My helmet was shot off or knocked off and I started looking for it, but the captain gave me a shove and asked "Do you want another clip?"

"Give it to me later," I said, "not right now." I took about 20 steps and a claymore went off about 10 feet to my right.

Between us and the claymore was a big anthill that took most of the blast, but it did hit five of us. Knocked us all over the place.

I was out for about a minute. When I came to Avillz was at my side, telling me it was okay, just be calm, and everything would be okay.

I thought the lieutenant had hit me in the head with his rifle or something. I was bleeding pretty bad, but I was able to walk if somebody would just show me the way. The first sergeant, James Scott, took me and another man to the LZ and we were under fire for the 400 yards out there. Soon I was in the hospital.

Later I found that 16 men had been wounded, but Skaggs was the only man to die. He was nominated for a top decoration but it doesn't seem like enough for a man like Skaggs.

This is a movie scriptwriter's dream of a story — a young soldier with only a firmly pressed foot between himself and a package of explosive death. The reporter's skillful treatment of the story casts the reader first in the role of the soldier and then as his rescuers — and always as the minute-by-minute observer of a tense drama.

MINE! CLEAR OUT!

OCT 15, 1967

CHU LAI, Vietnam, (IO) — "Mine!" screamed the young paratrooper. "Clear out!"

Spec. 4 Theodore Carlow of Perris, Calif., had gingerly put a foot down in the soft dirt as his outfit, the first platoon of C Co., 2nd Bn., 502nd Inf., 101st Airborne Div., swept a coastal area 360 miles northeast of Saigon. He heard a snap and felt three metal prongs sink under his foot.

"I knew right away it was a mine," said Carlow. It was an American-made "bouncing betty" of the pressure release type. Carlow kept a tight and firm foot on it — because to raise his boot meant to release the mine. It would jump waist high, explode with a shattering roar and spray bone-cutting steel pellets in all directions.

The first man to reach Carlow after he made his deadly find was Spec. 4 James Sullins of Lawndale, Calif., attached to Carlow's outfit from A Co., 326th Eng.

"I told him to stay still and everything would be all right," Sullins related. Carlow stayed calm and motionless as Sullins dug around the boot, looking for a way to disarm the mine. He was joined by S.Sgt. Harvey Reynolds of Orlando,

Fla. The others had retreated a safe distance away and were lying low.

"It's either a dud or a pressure release mine," Reynolds said. "It won't explode until his foot comes off."

"I'm going to cut your boot up the middle," Sullins told Carlow. If I stick you with my knife, grin and bear it. Don't jump up."

"I understand," Carlow said. Reynolds held the boot down as Sullins began to cut, as carefully and precisely as a surgeon. He slashed away the laces, the tongue and the back. Now only the sole was left. Reynolds next told Carlow to take his foot off the sole as he and Sullins held the sole down.

"Get those two rocks over there," he ordered. "Place them on the sole and make dammed sure you don't slip."

Carlow picked up the largest rock nearest him and laid it on the boot sole. Then he placed the second rock. Sullins told Reynolds and Carlow to take cover as he fused an explosive charge over the mine.

There was a blast like a thunder clap. It left a smoking hole four feet deep and five feet across.

This is one of the very few completely funny stories of the Vietnam War — but it could have easily wound up in the waste basket as a grossly offensive piece of bad taste. Not, however, in the skilled hands of Al Kramer, who gave the story the spontaniety of a barracks bull session without resorting to tasteless vulgarity.

PANTS AT HALF MAST FOR DEAD VC

OCT. 15, 1967 BY AL KRAMER

DUC PHO, Vietnam — It's not often a battle-tested American soldier gets caught with his pants down in combat.

But it sometimes happens — and it did to Pfc. Jimmy Holmes, 23, of Tallahassee, Fla.

It was a hot, sunny day as Holmes and the other men of the 2nd Platoon, 2nd Bn., 3rd

Brigade, 4th Inf. Div., searched the rolling coastland north of Duc Pho.

Not much was turning up, except the scores of tunnels and foxholes dug by a vanished enemy. That is until Holmes went into action.

You meet Holmes as he stands near an enemy soldier he has killed.

"Tell him how you got him, Jimmy," another soldier says.

"Hell of a fight?," you suggest.

"Go on, Jimmy, tell him."

"You guys leave me alone, I'm not going to tell him," Holmes answers.

"Go on, Jimmy, bet you're afraid to tell him," a chorus of other soldiers taunt.

An embarrassed Holmes turns to you and begins to explain.

"Well, you see, we were taking a break and I really had to . . . you know what I mean . . . when this guy pops out of one of them holes and heads straight for me . . . Man, was I scared."

"He really caught Jimmy in a bad defensive position," one of his buddies offers.

"And so?" you ask.

"Well no matter where I'm at or what I'm doing — I got my rifle with me, so I flopped down and let him have it."

Holmes shook his head and gave his one-man battle an epitaph: "You know, if that guy had let me alone, when I really wanted to be alone, he probably would have got away."

MSgt. Don Pratt, a veteran paratrooper and self-taught newsman, watched war become a spectator sport in which onlookers could be killed as easily as participants. Vietnam Bureau Chief at the time the Tet Offensive crashed into Saigon, Pratt sent his GI newsmen out for first class coverage and proved himself an outstanding reporter as well.

"TOURISTS! THE LAST THING WE NEED!"

FEB. 5, 1968 BY MSGT. DON PRATT

SAIGON — The citizens of Saigon have a new pastime — war-watching.

Maybe the initial terror of the Viet Cong attacks during the Lunar New Year holidays is subsiding, or maybe there's simply nothing else to do under the terms of President Nguyen Van Thieu's spartan martial law decree.

At any rate, reporters seeking scenes of action can find them by following the eyes and footsteps of ever-increasing numbers of civilians on the streets.

During a brisk battle near the presidential palace Wednesday hundreds of civilians lined sidewalks down the street. The more curious — or the least cautious — then inched forward until they were at the very edges of the lines of fire.

The next day, after the Reds were routed, two Caucasian couples strolled down the Nguyen Du where the communists dead still lay. Holding hands, they just let go long enough to photograph the grisly scene.

"Tourists," spat one newsman. "That's the last thing we need."

Thursday night, a group of Americans stood on the roof of the Plaza enlisted hotel and watched a fire fight in the streets below. A Navy chief, there as a sentry, counted eight grenade explosions and wondered about the civilian casualties in the thickly-populated area.

There were streets in the city, though, where there were no spectators, where there were no people visible at all.

Streets in Cholon, normally a morass of traffic, were utterly deserted.

The occasional crack of an unseen sniper's rifle explained why.

But in other streets where government troops decisively held the upper hand, spectators continued to gather.

Deadlines and deadly skirmishes were not all the hard-pressed Pratt had to worry about. One of his reporters was out of the bureau when the Viet Cong assault began. He was missing for most of three days and Pratt feared the worst. The reporter came back only minutes before 72 hours would have gone by and Pratt would have had to report him missing in action. Embracing his prodigal thankfully, Pratt was told the youngster had spent all that time hiding under his girlfriend's bed. Reverting from bureau chief to first sergeant, Pratt threatened him with sudden death if anything of the like happened again.

This hard-hitting, heartbreaking story tells of a mean and tragic paradox of the Vietnam War — how a youth with an appealing smile could transform into a guerrilla who kills.

"HE STILL HAD THE KOOL AID"

JUNE 30, 1968

BONG SON, Vietnam (Special) — "If they are big enough to hold a gun they are big enough to kill you," said Pfc. Jesse Diaz, of Santa Monica, Calif.

The 24-year-old paratrooper assigned to B Co., 2nd Bn., 503rd Inf., 173rd Airborne Brigade found out how true his words were recently when his unit was conducting a mission along South Vietnam's north central coast.

"We were searching a village for a suspected Viet Cong company," Diaz said, "and during the search one of the guys gave a package of Kool Aid to a young kid who didn't look over 15.

"We didn't find any enemy in the village so we moved on. Later that day we passed through the same village and all hell broke loose.

"VC were swarming all over the place hitting us with everything from AK47's to B40 rockets. Things looked tense for awhile, but our gunships moved in as the enemy wasted time in getting out of the village."

When B Co. swept through the village they counted 20 dead Viet Cong and assortment of weapons and ammunition. One of the dead turned out to be the same youth who was given the Kool Aid. He still had the Kool Aid in his pocket, but this time he clutched a brand new AK47 in his hand.

"He was probably hoping to use our water," Diaz said grimly.

The "dirty little war" was most hurtful toward the little people — the ordinary citizen whose backyards and farm fields suddenly became an arena of dust and flame. Bob Cutts told of a night of misery and terror for one small hamlet.

DEATH OF A HAMLET

JULY 2, 1968, BY BOB CUTTS

QUI HOA, Vietnam — Water pollution, traffic control, rezoning, population migration are not problems to the hamlet of Qui Hoa.

Smog? The 300 families who live there have never heard of it.

The air is fresh, the earth good, the breezes sweeping in off the China Sea bring enough gentle rain to keep rice green in the paddies, grass thick in the cow's grazing pasture. The rich markets of Qui Nhon City, bright with new treasures of a world the villagers have never seen, is only half a day's walk for the hamlet.

What more can a man ask from the gods than a kind place to raise his family?

But Qui Hoa is not kind to its villagers any more. Or, at least, the war that boils in the hills around Qui Hoa is not. It has poured down out of the hills, forcing the little people out of the valley. They have to run or be constantly on guard, constantly afraid for their lives.

War is no stranger in the little valley that nestles into the Blue Mountains, just south of the path that guards Qui Nhon City from the Viet Cong who command the hills.

The fishermen who live on the beach, close to their nets and boats, have learned to coexist with it: Each family owns two houses — one on the beach and one 500 meters inshore. In the daytime the beach is theirs, but at night each family retreats to its inland shelter as the Viet Cong come down out of the embracing hills after dark to forage.

If they find food in the fishing village, they leave the nighttime "refugees" alone. If not, they come looking.

It was a comparatively safe existence until Communists upset it.

The thrust to Qui Hoa's jugular came at 30 minutes after midnight on Ho Chi Minh's

110

Birthday. Twenty-four local farmers, the 169th Popular Force platoon, guarded the two main approaches to the hamlet — suddenly, where there had been blackness, a hundred shapeless forms materialized out of the grass in front of Tran Ly and his 12-man squad.

In one voice the VC, each marked by a yellow scarf around his neck, screamed "Xung Phong! Xung Phong!" (Attack!) and charged. Each of the formless shadows became a spitting fountain of fire as the AK47s and submachine guns opened up. When they got close enough, the grenades started coming in.

The squad opened with everything they had. The VC, just a handful of feet away, went down like mowed grass under the carbine and BAR fire.

But it was hopeless; the PF were too badly outgunned and outnumbered. The assistant hamlet chief, running from his home at the sound of gunfire, joined the fight without a gun. The only thing he could do was throw grenade after grenade blindly into the dark.

Ly's ammunition ran out. One BAR gunner was killed. Ly lost contact with the squad on the other side of Qui Hoa. He could not get response from the artillery battery on the radio.

It was, in the end, completely predictable. The VC pressed closer and closer, and two squads were within minutes of being wiped out. Ly and

Huynh Huu Ngoc, the young hamlet chief, ran to his home to save his family. The VC caught him, minutes later, and stabbed him to death in front of his wife and four little children.

As Ly's squad hid in the paddies around Qui Hoa, the artillery battery fired three star shells, which lighted up the hamlet beautifully and made it a lot easier for the VC to search the homes of Qui Hoa. That was the only "help" they ever got. The VC were gone at dawn, and the reaction force that finally arrived could only bury the four men that died in the attack, and chase the Reds further back into the hills. A few VC died in the chase, a measure of "revenge" was exacted but that company is still up there, still watching.

And within days, Qui Hoa began to die. The people, afraid now and unable to comprehend what the VC wanted from them, left the village in droves, packing their belongings in bundles and baskets through the pass to Qui Nhon.

No one is sure who owns Qui Hoa now.

"There just isn't anything we can do," says an American adviser. "Our forces are stretched so thin that we can't reinforce anywhere near fast enough. The guns are old, the ammo supplies are inadequate, and the support is unreliable at best. We do the best we can — that's all we can do."

Bill Collins saw the air war in Vietnam. He saw it in sweeping, cycloramic splendor. He talked to the Snoopy crewmen who saved a surrounded outpost; he heard the cynical banter of a Psyops pilot who played propaganda records, dropped leaflets and hoped for the best. And he saw lives saved when they could have been easily and casually erased.

"I'M GLAD WE COULD CHECK THEM OUT"

JULY 13, 1969 BY BILL COLLINS

There is a big, dark room out at Tan Son Nhut Air Base, on the north side of Saigon, where men are writing the immediate past, present and near future of their air war in Vietnam.

It is the 7th Air Force tactical control center, and it looks much like a house, with tiered rows of seats facing a big, screen-like plastic board that covers most of the front wall. It is clammy cool after the glare and heat of outside, and little

can be heard of the jets and turboprop planes landing and taking off a few hundred yards away.

A score of men sit in the artificial twilight, in the rows of seats, speaking in modulated tones into phones and radios and making ballpoint pen marks on forms and pads of paper. There are long bare desks in front of them.

In front, other men make and change figures and initials on the big drawing board with light orange and apple-green crayons (water soluble) to show which planes are on what sort of a mission in what part of the country. Still other men tend the banks of electronic consoles that flank the big board, their little lights winking like cat's eyes.

The hundreds of signals and symbols come in from, or are sent out to bases all over South Vietnam and beyond. They tell all that numbers can — which planes are where, what Allied units in what locations need help, how to get there, the results of each strike whenever available, what planes are ready for emergency call.

It is all part of a new supersophisticated kind of air war with a very simple goal.

"Our main business is saving American and Allied lives," said Gen. George S. Brown, 7th Air Force commander, "In this kind of war, it pays off for ground forces to make contact, then let the air and artillery handle as much of the fighting as possible. We offer the ground forces a service, and the more they can use it, the more lives will be saved."

It is all very hushed and efficient in the control center, and the thousands of numbers and symbols that flow through it each day will eventually become part of the war's history. To the statisticians and time-study analysts these figures, along with similar data from other services, may be the whole history of this conflict.

This would be lamentable. The most complete box score in the world doesn't really tell how the game was played. And in a time when man is turning more and more to computers for advice on everything from blind dates to the stock market to the defense of nations, he has yet to find the numerical values of courage, of fear, of willpower, of caring: The human ingredients in success or failure. There is no digital equivalent to Horatio at the bridge nor for the motivation of Benedict Arnold, nor the charms of Mata Hari.

And Brig. Gen. G.W. (Red) McLaughlin, former Tactical Air Control chief for the 7th Air Force, thinks the computers may be shortchanging his men in another area. He thinks they may even be fooling the time-study men.

"They say we can get our planes into the air and over a target where they're needed in 30 or 35 minutes," he said in a recent conversation. "But I really think we do better than that. Maybe 10 minutes better."

"We can divert pre-planned missions and have planes where they're needed sometimes in 10, maybe 15 minutes. Meanwhile, if it's a situation that calls for it, we scramble other planes from one of our bases."

"The scrambled planes may take anywhere from 25 minutes to, say, 40 to get there. But while they're getting there the aircraft we've diverted are already making strikes. Well, you can only make one strike at a time, anyway, and half the time in cases like this the scrambled airplanes have to wait their turn because they've actually gotten there too quickly.

"But how do you tell that to a computer? The only figure it gets are on the time lapse between the request for air and their arrival at the target. I just hope they can manage to get a fair answer out of those figures, for the sake of our guys."

Here are three stories which are unlikely to get proper treatment from a computer:

Russian tanks are rolling into Prague. Chicago's hotel rooms are full of cigar smoke as Democrats caucus on the eve of the presidential nominations, and its streets are full of tear gas as Mayor Daley's police brawl with a bearded, bedraggled army of protesters. It is Tuesday, Aug. 27, 1968, and nobody who isn't there has much time to consider the siege of Duc Lap.

The battle of Duc Lap is five days old and the handful of American advisers and what had been about 200 Vietnamese Civilian Irregular Defense Group (CIDG) soldiers are hanging grimly to their little hilltop camp, eight miles from the Cambodian border in Quang Duc Province.

Ringing them are about 3,000 North Vietnamese regulars, pumping away with mortars, rockets and smaller weapons. There have been ground probes and some of the enemy had gotten as far as the barbed wired barricades around the camp. For four days, these attacks have been beaten back. First Lt. Bill Harp and Sgt. Walt Collins weren't too sure they could do it again if the Reds came in force, nor was anybody else there. And now it looked like they were coming. Mortar fire, which had already wrecked half the buildings in the compound, was picking up. So was the small arms fire from the tree-line. It was already dark.

And then came Charlie, by the hundreds, shooting his AK47s, and with mortar shells slamming in — a banzai charge out of the old Japanese Army book. The CIDGs opened up with M14's and old carbines, but the Red river kept coming, running up the easy north slope of the hill.

And then there was Spooky. And there was some hope.

Spooky is the newest name for the oldest plane in the war, the C47, alias Dakota, alias Gooney Bird, alias Puff the Magic Dragon; the pre-World War II pioneer passenger liner they stopped making 20 years ago.

For this war the Air Force has added the letter "A" to its name and a minigun to its midsection, and the AC47 has become, of all things, a night fighter. And it has one of the best combat records of any aircraft in the country.

The AC47 has one big advantage over most planes and one big disadvantage. They are the same. It is a slow plane with endurance. Spooky can hang in for hours, blazing away long after the nifty jets have bulleted in, dropped their bombs and rockets, and headed for home. Spooky can also get shot at a lot more and a lot longer than its speedy grandchildren, the jets. On top of this, Spooky works the night shift, when Charlie makes the most of his trouble.

The name of the first Spooky pilot to reach Duc Lap that night isn't certain. It could have been Capt. Bill O'Brien, 33, from Akron, Ohio, or one of the 14th Special Operations Wing pilots, who have since departed Nha Trang. Whoever it was, Harp, Collins and a few other people want to find him and get him a drink.

"India (Harp's call sign), India . . . this is Spooky," came the voice from the airplane over the subsector headquarters radio. The voice was deep, nasal and laconic.

"OK, Spooky," Harp's voice was a little higher, tighter, "Papa says he's having a pretty hard attack down there." (Papa being the radio code name for the Vietnamese radio over at the Special Forces compound, a few hundred yards away.)

"You mean he's under attack at this time? . . . I don't see anything . . ."

"Yes, Spooky. He says it's a heavy attack."

"OK. We'll see what we can do."

Papa breaks in. There is a half-minute of static.

"Spooky, this is India! Papa says they're really getting hit over there, 50 meters from the barbed wire . . ."

Spooky turns lumberingly and swoops to the other side of the hill.

"Rog. We see 'em and he's right. Three hundred-and-sixty degrees. We'll work our way around the perimeter."

The ancient airplane turns again. The minigun vomits a stream of hot lead — 100 bullets a second — at the tide of NVA rising around the little hill. The minigun catches the Reds from above and behind. Some of the NVA try to turn back. They turn into a deadly shower that hits them in the chest, the face, the groin. Others try to breach the barbed wire perimeter. Some of these are shot in the back by Spooky's minigun. Some almost make it into the camp before the CIDG riflemen kill them.

Spooky sweeps around the hill and the minigun cuts a swath like a lawnmower through the attackers' ranks.

"Papa. Papa, how we do?" comes the voice from the plane. There is no answer.

"Papa . . . We shot number one or number ten?" Still nothing. "We shoot good or bad?" asks Spooky, thinking Papa may be dead.

"More of the same, Spooky! More of the same!"

Another turn around the hill, another 20,000 pieces of lead blazed at the Reds, now scattering and falling to Spooky's death-ray of bullets and rejuvenated fire from the compound.

Spooky on the air again: "I think we got a few of them."

Collins, talking now for Papa: "I think you did more than that. There still seems to be a lot of them near where you are now . . . about 50 (meters) to 100 out. Why don't you work that whole area over?"

"Will do . . . say, don't know how many of these bad guys there can be. In the last four days we've sure killed enough of them."

"Yeh . . . we should be giving you a body count tomorrow . . . you guys are gonna have a hatful of 'em."

"Well as long as we're helping you. That's the thing for us."

"Helping? Say Spooky, our Vietnamese commander here — I wanta tell you he's all man, and when he heard you were comin' tonight he stood there with tears in his eyes. And I tell you, he's all man."

"Roger . . . I think all of you guys down there must be. I wouldn't change places."

"I sure would . . . Say, Spooky, please be advised that our people have decided to give you a new name. You might want to pass it along to your uppers when you get home."

"OK . . . what's our name? Over."

"Guardian Angel, Spooky. Guardian Angel."

This wasn't the end of the battle of Duc Lap, but it was the turning point. Before it was over, AC47s had fired 714,000 rounds of minigun ammunition, and one afternoon Capt. Wayne F. Arnold, a forward air controller (FAC) from the 21st Tactical Air Support Squadron, hung his little O1 "Bird Dog" plane within easy range of the NVA guns for 2½ hours to direct 15 sets of F-100 Supersabre strikes on jungle-shrouded enemy nesting place.

The fight lasted 11 days. When it was over Harp, Collins and Capt. Tran Ngai, the camp commander. were still in control, and 776 enemy attackers were known dead.

"I thought we were all alone," Collins said a few days after it ended. "But sorta out of the blue. I had the whole Air Force protecting me."

Harp put it more simply: "If it weren't for Spooky, we wouldn't be here now."

It goes without saying that the U.S. Air Force has the most awesome collection of machines ever thought of. The fleets of F-4 Phantoms and other bullet-fast attack planes, lordly B-52 Stratofortresses that can erase whole acres of landscape from invisible heights, and monster transports like the C-141 Starlifter (not to mention the twice-as-monstrous C-5A) that can haul whole companies of men and equipment across oceans in jet time, are things as far removed from World War II aircraft as were the Flying Fortress and Lockheed Lightning from the hot-air observation balloons in Jules Verne's tales of the Civil War.

And amid these winged wonders, like a puppy at a horse show, sits the U-10 Courier.

It looks like your kid brother made it from a kit. Flying in it gives the feeling that you're riding the down off a thistle.

But the little plane and the men who fly it in Vietnam have a big, lonely and sometimes hairy job. They call it Psyops.

Psyops, which is short for Psychological Warfare Operations, is the forensic facet of the war. It's trying to do with words what the rest of the Allied forces are trying with muscle — convince Charlie and his friends from the north that he can't have the south, and that there are better ways to live than housekeeping in holes, easier jobs than dying for Uncle Ho.

Talking takes time, and this fits right in with the Courier's forte; the U-10 is about as slow a plane as you can find these days.

We took off from Bien Hoa Air Base at about 1 a.m. — Capt. Ron Shaeffer of Flight B, 5th Special Operations Sq. and his guest disc jockey. Destination: The jungle country and seashore about 80 miles east of Saigon.

There are two bucket seats. Behind them are two grocery boxes full of leaflets, one for the VC and one for the ordinary peasants. The ones for the enemy soldiers ask them how they like being hungry, tired losers and wouldn't they like to stop being suckers. The ones for the local citizenry are shaped like spending money (they even have a big dollar sign on the front) and mention that an easy way to pick up some money is to turn in their old VC and/or enemy supplies.

There are about 30,000 of each variety. There's a little chute on the right side of the cabin, and it's the co-pilot's (in this case passenger's) job to get turned around in the seat and stuff handfuls of the appropriate leaflets through the chute. Turning around in that seat is like turning around inside your underwear, and with a parachute it couldn't be done; so no parachute. Real modern.

But the other side of the rear cabin is something else — the answer to a hard rock bandsman's prayer. It's an amplifier and speaker system that can be heard for three miles or more on the ground with the airplane flying at 2,000 feet.

This is where the man in the right-hand seat gets to play disc jockey.

The little plane goes over and around a little clump of mountains, and there is the South China Sea, bluer than a bottle of Micrin, shimmering in tiny waves under the early afternoon sun. "One thing about this job," the pilot says over the intercom, "the scenery is great."

But the inhabitants aren't friendly. There aren't many of them — maybe a company or so — but they are all VC or VC supporters. The U-10 is there because intelligence reports indicate enemy elements are holed up in the thick jungle that starts less than a mile from the water. The pilot turns the plane into a wide circle and his companion hunts through the half-dozen tape spools on the dashboard for "No. 629," one of the top tunes on the Chieu Hoi chart.

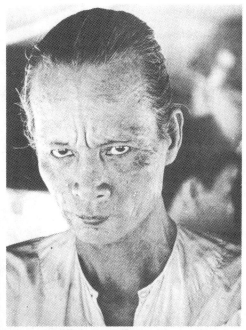

MEPHISTOPHELEAN FACE of a Viet Cong prisoner gave Stripes photographer Mike Kopp the shivers and a picture that won high praise and several awards, becoming one of the most familiar and famous of the war. The alert Ken George, a photo essayist trained at Syracuse University, made another fine portrait of a tiny refugee — a Montagnard baby in the Central Vietnam Highlands. This was a study of innocent and beatified peace in the face of war.

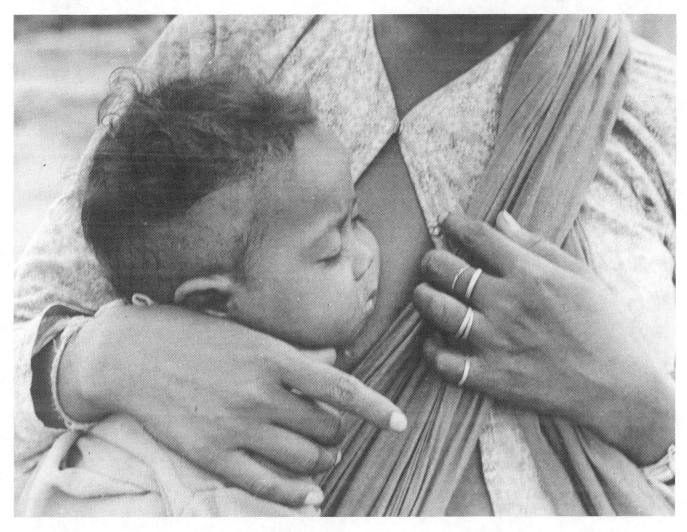

A MASK OF MUD is gamely borne discomfort for Pfc. Larry Martin as he maneuvers his tank over a plateau of muck in the highlands near Pleiku. Gary Cooper, with a camera, caught the same kind of misery cartoonist Bill Mauldin might have drawn on a sketchpad. It was one of many outstanding Cooper photographs.

LIFE WENT ON at leisure in rear areas like Saigon, although Red rockets and terrorist bombs often burst there and the "Saigon commandos," envied and despised by line troops, had to fight for their lives during the Tet Offensive. But a smiling ice cream vendor defied the laws of gravity and balance by carrying a tall stack of empty cones on her head and children were always in the Sunday crowd that flowed into the Saigon Zoo, turning a tangle of banyan trees into playground gear in an outdoor playground.

SOMETHING STRONGER than a fortified bunker seems to protect these soldiers, sprawling with exhaustion beneath a canopy of sandbags. This thoughtful, well-composed picture was made by Kim Ki Sam, brought from the Pacific Stars and Stripes Korea Bureau. At Da Nang, actress Ann-Margret needed a volunteer to join her in a wild frug and a Marine willingly danced up.

PS&S, Jack Baird

118

PS&S, Jim Becker

PROTECTING HIS WOUNDED MASTER, a scout dog stays at his side and glowers at the Pacific Stars and Stripes photographer who took this picture. The soldier still keeps a protective hand on his rifle, although a painful wound has taken him out of the war. Ugly drama like this was before the eyes of Pacific Stars and Stripes newsmen daily as they covered this skirmish or that large battle.

BLINDED, an Americal Division soldier hit by enemy fire in the Hiep Duc Valley takes firm grasp on the fatigues of a buddy who leads him to a helicopter that will take him to a casualty-crowded hospital.

120

HOLLOW LOG of a tree felled by age or war is a makeshift bridge but a slippery pathway for GIs making one of the dustpan sweeps for Viet Cong. Two suspects are rounded up, herded back to headquarters for questioning.

USA

DUSTOFF, they called it, after the blinding swirl raised by the rotors of versatile helicopters as they dropped in and out of battles to pick up casualties and save lives. Some felt that this was a jaunty nickname for missions that needed a more dignified definition.

The tape starts and music blares. You can hear it even with earphones on and the motor roaring. Then the music stops and a man's voice starts telling whoever is below that they're missed in North Vietnam and that nobody loves them here in the south. There is no visible response, which is just as well as far as the pilot and his pal are concerned. Charlie doesn't send in cards and letters. He sends bullets.

Then, about eight miles down the coast, there is a little village, Its borders are rectangular, its political conviction obscure. A few circuits of the perimeter playing "No. 124" (rough title translation:"Won't you come home Victor Charlie, Won't you come home?") and then it was time for the dollar-shaped leaflets.

While his partner chucked them down the chute by the handful, Shaeffer maneuvered the airplane in a series of sweeps calculated to let the little papers ride the breeze from the sea into town. "It takes four to ten minutes for them to get down from this height," he said. "Look at them waiting down there."

There had been only a handful of people within view when the plane first got there, but now the village streets were filling. From 1,500 feet up they looked like slow-moving fleas. Are Psyops leaflets really that big an attraction?

"Yeh," he said. "I think the main reason is that they use 'em for toilet paper. That stuff's pretty hard to get out here in the boonies. I just hope they read 'em first." It was hard to tell if he was kidding.

Three hours after takeoff from Bien Hoa, the little Courier finds a place in the line of big jets and turboprop planes streaming into Tan Son Nhut Airfeld and slips down onto the runway, turning off only a few hundred feet from touchdown. Probably no one on the base other than the control tower operator noticed.

The little U10 didn't even rate a parking space. The pilot, a big, easy-going captain, stopped just long enough to let off his passenger, check in with the operations desk, and then off for Bien Hoa.

For him it had been another lonely little flight. Other than the joy of flying itself, there was nothing much to it. There would be no mention of the 60,000 pieces of paper dropped or the three records played at the evening press briefings; no report on the results of this innocuous sortie. The only way he could have

gotten any attention would have been not to come back.

But if just one or two of those leaflets fall into the right VC hands down there in the jungle; if one recorded message strikes a responsive chord in the mind of a villager who knows something, then maybe some lives will be saved.

If you wonder why they call it the Bronco, you haven't flown in the OV-10.

After the fourth power dive and "four-G" pullout Chuck White finally showed some concern for the guy in the back seat. "How you doin'?" he asked, as if he didn't know.

"Fine," I lied. My cheeks were just coming off my shoulders, which in turn were slowly returning to their proper distance from my pelvis. I knew my face had been flattened for life, but I wasn't going to tell him.

"Good," said Chuck. "I'll show you some aerobatics." That brief series of rolls, inverted loops and other refutations of Galileo's pet theory will live long in memory. Dark memory.

But the wild ride wasn't the biggest thing Capt. Chuck White of the 19th Tactical Air Support Squadron showed that day.

Takeoff from Bien Hoa had been at 9 a.m., with the hour before it spent getting into flight gear (without help, this is a job for a contortionist) and checking out the plane.

It was designed as a counter-insurgency craft, but so far has been used mostly as a forward-air-controller and observation plane. It can carry a ton-and-a-half of armament, but in Vietnam most of its ordnance has been marking rockets.

There are two things the pilots especially like about it. It can go fast enough (280 m.p.h.) to make it tough for enemy marksmen to hit, especially at low altitudes, and it handles like a high-performance fighter. Its one notable disadvantage is that despite a lot of glass for the pilot in the front seat to look through, the rear seat isn't much more useful for ground spotting than a window seat on an airliner, blocked off as it is by the front cockpit, and the passenger strapped almost immobile into his ejection seat.

The spotting, flying and weapons control are necessarily up to the pilot, with the man in the back seat unable to do much more than pick up flying hours.

Chuck White had been in country about five months. Most of this time he had been flying the same general mission as this day's — observation and target spotting south and west of

Saigon for the Army's 199th Light Inf. Brigade. He had come to know the area and the people he worked with as well as a policeman knows his beat.

This beat is along the coiling Van Co Dong river and its tributary streams and canals. The river starts nearly 100 miles northwest of Saigon across the Cambodian border. It wriggles its way down through Tay Ninh Province, then passes close to the "angel's wing" of the border and cuts across Hau Nghia Province, bending slightly eastward to flow 12 miles south of Saigon and on into the bigger Saigon River just before the latter empties into the South China Sea. If this sounds like a likely enemy infiltration route from Cambodia toward the South Vietnamese capital, it is.

We were about five miles upstream from the Ben Luc Bridge, which links suburban Saigon with the Mekong Delta. As all along the lower reaches of the river, dozens of streams and canals crisscross the countryside here, all of them flowing slowly into the Vam Co Dong. The river itself winds in a series of horseshoe bends at this point.

"When we get past this bend we'll be in Charlie country," White said as we passed said bend. "There's not supposed to be anybody in this area. If there is, it's likely he's VC, though sometime the peasants get permission to fish or dig for eels."

White had been in touch with his ground contact for some minutes. So far all he'd had to say was "good morning." Then we crossed an intersection of a stream and a canal (the only real difference between these is that canals are straight and streams curl and bend like snakes) and something moved.

It was a sampan, nosing out from the bamboo banks of the stream. Then there was another, and another.

White told the 199th radioman about them and circled to make a closer check. When we got back there were more than a dozen little boats at the intersection. And making the circle White had seen something else — three people making their way across a field just to the north.

Neither the people nor the boats were supposed to be there. "There are two fire bases within range of this area," Chuck said over the intercom. "If these are bad guys we don't even have to wait for the Gunslingers (attack jets) . . .

Still, it looks a little wide-open for Charlie."

From the ground came word that the fire bases were ready, and that helicopter gunships were already in the area. All they wanted was the word to open up.

"Tell you what," White answered. "Do you have any national policemen around down there? These people look like they might just be civilians who've strayed into the wrong place. Maybe you can bring in somebody to check them out a bit first."

"OK, if you think so," came the voice from the ground. "We've got a chopper with an interpreter aboard on the way." Even as he spoke, the UH1 Huey was clattering toward the waterway intersection.

White held us in a circle as the copter landed on the north bank of the stream. The word came in less than five minutes.

The sampans were a fishing party that had gotten clearance at a village 20 miles upstream and had just drifted too far down. The three people in the field were a father and two sons walking home from a visit with relatives several miles away. None of these people had known they were in no-man's land, and none of them knew how close their ignorance had come to getting them killed.

"Well, you won't get to see any action," Chuck said. "But I'm awfully glad we could check those people out before they got blasted."

Then we headed over one of the sweeping curves of the river, and White proceeded to ruin what had been a pleasant, interesting morning with that series of bloody dives, firing four sets of marker rockets at old and apparently unused VC bunkers, and his finale of aerial gymnastics, "just to show what the old bird can do.'

It didn't occur to him to make further mention of the fact he had saved perhaps 30 lives. Yet if Chuck hadn't known the countryside as well as he did; if he hadn't been that familiar with its residents; if he hadn't cared enough to ask for a double check of those boats and that farmer and his sons, all those people probably would have been dead 15 minutes after he spotted them.

"We're here to save as many lives as we can," Gen. Brown had said only the day before over coffee in his Tan Son Nhut office.

Chuck White, the Jolly Green Midget of the 19th Tac Air Support, had just saved dozens — by caring.

124

This is the story of a surgeon who was taught to remove a gangrenous appendix, a ruptured spleen or an imbedded bullet — but found himself probing for a live grenade that had torn into a man's body and might have gone off if anything metal touched it. Anything like a surgical instrument. Spec. 5 Joe Kamalick stayed behind after the tent was cleared and got a story that none of the television medical dramas could have matched.

"BOY, THAT'S A RELIEF"

MARCH 22, 1970, BY SPEC. 5 JOE KAMALICK

CHAU DOC, Vietnam — Two X-ray films hung on the white wall of the operating room of the Chau Doc Province Hospital late Thursday afternoon.

They showed — in vague shape — the torso and leg of a man. The film also revealed — in sharp, clear lines — the shadow of an M-79 grenade round embedded in the man's groin.

The Vietnamese man was semi-conscious on the operating table, and the anesthesiologist stood near his head.

On one side of the man stood Navy Lt. Robert M. Ferrell, 28, of New York City, medical officer in charge of Military Province Health Assistance Program (MILPHAP) Team N-9.

He looked even younger than his 28 years. He held surgical scissors in each hand as he waited for the anesthesia to take his patient under.

Everyone cleared out of the operating room except for Ferrell, his assistant, Russel A. Waller, 22, of McComb, Miss., and Maj. Michael H. McCormick, 32, of Bend, Ore., operations officer for MACV Team 64 here.

They had intended to work behind sandbags but you don't keep hundreds of filled sandbags in an operating room as standard equipment. And building a blast wall would take too much time that the man on the table could not afford to lose.

Instead, three men were wearing two flak jackets each. One covered the chest and the other was improvised around the waist.

Their eyes, faces, necks and arms were exposed. If you have ever seen an M-79 round go off then you know there was nothing between the round and Ferrell's face but 18 inches of air, a cloth surgical mask and one layer of sweat.

"When you get a hold of it, don't move it around too much and try to bring it out the way it went in, along the same path," said McCormick.

McCormick was on the operation as "an explosive ordnance disposal" adviser. But he is not an EOD specialist. "I'm just a grunt," he said. "But I know something about M-79 rounds."

The man on the table slept quietly under the anesthesia. Ferrell said, "OK" and bent over the ugly wound.

He skipped through a half inch of skin over the projectile, his hands trembled once for a second and stopped.

It happened very quickly. He cut forward again, then twice more, reached inside the wound with the scissors, clasped the round at its base and backed it out the hole it had made.

When it cleared the man's body, McCormick said something like "There it is, all right." But no one was listening very closely. All eyes in the operation room watched the round at the end of Ferrell's scissors as he moved it over a stainless steel pan McCormick held and then laid it very gently on a gauze pad at the bottom of the pan. McCormick turned quickly and handed the pan to someone just outside the door. "Choi oi" said Ferrell. That is the Vietnamese equivalent of "holy cow."

His hands went down to his sides and he let out a long breath, a breath he had been holding for some time.

When you've just removed a live, armed round that could have killed or maimed you, what do you say? Something suave and cool? Maybe in the movies where a live round isn't live at all.

"Boy, that's a relief," said Ferrell as he pulled the cloth back from his face.

McCormick and Waller need not have been in the operating room. Ferrell had wanted to go it alone, just to minimize the unsavory results if the round had detonated. Some M-79 rounds are set for air burst and will explode at the touch of metal like surgical scissors.

Neither McCormick nor Waller would let him do it alone. But the moment of truth, thus having passed, was really Ferrell's alone, even though all three men ran the same risk.

Ferrell had to do the cutting and then grasp the round — a decision and a move that could have meant he would never again lay eyes on Washington Square.

Ferrell had asked for a cigarette and was

leaning against a table. Someone asked, "Did they teach you how to do that at Cornell, doc?"

Ferrell just laughed, a good humored laugh but one that still carried a nervous note. Ferrell has less than 64 days left in the country.

"What are you drinking tonight?"

The men laughed. Ferrell seemed more nervous than he was during the operation itself, as if it were just getting to him.

"A lot. I don't care what it is, just a lot."

Everyone laughed again, louder and with a little more gusto. The tension was finally gone.

Spec. 4 Seth Lipsky was the first newsman to get into surrounded Dak Pek, a torn, Stygian landscape full of flayed trees, smashed bunkers and brave but tired men. Lipsky moved over the blast-deadened terrain, listened to the weary voices of the defenders and saw what they could see — the ghosts of violence.

"TONIGHT I WANT THE VC TO COME"

APRIL 18, 1970, BY SPEC. 4 SETH LIPSKY

DAK PEK, Vietnam — Wednesday night there were flares and a moon over the complex of fortified hills here, but in the command bunker most of the time there was only a flickering candle.

By the candle there was an ashtray of butts and Sgt. Doug Hull, a Green Beret adviser, was hunched over a radio explaining how he felt.

About the only personal belongings Hull had left were his boots, trousers and undershorts. The rest had been burned or buried in an enemy sapper attack Sunday.

Incoming rounds were hitting regularly 20 meters away, and a night or two before a 122mm rocket had hit just outside the door. Still Hull was saying this was where he wanted to be, out practicing his profession with soldiers he respected and civilians, he said, he loved.

With a blanket on the concrete floor, Sgt. Charles Young, 21, was nursing his foot and trying to get some sleep. Three days ago he'd gotten a rude awakening. He was in the main U.S. bunker when a satchel charge blew it all in on top of him.

"You felt like a rat in a trap," he said. His buddies dug him out, but four nights later they were still prying open the trap.

Out atop a bunker in the night, advising the process, was Green Beret Capt. Gordon Strickler. From atop the bunker, he could see the other hills only dimly.

Somewhere on the black silhouette of a western hill there was another American soldier. He was calling in over the radio in a nervous voice: "It's quiet out here. Yeah. Almost too quiet."

It was quiet out there, but a plane was droning in the night sky. The blinking plane was a Stinger and suddenly a stream of red flashes came streaming down from the sky. The hills lit up with explosive bullets striking. The sound of the guns, an eerie, brittle speech, echoes across the valley.

From a distant hill the watching soldier said that was frighteningly close. But from another hill the air-controlling radio man told him to keep calm.

The air-controlling radio man was 1st Lt. Don Andrews. He had a bandage on his head where, he said, he had stuck his ear in a fan. He also had a map, marked and numbered and he and Sgt. 1.C. Thomas Weeks said they could read the map. That afternoon Weeks called the numbers out to Andrews and Andrews wrote them on his pants. "My pants," Andrews explained, "is like a damned secret document."

It was not learned whether Andrews was reading off his pants leg in the night. But apparently the fire was accurate, because every time the fire came down they called back up and told him "looking good, looking real good."

Somewhere on one of the many fortified friendly hills in the Dak Pek camp a Civilian Irregular fighter named A Jong was making the rounds of his platoon. For his role in leading a charge to take a hill back from the enemy Tuesday, they call Jong "the camp hero" and put him in for a U.S. Silver Star.

"Tonight," Jong said, "I want the VC to come and I wait."

But only the most aggressive fighters wanted the VC to come that night. On the far side of the complex, they said, they could smell the ghost of his last visit — the stench of enemy bodies still on the ground. When the VC comes, people at Dak Pek die, and that is the unforgettable fact of the night at Dak Pek.

And then the president of the United States said, "Tonight, American and South Vietnamese units will attack the headquarters of the entire Communist military operation in South Vietnam." When they did, and the signs along the roadway changed from quo'c ngu' to another language, Pacific Stars and Stripes followed them again. Two reporters at the Stripes bureau in Saigon, unborn when the first staff moved into an office in downtown Tokyo, were not dismayed by a story that broke with jolting suddenness. They merely climbed into the first available vehicle — a station wagon — and drove up to the war. Here is their story — the kind of mud level war that Ernie Peeler reported, the kind that Spec. 4 Paul D. Savanuck was seeking when he was killed in Quang Tri Province a year before.

IT'S EIGHT CLICKS BEFORE SOMEONE KILLS YOU

MAY 2, 1970 BY SGT. PHIL McCOMBS AND SPEC. 4 JACK FULLER

WITH VIETNAMESE FORCES IN CHIPHU, Cambodia — The young man dressed in faded, neatly-tailored camouflage fatigues bent over his plastíc map and clutched two field telephones, one to each ear. He smiled.

The young man was an American Special Forces soldier, and he was working on his map at a dusty intersection in this deserted little town 12 miles inside Cambodia on Highway 1, about 55 miles northwest of Saigon in the so-called "parrot's beak."

The town is deserted because there is a big battle raging in this area — somewhere west, north and south of here — and the Cambodians who live here thought it best to get out of town for a while. The little ribbon of highway stretching to the South Vietnamese border to the east is the only way in — or out.

As you drive along that little ribbon of highway you can see the battle on both sides — columns of smoke rising from treelines across the flat rice plains and walls of dust sweeping along at great speeds.

If you look closely at the speeding walls of dust, you can see that they mark the progress of big formations of South Vietnamese armored vehicles dashing across the open spaces in formation.

In the dust and smoke you can see helicopters buzzing around — some flown by Vietnamese and some by Americans. The Cobra gunships are all flown by Americans.

There are other American advisers here and there among the Vietnamese and some of them don't like to have their pictures taken — like the ones clustered around an odd-looking, unmarked helicopter sitting in a field by the road. They were talking with a group of Orientals, some in civilian clothes, and sent a man with a Tommy gun rushing over to insure no photos were taken.

We drove along that highway — through the strangely deserted little villages with strange names like Bavet, Kno Koki and Prey Phdau — not knowing if there were any Viet Cong checkpoints ahead.

There were several Americans who waved goodbye to us as we crossed the South Vietnamese border into Cambodia in our station wagon.

"You can go two miles OK but then it's dangerous," one warned. He was wrong. You could go 14½ miles before it got dangerous.

Here in Chiphu, the tanks roll into the center of town tearing up the asphalt, which is melting

127

in the blazing sun, and kicking up clouds of dust around that American Special Forces adviser.

There are trucks loaded with troops — Vietnamese Special Forces, Rangers and irregular strike forces. The troops think they have arrived at the front and everyone is giving everyone else funny looks.

The "front" is probably where you can't drive any further west into Cambodia without getting killed or captured.

But the Special Forces adviser won't talk, won't even give his name, and certainly won't tell where the front is. He answered only one question.

"How much further can we drive before someone kills us?"

He gazed thoughtfully for a few moments into the middle distance and said softly, "eight klicks."

Eight klicks — something like five miles — and you come to a bridge destroyed by the Communists. There are tanks waiting to move west as soon as it's repaired.

McCombs and Fuller would both write of the war as successful novelists.

He only wanted to live, this small being called Luu Quan, but war and those who waged it blighted his life. In few but telling words, as exact as the stanzas of a poem, one of the best correspondents Stripes fielded in Vietnam told of how war bullied "the little people."

THE LITTLE WAR OF LUU QUAN

JUNE 16, 1970, BY SPEC. 4 STEVE WARSH

BA REN, Vietnam — Battered pail in hand, the dwarf ambled toward the nearby well to draw water for making what would be his morning meal.

Luu Quan, 35, a life-long resident of this roadside village 16 miles south of Da Nang had done so countless times before.

And countless times before, he had shared that meal with his wife, Pham Thi Diem, 37, and his son — also a dwarf — Luu Sau 8, in their wood-frame hut.

And countless times before, blue denim workshirt hanging to his twisted knees and white towel wrapped like a turban around his head, Luu had walked the few hundred yards through crowded alleyways and across Route One to his job at the prosperous village marketplace.

His job — a simple one — sweeping and mopping the one-story pavilion-like concrete building, for which he was paid a salary by the village chief.

But a nightmare four days earlier changed the routine.

This morning, the fetching of a pail of water was all that was normal.

This morning, the village marketplace still stood, fresh from its recent use as a morgue.

This morning was four days after Communist mortars sent Luu and his family scurrying in the middle of the night into a sand and dirt bunker next to their hut.

Unhurt by the mortars, the family huddled as Red terrorist gangs darted in and out of alleyways hurling grenades and satchel charges into homes and bunkers. According to Luu, a lone Viet Cong ran up to his bunker and then left suddenly, telling the family to stay inside or they would be killed.

Frightened by the Communist terrorist, Luu decided to move his family to safer quarters — nearer the Ba Ren Bridge where Vietnamese militiamen and American Marines had compounds.

Luu is not sure of what happened next except that he and his wife became separated from their son. They moved to a nearby schoolhouse while their son remained in the bunker.

Minutes later, Luu said, two VC threw a grenade into the bunker, killing Luu Sau and demolishing the structure. A day later, poking through the rubble at the entrance of the bunker with a spade, Luu would find two mangled hands — all that remained of his son.

Luu and his wife escaped injury.

With almost all his possessions gone, his hut burned to the ground and his only son dead, Luu is not optimistic. He says he is afraid that the VC will attack Ba Ren again. Luu says that he will fight if they do.

This is descriptive war reporting at its best — writing that acquaints the reader with the discomfort of dirt and mud, along with gripping and authentic soldier talk. Note the way the reporter skillfully sketches in the surrounding war scenery, like the details of a photograph being developed.

'IT'S LIKE COMING HOME ... ALMOST'

JUNE 29, 1970, BY PETTY OFFICER 3RD CLASS RON SHAEFFER

EN ROUTE TO VIETNAM FROM CAMBO-DIA — A young man sat in the gun turret of an armored personnel carrier and scanned the jungle ahead. His unit, leaving Cambodia for a camp inside Vietnam, worked down a mucky red, jungle road. The man's clothes, mustache and glasses had a reddish tinge, and his hair was matted with dirt.

The armored vehicles ground steadily down the road, past the straw houses of a Cambodian village, past fields with bamboo fences, past children making the peace sign.

Ahead, on the left, stood a bullet-riddled sign, "Welcome to Vietnam."

Each truck slowed and a crewman threw a colored smoke flare at the sign. Some men let out whoops and raised rifles as they crossed the border. Spec. 4 Mike Dempsey continued to scan the jungle from behind his gun.

"I've left some feelings back there," he said. "Too many friends . . . too many people messed up."

Dempsey had been in the field in Cambodia for 51 days, doubling as a medic and .50-caliber machine gunner.

"We had tracks that hit mines all the time," he said. "But mines weren't what hurt us. We've got a good, heavy plate under us. A mine can knock you off an APC, but it won't kill you. Mines weren't the problem. It was the RPGs."

Rocket propelled grenades, launched from a bazooka-like device held by one man, can go through an APC, scrambling anything inside, he explained. Sometimes RPGs land on top of a vehicle, sweeping away the men sitting on the deck.

"They come from the jungle, and you don't see the enemy," he said. "It's frustrating. About the only thing that helps is a body count, but even that doesn't matter if your friends get hit."

The medic/gunner pointed to the man who rode on the deck at the rear of the track. "Kreuger knows . . . Krueger's seen it all," he said. Kreuger, too, was covered with red dirt.

An M-16 was in his lap. He stared straight ahead. His eyes said he was not going to talk for a while.

Dempsey told how earlier in the week an RPG round had evidently been fired at his track, but instead the round hit another APC that had just pulled into the line of fire.

"The round hit the cupola (gun turret). It killed the man on the deck . . . blew him down there," he said, pointing to the interior of an APC. "In the cupola there was this shake 'n' bake (slang term for a man who is promoted to E-5 after a 16-week NCO school).

"One of his legs was blown off. The other one was pretty well wasted. So was one arm. I've seen a lot, but this was the worst. I had the dry heaves. But this guy, man, he was a cool dude. I started to apply a tourniquet and told him to go ahead and grab my hair and pull and he said, 'Doc, don't even bother. . . . I don't feel a thing.' And this guy lived. He made it."

Along the road, the jungle vegetation thinned and gave way to short ground cover, punctuated with tall, bare trees. Clusters of men and machines were in the distance.

Spirits picked up as Katum, Vietnam, came into view. "Six more months," Dempsey said. He said he wanted to return to school and to the New York City motel he managed for his mother.

At the camp, the tracks rolled slowly past the band, playing "Saints Go Marching In." Soldiers exchanged optimistic gestures. Cold beer was handed to some of the men on machines.

"Kind of good to get back." Dempsey said, wiping the dust from his glasses. "It's like coming home . . . almost."

A fine story penned in Saigon offered exhibit-A proof that dogmatic Communists are very often their own worst propaganda enemy. A witty and topical headline, written on the Pacific Stars and Stripes copydesk in Tokyo, was a perfect lure for Page 1 readers.

HANOI ROCK GROUP — THEY WON'T LET IT BE

FEB. 3, 1971, BY SPEC. 4 HOWARD LAVICK

SAIGON — The leader of a North Vietnamese rock-and-roll group and seven members of his band were sentenced to prison by Hanoi Municipal People's Court for "disseminating depraved imperialist culture and counter-revolutionary propaganda," according to a Jan. 12 article in the Hanoi Moi newspaper.

A translation of the article, distributed by the Joint U.S. Public Affairs Office in Saigon Monday, said the band leader, 37-year-old Phan Thang Toan, was accused of "gathering a number of bad elements and forming them into a band to play 'golden music.' When they performed for money at wedding and engagement parties, they sought ways to sneak in some 'golden music' in order to popularize the music and to feel out the tastes of the youths."

The article also said the group had smuggled American records into Hanoi and taught themselves how to play the songs. "They industriously copied the manner in which the songs were sung — heart-rending, provocative and romantic — in order to spread them and seduce youths.

"They (the band) held frequent musical parties in places decorated to look 'mysterious,' which reflected the flattering words they used and the stories they told each other about the dissolute, degrading and orgy-filled life of the capitalist class," the article said.

According to the article, Toan and his group were accused of "enticing a certain number of young boys and girls who loved music but who were artistically immature, and caused them to follow their clique. They encouraged and induced them to live a depraved life.

"Toan and his gang's misdeeds cannot escape the people's notice," the article said. For leading a "depraved, cowboy life and having ultimately committed hooliganism, theft, rape or blackmail, or for having engaged in counter-revolutionary propaganda . . . because of the seriousness of the above case, the court sentenced Toan to 15 years' imprisonment and the forfeiture of his citizenship rights for five years after his release," the article said.

The band members received lesser sentences, ranging from 12 years to 18 months imprisonment as well as loss of citizenship after their release, according to the article.

By contrast, Stripes reporters were instructed to write straight reports and exclude emotions or feelings in their stories — something that was frequently difficult to do under fire. It was hard for Gary Cooper to "write it straight" when he was pinned down and nearly overrun in an ambush and for Gene Young when he lost a good friend in a firefight. For the most part, correspondents stuck to being reporters, despite pressures from some commands to make them propagandists.

This was unbelievable but true — a strange and elaborate hoax engineered by two look-alike brothers.

"I CAME TO KEEP MY BROTHER OUT OF TROUBLE"

MAY 20, 1971, BY SPEC. 4 LARRY MYERS

CHU LAI, Vietnam — A 22-year-old American who came to Vietnam three weeks ago masquerading as his younger brother, an infantryman with the 196th Inf. Brigade, was expected to return to Saigon Wednesday to await transportation back to the United States.

Wes Storer arrived in Vietnam in late April in place of his brother Glenn, a specialist 4 who was to return here to complete his tour after two weeks of Stateside leave. Glenn, 21, was a draftee, his brother said.

"I came to keep my brother out of trouble. He said we were just wasting lives and it wasn't worth it. As the time came to go back, we just decided that I would come back in his place and serve the last six months of his tour," Wes said Tuesday evening at Chu Lai.

He arrived in Saigon complete with his brother's ID cards and leave orders, he said. After three days of waiting at Tan Son Nhut airport, he caught a flight to Chu Lai and returned to his brother's unit, the Echo Recon. Co. at Hawk Hill, south of Da Nang.

"I didn't have any trouble playing the role of the soldier," said Storer, who has never served in the military. "I just saluted when everyone else did, ended every sentence with 'Sir' and acted stupid the rest of the time.

"Before I left I memorized five or six pages of information my brother gave me, mostly slang and things," he said.

Storer was turned over to military police on April 24. He spent several days in a cell until MPs verified his identity with his hometown sheriff, according to Maj. Verner N. Pike, 23rd Inf. Div. acting provost marshal.

"One of the guys was afraid that I would get hurt, so he went to the first sergeant and told him who I really was," Wes related.

When they found out he was a civilian, military police released Storer, but he volunteered to remain with them until his passport was forwarded here, he said.

"He's a good boy, and he's helped a lot around the company," Pike said. In addition to working for the MPs, Storer also spent part of his time working for the USO here, he said.

(Meanwhile, AP reported the father of the two brothers, Carleton R. Storer of Yarmouth, Maine, said the younger brother is now en route to Vietnam.

(Storer said Glenn was shipped out of Ft. Devens, Mass., late Monday.

(He said that a few weeks after Glenn's leave ended, federal officials notified him that someone was impersonating Glenn in Vietnam and asked him to verify identification. "It was then he learned that all this switching they'd been kicking around had become a reality," Storer said.)

An Army specialist, Jerry Van Slyke came from professional fighting stock — his father was a career Marine. He could almost feel the haft of an unorthodox fighting tool as he wrote one of the most striking, off-beat stories of the Indochina War.

SWORD OF THE SAMURAI

JULY 4, 1971, BY SPEC. 4 JERRY VAN SLYKE

The three North Vietnamese soldiers, unaware of danger, sat huddled around the little fire. The coals cast a ruddy glow along the hard-packed dirt floor of the hut as the sun probed through the trees. The unique odor of Vietnam — stale rice and dirty wood smoke — permeated the air. Chattering, the three soldiers ate hard lumps of rice with their fingers. Then, one saw the two Marines hidden in the brush a few feet outside the door of the hut. Everything happened at once.

With a shout to his companions, the North Vietnamese triggered an automatic burst at the two Marines. A Marine squeezed off a quick shot with his M-16. With a wet crack, the bullet snapped the enemy soldier's breastbone and tore through his chest.

Another NVA ran toward the back of the hut, firing his rifle ahead of him. A third Marine hidden in the brush there killed him with a single bullet.

The last enemy troop, armed with a bolt-action rifle and long bayonet, charged straight at a Marine in front of him in a desperate bid to survive the death trap.

The Marine he charged was Sgt. George J. Weaver, a Japanese adopted by an American family and a naturalized American citizen. Weaver was an unorthodox Marine. In addition to his rifle, he carried a long, sharp samurai sword in the tradition of his ancestors.

It all took only a few seconds, but it seemed longer — much longer.

Weaver's hands were moist on the sharkskin hand-grip of his sword. The steel slid easily and smoothly out of the scabbard. His years of studying kendo paid off. The blade sliced through the air and a dead NVA fell to the ground.

As the echo of the gunfire faded away, there was a muffled scurry of activity for a few seconds in the village around them. It did not take the civilians long to gather their children and crawl into the family bunker.

An unnatural calm spread over the village. No voices floated through the air in sing-song Vietnamese. Dogs were quiet. Nothing moved.

A quick search of the bodies revealed one of the enemy soldiers to be a man named Li who had been living with an old woman he claimed was his mother and another man, named La-ri, Li had said was his brother.

A few minutes later, Weaver and his men were looking over Li's abandoned hut. The "mother" and "brother" had vanished.

Li and La-ri had been posing for months as friends of the Marines, bringing the Combined Action Platoon's (CAP) 12 men fresh vegetables and fruit and puppies for pets.

At midnight the same day, the enemy launched an attack. Mortars crashed, rockets blasted into the little compound. One hit the small tower the Marines had erected and killed the Vietnamese militiaman and seriously wounded a Marine who had been manning it. Firearms crackled, increasing in intensity until the gunshots were one continuous sound.

But the CAP survived.

When the NVA blasted a hole in the wire with bangalore torpedos, a machine gun was waiting for them. When they threw planks across the wire to run across, claymores thundered. The CAP survived. The Marines had known much of the enemy's battle plan.

They had known because Weaver had his own private spy service. Finding official intelligence too inaccurate, clumsy and too slow, Weaver started his own system, employing at one time five fulltime agents and several more auxiliaries.

The villagers both respected and feared Weaver. Although he was friendly and they knew they could count on him for help, he was a formidable-looking Marine.

About 5 feet 6, he always wore his sword and carried his rifle. He was never without them. He wore jungle boots and trousers and a green undershirt. Over this he wore a knee-length, blue Japanese coat, open at the waist with a grenade-filled cartridge belt visible underneath.

His hair was piled on top of his head in samurai style, with a bamboo stick through it. Two bandoleers of cartridges crossed his chest to complete his wardrobe.

People used to gather discreetly to watch Weaver practice with the sword. Perhaps they smiled at the unusual footwork of a Japanese samurai, but they stopped when he slashed flying insects out of the air.

Weaver used to spend the afternoons walking around the village, talking to people and sharing a Coke with some kids now and then. Some of the kids were his best agents.

Often he stopped at a house and was invited for dinner. Then, he would squat with the rest of the family, carefully adjusting his sword and hitching the sides of his happi coat over his legs, and eat rice and water buffalo.

Some of his most pleasant afternoons were spent in the company of an old man whose name no one really knew. They called him Old Man Seka and he was the town drunk and the whole village looked down on him for his drunkenness.

Old Man Seka's family had been killed by Viet Cong terrorists and his house had been burned. The old man still lived in the burned-out shell of the house, a hollow, beaten old man in a hollow, roofless old shell of a house.

Weaver loved him.

But, the war was Weaver's reason for being in the village, and each day, toward dusk, he would leave the old man and walk back to the CAP to get ready to fight the war.

Early each morning, after the compound had been cleaned and the night defense weapons secured and stored for the day, two three-man killer teams would patrol the area until noon, and two more from noon until dark. This system gave each of the CAP's men a patrol each day.

Weaver invariably led one of the morning patrols.

Weaver picked his men carefully and many times they tracked single or small groups of NVA soldiers as far as five or six miles, almost always with deadly results.

On one of these trips, Weaver almost bit off more than he could chew, and added to his reputation with the sword.

The patrol had discovered a small, deserted hut, but, checking around, one Marine found Communist literature. Another found tracks made by the tire-soled "Ho Chi Minh" sandals.

Weaver reported the situation to the CAP by radio, and the three Marines set off in pursuit — and into a trap.

Moving quickly, but cautiously, down a trail through a large bamboo thicket, the point man stopped and raised his hand. Without speaking, he pointed at the ground beside the trail on one side, then the other. There were footprints leading off into the brush, while other tracks kept going along the trail.

The three squatted while Weaver thought. From experience, he knew an ambush had been set up ahead on the trail. The NVA was attempting to draw them out.

There was a quiet, metallic rasp as Weaver slid his sword out. He thumbed his rifle on full automatic. The other two already had their rifles set and each held a grenade in his hand, the pin out and the spoon held firmly under the thumb.

Silently, Weaver motioned them to slip off the trail and circle around to get back. When neither man understood clearly, Weaver took the point himself.

Cautiously stepping through the brush, the little party glided through the bamboo. Suddenly Weaver froze. Twenty feet ahead of him was an NVA soldier leaning against a tree, a grenade launcher in his hands.

As long as they remained motionless, the man would not notice them through the bamboo. But remaining motionless would not get them out of the trap. Just then, fate took the decision-making process out of Weaver's hands.

The radio crackled noisily.

The NVA jerked around with a shout and fired a quick round at Weaver who was charging him. The grenade missed and bounced around the bamboo, failing to detonate since it had not traveled far enough for the fuse to ignite.

The NVA turned to run and Weaver's sword arched downward. It hit the launcher.

The other two Marines, meanwhile, had thrown their grenades through the bamboo and each fired a burst at the ambush squad.

"Run!" Weaver shouted, and the three raced through the bamboo with bullets whistling around them. They leaped into a ditch and Weaver quickly checked his map and called for fire support.

Years later, it seemed, the request came through and a round of white phosphorus came whistling in several hundred feet away. The NVA quickly began to leave the area. They knew what was coming.

Weaver adjusted the mortar fire and called for another round of white phosphorus. It came in on target and he called for a barrage of high explosive rounds. They crashed in, followed by a barrage of smoke to set up a screen for the Marines to slip away under. By the time the second barrage of explosives thundered in, Weaver and his companions were a quarter of a mile away.

Back at the CAP, the ragged three puffed into the compound, worn out.

"How did you get that, Weaver?" someone asked.

Weaver looked down. The NVA grenade launcher he had hit was still stuck on his sword.

A few years before one of these stories was written, a Stripes newsman in Bangkok saw a small object in a shop window — a finely carved ivory figurine that looked like an Old World chesspiece. The shopkeeper told him it was an antique opium weight, placed on one pan of a brass scale to make sure a buyer got every paid-for ounce of precious white powder. Legal or disallowed, the poppy fields indifferently flourished and the drug trade had been traditional in Southeast Asia for centuries. Late in the Indochina War, drugs hit American ranks with horrendous impact. Pacific Stars and Stripes launched a long-running public service series called Cold Turkey — taking the name from a slang term for the convulsive effects of drug withdrawal. Rather than sermonizing, the newspaper inquired — asked drug users and those close to the problem to write letters and describe their experiences. Reporter teams were dispatched to the scene of the crisis.

"HE'S SO DAMNED YOUNG ..."

AUG. 22, 1971 BY HAL DRAKE

SAIGON — Walk through the 6th Convalescent Center at Cam Ranh Bay, 190 miles northeast of Saigon, and you see troubled youngsters with faded eyes. Youngsters who sought La Dolce Vita via the capsule and the needle — who are here to shudder off the effects of heroin and watch the world swirl back into focus.

So damned young — all of them. Not long ago, a venerable greyhead of 24 came in. He had been a night worker at an air base. His co-workers had wondered about him. He would come in, braced and erect, ready to do a steady and efficient night's work. But by morning he was a quivering wreck.

After six months of unspoken suspicions, the truth came out. With only a few days to go before he went home, the sergeant admitted he was on heroin — 16 vials a day. He was living with a Vietnamese woman, also addicted, who tied him to stiffen his veins and then turned the needle on the sergeant and herself. Now he lay in Ward 21, a withered and malnourished stalk of a man.

A young GI counselor and social worker tried his best to draw the sergeant out — to probe hurtful disorders of character and deep emotional wounds.

Nothing — only rigid silence. Nothing until the day the sergeant glanced up and asked with frightening suddenness: "What could you do the 440 in?"

"Fifty seconds," the college-trained counselor replied.

"Bet I could beat you."

"Let's go," the counselor said, taking a firm grasp on a heartening flicker of interest.

"No, I can't run like I used to."

"It's no wonder you can't after 16 vials a day."

The sergeant acted as though he hadn't heard, and the counselor could tell he had slipped away again. He glanced off absently and looked vacant and dejected. "You don't matter anyway," he said finally. "None of you matter. F --- all of you."

The sergeant, the counselor learned later, was a university graduate who had set a state record in the two-mile run. One hell of a runner. Once.

"He meant it, too," the counselor said, "that business of what we could all do to ourselves. If you're like that you don't care about anything but a hit. It's your wife, your scotch and water, everything. Stay up for a month, come down for a day. Man, I do my best to reach out and help but there are so damned many . . ."

More than 100 years after drugs first ravaged American ranks, there is another plague of addiction in another war. During the Civil War, both Union and Confederate hospitals made wide and indiscriminate use of morphine, an opium derivative developed in 1830 and named, because of its restful, pain-killing effects, for the Greek god of slumber.

Only in war did doctors discover its drawbacks — that the human systen could develop a tolerance and then a craving for it. After the surrender at Appomattox, thousands of shuddering derelicts in faded blue or ragged gray wandered the streets of New York, Atlanta, Chicago, Mobile. For decades morphine addiction would be called "the soldier's disease."

In 1896 German scientists produced a refinement of morphine called diacetylmorphine — trademarked as Heroin. It seemed like a marvelous discovery at the time. It could ease the convulsive coughs of bronchitis and other respiratory ailments. It could put a shocked and agonized patient into instant euphoria.

In one of the most terrifying miscalculations

134

in medical history, it was reckoned to be useful in easing addicts off morphine — until heroin itself was discovered to be the most addictive of all opium-based drugs. In future years doctors would declare it too dangerous for any medical use at all. Most countries would ban the manufacture, sale, use or possession of heroin.

Why did an outlawed drug pollute the ranks in another war? A veteran military police officer shrugs and explains it grimly and simply:

"What is totally banned and prohibitively expensive at home is cheap and plentiful here. Christ, they can get it as cheap as $1.30 a capsule. We couldn't begin to choke off all the supply sources. A lot of these kids come over there down on the Army, down on the war, down on everything. They face terrible danger or day-in, day-out monotony where the routine is the same and there's never a Sunday or weekend. They grab at this thing as a lark and think they can kick it later . . ."

Could he have been talking about the shriveled black youth who lay on a cot at Cam Ranh, shivering as convulsive chills lunged through him? A stranger visited the convalescent center and spoke with the youth, plumbing for paradoxes. The youngster, though black, wasn't poor — his father was a prominent civic leader in Newark. While he was down on the Army in general and Vietnam in particular, he couldn't complain too loudly — he was a young regular.

He was a fantastic and inventive liar, although not a very clever one. He was on his way home for a 200 — a for-the-good-of-the-service discharge — instead of a court-martial that could have resulted in a long sentence and a dishonorable discharge. He was here because of something that had demolished his youth and character — something that had made him lose all sense of time, dimension and consequence . . .

He was using smack, he said — snorting 11 capsules a day.

No, said a young captain, his company commander at a transportation outfit in the Saigon area.

"He was a shooter. He used the needle. We caught him three times with drugs and syringes. He said he could stop whenever he wanted to but he never could. They never can. I know. I've got a big problem in this company. People like that can get it from friends, pushers, mama-sans who come right up to the fence. I got to the point where I stopped picking it up — I was more of a policeman than a company commander. They'll get caught sooner or later. I could pull a surprise shakedown and pick up a hundred (drug capsules) today."

The youth, he relates, was picked up in February for stealing a camera and assaulting an MP. His hands had dropped numbly and automatically on the camera because it was salable and he needed money for a hit. He did his pitifully frail best to battle a burly MP because he faced discovery of both the theft and the syringe that was found on him. Court martial charges were placed but never pushed. Later there were AWOL and drug arrests. But as long as he could stay in another dimension, the youth couldn't have cared less.

A pair of nimble and conscienceless hands was plundering footlockers and personal possessions shelves not only in the youth's own company but in two others down the road. A stolen fan and cassette were traced to him. More charges placed. At this point he could have been a scapegoat for other thieves — because whenever anything vanished, it was a conditioned reflex for angry soldiers to seize the youth by the lapels and say, "You little (offensive term defining incest), where's my radio?"

"How come everyone comes to me when something gets gone?" he would wail back.

"He made so many enemies so fast that I actually feared for his life," the captain recalls. The youth had been pulled off any jobs that required trust, initiative or responsibility. He was the floor sweeper, the CQ runner, the name automatically called when a malodorous detail had to be performed. Half or three quarters of the time, the captain related, he couldn't even be trusted on those.

He would disappear and turn up in one of the three company areas, where he was about as welcome as a storm cloud over a picnic ground. Two or three times soldiers with something less than homicide on their minds used the most basic means to discourage the youth's presence. He stumbled back to his barracks with a cut and swollen face.

The charges piled up; AWOL, breaking arrest, larceny, assault, possession of drugs, He never ate and became gaunt and wasted. He stayed up with whatever could be begged, borrowed or stolen. When he was caught in the act or cornered by evidence there was an Academy Award scene with the same changeless script.

I'll kill myself if I have to go to jail," he would sob desperately. "I only made one mistake. Give me a break."

Other times his remorse and self-disgust were genuine. In his barrack, where he was a social leper, he would shake his head and say to everybody and nobody: "I've got to come down. Jesus, I've got to come down. My old man can't see me like this . . ."

A few tried to help him, even though he had disavowed any friendships that weren't useful on payday. He had his own crowd — fellow addicts who used him as a runner and buyer. He was caught once thrusting money through a fence to make a purchase. He stacked up $500 in debts — and was known to steal from the man he borrowed from in order to pay him back.

One friendly hand the youth pretended to accept but actually spurned was that of his first sergeant, a paunchy veteran of 20 years service.

"I tried to help him, the captain tried to help him, a lot of people did. No good, no use. A man makes his own breaks. If he wants to stay up,

he'll stay up. If he wants to come down, he'll come down.

"We caught him twice with syringes. Three vials under his pillow. I tried to get him to work, he wouldn't work, not even dayroom orderly. I asked him to go on the amnesty program. He agreed, then backed out. Said he'd been off three weeks. That was a lie.

"In a way, I felt close to him because he kind of reminded me of my son. He'll be about the same age in September. I worry about him like I worried about this kid.

"He told me he was coming down his last week here. But I caught him the day before he left, shooting in the arm."

The youth departed, and nobody expressed profound regrets; it was good riddance to a grifter and a barrack thief. But one man, recalling the skeletal youth with the vacant and furtive eyes, said:

"I can't say anything good about him, and I can't say anything bad. But no matter what he did or what he stole or how he lied, you got to feel sorry for him. It's just that he's so damned young — only 19."

BUSINESS AS USUAL AT BUNKER 590

SEPT. 5, 1971 BY SPEC. 5 STEVE MONTIEL

LONG BINH, VIETNAM – Buying heroin at this sprawling U.S. Army base takes less than 15 minutes of bartering across concertina perimeter wire.

I know because I did it.

The cost for one vial of heroin: A waterproof bag with an old, ripped poncho stuffed inside.

The place: Down the hill from U.S. Army Vietnam Headquarters along the perimeter between Bunker No. 590 and the highway to Vung Tau.

I first visited Bunker 590 on a Saturday morning 10 days before payday, a slow time of the month for the heroin business, a time when a GI can trade three rolls of toilet paper for a vial of heroin.

A half dozen empty vials were scattered on the ground in front of the concrete bunker.

A small patch of chicken wire dangled from a corner of the bunker. Two empty vials, like fish caught in a net, rested in the warped wire.

Across the road three Vietnamese boys and a girl, who might have been 10 to 13 years old, sat on a small rug, minding their open-air stop-and-shop heroin store. Two of the boys wore U.S. Army field jackets.

Two boys on motorcycles patrolled the road, Highway 317, on the look out for military or national police who might disrupt sales.

A narrow, dirt path snaked away from the road to Ben Go village, described by one MP as a no-man's land for police.

That afternoon about 5:30 I stood behind a row of hootches near Bunker 590, took off my fatigue shirt and untucked my white tee-shirt.

I clutched the bag with my right hand as I cautiously rounded the end hootch.

I cast furtive glances over each shoulder as I walked the 50 yards to Bunker 590, overacting, no doubt, but I had been told to appear nervous.

By the time I arrived at the bunker I did feel nervous.

I sat down between the front of the bunker and an RPG screen and waited for one of the children across the street to see me.

Five minutes later I was still waiting. The children were playing a game away from the highway toward the village.

Finally I walked 25 yards to the two rows of concertina perimeter wire.

One of the boys, the tallest of the group, ran across the street and stood opposite me on the other side of the wire.

I lifted the bag so he could see it and held up two fingers for two vials of heroin.

He motioned me to step through a narrow gap in the first row of rolled barbed wire and into the space between the two rows of concertina.

I stepped over strands of barbed wire strung close to the ground and stood in front of the gap.

I grabbed the bag with both hands and heaved it high over the first row of wire. It landed on the outer row.

Three other boys crossed the road to help the tall boy fish the bag out of the wire, and I retreated to my station in front of the bunker.

The boys scampered back across the street without the bag when a Vietnamese Military Police vehicle approached. The MPs stopped to talk with the children for a minute or two and then left.

The children scurried back to the wire again. The three small boys boosted the tall one up to the top of the concertina. The tall one scooped the bag out of the wire and carried it back to the rug across the street ,and opened it.

He handed it to a young girl, who took it to a bush about 50 yards off the highway and returned with a small object that she gave to the tall boy.

I stood and held up two fingers. The boy held up one. I again flashed two fingers, and he again held up one.

Then I nodded my head and settled the bargaining by sticking up my right forefinger.

The boy ran to the wire, and I walked to the inside row of concertina. He tossed the vial over both rows of barbed wire, and I caught it in midair.

We waved to each other and departed.

Military Police confirmed that the white, powdery substance in the vial was heroin.

These young dope peddlers are good businessmen, police sources said.

They don't want to lose customers.

The series took weeks of hard work and unified staff effort — well rewarded when the Public Relations Society of America presented the newspaper with the 1971 Silver Anvil Award for making "a significant contribution in the attack on the drug abuse problem throughout the Far East."

Drawdown, pullout, however it was defined, the American presence in Vietnam was thinning out — but in early 1972, when the North Vietnamese launched a ferocious offensive, there was plenty of war left for the last few. Stripes reporters didn't sit it out in Saigon. One got right next to the bleeding and another was repeatedly ordered to get out of an endangered city — and one other saw a poignant and horrifying vignette on a roadside.

"A SHELL FRAGMENT GRAZED MY KNEE ..."

APRIL 8, 1972 BY SPEC. 4 KEN SCHULTZ

DONG HA, VIETNAM — I was lying in a roadside ditch next to bleeding soldiers and newsmen.

Only moments before, I had been taking photographs of South Vietnamese Army tanks raking North Vietnamese Army positions 50 yards away while tactical air strikes pounded

NVA forces around this northern battlefront city.

Now, along the roadside, I was busy tying a makeshift bandage from a handkerchief to a wounded newsman's knee and almost at the same time taking photographs amid the confusion and shelling.

One scarcely had time to bat an eyelash between the moment an American officer first sighted 10 NVA tanks moving south on Highway 1 north of the city and the time the shelling began.

The sound of an exploding mortar round suddenly rent the air, and a shell fragment grazed my knee as I dived for a nearby hole.

During a brief lull in the shelling I ran to the command center, an armored personnel carrier sprouting antennas.

Several other newsmen there to interview American advisers were wounded by the mortar round.

One adviser had been hit in the back, a newsman in the neck and another in the leg and face. Nearly everyone there had some sort of injury.

The wounded had to be moved from there because the fire was becoming more intense. The thump, thump, thump of incoming rounds was all around.

The wounded were pulled back about 50 yards and everyone fell into a roadside ditch.

Suddenly a tank hovered overhead on the road. Its huge barrel stretched across the ditch.

An American officer wearing a .45 pistol appeared and ordered the wounded soldiers and newsmen onto the tank. Then the rest of the newsmen climbed aboard.

The tank sped through the empty streets of Dong Ha past the rotting bodies of three NVA soldiers and south to a checkpoint where the wounded were transferred to other vehicles.

DEATH IS NO BIG THING

APRIL 25, 1972 BY HAL DRAKE

BEN CAT, Vietnam — The little tableau had arranged itself perfectly and told of death — sudden, violent and casual.

About 10 feet from the road-side was a clump of bushes, a thorny mesh of wire, a bit of torn, bloody shirt — obviously, a badly selected ambush position.

The dry, red earth was tracked. Something slack and heavy had been dragged through it. It had lost identity as person or being — it was just a body, an object with a splintered head and a torn arm.

How had it happened? The way it always does — a carelessly selected place to hide and kill, a rapping exchange of fire, another abrupt and nameless death.

The shirt of the Viet Cong had been twisted up and the trousers dragged down as he was briskly pulled to the knoll beside Highway 13 and deposited there like a bundle of old, unwanted clothes. It was an appallingly undignified death — one that excited no interest, curiosity or

compassion in the little settlement outside this town 25 miles north of Saigon.

A little girl smiled at the Americans who stopped by the roadside. Her half-naked little sister toddled and beamed beside her. An old man squeaked by on a bicycle, not even glancing at the bloody, disheveled form beside the highway.

The black-uniformed Popular Forces men who had killed the Viet Cong slouched around, their rifles and carbines slung carelessly over their shoulders like fishing poles. Farmers who have been cast as soldiers, they had just finished a tiring and dangerous night's work.

A few townspeople walked under the archway to the settlement and crossed the highway to what appeared to be a town hall. They gave the body a glance and a mutter — nothing more. Some sought shade and restful conversation in a tea house, perhaps talking of the dim thunder up the highway, where South Vietnamese and Communist forces grappled on the approaches to the embattled provincial capital of An Loc.

Someone would carry off the body. Someone

always did. Grief would be private and cautious, for the bereaved could be tracked and questioned as Viet Cong suspects themselves.

But the Popular Force men were getting ready to turn in. Patrons drank in the teahouse, and in one home there was the voice of an angry mother, a slap, a crying child. Life went on —

for nothing really bizarre or disturbing had happened the night before.

The horror of it was that there was no horror.

Death was nothing extraordinary. It had passed this way too many times, and was something as causally inevitable as birth or dawn.

KONTUM: THEY SAY GET OUT

MAY 19, 1972 BY SPEC. 4 JIM SMITH

KONTUM, Vietnam — "I'm not going to tell you again, young man. I want you out of here," said the American colonel. It was the third time I had been told to leave Kontum City.

"Get your gear and get on that chopper," he said.

But by the time I shuffled to the chopper pad with flak jacket, helmet, camera and suitcase, Monday's last chopper had lifted off. Time bought. Two more days in Kontum to drink in thé sights and sounds. Maybe for the last time.

Kontum is a city in crisis. Refugees streamed though the MACV Team 41 compound and were evacuated on choppers to Pleiku in almost continuous sorties for the last week.

In the compound Montagnard special forces troops played volleyball and listened to American cassette tapes and radios between guard shifts on the perimeter. Their American advisers, most of them former Green Berets, drank pineapple juice and vodka, ate C-rations and joked about old times.

Along the road civilian trucks passed crammed with refugees making a desperate attempt to flee the city. The same trucks would return later in the day, their grim-faced drivers moaning about "Beaucoup VC . . . No can do Pleiku."

A mile up the road is the chopper pad from which B Troop, 7th Sq., 17th Air Cav., flies its daily missions.

Cobra gunships belly in with a whoosh, are quickly rearmed and refueled and leap off again.

Some Americans relaxed on the skids of their Hueys drinking cold water from Coke cans and listening to transmissions from the field.

In the shade of one chopper, some ARVN infantrymen played cards for stakes of 100 piasters and sucked water from their canteens and chewed on fruit.

Inside the city the black market hootches were deserted. No trinkets for sale in Kontum City. Some cafes stayed open, but business was slow. Very slow.

An American adviser wheeled a truck into town to evacuate the family of a Montagnard soldier. The whole village wanted to go. Many already had their meager possessions packed.

"No," the sergeant explained, "only the immediate family of the soldier can be evacuated."

Some small, crying boys were helped down from the truck.

"Tell them I'd like to take them all out," the American told his interpreters. "But I can't. Tell them! Oh Jesus, I wish I could take them all out! Come on, let's get out of here! I feel sick."

Sleep Monday and Tuesday at Kontum was interrupted by the rumble of B52 strikes around the city, the thunder of artillery and the pop-whistle of illuminations. There were no contacts . . . No enemy in the wire.

"This is the calm before the storm. You'd better believe the enemy is coming in strength," a U.S. adviser warned. "You'd better get the hell out of here."

On Wednesday afternoon I swam in a pool at Pleiku. Kontum City seemed a million miles away.

Not far from Saigon, on a highway Americans called Thunder Road, North and South Vietnamese fought for ownership of a besieged town called An Loc. But it was Sunday morning and many of the capital's citizens sought out restful leisure in the shade of the Saigon Zoo — much in the same way the ancient Greeks had watched the Olympics as outnumbered Spartans met the invading Persians and fought for their country's life. But the war was close, nerves were raw and a common civic sound shook everyone. Authorship of this short masterpiece, filed from the Stripes Bureau in Saigon, has unfortunately been lost.

A DOWN TO EARTH SOUND

MAY 17, 1972

SAIGON — A light drizzle, more like a thin mist, was falling in Saigon's zoo. But the zoo brimmed with people determined to enjoy their day of rest.

Small groups of people tiptoed carefully around mud puddles, holding their pieces of sugar cane high overhead — as if keeping them from the mud.

They wandered aimlessly, stopping to peer into seemingly empty cages and pits. The occupants had gone in from the rain.

In the distance an occasional rifle or pistol shot shattered the afternoon peace.

A leisurely walk in Saigon's zoo is a pleasure. The grounds are a unique splash of green in this city of sunfaded beige and grey.

Photographers, their dilapidated Polaroid cameras swinging from their necks, shout their services to passers-by.

Small children, some naked and some nearly naked, race from puddle to puddle. Splashing is more important than candy or a handout.

The trees, the shrubs and the flowers give off a pleasant country-fresh odor. What Communist threat?

Suddenly a loud bang and everybody freezes and draws closer to the earth. Moments of tense quiet.

Then another crack, and then loud cursing and the young boy kicks his rusting motorbike. And it backfires again.

An experience like this was a never-in-a-lifetime thing to most newspapermen — and Sgt. 1st Class Frank Castro, Stripes bureau chief in Saigon, later said he could have just as well done without it.

WE WERE WAITING FOR THE EXPLOSION ...

JULY 4, 1972 BY SGT. 1ST CLASS FRANK CASTRO

"Get out! Get out!"

There was a rush of air from the rear exit of the giant Pan American Boeing 747 jetliner, flung open as five shots were fired in the compartment behind me and a would-be hijacker was blown apart by a .357 magnum at point-blank range.

We got out. There were about ten people in front of me and we flung ourselves into the rubber chute that dangled from the plane like a slack tentacle, sliding about 20 feet to the hard runway at Tan Son Nhut Airport.

The wind blew the slide sideways and several people fell about 10 feet. The man in front of me fell on his forearm but refused help. We ran stumbling from the screaming engines of the big jet.

It was over, suddenly and at last. I had braced myself for an explosion. None came.

That's what I was really expecting — an explosion. In those last confusing moments, when you are suddenly stung by fear but not locked rigid by it, the plane swung into a rapid, twisting descent, the kind that brings bursting pain to your ears, landed and rolled to a screeching stop on the tarmac.

Once on the ground, we heard those shots from the rear compartment — they came to me as two muffled pops — and felt the cold splash of air. I thought an explosion had been fused. So did others. We slammed onto the floor and into seats. And, I guess, after we got out we ran about 200 yards, all the time waiting for that damned explosion.

It had started out as a routine and depressing return from a rest and recuperation leave that was all too short. I saw my family, and other men met their wives. It was about 3 a.m. as we trudged out to the silvery jumbo jet that would fly us back. In a corner near the loading entrance, there was a young guy who appeared to be Vietnamese. He was listening to a tape recorder, was well dressed and appeared to be at ease in an American atmosphere.

The flight to Guam was long and as we went on to Manila, the stewardesses dished up coffee and rolls. I wonder if the little guy with the tape recorder ate his rolls — you just don't pay much attention to little details like that.

A young woman with a child that looked about 18 months old came aboard in Manila. I will long remember both of them, particularly the little boy.

About 45 minutes out of Manila, funny things began to happen. The stewardesses were suddenly too busy and they had a lot to whisper about. Flight Director Bill Wilcox walked down the aisle, making light and easy conversation, but his face was a mask of concern.

"Got any pix of your wife?" he kidded. "No? I'll show you some." And damned if those GIs didn't roar at that old line. We were given customs forms and I begged a pen from a pretty stewardess who looked like a Filipina.

She walked back to the rear compartment and that guy with the tape recorder grabbed her. Before GIs back there could react, he shouted "I have a bomb!"

I was in the forward section and this drama was unknown to me. But in the next hour and a half, we all became acutely aware that there was trouble.

As we made the steep and eratic descent, the little kid started crying because his ears were popping. His embarrassed mother rocked him and a pale-faced stewardess played with him a few minutes. The child soon slept. Those stewardesses were marvelously cool and efficient all the way.

The mother, carrying the child, slid with him down the chute. After I finished sliding, tumbling and running, I suddenly noticed an inch-long gash in my little finger and my wedding band was dripping blood.

The hijacker came out, too, the hard way. Capt. Gene Vaughn, the captain, had flung a stranglehold around him while two other passengers wrestled with him and one more passenger, as Vaughn shouted, "Shoot him," jammed the pistol into his belly and triggered the shots. The hijacker had tried to stab Vaughn but only ripped his right shirt pocket. Vaughn grabbed the supposed bomb, fielded it to a GI who hot-potatoed it to another American, Don Zile, a Special Services employee who jumped from the plane with it, ran 100 yards and threw the object into a grassy area. He said his main fear was dropping it before he got clear of the plane.

The hijacker, thrown from the jetliner, landed on his face, but had died instantaneously from the gunshots. I looked at the body a few minutes later. That good-looking blue silk suit and his white shirt and tie were a smear of red. All of the shots hit him, and he was literally disassembled.

I saw the woman and the little boy in the customs room of the terminal about six hours later. The baby was happy and laughing as the ground stewardesses played with him, but the mother was still pale and shaken. But so were we all.

I recall saying a couple of days before that I thought the death penalty for hijacking was too severe. Now we all talked about it and an Air Force colonel said, "He paid the price."

It was a consensus: the best thing happened to the son-of-a-bitch.

Castro's horrifying story was picked up by the Associated Press and sent all over the world. In a few days, letters from AP subscribers in the States started coming in, a lot of them laudatory but many protesting what one editor called the "cruel and insensitive" last line. Castro, still shaky but thankful to be alive, defended what he had written and said he wouldn't change a word. "I defy anybody to go through something like that and not come out feeling the same way," he said.

Back home, the drawdown war had moved to the inside pages of most newspapers and was at the bottom of the six o'clock news. But Americans still died.

AB PAYDAY: THE REDS CASH IN

AUG. 3, 1972 BY SPEC. 4 ALLEN SCHAEFER

BIEN HOA, Vietnam — Tuesday was going to be a good day — payday.

A U.S. Marine lance corporal left the air terminal, where men were already lining up to get their checks from the paymaster, and walked in the predawn darkness to pick up the collection box for the orphan and refugee fund the air group supports.

As he neared the office at 5:10 a.m., a 122mm rocket screamed through the black sky and exploded 10 feet from him.

The Marine died almost immediately. A chunk of steel had punctured an artery.

At the same time, 400 yards away, another rocket smashed into the air terminal, blowing a sleeping Leatherneck from his bunk in an office there.

One soldier, hearing the rumble of the incoming rounds, had taken shelter in the corner of the building when the rocket exploded overhead and seriously wounded him.

In the early morning attack that killed one American and wounded 16, Communist gunners rained 71 Russian-made 122mm rockets into the American side of the giant air base 15 miles northwest of Saigon, according to sources here.

The rounds peppered the area in an in-discriminate pattern that included runways and living quarters.

Three of the projectiles hit a Marine ordnance shop where two soldiers were sleeping. Unhurt by the explosion, the men battled to extinguish the fire that eventually leveled the building. Other rockets hit open revetments where rows of jet fighter-bombers were parked, slightly damaging three planes.

"I woke up, and it sounded almost like there were mortars being walked into the base," said Col. Dean Macho, commander of the Marine Air Group which had moved to Bien Hoa in mid-May with two squadrons of A4 Skyhawks.

Macho, 49, of Colorado Springs, said flight line operations were delayed as workmen swept the runways and aprons clear of a layer of shrapnel and rubble.

Tuesday's attack was the first major one since the Marines arrived at the air base, the commander said. A few rockets hit the installation in late May.

The 122mm rocket, which has a range of about 4½ miles, can be launched with a standard tube or a makeshift bamboo trough.

First reports indicated that many of the rounds were fired from the north, and Macho said the first mission of the day was in an area five miles north of the base.

In Paris, the ponderous Indochina peace talks suddenly picked up pace and North Vietnamese delegates told chief American negotiator Henry Kissinger they would sign a ceasefire — perhaps because, as one official in Washington suggested, the United States had applied the persuasive cudgel of B-52 raids on Hanoi. Would the standdown be a lasting and meaningful step toward a political settlement of a long war? To the Americans left in Vietnam, the dynamics of that were out of their hands — they knew only that they were going home. Sgt. 1st Class Frank Castro — who wrote well of far happier happenings than attempted skyjackings — turned out this history-under-pressure account of GI reactions.

"NOBODY WANTS TO BE THE LAST GUY KILLED"

JAN. 26, 1973, BY SGT. 1ST CLASS FRANK CASTRO

SAIGON, Vietnam — Relief, happiness and, for a few, the dread of being the last casualty, were the prevailing attitudes among GIs when they learned of the ceasefire agreement that will

PS&S, Jack Preston

SHELLFIRE BATTERS the besieged Special Forces camp at Ben Het, six miles from the Laotian-Cambodian border, and there's little this GI can do but stay in his bunker, keep his head down and sweat it out. The gutsy Bob Hodierne got in and out of the hotplate position by helicopter and put his camera up as others were ducking sharp bursts of iron. Some of the worst obstacles, as the hapless GI below discovered, were the underwater potholes that could give him an unexpected ducking. A buddy grins at his discomfort.

LONG-STEMMED TEENAGER Claudia Garcia found herself well watched after a USO show for 82nd Airborne Division troopers in Vietnam. She also found a friend — one of the many stray pups adopted as mascots.

144

PS&S, Paul Harrington

INDIFFERENT TO DEATH, South Vietnamese Popular Forces militiamen walk past the Viet Cong they killed in a brief gunfire brawl the night before. Nobody in a small roadside settlement pause to mourn or pity the dead, for this was just another corpse and many had been seen before on the battleground route that led to **An Loc.**

145

THIS WAS A HOME in the hapless hamlet of Chon Thanh, ripped by Red rockets because it was just below An Loc — the city that died after weeks of desperate fighting. With no roof or wall left, this woman joined other refugees who boarded inhumanly-heaped buses or walked to Saigon. In Vietnam, Korea — every war — it was the same.

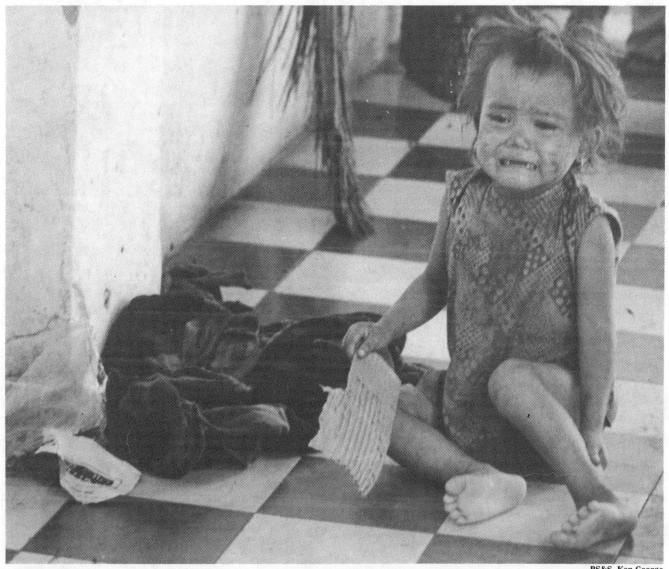

CRYING HELPLESSLY as her mother dies in a hospital outside An Loc, this little girl can only wonder and weep about the violent and bewildering world of adults. As always, war struck hardest at the innocents.

WITH NOWHERE TO GO but an American Red Cross refugee camp, these dispossessed Montagnards from the Vietnam Central Highlands — a few of the 21,000 forced to flee by the North Vietnamese Easter Offensive — are still fastidiously proud, bathing where they can as the war rolls over the homes they left.

148

IN ANOTHER WORLD, these little girls would trade toys and learn how to ride tricycles — all in the carefree, never-seen-or-known world of peace. Now, forced from their homes, they can only search each other's heads for vermin in a dirty and overcrowded refugee camp. No grief or discomfort shows on their faces and this was what often moved Americans to tears — the terrible stoicism of children hardened to maturity before their time.

be signed Saturday.

Saigon spokesmen, meanwhile, were guarded in comments about an end to hostilities, saying that after the pact is signed ARVN troops will "continue to protect the people and defend our lands." They said combat operations would go on until the signing.

On the American side military planners quickly dusted off plans for a 60-day withdrawal that no one expects to have difficulty completing.

"Everybody's just happy right now," said Air Force Tech. Sgt. Tommie Scott after hearing President Nixon's broadcast Wednesday morning. He said his first feeling was of relief and his first thought was of "going home!" Scott has been in Vietnam nearly six months. This is his first tour.

It was the same with nearly every American soldier interviewed. All expressed happiness for the prisoners of war who will soon get their freedom.

Saigon spokesmen said their forces have been alerted to be on the look- out for released prisoners.

Fliers in F Troop, 9th Cav., heard the President's speech while standing near their aircraft, grounded by bad weather. The outfit with its Cobra gunships and light observation "Loach" helicopters has been patrolling the Tay Ninh area in recent months and the fliers say the action has been deadly.

"It was a sort of chilling," said Chief Warrant Officer Bob Monette as he recalled first impressions of the announcement. "We all had our transistor radios on. We expected a cease-fire and — finally, after all these promising talks — there will be one. I know there were some goose bumps and some very proud guys standing around out there.

"We rounded up a couple of bottles and everybody had about a half-ounce toast . . . then the weather lifted and we went back to work."

The fliers recalled numerous incidents they say makes them hesitant about flying during the remaining days. Monette recently flew his crippled Cobra back to Bien Hoa AB and "had a heart attack when I saw the damage."

A missile had blown part of the chopper's propeller off. More recently several cavalrymen have been wounded by enemy ground fire and several other craft have taken multiple hits.

"Nobody is refusing to fly," assured Monette. "But nobody wants to go out and become the last guy killed in action."

The fliers also would not discount the possibility of flying after the treaty is inked. "We are all set to start packing. But who knows, we may get called out to save some American advisers who are about to get overrun," one said.

But for most American soldiers the greatest concern is packing up and going home or to a new assignment. A few did express disappointment at the prospect of leaving Vietnam.

"I was going on R and R next week," groaned one disgruntled airman. "Now I'll probably get shipped to Thailand and who knows when I'll get to go home. But I'm glad the fighting is over!" he quickly added.

Air Force Tech. Sgt. William Rittmeister, here only three months, said: "It is great news. I don't want to be here and I think that the Vietnamese, with a little initiative, can take care of themselves."

"I knew what the President was going to say. Well, we all suspected. But I had to hear him say it. And when he did it was a pleasant surprise," said Army Capt. John Conway.

According to personnel experts at U.S. headquarters, anxious soldiers began clamoring for assignment information almost with the President's last words.

"We have carefully made plans and nobody is going to leave here without an assignment," a personnel specialist said. He said that his next weeks would be spent on the phone getting new duty station orders from the Pentagon.

"I was just amazed at first," said Spec. 5 Bill Busche of the President's talk. "When this round of meetings started many of us were pessimistic and then here's the President telling us all the plans!"

"I just hope it hasn't all been a waste," whispered a sergeant who is on his third tour. "I was with the infantry in '67-'68 and I lost a lot of friends. I don't want to think that 50,000 or 60,000 Americans died and few hundred thousand were wounded for nothing."

Another soldier ventured: "I think that if the South Vietnamese take a firm grasp and if they have learned anything from us, they can take care of themselves. I hope that the training and experience and material we have given them pays off."

Deprived of the heady euphoria of a victory parade, Americans could look forward to only one rousing moment — welcoming home other Americans who came out of a dense and massive prison in Hanoi. Their first stop, after C-141 transport planes brought them out of the North Vietnamese capital, was Clark AB in the Philippines.

THE DAWN'S EARLY LIGHT

FEB. 3, 1973, BY HAL DRAKE

CLARK AB, R.P. — A flightline bystander remarked the other morning that it would be ideal if released American prisoners of war, taking their first steps back into a beautiful and unfamiliar thing called freedom, landed here by the dawn's early light.

It would show them they were out of the Hanoi Hilton and back in the world of sunlight, he said, and a dawn glowed to life to illustrate his point.

There was a sheet of ashen gray clouds over a frowning promontory called Mount Arayat. In one long rent through the sheet, the sky was visibly pink, then reddish and white. It glowed blue at the first sunburst. A golden flow of molten sunshine spilled over the Military Airlift Command terminal and the bulky, camouflage-dappled transport planes along the flightline.

But it was all wishful speculation. No one knew when the first plane bearing returnees from Hanoi would land — on what day or what time of day. If they land in sunlight, they will see the ageless features of a military post and faint signs of a world that has changed greatly while they were away.

They will see an estimated crowd of about 300 newsmen along the flightline, many of them on flatbed trucks that will serve as makeshift camera platforms. Behind that, there is a long, tin-roofed, cinderblock building that serves as an Air Force mail terminal and freight warehouse — U.S. military, contemporary and uninspired.

A crowd of other persons is expected — those who come to welcome and watch.

There will be no time for gestures of gratitude or sympathy at planeside. The returnees will walk or be carried into blue ambuses — buses converted into large-sized ambulances. In the more attractive and modernistic terminal is a snack bar filled with dietary luxuries many returnees left long ago — hot coffee and hamburgers.

The returnees will be whisked past those. They will be fed a soft, balanced diet for stomachs made delicate by long privation.

On the way to the hospital, there will be a quick, flashing glimpse of the base — stately banyan trees, bungalow-like quarters, spacious lawns that are yellowish brown in the long dry season.

There is the People's Place, a plain, whitewashed building that is a hangout for youngsters who gather to speak a new tongue — they crash, rap and listen to soul. The sign outside might incite the interest and curiosity of those who had been away for a time — it shows the world resting in a black hand. A small, green-lettered shingle says ECOLOGY — a term that could be strange to some.

All of these things may be passed and seen — some to be dearly welcomed and deeply puzzled over.

At the hospital, where returnees will be briefly confined for medical checks, there will be a brisk, efficient business of debarking at the concrete receiving dock and passing under a covered walkway into the five-story building.

Returnees will be moved into two- and four-man rooms, "configurated," as the military says, so that broad picture windows face expansive scenery.

The returnees will look out at a ring of mountains, a sprawling base and an overseas American community — and savor the taste of a sweet, strange thing called liberty.

The story promised to be one of the most touching and dramatic in years and fulfilled every expectation. Reporter-photographer teams flew back and forth between Tokyo and the air base 50 miles north of Manila, and some of the hardest work was done by darkroom men in the home office. They would wait at Yokota AB in the western suburbs of Tokyo, often for hours, to pick up film correspondents had put aboard aircraft at Clark. Then it was a long drive back to the city to print pictures for the next day's papers.

"GOD BLESS AMERICA"

FEB. 14, 1973, BY SPEC. 4 TOM LINCOLN

CLARK AB, R.P. — One hundred fifteen American pilots, released a few hours before from the darkness of a Hanoi prison, landed under an overcast sky at this base late Monday and walked into the sunlight of a vibrant, triumphal welcome — one in which the spirits of many returnees seemed to glow brighter than those of the 2,000 persons who turned out to greet them with cheers, banners and chants.

Several hours later 26 other Americans, including a civilian who had been a Viet Cong prisoner for a month less than nine years, were brought from Saigon on a C9A medevac plane after an earlier release had been stalled by hours of tense negotiation. All but one man walked from the plane. The 19 servicemen and seven civilians, tired but happy, were greeted by the tireless crowd. One greeter waved an American flag at them.

Hospital authorities said initial examinations showed the men to be in good health. Their morale and discipline was very good, a statement said. They were allowed to conduct reunions among themselves and to pick their own room assignments.

The first man off the first of three C141 transport planes which flew from Clark to Gia Lam airfield outside Hanoi and then back to this base 50 miles north of Manila was Navy Capt. Jeremiah A. Denton, a Navy pilot who had been held by the North Vietnamese since July 18, 1965. Pausing at the bottom of the yellow ramp that was rolled up to the giant aircraft's midsection, Denton stepped to a loudspeaker and delivered a warm and simple message of gratitude.

"We are honored to have had the opportunity to serve our country under difficult circumstances. We are profoundly grateful to our commander-in-chief and to our nation for this day. God Bless America."

For the second man off the plane, long imprisonment had been a stressful experience that brought crushing personal difficulties. Navy Lt. Cmdr. Everett Alvarez Jr., who was shot down Aug. 5, 1964, and was held in communist captivity longer than any other American pilot, bounded briskly but expressionlessly down the ramp to follow Denton in exchanging salutes and handshakes with Adm.

Noel Gayler, commander-in-chief Pacific, and Lt. Gen. William G. Moore, 13th Air Force commander.

Then he strode down the carpet that would be a pathway of honor all afternoon and stepped into a blue ambulance bus.

Three of these waited beside the tail of the huge Starlifter. Thirty-seven men off the first plane — some noticeably limping but all making a prideful effort to walk with a square-shouldered, upright stride — boarded the first two buses. Three others, on stretchers, were carried down a ramp that thrust out of the tail and put aboard a third bus.

A gesture by one returnee brought applause even from the crowd of newsmen who were closest to the aircraft and were trying in a brusque, impersonal way to assemble notes for a difficult story. Capt. Galand D. Kramer, imprisoned for more than six years, pulled from under his jacket a crude, blue-lettered banner that looked as if it could have been made from a pillow case. It read, "God Bless America and Nixon."

Lt. Col. Richard F. Abel, a public affairs officer who flew into Gia Lam with an advance party and came back with the first planeload of returnees, said Kramer showed another such banner — lettered in Vietnamese — to his former captors as he was repatriated.

On the plane, Abel said, he noted that long imprisonment had not erased a sense of unity or military propriety among the returnees, telling of how Denton informed the others that Gayler and a color guard were waiting for them and that he, for one, intended to salute both. He then glanced around with an unspoken question. After the plane landed at 4:12 p.m. and Denton debarked first as senior officer, every man who followed saluted the officers and then the colors.

The others debarked in "shoot down order" — by date of capture. After Alvarez there was Cmdr. Robert H. Shumaker, shot down Feb. 11, 1965 — and then Lockhart, Vohden, Morgan, Harris, Butler, Peel, McKamey, Guarino, Kari, Tschudy, Daughtrey, Schierman, Collins, Knutson, Cherry, Lilly, McKnight, Pitchford, Crayton, Myers, Rehmann, Kramer, Miller, Wilber, Osborne, Guenther, Hawley, Jackson,

Lerseth, Geloneck, Arcuri, Higdon, Giroux, Anderson, Cook, Klomann, Madden.

Dressed in gray jackets, blue slacks and black shoes furnished by the North Vietnamese, they were greeted by a crowd that numbered about 2,000 and started as a small knot of people on the sandy northern edge of the runway.

Base officials had discouraged but not banned such demonstrations, in line with President Nixon's belief that noisy welcomes might upset returnees and interfere with their privacy.

At one point before the planes began arriving, air police ordered the crowd, mostly housewives and children, to move back 200 feet. Then they told them to leave and assemble beyond a nearby gate, saying that jet blasts made the area dangerous. The angered women refused to budge and threatened a sit-in.

One Air Force wife said "Eight years the VC have been saying that nobody gives a damn and we came out to show (the returnees) that somebody does. They're (the air police) getting as bad as the Viet Cong . . . we just want those boys to see our signs and hear our yells. When one of those boys goes down we go into church and start praying. These are our men. This is our family coming home."

Apprehensive air police allowed them to move back to orange nylon cord that cordoned off the flightline. As the afternoon wore on and the Starlifters neared the airfield, the crowd swelled and stood its ground and braved blasts of sand as the first aircraft landed. As each returnee appeared, the deafening chant "Wel-come home! Wel-come home!" was raised.

On the plane, Abel said, several men offered self-composed prayers — "Thank God I am alive and I am going home . . . I wouldn't have made it if it wasn't for Jesus Christ — to look up and see Him."

They also interestedly studied a POW list printed in Monday's Pacific Stars and Stripes. Their names and those of others slated for freedom were on it.

Lt. Cmdr. Milton S. Baker, who rode back wih that group of returnees, said he was closely questioned about many things — fashions, military ranks and women's lib. One noticed short collars on his shirt and asked if that was the style now. No, Baker replied, they are longer. He was grilled extensively about sports.

The third and last group was "very healthy and very, very wonderful," said an Army officer who was also in an advance party that landed early Monday at Gia Lam. Speaking for 35 returnees, Navy Capt. James A. Mulligan said the men in his group had sustained themselves through faith and added: "Thank you for keeping your faith with us and making this wonderful day possible." Mulligan had been in enemy hands since March 20, 1966.

Darkness fell, but the crowd gamely hung on — still waiting for the plane that was to have appeared first that day. A C9A Nightingale of the 9th Aeromedical Evacuation Sq. flew to Saigon early Monday to make a routine but dramatic pickup of patients — 27 men who had been held months into years by Communist units in South Vietnam.

Complications developed. Eight U.S. Army helicopters sat for hours on a rubber plantation while fine points of protocol were discussed.

At one time the Americans were in sight of the helicopters when the Communists turned them away and argued some more. Finally, they were placed aboard and flown to Saigon, where all but one man, a civilian who elected to stay in the South Vietnamese capital, boarded the Nightingale and were flown to Clark.

It was 11 p.m. when they arrived and were inundated by waves of cheers.

For Maj. William H. Hardy of Fayetteville, N.C., freedom ended an ordeal that began June 29, 1967, when he was seized in Bien Hoa province while arranging delivery of supplies for the U.S. Agency for International Development.

Pvt. Ferdinand Rodriguez, a youth of 19 when he was reported missing on April 14, 1968, emerged from the plane a man of 23. He had been in Vietnam less than three weeks when he vanished, Rodriguez' parents live in Brooklyn.

It was Maj. Raymond C. Schrump, also of Fayetteville, who spoke for the group, greeting Gayler and then turning to the crowd — even noisier now because aircraft noise had diminished.

"It has been a long time. I want to thank each and every one of you for such a very, fine welcome. Thank you."

Among the 26, the man held longest in captivity was a civilian — 38-year-old Douglas Kent Ramsey of Boulder City, Nev., who was captured in the vicinity of Hau Nghia Jan. 5, 1966. Yet Ramsey walked down the rear ramp of the ambulance plane and boarded the bus with steady step.

Capt. David E. Baker came off the plane on a stretcher, but crossed his hand in a kind of prizefighter's handshake to acknowledge a drumroll of cheers.

"Pinch me, major," one youth pleaded. "I don't think this is real."

Like the returnees from the north, they were taken to the hospital at Clark, where they, like the earlier arrivals, feasted on forgotten luxuries like steak and eggs, along with ice cream — the latter so popular that it was devoured in the mess before regular dishes were served.

When a dietitian asked a man on crutches to sit down to be served, he replied:

"No, ma'am, I've been waiting seven years and I'm not about to sit down for someone to wait on me."

"THE FIRST THING I'M GOING TO DO ..."

FEB. 21, 1973 BY HAL DRAKE

CLARK AB, R.P. — The last time Maj. Jay R. Jensen saw his little girl she was a moppet of 10. She has yet to turn 17, but is already married — and Jensen is a grandfather.

That happened last December, Jensen told a newsman Monday — one of the many unseen landmarks of the life he passed in the darkness of a North Vietnamese prison. Shot down when his F-105 jet aircraft was hit by a surface-to-air missile on Feb. 18, 1967, he was liberated six years to the day later — walked aboard a C-141 StarLifter Sunday at Gia Lam Airfield, outside Hanoi and was flown with 19 other former prisoners of war to this base 50 miles north of Manila.

His daughter's marriage and motherhood got only short shrift in his conversation — as did the doleful fact that his wife divorced him three years ago.

"I was repatriated the day I was shot down," Jensen related, "exactly six years later . . . I feel that I have spent six years in hell and that I have been resurrected and I'm going to start a new life."

One of the 20 returnees who arrived at Clark AB Sunday, Navy Lt. James W. Bailey, flew home Monday to be with his critically ill father.

Homecoming officials said the other returnees were spirited and healthy, and said their processing at the base hospital would be completed in time to move them late Wednesday to hospitals near their Stateside homes. Some officials believed all or most might fly out Tuesday.

Jensen and five other returnees from North Vietnamese captivity met a like number of newsmen who were allowed brief, carefully monitored interviews and agreed to share what they heard and wrote with their colleagues.

Capt. Michael C. Lane, whose parents live in Atlanta, was told the miniskirt was out and mourned its passing.

"I only saw one in London — before I was shot down," Lane said.

Capt. Kevin J. McManus, whose wife lives in Falls Church, Va., told of marrying her only three months before he was shot down in June of 1967. They had only four days together before that.

"She's never even cooked me a cup of coffee," McManus said. But a long-distance phone call from the Clark Air Base hospital to Washington, where Mary J. McManus works for the Republican National Committee, told him that, "she hasn't really changed and that's what really counts."

"My wife and I had one goal — to have 16 kids. After that, it doesn't matter."

Air Force Capt. Herbert B. Ringsdorf, Elba, Ala., told of having an "understanding" with a girl before he was shot down and captured on Nov. 11, 1966. While he sat out a time-capsule existence, she married someone else.

Navy Cmdr. James G. Pirie, Birmingham, Ala., had been away since June 22, 1967. He told of a small feast set before him and his fellow returnees at the base hospital — "things we had literally dreamed of" — and how he used a knife and fork for the first time in six years.

"I didn't have any trouble," Pirie said.

Five years was a long time for Capt. Edward Mechenbier, Dayton, Ohio, and for McManus — the "backseater" of the F-4C Phantom Mechenbier piloted when the two Air Force Academy classmates went down together on June 14, 1967. One thing sustained him, Mechenbier said — his strong belief in God and his assurance that his wife, Claudia, was praying for him.

All of the men talked of binding up the loose ends of lost years — particularly Jensen.

"I've put six years of time and study on planning an extensive wardrobe," he said. "And I plan on taking a little bit of time and expert advice on picking it. I will have to do that immediately if I'm going to do anything else.

"One of the first things I want to do is go on vacation with my children. Plan an extended vacation as soon as they're out of school. I hope to get as much leave as I can possibly get. I hope to take them around the world. I'm going to take every day I can get."

Besides marking it as the most significant anniversary of his life, Jensen will remember that Sunday outside Hanoi for something else — being taken to the airport in a bus and viewing "the most beautiful airplane in the world," along with another sight that six years before would have been routine and mundane.

"It was pretty good to see American uniforms," he recalled, "and awfully nice to see smiling faces . . .

"When they started those engines, we cheered, and when they lifted off, I believe it was our voices that lifted it off."

Rules governing the interviews banned discussion of wounds or injuries suffered by prisoners or any revelations of prison life that might bring reprisals on those still interned.

Mechenbier said the prisoners drew strength from one another — each understood and confided in the other man. There were three conversational don'ts — women, religion and politics — but they were little observed, Mechenbier recalled. There was little of the light banter fighter pilots might exchange at a bar — discussions were often deep but at the same time "amazingly controlled and rational."

There was also black humor — jokes about the dolorous routine of prison life.

Asked to express his thoughts about the meaning of prison life, Mechenbier pondered and then harkened back to Ernest Hemingway's definition of sex.

"If you've never done it, then words can't express it. If you have, you don't have to have it described."

Asked what kept them going?

Mechenbier:

"Like so many men, belief in God and religion was something I could turn to. But the strongest thing was my wife. It means a lot to know that someone back there is praying for you . . . you get a lot of strength."

Lane:

"My release was always just six months away. We always used that sight. We counted things also one day at a time. At no time did we despair."

Jensen:

"The thing that kept me going was faith. Most of all, faith in my God, faith in my country, faith in my fellow prisoners and faith in myself. I think the faith we had in each other, we kept each other going."

While a bond of closeness between him and his fellow returnees will last a long time, Jensen said, all have decided "to get as far away from each other as possible."

"We know each other better than our wives did."

All six men have lost the better part of a decade. What to do now?

"I've sort of adopted a wait and see attitude on everything," Ringsdorf shrugged. "I've decided there is no way I can catch up on six years in just a few months, so I won't even try to make a concentrated effort on that. I'll just let it come back along to me."

McManus wants to go on flying. So does Pirie.

Lane said he had "972 alternative plans," but is now focusing on a degree in international relations and a position as an air attache.

A reserve officer, Jensen is only a year and a half away from 20 years' service. He doesn't particularly want to fly again — a hoped-for ROTC assignment to Brigham Young University would suit him fine.

Mechenbier did not say he would stay in the Air Force nor exclude the possibility of his getting out. He has been told there is a whole cornucopia of opportunities on the outside and wants to look them over.

As the last American uniforms left Saigon, Pacific Stars and Stripes closed its bureau and would cover the last years of the war, as the fragile cease-fire was shattered, through remote reports filed by wire services. If Stripes reporters no longer went to the war, the war came to them — the torrent of refugees that poured out of South Vietnam as a damburst North Vietnamese offensive burst toward the suburbs of Saigon. A writer with a gift for compassionate description, Jim Lea told of history's foundlings — the thousands in a stopover settlement called Tin City.

SAIGON WILL FALL, REFUGEES SAY

APRIL 28, 1975, BY JIM LEA

ANDERSEN AFB, Guam — "Has Saigon fallen?" The man is a doctor but would not give his name because, "I have relatives there still."

Not yet, he is told.

He watched for a moment while his oldest son played a game familiar to 17-month-old children everywhere. The boy threw a plastic toothbrush case to the floor and waited expectantly for Mrs. Gerry Covey, a Family Services Volunteer, to pick it up. She did and the boy threw it down again and waited for her to pick it up once more.

Thirty feet away, in a room filled with diapers and baby bottles, the doctor's wife sat resting quietly while tired Andersen housewives — who leaped to their feet, alert, wanting to help, each time a new Vietnamese face appeared at the door — changed the diapers of the doctor's youngest son, all of four days old.

"It will fall," he said quietly.

All the people who are fleeing Saigon say it will fall in days. Panic, they say, is teetering on the edge of explosion.

Order at the gates to Tan Son Nhut is crumbling, the doctor said.

"People who are in cars with Americans are allowed through the gate, but people who are not with Americans cannot drive into the base," he said.

"My family and I were together, but we became separated," a woman said. "They came on a plane before me and I can't find them now.

"Certainly Saigon will fall. Yes, the Viet Cong will attack.

"Saigon will fall within a week."

Some of the people aren't worried about Saigon, only about their now and tomorrow.

"They only gave me 40 minutes to pick up my clothes," said a woman who had spent 20 minutes trying to call her husband in the United States. "I could only bring one suitcase. There wasn't time for more. Now I lost my suitcase."

"I would like to go to Australia," another doctor said. "I don't think I can work in the United States, so I want to go to Australia. Canada, if not there.

"I hear they need doctors in rural areas of Australia and I am a doctor."

"HER FATHER WAS LEFT BEHIND"

MAY 7, 1975, BY JIM LEA

AGANA, Guam — A girl who is 5 or 6 squatted in the sunlight of a beach she did not know existed a week ago, building a sand castle and surrounding it with a wall of small shells and pebbles.

A reporter who watched her for a while picked up a hermit crab in its burrowed home and dropped it inside the tiny wall.

The girl stopped at her play and watched the crab drag its shell to the wall and try to scale it.

She looked up at the reporter and did not smile. Then she knocked a hole in the wall, kicked away the castle of sand and moved down the beach to sit beneath a tree and look at the sea.

"Her father could not come with her," said a man sitting nearby. "He pushed her onto an airplane, but there was no room for him.

"Maybe he left later."

Staff Sgt. Dale Clements, from Kingston, N.H., spent the first 36 hours of Operation New Life on his feet. Since then, he has slept only a

156

very few hours, sandwiching naps between escorting newsmen who are here to cover what is happening on Guam.

When he is not attending to that Air Force duty, he is working at humanitarian pursuits, attempting to unite families torn asunder by the airlift which has snatched thousands from what they were certain would be death.

The only reason he can put himself to what he is doing — and he is by no means alone — is that "everybody has to help."

Perhaps one of the reasons is that he remembers a boatload of refugees who landed not too far from his New Hampshire home 3½ centuries ago.

They came in a craft called the Mayflower.

The airline stewardess who was a long way from the dust and heat of the sprawling tent city U.S. Seabees erected at Orote Point in eight days summed up what appears to be the general opinion in the United States of Operation New Life.

"Those people should have stayed where they were. There were so many children who had no choice in the matter. How do we know they would not have been better off under Communism? We should never have become involved there in the first place.

"The people should have stayed in Vietnam. We have our own problems here. They don't speak English. They don't know our way of life. They aren't Americans."

She has lost sight of some facts, perhaps. Whether or not we should have become involved in Vietnam is not the question now. We did. This nation has since its birth absorbed refugees from everywhere and has become stronger for it.

But, perhaps she doesn't remember a ship called the Mayflower. Her ancestors did not arrive from that direction. She is third-generation Japanese.

Some people are saying that Operation New Life is the result of a national guilty conscience over Vietnam. There are thousands of soldiers, sailors, Marines, airmen and their wives, husbands, sons and daughters here who do not agree.

"What's this guilty conscience?" said a 25th Inf. Div. soldier from Hawaii who has come here to join other soldiers from a dozen Stateside bases, Air Force doctors and corpsmen from Mississippi and Texas and Japan and scores more American servicemen from many places.

"We ain't got a guilty conscience over nothing. We fought the war. We didn't run away. It wasn't our fault we lost and it wasn't these people's fault either. Now they need help and we want to help."

He ended the angry soliloquy with a foul word.

The 25th was one of the first U.S. units committed to battle in Vietnam a decade ago.

A Marine, a soldier and a sailor stood on the flatbed of a truck loaded with blankets at Asan and tried to reason with a Vietnamese who was ordering them not to distribute the blankets to the mob of other Vietnamese who were reaching for them.

"This is not the proper way to do this," the Vietnamese shouted. "I order you to stop. The blankets must be distributed through the proper channels."

"Hey, buddy!" the Marine said, trying to keep his cool. "I was told to pass 'em out."

At the edge of the mob, a woman who wore the black trousers and white blouse of the peasant of what had been her country stood clutching a blanket.

"We don't have enough blankets," she said. "Someone told us we must see the barracks chief to get a blanket but we cannot find the barracks chief."

Tears began rolling down her cheeks which already were lined with too much worry and too much toil and too little sleep.

"Is this the way it will be here, too? I did not want to leave. I do not speak enough English and I do not know anyone. But I know I would have been killed if I had stayed. All we want is freedom, but where will we go? What will we do?"

She began to wail and a sailor came from somewhere and put his arm around her shoulders and led her off to an American woman volunteer to find comfort.

"We did not know there was a place here to eat," the man told Army WO Erv Deaton, who spent six years in Vietnam, part of them wearing a green beret.

"Bring your people here," said Deaton, who says he has been so long away from home that home now is "wherever I hang my hat."

He is a member of the Army's 515th Ord. Co. and he and another warrant officer now operate the messhall at Asan. It is not an Army messhall, though. It is Army and Navy and Marine.

"Everybody's doing a great job. The food isn't exotic, but it'll keep people from being hungry. As long as there's somebody who wants to eat, he gets a meal.

"This has been one time when the military has talked about something one day and has done it the next.

"It's just great. The guys who are working here are really getting an experience. They've been working in the peacetime Army for a long time and sometimes it seems there are only 'make-work' jobs to do.

"Now they can see how important they are."

Ask many Vietnamese here who they would like to meet in the United States and they say, "Ed Daly."

Daly is the president of World Airways who took the last refugee flight from Da Nang a month ago and made his own rules to get orphans out of Saigon.

"He started this thing," said Pham Van Huu. "If he had not done what he did I think it would have taken the American government a long time to get this started.

"I would like to thank him."

Scores more of Huu's fellow refugees feel the same.

The woman said her name is Kim Hoa and she is not afraid to identify herself, "because we are out of there now and there's nothing they can do to us." She came to Asan with her family of 24.

"We'd like to go to Hawaii," she said. "We don't want the Americans to feel bad about the Vietnamese. We are willing to work and we will live now the way the Americans want us to live.

"We'd like to open a cafeteria in Hawaii. We had a cafe on the beach at Vung Tau. If we cannot do that, though, we can farm.

"The Americans we have seen here work like they do not care about themselves. We want to work, too. We would like to become Americans if they will let us.

"Can we do that?"

There is some good and some bad in any undertaking the size of Operation New Life. It is unfortunate that not enough can be said about the good. It is unfortunate, too, that there must be some bad.

"You can't just walk away from these people," said Marine Pfc. Pren-tice Patterson, from San Diego. "Nobody wants to go home until we know we've done all we can.

"The thing that really makes you mad is that some of these people are getting ripped off.

"This morning there was a guy here selling things. He was charging $2.50 for a pair of 50-cent rubber slippers. We asked him why he was ripping the people off. He said, 'Hey, man. I gotta make a living.'

"We threw him off the base."

Words like "marvelous" "outstanding!" "fantastic!" do not adequately describe what is happening here.

The only thing which can be said and come near the true picture is:

No matter what happens after these refugees pass through Andersen AFB, Asan, Orote Point, the Naval Air Station, the Naval Station and the several construction camps which have been turned into temporary homes for them, they will leave here knowing that they have seen an untold number of Americans being Americans.

Saigon fell.

With shattering suddenness, North Vietnamese and Viet Cong forces picked off the citadel of the politically bankrupt South Vietnamese government, which had as its dirge the calm plea of acting president Duong Van Minh.

"The Republic of Vietnam policy is the policy of peace and reconciliation, aimed at saving the blood of our people. I ask all servicemen to stop firing and stay where you are . . . We are waiting for the provisional revolutionary government to hand over the authority in order to stop useless bloodshed."

Those crisp syllables, spoken on April 30, 1975, were like the tones of a bell, tolling off the last hours of a long war. Within a few hours, the streets of Saigon swarmed with green-helmeted

Hanoi regulars and irregulars in the peasant dress of the Viet Cong.

Saigon died alone. No American aircraft flew out to oppose the enemy who no longer fought the wily, stranglecord war of the outgunned guerrilla, but swarmed over the crumbling defenses around the capital. They were backed by tanks, artillery, mortars, lacking only what they had done without for the entire war — the canopy of air cover.

Stripes told of it in a red headline:

IT'S OVER

The following year, the last American air units in Thailand — a launching pad for wartime strikes against North Vietnam — nodded to Thai government demands and ended a long presence on the Southeast Asian mainland.

To Bob Cutts, who had been the first newsman to fly on a raid over the north, a lot of good people deserved not a passing nod from history but a last hurrah.

OVER ... AND OUT

JULY 21, 1976 BY BOB CUTTS

So it's over.

You will probably notice it most by the silence they leave behind them; the silence of the villages sleeping in the moonlight, the silence of voices that do not speak or laugh or whisper into a lover's ear anymore.

It's over, at last.

"Cannon Two-One, I have my Sabres holding at 7,000. The .50-caliber on the ridge is giving 'em heartburn — watch out for him. I also have a few tourists on the road 'bout a click south of you. I think it's Charlie. Wanna use up your 20-mike?"

"Roger, Fox Three, we'll get right on 'em."

We roll up high and lazy into the sun like a cat stretching, flashing belly-silver for an instant and then falling, hurling ourselves at the Earth.

The 16 big cylinders fall off to a grumble as the throttle slides back; the hand guides the blunt ugly nose of the Skyraider down, down, the rows of waiting gun barrels out on the wings just a discretionary matter of a few ounces of pressure under the thumb.

Two black dots are running on the dirty brown road, and we are here for the kill. I am the hawk, I am the eagle, it will all be so easy ...

"Whoops. Can't do her, Fox Three. Looks like a woman and a child."

We roll up and out suddenly, the gravity pressing at us, and I am ... confused. I could see only two dots.

But it's over now.

That was the way it used to be. For years and for seconds they went up those aluminum ladders, their bodies in the armor of a technological war: flight suit, gravity suit, seat belt, shoulder harness, parachute, survival vest, life jacket, helmet and face mask, oxygen hoses and radio wires and, for the bottom line, a pistol and a knife. Some carried a medal, some a mezuzah. Some carried only faith in themselves and their birds.

They all carried fear.

The chocks were pulled, the crew chiefs waved them off, the big engines sang their choruses of thunder to the skies and then they were gone . . . some, forever.

Over the tarmac, down the asphalt, up through that diamond blue Southeast Asian air, for all those years and seconds, they did it again and again and again. Old men — some too old really for this game, going into their third war now but unwilling to leave the game to the younger ones. Young men — some too young really, but not willing to let the fear show through.

And other men who simply knew the game and knew it had to be played, whether they themselves won or lost. Because it was What They Do.

Who were they? You knew them. They were bearded revolutionaries who stood at Saratoga, they were farmboys who died at Gatlinsburg. They were Depression kids who went down on the Lexington, they were teen-agers who left their bodies broken and bleeding on Heartbreak Ridge.

They were John Kennedy and, yes, Lyndon Johnson. They were Alvin York and Pappy Boyington; the kid you double-dated with the 10th grade and that guy you got drunk with that time at the club back at, let's see, where was it now, Udorn? Ubon? Korat? Nakhon Phanom? U-Tapao? Funny, already the names are fading from memory . . .

They were men. They did what they had to.

159

They did it proudly, they did it well. They were never there just for the killing, you just remember that.

They were all there because all of us once had a dream that anybody who wanted to be free should be. They were just the ones who were caught in the crush between the dream and the reality, in their sleek, fast, beautiful machines, where the killing — and the dying — had to take place.

They were there because you sent them, America. No matter what you feel or believe, never forget that they went and that they served you, well and to the last measure.

If they are home now, and there is nothing left in the skies of Southeast Asia to remind you of them but the silence and an occasional distant roll of summer thunder — it is with pride that they returned.

They were men. They did what they had to. Damn well.

WITHOUT WAR

TO 1984

IT'S OVER

Most Yanks Got Out

Compiled From AP and UPI

SAIGON—The United States pulled out of Vietnam Tuesday. All but a handful of Americans fled the country aboard Marine helicopters by early Wednesday and left it up to the Vietnamese to find peace.

The Americans were ordered out Tuesday by new President Duong Van Minh to meet one of the Communists' major conditions for peace talks — an end to the U.S. presence. Political sources said the Communists and the Saigon government had agreed in principle to call a cease-fire.

President Ford then ordered Marines to evacuate the last Americans assigned to the U.S Defense Attache's Office within 24 hours. Ford promised in his statement that force would be used only to protect lives.

Aboard the USS Blue Ridge, command ship for the evacuation, a correspondent said the Navy announced 4,582 persons, about 900 of them Americans, had been lifted out by the evacuation that began at mid-afternoon Tuesday. Forty ships of the U.S. 7th Fleet were gathered in the South China Sea for the task.

Former Vietnamese Premier, Vice Air Marshal Nguyen Cao Ky, natty in his khaki safari suit with maroon scarf around his neck, stepped aboard the command vessel. He said nothing to reporters.

Naval spokesmen said Mrs. Graham Martin, wife of the U.S. ambassador to South Vietnam, arrived before the first official wave of helicopters left three carriers off Vung Tau for the evacuation run.

The few Americans remaining in Saigon apparently were mostly newsmen.

The departure ended an era that cost the United States 14 years, $150 billion and more than 50,000 lives —the last of which in combat were two U.S. marines killed in a Communist attack on Saigon's airport early Tuesday that spurred the pullout.

The evacuation came 17 days
(Continued on Back Page, Col. 1)

PACIFIC STARS AND STRIPES

AN AUTHORIZED UNOFFICIAL PUBLICATION FOR THE U.S. ARMED FORCES OF THE PACIFIC COMMAND

15¢

Vol. 31, No. 120   Thursday, May 1, 1975

A U.S. Marine points a rifle at South Vietnamese trying to climb over the wall at the U.S. Embassy Wednesday in desperate attempts to get aboard the evacuation flights. Marines guarding the embassy had a tough time keeping order as the Vietnamese panicked and tried to throw themselves over the walls and wire fences. (UPI)

SAIGON (AP) — The Saigon government surrendered unconditionally to the Viet Cong Wednesday, ending 30 years of bloodshed.

The surrender was announced by President Duong Van "Big" Minh in a five-minute radio address.

As he spoke, the city of Saigon fell quiet and shellfire subsided.

Minh said:

"The republic of Vietnam policy is the policy of peace and reconciliation, aimed at saving the blood of our people. I ask all servicemen to stop firing and stay where you are. I also demand that the soldiers of the Provisional Revolutionary Government (PRG) stop firing and stay in place.

"We are here waiting for the provisional revolutionary government to hand over the authority in order to stop useless bloodshed."

On the same Saigon radio broadcast, Gen. Nguyen Huu Hanh, deputy chief of staff, called on all South Vietnamese generals, officers and servicemen at all levels to carry out Minh's orders.

"All commanders," Hanh declared, "must be ready to enter into relations with commanders of the Provisional Revolutionary Government (Viet Cong) to carry out the cease-fire without bloodshed."

South Vietnamese officers said they had no other choice.

The surrender came within hours of the evacuation of all Americans except a handful of newsmen from Saigon

Reaching the decision to pull out, Page 3. Other coverage on Pages, 6, 7, 12-13.

and the closing of the U.S. Embassy which was later looted along with the residence of U.S. Ambassador Graham A. Martin.

South Vietnamese officers complained that the U.S. evacuation had panicked the army and that many top officers and most of the air force had pulled out, leaving the armed forces depleted and Saigon an open city, as Communist-led forces closed in.

(A few people appeared to brave the around-the-dock curfew minutes after the announcement, UPI said, but shellfire continued and there was sporadic small arms fire in the heart of the city after the president's brief address.

(Minh spoke as Communist forces fought toward the very center of the city, which by mid-morning had seemed to be in a state of panic and imminent collapse.

(Police were ordered to raise white flags over their stations.

(The U.S. Embassy was burned by looters.

(They carried away desks, chairs and typewriters from the building the Americans had evacuated.

(Vietnamese still waited in the Embassy compound for evacuation. Among them was an American with his Vietnamese wife and children, UPI said.)

Despite the U.S. evacuation, it was certain that the Saigon army would fall anyhow whether the Americans stayed or not.

More than a dozen North Vietnamese divisions were ringing Saigon while the capital was defended by less than a division of green troops.

The Viet Cong had rejected a cease-fire and negotiations proposed earlier by Minh and demanded in effect an unconditional surrender to include these terms:

—The withdrawal of Americans.

(Continued on Back Page, Col. 1)

Sgt. 1st Class Steve Greene, one of the most talented and enterprising newsmen Pacific Stars and Stripes ever had, sought out an adventurer many people thought should have been certified as insane — and got a stirring and colorful interview with the man who skied down deadly Mount Everest.

A POINT BEYOND MADNESS

AUG. 30, 1970, BY SGT. 1ST CLASS STEVE GREENE

"If anything happens to me, bury me here. I'll have the greatest tomb on Earth."

Yuichiro Miura took a long time getting dressed on the morning of May 5. This was the day he had waited for, planned for, over a long three years. He might have smiled at the American expression that he was on top of the world in more ways than one. He flexed his muscles, grinned to himself, and went out to face his own personal moment of truth.

"The snow ran out at the 26,000-foot mark. Or I should say the ice ran out. At that height, you have a steady wind comparable to the jet stream. It carries the loose snow off the peak, leaving nothing but bare rock for the last 3,000 feet to the top. This was as high as I could go for what I planned to do. The peak was a mere 3,000 feet above me. The view looking down was more awesome now than looking up."

Miura adjusted his sun goggles, gripped his poles, took a deep breath of the oxygen being fed to his lungs from the tank on his back, and had final, terrifying, thoughts about being the first man in history to attempt to ski down Mount Everest.

"There is a point beyond madness which every mountain climber reaches, usually at the half-way mark. You look down, remembering all the narrow escapes, the tragedies and superhuman labor it took to get that far. Your eye picks out the erratic line of base camps as they zig-zag up the mountain, each one a silent tribute to your will.

"And then you look up ... up to the peak, majestic in its awful lonesomeness. And you know you've got to humble it. Not only for yourself but for the greater cause of the thing we call the human spirit.

"And somewhere between your head and your heart, you remember Hillary and Tenzing ... and, suddenly, you're not alone anymore."

The Sherpa guides thought Miura was crazy when they discovered what he had in mind.

They looked at each other and called him the "Japanese Yeti" — the Nipponese abominable snowman, a reincarnation of the Sherpa guides who have lost their lives on the treacherous slopes of the world's highest mountain.

Skiing had been Miura's life since he was 5. He had been a sickly child in Aomori, across the straits from Hokkaido in Japan's north country. And his father had taken him hiking and skiing in the Japan Alps at every opportunity in an effort to build his strength.

"My original intention was to become a veterinarian and I actually spent three years as an assistant professor at Hokkaido University before becoming involved in professional ski racing." Before ... deciding to become the fastest man on skis in the world.

If you are going to become the fastest man in the world on a pair of skis, you must seek the steepest slopes in the world to hurtle down. And Miura hung it all out in death-defying runs down Mount Cook in New Zealand, Mount Rainier in Washington, Mount McKinley in Alaska and even on the Columbia Glacier in Canada.

"I had a world record going for me at a speed race in Chiavenna, Italy, in 1964, on the southern slope of the Matterhorn. But I didn't hold it long. I was clocked at 106.8 mph going through a 100-meter electronically-measured course. This was six-tenths of a mile faster than the record established the previous year. But I fell before going through the finish gate and wound up taking seventh place. I came close to the 100 mph mark a second time during a run down Mount Fuji in 1966, but I opened my drag

163

chute too early and it slowed me down to a snail's pace of 50 mph in a matter of seconds."

You must open a back chute quite early on a downhill run, Miura explained, for if you gather too much speed you stand the chance of having your arms pulled from their sockets when the chute opens.

"It isn't the same as a sky diver jumping at relatively low altitudes in what we call heavy air and reaching a maximum terminal velocity of approximately 120 mph At the higher elevations used for speed skiing — 10 to 15 thousand feet — the air resistance on a moving body is only one-third as much as that on the sky diver. Which means that, in theory at least, the skier could hit speeds as high as 300 mph. At that speed, a drag chute would be absolutely worthless."

Mount Everest, the greatest mountain of them all, was the final challenge that drew Miura like a magnet — and nearly drew him to his death.

"We started out from Katmandu on March 5, 1,000 of us, to launch the most massive attack on Everest in history. The planning alone had taken three years to complete and the group was determined to plant the Japanese flag on the summit. My interest in the venture was solely to establish a new speed skiing record.

"Our group progressed slowly, established our base camps as we struggled upward, leap-frogging our way from camp to camp up the 40-degree incline of Everest's south col or cone.

"Fear was a constant companion. We remembered that 30 climbers had lost their lives on Everest's craggy slopes since 1928. Our expedition was to swell that figure.

"Death struck six of our Sherpa porters who were crushed beyond recognition when a massive ice avalanche tumbled blocks weighing several tons each on top of them. The tragedy occurred at the same spot in the same manner where John E. Britenbach, the American climber, lost his life in 1963. We lost two other guides on the ascent when they suffered fatal heart attacks.

"We buried our dead and continued clawing our way up the mountain, like so many insects on the carcass of a great dead beast. But we were to find that our beast wasn't quite all that dead."

And then, three months after they had begun their journey up Mount Everest, the snow ran out. The jet winds took over and swept the remaining 3,000 feet clean for those four mem-

bers of the party who would continue on to plant the Japanese flag on the summit.

"Our four climbers made Japan the sixth nation to reach the top, if you credit the claim of Red China. They later reported they found nothing on the summit to indicate that anyone had been there before. The only thing we did find to establish proof that others had been this high was a pile of some 100 used oxygen bottles buried at varying depths in the ice and snow."

Saburo Akai, president of the Akai Tape Recorder Co., had put up $500,000 to get Miura to this spot on Everest from which he would make his speed ski run. Six men had lost their lives. It would be the best chance of his life to set the record he had climbed so many mountains to obtain.

Miura donned his normal ski suit and then strapped on a nylon air-cushioned life jacket. He put on a specially modified pilot's helmet with a two-way speaker, an oxygen pack consisting of three tanks containing enough air for 20 minutes . . . and, finally, a drag chute with the rip cord extending to his right hand.

Sun goggles, ski poles and a standard pair of skis completed his outfit.

At precisely 1:07 p.m., Miura dug his poles into the icy crust of Mount Everest as the cheers of the Sherpa guides and members of the Japanese expedition floated across the awesome slopes and hung in the frigid air. He shoved off.

In six seconds he was traveling at a speed of 111.8 mph with a pull of approximately five times the force of gravity on his body.

He popped his chute.

And then it happened.

The snarling crosswinds that flail the face of Everest like a great invisible howling beast chose that moment to center their fury on the brash mortal who had so brazenly invaded their domain on a flimsy pair of skis.

As the Sherpas watched in horror, Miura's chute began to whip violently from side to side, caught between the force of the 100 mile-an-hour down-hill plunge and the wind that came howling up the draw between Everest's two cones.

A titanic battle began between the lone Japanese man and the elements he had dared challenge.

Miura was in trouble. And he knew it. He was racing to his death. His breath came in great ragged gasps like some dying animal as he sucked at the oxygen on his back. The banshee winds howled around him, lashing him, tearing at the frail strings that linked him to his drag chute . . . whipping the chute back and forth behind him like a cat would sling a rodent . . . pummeling it like an invisible fist might punch a great bag.

Below him, rushing at him at blinding speed was the deepest crevasse on the mountain. He had dropped rocks into the crevasse on his way up and never heard them hit bottom. This bottomless pit was now directly across his path of descent, less than three-quarters of a mile away. He was speeding at 100 miles-an-hour toward eternity.

Now crouching, now being jerked erect by the wind-whipped chute; twisting, turning, dodging the half-buried rocks in the flying snow, Miura careened down Everest like a drunken puppet being manipulated, tortured, led to his death, by his enemy the wind.

And then, as if his strings had finally frayed through, the puppet fell.

"When I stood at the beginning of the snow-line at the nearest point I could get to the top, I was completely empty-minded. I seemed that I even forgot where I was and why I had come to Everest. It was something akin to a spiritual state of perfect selflessness or ecstacy, though that would probably be an exaggeration. All I know is that my mind was empty. No fear. Nothing.

"When I opened my chute I felt no resistance at all. I just kept slashing down the slope, down Mount Everest, like a rock. Thirty seconds later I knew I had little chance of surviving. I knew it was sayonara to my life and I wondered what would happen to me after death. I felt no fear, only curiosity as to my death. A sort of empty loneliness engulfed me as I plunged down Mount Everest to my doom. Was my life a dream? The word 'dream' kept flashing into my mind as I shot down the mountain out of control. I knew I couldn't survive."

Miura fell at a point only 437 yards short of the crevasse. His chute billowed in the fist of the wind but it was useless in stopping his plunge toward the icy pit. He slid and tumbled and ploughed a path down the frozen slope at a bone-shattering 80 miles an hour now.

"I could hear the Sherpas crying and praying for me, their voices piercing through the microphone and into my helmet radio as I tumbled and ricocheted off the rocks and ice mounds.

"I lost a ski and saw it fly away from me in a cloud of snow and now I knew, like the Sherpas, that there was no hope left. I thought of the crevasse in front of me."

One-hundred, 200, 300 yards, down, down, down, turning, tumbling, grinding, sliding, the orange and white-striped chute whipping from side to side behind him, Miura fell. Suddenly looming in front of him, rearing up to meet him out of the snow, beckoning his body for one final crushing embrace was a massive rock formation.

His chute swung in a great arc behind him as the treacherous wind twisted, guided his body toward the mammoth mound of jagged rock marring the icy slope like a black iceberg on a frigid seascape.

And Miura lost consciousness.

There had been hope, a prayer, a flickering undying possibility that Miura would survive until he hit the rock. But now as his body smashed against the icy granite, embracing its deadly ragged contours for what seemed an eternity, there was no hope.

Where there had been prayers and tears and loud lamenting on the slopes, now there was silence. It was as if the Sherpas and the climbers and the cameramen who tracked Miura's race with death had lost consciousness too.

Akira Kotani, the famed Japanese photographer of mountains and men, had tracked the horrifying descent of his countryman down Everest through the long lens of his camera and now it was as if he had switched to an agonizingly silent frame-by-creeping-frame slow motion camera.

He saw, as if it would be burned on his brain forever, Miura's lone ski strike fire from the rock and break into matchstick fragments filling the air around the rock like so many insects darting to safety . . . and Miura's body, released by the wind and the crushing force of gravity, hurtle up and over the mound of stone and down the other side . . . followed by the still-billowing chute that had not saved him from this peril.

And on the broken puppet fell . . . toward the bottomless crevasse now inching into the left-hand corner of Kotani's lens as he tracked Miura's tumbling unconscious form.

Then the wind stopped! It was as if some unseen hand, a spirit of a long-dead Sherpa, finally stayed the fickle chute! But did it matter . . . that Miura's plunge had suddenly ended only on the lip — a mere 100 yards away — of the precipice? Had not his life already flown? Had he not said to bury him here?

Miura's body lay still in the snow, crumpled in the snow, the chute holding the puppet strings taut in the stillness that enveloped the scene like a white shroud.

Kotani's longest lens zeroed in on the still body like a great eye probing for life, waiting, begging for a breath to fog the glass. An eternity passed.

"I thought I had died and by some miraculous quirk of fate I had been reincarnated into my former self."

It was only a tiny movement. And hearts stopped on the slopes. And then an arm, one arm, raised slowly.

"There is a Japanese word 'natsukashii' which means 'happy to meet an old friend again.' It was my first thought when I came to in a heap in the snow and knew I was alive."

The arm fell . . . and then — it seemed like hours to those watching from so far away — it rose again. It hadn't been a dying reflex!! This time the gesture carried a message to those on the slopes! Miura was alive! He had cheated the mountain and the wind and the looming crevasse.

A great cheer of joy swept across the ice and snow toward the first man to ski down Mount Everest. The mountains rang with the shouts of those who hurried to lift him from the snow.

It was a miracle. A miracle that he had fallen. A miracle that he had hit the rock that slowed his descent. A miracle that he had stopped so short of the crevasse. A miracle that he had suffered not one broken bone . . . or even a single cut. He was, indeed, the abominable — albeit a bit bruised — snowman.

"If it had worked out as we had originally planned, I would have skied down the mountain, stopped before the crevasse and used the ropes to come down the rest of the way. And it would have meant merely that a Japanese named Miura had skied down Mount Everest.

"But now I realize that I knew I couldn't survive when I got under way and that I miraculously escaped death only because I fell. And when I came to on the slope and knew that I had survived, I felt how good life was and how happy I was to be alive and how happy I was to be the person that so many people were pleased at welcoming back to life after my near-disastrous journey down Mount Everest.

"I found I had reaped a harvest of comrades who were willing to risk their lives with me. And I had met an old friend again, myself."

The persistent legend of the Tibetan yeti — the man-ape who supposedly roamed the Himalayas — briefly invaded Japan. A Stripes reporter gave the story appropriate doubt and tongue-in-cheek treatment.

JAPAN HILLFOLKS SPOT BASHFUL 'YETI'

DEC. 12, 1970

TOKYO — Has the Tibetan yeti immigrated to Japan?

Five persons around Mt. Hiba, a national park and farming area in Hiroshima Prefecture 600 miles southwest of Tokyo, claim to have seen a "short, hairy, ape-like creature" who thus far does not seem hostile or harmful. Matter of fact, he took off faster than the people who saw him.

Prefectural police said he was first seen (well, possibly) June 30 by Shigeru Iori, a 47-year-old farmer who claims he stepped up to greet a short, hunched figure who was shuffling along the foot of the mountain. The figure turned toward him, Iori said, and he (Iori) stared in slack-jawed astonishment at a creature that stood about five feet tall and "looked more like an ape than a man."

Iori said the strange being had bowed, stunted legs and was covered with thick dark hair. His face was similar to a human face, Iori said, but he had a flat head with short, bristly hair.

Four other persons, mostly farmers, have seen the terrifying and terrified creature since then. He vanishes in a flash when he sees people.

He kept well out of sight when nine members of a Kobe University expedition club probed the highlands for him. They saw only six "tracks" of the creature, allegedly found by a 47-year-old construction worker. A plaster casting of one of these was sent to Hiroshima Prefectural Police. Laboratory workers noted its startling similarity to a human hand.

Yukio Omae, chief of police in the town of Shohara near the mountain, said that if it is a yeti who has found he likes the smaller mountains and greener pastures of Japan, he can go his own way. But the first time he goes after people or cattle, he's had it — Omae will take out police dogs and find him.

In 1967, longtime Pacific Stars and Stripes Entertainment Editor Al Ricketts got a rare exclusive — an interview with reclusive Japanese novelist Yukio Mishima. Many hailed the author of "The Sound of Waves" and "Temple of the Golden Pavilion" as the most brilliant of his time. Others called Mishima a demented dreamer with a mind full of bloody murals from Japan's violent past.

Perhaps one story explains the other.

MEET YUKIO MISHIMA

JULY 2, 1967 BY AL RICKETTS

In a fashionable residential section near Tokyo International Airport, where sleek jetliners shatter the afternoon calm, a slightly built but muscular Japanese daily contemplates the tiled rooftops below from the sundeck of his Spanish style home.

At 42, novelist-playwright Yukio Mishima, sometimes called "the Japanese Hemingway," is probably one of the best-known Japanese exports since transistor radios.

Yet, with 33 plays, 16 novels and many short stories (including "The Sound of Waves" and "The Temple of the Golden Pavilion") already under his belt, Mishima is just hitting his literary stride.

He is currently at work on a four-volume novel — all about reincarnation — that he estimates will take him at least another five years to complete.

A recent venture into movie-making produced an artistic hair-raiser that invariably leaves Western audiences limp with its grim close ups of a hara-kiri ceremony. The shock of this scene is intensified by the poetic, and equally realistic, love scenes which precede it.

"Yukoku" (Patriotism), which Mishima produced, directed and adapted from his own gripping short story (he also cast himself in the only male role), concerns a Japanese soldier's suicide when faced with the betrayal of his country.

Hoping to learn just a little bit more about what makes Yukio Mishima run, I journeyed to the literary lion's Spanish castle and bearded him in his den.

A smiling Japanese maid opened the wrought iron gate that protects the 10-room Mishima manse from the public, then led the way past a seven-foot classical statue that stands poised on a circular tile zodiac in the middle of the front yard.

We waited briefly in a scaled-down, high-ceilinged room that might have been lifted right out of a home in Madrid, until the door opened and the jaunty author — a battered black briefcase clutched in his hands — bounced into the room.

"I guess you are wondering about this black case," said Mishima, while we took a short tour of the house. "I always carry it with me, even from room to room. It's full of notes, phone numbers ... important things that I might otherwise misplace."

Mishima speaks a precise, almost Oxonian English and when he wants to make sure he is being perfectly understood he tends to pace hiself like a long distance runner. Sipping slowly on a cold glass of beer, the wiry body-

167

building enthusiast reflected on the subject matter in "Yukoku."

"In the '30s," he explained, "suicide was considered an honorable death. It was a symbol of a strong will and proof of great courage. The Western mind, I know, finds this hard to understand. After the war, even the Japanese tended to look back on kamikaze pilots with little respect.

"Although that post-war attitude is changing today, I'm afraid the youth of Japan still has little belief in the old principles. I talked to a group of Japanese students not too long ago . . . and I was shocked.

"They told me that they didn't want to die for their country, that they didn't think Japan should arm and take part in her own defense . . . I don't understand that kind of thinking."

In spite of his doubts and fears. Mishima, it seems, is a man who has come close to finding his own personal satori. Once a pub-crawling playboy, he now devotes his time to his wife and two children, his work (he writes every day from midnight till 6 a.m.) and to shaking his head at modern Japan.

"We borrow all the wrong things from the West," says Mishima. "We are a mixture of contradictions and cultures. And we haven't had a literary revolution since the '30s. Today? We don't have any serious young Japanese writers today."

Even his spare time, which is drastically limited, is occupied with things that don't accurately mirror either his upper-class family background or his role as spokesman for the "modern" Japanese.

(His father and his grandfather were government employees and young Yukio was trained for the same profession. "I tried it for about eight months," smiles Mishima, "and then I gave it up.")

You're not likely, for example, to find the globe-girdling author wheeling down the highway in an expensive Jaguar or competing for a tee off time at one of Japan's many crowded golf courses.

"Before the war," says Mishima, "golf was an expensive hobby. It was the sport of the bourgeois set. Now, the courses are overcrowded. The game belongs to the common man . . . And I can't bear the thought of watching a young girl carry a heavy golf bag around the countryside."

(In Japan, most of the caddies are female.)

These observations were offered with a faint trace of a smile as he rose to remove an ancient samurai sword from its faded cloth cover. He then demonstrated the Japanese art of "iai" — unsheathing and resheathing a razor-sharp blade — eyes straight ahead — without losing a single finger.

Mishima is also an accomplished kendo man and just as he belts an opponent with a swift stroke of the bamboo kendo pole, he is just as likely to throw a fast verbal curve at an unsuspecting guest who wonders how seriously he takes reincarnation.

"I don't believe it!" Mishma chuckes, practically slapping his thigh at the thought. "I don't believe in reincarnation . . . I just use it to tie my stories together."

Three and a half years later, Steve Greene was told that a "crazy man" was haranguing troops from a balcony at the Ground Self Defense Force Eastern Army headquarters in nearby Ichigaya. Greene rushed over and returned several hours later — his shoes and trouser cuffs stained by blood that had seeped out of a shuttered room — to write a straightforward account of one of the most bizarre and horrifying events of the decade.

MISHIMA KILLS HIMSELF IN FINAL ACT OF PROTEST

NOV. 27, 1970 BY SGT. 1ST CLASS STEVE GREENE

TOKYO — Yukio Mishima, well-known Japanese author and playwright, died Wednes-day by ritual disembowelment and decapitation in a bizarre act of protest which left the nation stunned.

Mishima and four members of his private

army, Tate-No-Kai (Society of the Shield), slashed their way into the office of the commanding general of the Ground Self Defense Force Eastern Army at his headquarters in Ichigaya base, wounding eight soldiers with swords before reaching their objective.

The group lashed Lt. Gen. Kanetoshi Mashita to a chair and presented him with a list of demands after inflicting wounds on four of his staff officers including Maj. Gen. Akira Yamazaki, his chief of staff.

Mishima demanded that Mashita gather his troops in front of the headquarters building by 11:30 a.m.; that he let Mishima and his group introduce themselves and deliver a speech to the soldiers; that other members of his group, excluding the five already present, be allowed to attend the meeting and listen to his speech, and that he not be interrupted in any manner by tear gas, loud speakers or any psychological attacks.

Mishima accompanied his demands with the promise that if they were accepted, his group would release the commanding general within two hours. He warned that if the terms were not met, he would kill the general and commit hara-kiri (suicide) himself.

After approximately 1,500 of the bases's 4,500-man complement had been assembled in front of the building, Mishima appeared on the balcony fronting the general's office and delivered a 10-minute speech.

Attacking demonstrations conducted by Japanese leftists on Anti-War Day Oct. 21, Mishima said, "Protection of Japan's life and culture can be achieved only by the Emperor and the Self Defense Forces.

"I have waited for the day the members of the Self Defense forces would rise, but no one has risen. I am still waiting for them to so," said the 45-year-old novelist.

The JSDF must guard the law, said Mishima, but the present law does not allow them to do it. It is up to the SDF to change the law, he said.

Denouncing Japan's present body politic as corrupt, Mishima concluded his speech with the traditional war cry of the old Imperial Japanese armed forces: "Tennoheika Banzai!" (Long live the Emperor).

Mishima then ducked back into the barricaded office and stripped off the tunic of his uniform and knelt on the floor facing Mashita.

"I told him, 'Don't do such a silly thing,'" Mashita later told the newsmen, "but he wouldn't listen.

"He turned the sword point toward his stomach, staring at me without speaking. Then, with a shout, he plunged the blade into his abdomen and drew it across him."

He was immediately beheaded, as prescribed by samurai tradition, by Hissho Morita, 25, a Waseda University student and Mishima's second in command. Morita then followed his leader in committing hara-kiri and was beheaded by another follower, Hiroyasu Koga, 25, police said.

Koga and the two other members of the raiding party — Masayoshi Koga, 22 (no relation), and Masahiro Ogawa, 22, freed Mashita and were arrested as they left his office.

All three were charged with homicide at the request of another person, unlawful entry, unlawful confinement, inflicting bodily injuries and violation of the Firearm and Sword Control Law.

At approximately 3 p.m., Yasunari Kawabata, Nobel Prize-winning novelist and longtime friend of Mishima's, arrived at the headquarters to pay his final respects, but officials would not let him enter the office.

He told newsmen he never thought Mishima would die "such a miserable death," wire services reported.

This is Jim Lea again — still a probing observer and a master of atmospheric prose as he gives readers a brief, edge-of-border look into an ideological monolith that would be largely forbidden to American travelers for the rest of the decade.

A PEEK THROUGH THE BAMBOO CURTAIN

FEB. 19, 1971 BY JIM LEA

HONG KONG — The rain has grayed and sullied the land, but there is evidence that, in spring or autumn, it would be a lovely place.

The valley is wide, flat, threaded by a sluggish stream and calicoed with vegetable fields. There is a constant quack of duck voices conversing in their pens beside the mossy-roofed houses, but the sound melts into the overall scene and soon becomes familiar.

Occasional foreign sounds shatter the peace. There is the clatter of an early morning train on the Kowloon-Canton rail line, the roar of a truck motor as it is geared down for the Sheung Shui checkpoint.

The policemen who man the Sheung Shui checkpoint on the edge of a buffer zone which stretches two miles to the Chinese border are young, powerful-looking men. They are dressed in heavy, navy blue peacoats and boots and light green trousers. The left pocket of their coats is cut wide, hiding the butts of their pistols, but allowing easy access.

They move from the station and wait beneath the wide overhang of roof until the truck is abreast of them. One walks slowly to the rear of the vehicle while two others wait for the driver to lower the window. He gives his destination, shouting to make himself heard over the sound of the rain and the din of the ducks in a cage over the cab.

One of the Chinese policemen answers and the topheavy truck rumbles south.

"Many trucks come from the north every day," the corporal in charge says, watching the truck disappear past the road sign which screams to travelers from the south, "FRONTIER — CLOSED AREA. Entry prohibited without a written permit. by order, Commissioner of Police."

"They bring vegetables and ducks and eggs, very good eggs. Sometimes we stop them for a search. Not often."

The trucks already have been searched, further up the road, at Lowu or beyond the river which separates Britain's New Territories from China.

"And," the corporal turns suddenly to the visitor as though he has just realized that the man is there, "what are you doing here?"

He listens without expression to the explanation of the mission of the British Red Cross minibus which has left the visitor — who had no police pass — there before continuing on to Lowu to deliver food packages to the Chinese Red Cross for two Germans, a stateless person and four Americans in China.

"I saw no packages in the truck."

He knows there were packages. They have gone to the border every month for 15 years. He is playing some sort of game and, before he realizes it, the visitor is hooked and the corporal begins to reel him in.

"The Americans do not receive the packages, you know. They are not given to them."

Americans who once were detained in China have confirmed that the packages are delivered. For the sake of argument, the visitor says only that with the political climate between China and America being what it is we can only hope that they are delivered, can only trust in the basic humanity of the human beings who control the lives of the men who are detained. He has walked into a conversational trap.

"Yes, you can only trust. It's not very much, you know. You do not recognize that China exists so you can only trust. It isn't good that there is no conversation between you."

The corporal looks up the road at the truck approaching empty from the markets of the south.

The visitor, seeking a way out of the conversation, remarks on the predominant color of all the trucks. The corporal smiles a small smile.

"You see. You don't understand. It does not mean what you think it means. Red is a lucky color to Orientals. In many places — even in China — it means only luck, nothing more."

When the truck has passed through, the driver scowling at the stranger who stood beside the corporal — instant distrust seems to be a failing of both sides — the policeman continues.

"China and America will be friends again very soon. You must, you know. China is much too large to be ignored forever. Historically, you are friends. You both had revolutions.

"But, you must stop threatening with your military and you must talk. China is not afraid of your military. China is so big that she has never been afraid of big things.

"Taiwan is the problem. There cannot be two Chinas. It is a ridiculous situation. You must become friends again with one China."

A small border incident ends the conversation.

An old man, his bicycle loaded high and topheavy with baskets of radishes, pumps through the gate from the north, his brown, bare legs straining against the pedals looking like old ivory. An empty truck, its vegetables deposited in the stalls of Fan Ling or Tai Po or markets farther south, is stopped at the gate.

The old man pedals forward, directly into the truck. He shrieks at the driver, shaking his fist, and the driver, shaking his fist, also, shouts back. The policemen separate them, help collect the radishes which have spilled, then push the old man and his bicycle back away from the truck.

As soon as the driver crawls back into the cab, the old man starts forward again, squeezing between the truck and the gate stanchion. The driver shakes his head in disgust and pulls north.

"Now," the corporal says, coming back from the confrontation which the old man from China has won, "perhaps you will take no more photographs. The people who pass here may distrust you.

"Perhaps," he indicates a concrete guard post some distance from the station, "you will wait there for your friends. We would not want your cameras and intentions to be misunderstood."

A Pacific Stars and Stripes photographer barely jumped clear of a deliberately-aimed motorcycle.

Newsmen frequently dodged bricks and rocks or found themselves wedged between police trying to clear ground for New Tokyo International Airport and rioting farmers who felt they had been unfairly dispossessed by pushy bureaucrats. Radical students jumped in and turned Narita, a one-time pasture for horses that pulled the emperor's coach, into a battleground on which three policemen were slain.

"This is the closest damned thing you'll find to a war," said Air Force Tech. Sgt. Paul Harrington, the photographer who had dodged the two-wheeled assault.

The battle lasted for weeks into months. Here is one of the first and best Stripes reports.

RADICALS WIN ROUND ONE

FEB. 24, 1971 BY SPEC. 4 JERRY VAN SLYKE

NARITA, JAPAN — "Yukio Mishima loved Japan! Yukio Mishima sacrificed himself for Japan. Would you do the same?" the angry old man shouted. "Or aren't you actually turning your backs on Japan and playing China's game?"

Across the valley from the old man, nearly a thousand members of the Revolutionary Marxist Students League (Chukaku) were encamped, attempting to stall construction of the new Tokyo International Airport a few miles from Narita City and about 35 miles east of Tokyo

"Yukio Mishima was a dirty fool," the answer floated back harshly.

"You are not fit to speak of Yukio Mishima," the old man — Bin Akao, leader of the right-wing Great Japan Patriotic Party — screamed back at them, and he went on for more than an hour, telling the students to go home.

They did not, but the more than 1,300 National and Prefectural Police and New Tokyo Interna-

tional Airport Corp. Guards who had come to chase them away did leave.

Chiba Prefectural Governor Taketo Tomono, who Saturday had ordered police to forcibly evict the students and six farm families from land earmarked for construction of Tokyo's New International Airport, called police off at mid-afternoon because of fears of violent counterattacks by the radicals and the farmers they support.

Original plans had called for police to move at daybreak on six fort and tunnel networks from which the students and farmers have vowed to fight to the death to save 33 acres of land at the northwest end of the new airport's main runway. They held off, though, as nearly 1,000 snake-dancing, chanting students prepared for battle.

At mid-morning, police reported that they had discovered 10 shotgun shells near the students' barricades. Earlier, officials had voiced fears that guns and ammunition stolen last week by an ultra-left student group had found their way into the network of tunnels at the airport site.

At 1 p.m., 20 prefectural police and airport guards marched into the valley stronghold and read an eviction notice signed by Tomono. The students replied with obscenities and indecent gestures. The police retreated.

Tomoro ordered a halt to police operations about 3 p.m.

The attempts to oust the protesters were to continue Tuesday. Tomono has promised construction officials that the students and farmers will be gone by March 14.

The United States held a long stewardship over Okinawa, an island that had been part of Tokyo Prefecture before it was seized as a prize of war in 1945. Even while Okinawa and 72 other islands were under American administration, Washington acknowledged that a former enemy held "residual sovereignty" — and that their return to full Japanese control was a promise. After 26 years, the pledge was fulfilled by an exchange of signatures — comprehensively reported by Jim Lea.

"WE BOTH HAVE MUCH TO BE PROUD OF THIS DAY"

JUNE 19, 1971 BY JIM LEA

TOKYO — The U.S. and Japanese governments Thursday signed a 1,978-word agreement which will put Okinawa, 72 other islands and 978,000 people under Japanese administrative control.

It brings to an end more than two decades of American rule in the Ryukyu Islands.

The 29-minute ceremony was relayed between Tokyo and Washington by Intelstat communications satellite, the first simultaneous broadcast of any treaty-signing proceedings.

While thousands of leftist students threw homemade bombs and burned automobiles less than two miles away to protest the treaty, Japanese Foreign Minister Kiichi Aichi began signing the reversion document at 9:16 p.m. in the reception hall of Prime Minister Eisaku Sato's official residence. Simultaneously, U.S. Secretary of State William P. Rogers signed an identical copy of the agreement in the State Departmen's Jefferson Room in Washington.

Aichi sat at a white brocade-covered desk in the vaulted-ceilinged, Japanese and American flag-bedecked hall and Rogers, with Japanese Ambassador to Washington Nobuhiko Ushiba seated beside him, sat at a desk historians believe to be the one used during the signing of the Louisiana Purchase agreement in 1803.

Rogers finished signing first, at 9:17 p.m.

Sato recalled during a short speech following the signing that "I had once stated that the post-war period will not have ended for Japan as long as Okinawa had not been returned to the motherland.

"I am confident that the time has now arrived when ... Japan can truly be said to have emerged from the post-war period and is ready to move forward to face the new era of the 1970s, particularly the new Pacific Age."

In Washington, Rogers read a statement from President Nixon, who did not attend the ceremony, in which the President said, "We both have much to be proud of this day.

"The friendship and mutual respect which enabled our negotiators to resolve the many difficult issues will, I am sure, enable us to work together in peace for the continued progress of our two countries and for that of the entire world."

Speaking for himself, Rogers said, "We Americans have tried to exercise our stewardship over those islands and people for the past quarter of a century conscientiously and constructively.

"We take pride in that stewardship. However, we take even greater pride in carrying out our pledged word to the people of Okinawa and to the people of Japan."

Although the agreement does not mention nuclear weapons — a major bone of contention among opponents of the document in Okinawa and Japan — in any of its nine articles, both Sato and U.S. Ambassador to Japan Armin H. Meyer either mentioned or alluded to the nuclear weapons question in statements during the ceremony.

"Fundamental agreement was reached in the joint (Nixon-Sato) communique issued in the fall of 1969 which called for the reversion of Okinawa during 1972, free of nuclear weapons on the same level as mainland Japan," Sato said.

Meyer assured the Japanese and Okinawans in his statement that the "return of Okinawa will be on a completely homeland level."

Under the agreement, U.S. bases in Okinawa will be operated under the U.S.-Japan Treaty of Mutual Cooperation and Security which requires the United States to conduct prior consultations with Japan before bringing nuclear weapons into the country.

The United States repeatedly has refused — as it does elsewhere in the world — to confirm the existence on Okinawa of nuclear weapons. However, a few hours before the signing ceremony, a Japanese Foreign Ministry spokesman said that $70 million of the $320 million Japan will pay for U.S. assets in Okinawa will be spent on the removal of nuclear weapons.

The ceremony ended after Aichi and Meyer signed six documents related to the reversion agreement.

The ceremony in Tokyo was attended by about 50 U.S. and Japanese officials including Sato's cabinet, U.S. Embassy Minister Counsellor Richard Sneider, Lt. Gen. James P. Lampert, high commissioner of the Ryukyu Islands, and Lt. Gen. Gordon Graham, U.S. Forces Japan commander.

Speaker of the Ryukyus Legislature Katsu Hoshi and Seiyu Hirata, Government of the Ryukyu Islands (GRI) high court chief justice, were the only Okinawans who attended. GRI Chief Executive Chobyo Yara declined Sato's invitation to attend the ceremony because, he said, many Okinawans are unhappy with the agreement because it does not spell out provisions for a nuclear-free Okinawa and allows the United States to maintain bases in the islands.

Under Secretary of State U. Alexis Johnson, Secretary of Defense Melvin R. Laird and Adm. Thomas H. Moorer, Joint Chiefs of Staff chairman, attended the ceremony in Washington.

While the ceremony was taking place, more than 50,000 leftist students, labor unionists and Japan Socialist Party members who had held rallies during the afternoon at some of the capital's largest parks, began marching through the streets to protest the agreement signing.

The worst incident of violence seen in demonstrations so far this year occurred at Meiji Park, less than two miles from the official residence, just moments before the signing took place. Twenty-six policemen were injured near the park's National Stadium when demonstrators threw a homemade bomb at riot squads.

A police spokesman said the bomb was believed to have been made from a piece of pipe filled with explosives. Three of the policemen reportedly were injured seriously.

The protesters also overturned four automobiles in the Meiji Park area and set them afire. Earlier in the evening, students and police clashed near Shibuya Station and several firebombs were thrown. Sporadic clashes continued until after midnight.

Police said Friday that 732 demonstrators — 131 of them women — were arrested in Tokyo. In addition to the fire-bombing incidents, police said the demonstrators stormed onto commuter train tracks at Shibuya and paralyzed Yamanote and Chuo line traffic for more than an hour.

Demonstrations and minor outbreaks of violence also were reported in Naha, capital of Okinawa, where several thousand protesters pelted police with bottles and rocks. One thousand riot squadsmen were on duty there, while more than 12,000 had been mobilized in Tokyo.

Demonstrators in both places demanded that the islands be returned unconditionally, with no U.S. bases remaining. Twenty students were arrested in Okinawa.

Although the agreement was signed Thursday, the actual date of reversion has not yet been set. The Japanese are asking for April 1, 1972, but the United States votes July 1, 1972. The agreement must first be ratified by the U.S. Senate and the Japanese Diet (parliament), and will become effective two months after that ratification.

Under the agreement, the United States will turn over to Japan 47 bases with a total of about 14,500 acres of land, "about one-seventh of our current holdings," a U.S. official said. Many of the facilities to be returned are now operated by the U.S. Marine Corps, but the official said that there would be no reduction of Marine forces on the island.

"We have not reduced the number of personnel and have not diminished the strength of our military effectiveness by this agreement," the official said.

The only military unit to be withdrawn from the island as a result of reversion is the U.S. Army Pacific Intelligence School, the official said, "because there is no provision for third-country national training."

Although the agreement does not list them specifically, the Senkaku Islands are included in the area to be returned to Japanese control. The uninhabited islands, which are believed to be rich in oil deposits, are claimed by Japan, the Republic of China and Communist China.

"We received the Senkaku Islands from Japan under the peace treaty and we are returning them in the same context," the U.S. official said.

The reversion agreement allows the Voice of America radio station to continue operation in Okinawa for five years, but specifies that the U.S. and Japanese governments will begin consultations on the future of the station two years after reversion.

It was the Age of Aquarius and Zumwalt — of democratic quarterdeck discussions between officer and enlisted man and court martials for long hair and frowsy beards. The concussive changes that had rocked American society made their inevitable way into the military and the old values of discipline and patriotism seemed like period pieces of another time. Viewing it all as an odd and picturesque social phenomenon, a Stripes reporter was colorful yet restrained as he wrote this yarn — a story that would itself become a period piece as the trend reversed and the old values came back.

COFFEE HOUSES CENTERS OF GI PROTEST

JUNE 19, 1971 BY SPEC. 4 RICK HOWELL

MISAWA, Japan — He leans over his cola-colored drink for the bag of popcorn. Popcorn sells big in the Owl Coffeehouse, or so it seems. At least, somebody always has a bag.

He reaches his popcorn, opens it and offers the snacks to the people in the room.

One of the two bartenders is stoking the fire with thin, wide but short boards. The old wood burner sits in the middle of the club, but out of the way.

The tables and small inverted "L"-shaped bar are on one end of the peace-postered room. The other end holds a collection of tables and chairs and a small stage partitioned by four-foot-high wooden panel from the rest of the room. The stage is filled with band equipment — a drum set, guitars and amplifiers.

The guy with the popcorn has an Air Force regulation haircut and wears wire-framed glasses. He's talking to a civilian — young, long-haired and also wearing wire-framed glasses.

The conversation is varied, but in the Owl Club, if you're not talking about music, you're generally talking about peace or complaints against the military or seeking advice on how to get conscientious objector applications.

The club, a few hundred feet outside the Misawa AB gate is a gathering place for the anti-war GIs and members of the peace movement. It serves as headquarters, at least a mailing address, of the underground newspaper "Hair."

The atmosphere is quiet, even though Steppenwolf is blasting sounds from the small phonograph behind the bar.

Large and small posters cover the walls along with hand-drawn signs declaring "No Agnews is good news" and "Nixon" spelled with a swastika for the letter "x." Pencil-drawn faces are scattered on the walls.

A shelf winding its way along the wall, about mid-thigh high, is blanketed with underground newspapers from throughout Japan. They range from near professional to crudely mimeographed gripe sheets.

Examples:

"Freedom Rings" is from the Tokyo area. It prints: "If you believe something, brothers, don't be afraid to say it. But if you say something, don't back down and change what you say to appease the man."

"Yokosuka David," from the Yokosuka NB area: "All these papers and groups have one thing in common. They all hate military and establishment pigs and are unified to this cause."

"Fall In At Ease," also from the Tokyo area, is one of the more professional-looking papers. It carries articles by Black Panthers Eldridge Cleaver and Bobby Seale and features cartoons and photographs.

"The Stars and Bars" is a mimeograph sheet that prints letters from the Iwakuni stockade.

Other papers include the "Semper Fi" from Iwakuni, "Itazuke YAD" and "Hair."

Editors of the papers, if they are known, claim they lead a precarious life. They're in the military while working on basically anti-military papers.

Cpl. George Bacon says he was shipped out of Japan to Vietnam for allegedly working on "Semper Fi."

In a letter to the "Playboy", he said the officers "resorted to a method frequently used to deal with dissident GIs — the punitive transfer. In less than two months, five of us suspected ringleaders were transferred."

The Iwakuni information office said Bacon was transferred routinely "to fulfill a quota in his specialty to the 1st Marine Air Wing in Da Nang." He was given 24-hours notice before his transfer, said the office, "which is a very normal thing."

Asked if Bacon's was a punitive transfer, the office said, "No, we don't have anything by that name. The officer that made a punitive transfer would be arrested."

"The last editors of 'Hair' were busted," said one of the anti-war movement members at the Owl. "The paper used to be printed on the base." The papers, by regulations, may only be printed off-base.

"The base officials found out who they were and transferred them," he said. Since then, "Hair" has been revived, "now prints off-base and plans to go offset soon."

The Misawa AB information office denied that the paper had ever been banned or printed on base. "They just stopped printing," he said. "We don't know why. We don't worry about it that much. It's not that big a thing."

He said, "No action has ever been taken against anybody who has worked on the paper."

The editors of "Hair" say the GI anti-war movement is growing, at least in the Misawa area. "Some GIs who have spent their off-duty time running the bars downtown have begun to favor establishments that are sympathetic to the anti-war movement, the most prominent of which is the Owl Coffeehouse.

"Representatives from the Pacific Counseling Service in Tokyo are frequently visiting Misawa to assist GIs who have requested conscientious objector applications and in anti-war activities," said a recent edition of "Hair."

"There has been an increase in the number of conscientious objector applications submitted and processed," it said.

Both Iwakuni and Misawa spokesmen denied any increase in conscientious objector applications on their bases.

"We have established close relations with GI and civilian anti-war organizations in Japan and in the States," the editors of "Hair" reported.

The papers, most of which carry the notice, "This is your personal property. It cannot be legally taken away from you," use their papers as a forum to express their anti-war stands and for airing gripes against the military.

Two people at the bar are munching on popcorn and talking about getting a band together. Somebody else throws a Janis Joplin disc on the record player.

Three people are sitting in chairs around the small tables. Their conversation is barely audible. Only pieces of it are heard. "I was worried. They had everybody there, man. The company commander . . ."

"Don't worry," said a voice from somewhere in response. Somebody said something about a lawyer.

Someone leaped over the partition to the stage and beat drums quietly to the Janis Joplin record.

The times, they were a-changin', and this, too, would pass away. Coffee house sheets became curios in only a few years. Among dissident GIs, few became as famous as the pair apprehended going through a military customs check at Iwakuni MCAF with a color picture of themselves beside a large bag of hashish.

Americans in Japan had for years enjoyed a big plus — a rigidly fixed currency exchange rate that transformed a single dollar into 360 Japanese yen. The dollar was king on the currency market and foreign economists felt that it was unfairly strong against the stable yen — the reason the Japanese were pressured to take the fetters off the yen and allow it to find its own level against the dollar. Resisting for years, they finally gave in — and Americans suddenly found themselves with less yen in hand, when they could find it at all. Onbase banks were closed or yen sales halted as officials sorted things out. Americans who lived offbase made desperate promises to landlords and bachelors had little to make whoopee with as the exchange rate — far less than 360 to one — capriciously varied from day to day. This report relates how rain fell into a lot of lives.

"I HOPE YOU GOT YEN, GI"

SEPT. 1, 1971, BY STAFF SGTS. PAUL J. HARRINGTON AND R.R. KEENE

TOKYO — "I hope you got yen, GI," were the next words she spoke after "welcome."

It was that way around most U.S. military bases in the Tokyo area Monday afternoon and evening after U.S. Forces Japan announced suspension of all on-base yen sales until further notice.

Restaurants, bars, hotels and any businesses catering to the yen converted from the American dollar, were having problems.

It was impossible for many American military and dependents to even negotiate a taxi off base.

Bank tellers at the Chase Manhattan at Yokota AB complained that at least 100 persons ignored the "No Yen Sales" posters on the doors and inside, and asked if it were possible to purchase yen.

Sgt. Dennis Anderson of the 6100th Air Base Wing, carried his $500 for purchase of a car and insurance in his hands. It was useless.

"I have to change this into yen to pay for everything. I think it can wait," he hoped. "I'm wondering about the six other guys in my shop who live off base. Their rent is due in yen. They are really in a bind."

Also standing in the lobby of the bank were Chief Master Sgt. Albert H. Allendorf and his wife, Mattie, who had hoped to do some shopping on their 10-day leave from Okinawa.

"They say (Yokota bank tellers), we can change money at a Japanese bank," he explained. "I haven't got enough yen to get a train or taxi to one."

His wife frowned, "I usually get my hair done on the economy, I guess I'll have to go to the base beauty shop."

On the strip of businesses facing Yokota's fence, authorized money changers like the Pony Co. Ltd., which sells electronic items, posted signs saying purchasers were getting an exchange rate of 336 yen to $1 and the only checks accepted were traveler's checks.

One salesman said, "Every day the stores are very crowded, even before paydays, but not since the yen changed. Now business is bad all along the street. People come in and look, they find out that everything is 6 percent more and they say, 'Wait a minute, we'll be back!' That's the last we see of them.

"We businessmen are hoping the yen will stabilize fast and things can get back to normal."

Illegal yen conversion on a small scale was being done at some bars in Fussa, Tachikawa City, and Asaka, located outside North Camp Drake.

Small bars would not convert yen openly. In many cases the hostesses would change yen for the customer. The prices were high. 300 to 320 yen to a $1; however, most would not change anything larger than $10.

A GI read a notice from his command saying they were doing everything possible to solve the problem and that yen sales on base would start immediately upon obtaining a decision from the "proper authority."

He shook his head, "The rent is due, the insurance is due, the maid needs to be paid, and I'm dry. Whoever 'Proper Authority' is, I hope he hurries!"

Thirteen years later, the dollar-to-yen rate had yet to settle — and was still as hard to keep up with as a handball in flight. Many of the bars and restaurants that had catered to American patronage were dead, slain by their own currency as the flabby dollar got weaker yet.

The Okinawa Reversion agreement had been signed, the Japanese held the helm of government and Prime Minister Eisaku Sato praised the historic moment the Japanese regained in peace the territory that had been lost in war. The bitter past seemed cleanly buried — and yet, all over Okinawa, there was an unwanted legacy of the last war. Beneath streets, gardens, farmfields and schoolyards, there were tons of old ammunition — iron-jacketed explosives that had landed as impotent duds during the 1945 battle for the island but could burst to lethal life at anytime, killing long after they were meant to kill. It happened on a quiet street in Naha, and Jim Lea was there to paint a dark mural of tragedy.

DEATH REVISITS THE OLD NEIGHBORHOOD

MARCH 5, 1974, BY JIM LEA

NAHA, Okinawa — "Who do you blame for this?" A young woman asked no one in particular. "Who'll take responsibility?"

"You can't blame anybody," a young man standing nearby answered. "It just happened. Like a typhoon."

"The war," an old man mumbled. "The war is responsible."

They stood at a police barricade Sunday, watching as police and construction workers sifted through tons of mud and chunks of stone and shards of steel and broken dreams Sunday in Naha's Oroku District.

Oroku normally is a quiet place.

Except for an occasional clash between radical student groups which have headquarters or hideouts here, there is little excitement.

Saturday there was tragic excitement and Sunday the quiet was deathly.

Thirty-foot-long, foot-wide steel girders weighing nearly a ton lay twisted like tinfoil. A steam shovel, crumpled and split, lay like some child's discarded plastic toy.

The floor of a nearby house was covered with bits of broken furniture and piles of grey, drying mud. Loose sheets of corrugated tin which had been a roof before mud and rock came crashing through it creaked in the afternoon quiet.

In the playground of the St. Matthew Episcopal Church Kindergarten a swing which was three-year-old Miho Miyamoto's final happiness was bent into uselessness.

Saturday, as she played on it waiting for her mother to finish a kindergarten parents' day program, a ghost of World War II blasted into her young life and buried her.

Police who now have found more bits of shrapnel and a 27-inch-diameter steel baseplate, now say the explosion which killed Miho and three other persons in Oroku Saturday was a 1,100-pound land mine.

Five hundred mines, officials said, were laid in Oroku in March 1945 to protect the Japanese Imperial Navy's final command post. At least 40 of them weighed 500 kilograms (1,100 pounds each). The rest weighed 150 kilograms (330 pounds).

"They should have done that before," someone said Sunday, watching as two policemen moved gingerly over the muck in a shallow blast crater with a metal detector.

"How could they have known before?" someone else asked.

In the first confused hours after the explosion, there were reports that a kindergarten teacher had been killed. Officials said Sunday no teachers died.

Josho Maeshiro, 56, did. A construction worker, he was standing near a pile driver which was pounding a steel retaining wall into a sewer excavation and detonated the mine.

He was thrown over a six-foot-high fence and died in the entranceway of a house more than 100 feet away.

Akiyuki Kakazu, 45, died in the seat of the pile driver.

Tsunemasa Maehara, 32, was driving through the area in his light van taxi. A 30-foot steel beam smashed through the front seat and he died five hours later at Naha's Red Cross Hospital.

Thirty-two other victims lie injured in four hospitals.

One of them, another three-year-old girl, was unconscious for more than 24 hours after the blast. Hospital officials said she is in serious condition, but will survive. As bystanders watched the cleanup crew Sunday, many of them wondered — some aloud — if any more World War II souvenirs lie beneath Oroku.

"People who were here during the war thought all the mines had been detonated or removed," a policeman at the scene said.

"But," he added, "nobody knows for sure."

177

This story sparked a lot of criticism from elders who felt the newspaper shouldn't have printed a report with a negative kind of message — for cool and intelligent criminals, crime sometimes did pay. Yet it was the last chapter in one of the most colorful and exciting crime stories in years.

FUCHU BANDIT RIDES HOME FREE

DEC. 11, 1975 BY HAL DRAKE

TOKYO — "I'm terribly sorry," detective Kazuo Kitano told his fellow officers as a grandfather clock near him tolled midnight Tuesday. "We did all we could have done, didn't we?"

Kitano was dry-eyed, but it was a time for tears — a national loss of face for Japanese police who, after seven years of effort, thousands of hours of careful and incisive investigation and the questioning of more than 100,000 suspects, had to give up and admit defeat.

The fabled Fuchu bandit, the unseen suspect known only by a composite photograph, went free. As minutes crumbled away and one detective tiredly crossed off Dec. 9 on a calendar, the statute of limitations ran out on the Dec. 10, 1968, robbery in which a daring young man on a motorcycle stole almost a million dollars in an audacious deception and masquerade. He could no longer be punished by criminal law and a challenge to lawful authority would go unpunished.

The scene was Fuchu Police Station on the outskirts of metropolitan Tokyo and Kitano addresssed a special squad assigned to the case for the last time. It broke a dream for him — he had once said he wanted to catch the bandit, look him in the face and "drink to my heart's content." Now it was not to be.

Where was the bandit? Where was the money? They did not know. There was nothing to do now but follow the ritual of tradition — apologize to the people of Japan for failure to catch a brazen thief who might still be among them.

Kuniyasu Tsuchida, superintendant general of the Tokyo Metropolitan Police Dept., did the same and paid an offhanded tribute to the bandit by calling his crime "important and unique" — and as of midnight, unsolved.

Tsuchida accurately described the crime. Every schoolboy and reader of lurid weekly magazines knew its details by now — how the bandit first sent threatening letters to the Kokubunji branch of the Nippon Trust and Banking Co., then dressed in a mockup police uniform and jumped astride a white-painted motorcycle to intercept a bank car as it carried three duraluminum chests full of Japanese yen, totalling by current rates more than $1 million in exchange value, to the Fuchu plant of the Tokyo Shibaura Electric Co. The money was to be paid out in yearend bonuses.

Flagging the car down outside, of all places, Fuchu Prison, the imposter told four occupants the car might be wired with dynamite. They scrambled out and he crawled beneath the auto and set off a smoke bomb — something that sent the four unarmed guards running into roadside bushes. Before they knew what had happened, the "policeman" was behind the wheel and the car was gone — along with the money.

The bandit had everything carefully planned. Another car, its motor running, was waiting at a nearby cemetery. The bandit abandoned the bank car, transferred his loot to the other one and drove to a nearby woods, where he emptied the chests and left them — one of more than 60 items he indifferently abandoned for police to find, including pieces of his disguise. All were useless as clues.

One of the most intensive manhunts in Japanese history began. Everyone from rookie patrolmen to hard-eyed veterans of the detective force in Tokyo, Osaka and every major city and small town in Japan joined the hunt. Suspects were questioned, clues carefully sifted and every tip carefully checked. Police overseas reported any flush, big-spending Japanese who answered the description of a face posted all over Japan — a composite one drawn from the descriptions of the four bank messengers.

Hachibei Hiratsuka, a top cop who had broken some of Japan's most famous cases, was placed in charge of the special squad that set up at the Fuchu station and had no other job than to solve this one. Hiratsuka was a kind of Captain Ahab, vowing to stay on the case until it was solved, even though he lost retirement money he would have gotten for turning in his badge.

178

LITTLE REFUGEE can only look at the world with sad and puzzled eyes, wondering what became of the life she knew and what lies ahead in an unknown world — the plight of thousands who fled Vietnam as the communists closed in on Saigon and called it Ho Chi Minh City. At sea, warships became rescue craft and ships like the guided missile cruiser Fox boarded fishing boats or any frail or flimsy craft refugees could flee in. These Fox crewmen pluck 27 refugees from a 40-foot boat. On that same day, the carrier Ranger picked up 137 young and old refugees in the South China Sea, the tragic trough for those who fled a lost life.

PS&S, Ken George

USN, Pat Winter

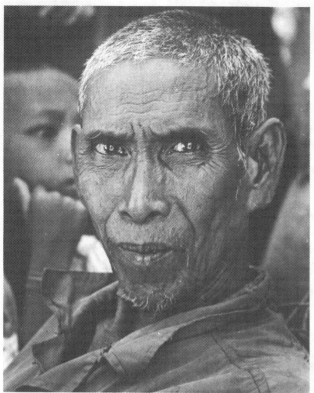

PS&S photos, Ken George

VERY OLD OR APPALLINGLY YOUNG, Vietnamese refugees crowded halfway points like the Philippines, where an elder with a face weathered by stress could look thoughtful as both he and a younger foundling pondered life in the United States or whatever country would take a man who had lost his own. It was often easier for children to put aside confusion and sadness and make the best of whatever came — such as these youngsters who boarded a beached "Boat of Freedom" and made a playhouse of it. Unlike their elders, they would forget easily and grow up as different children in a new land.

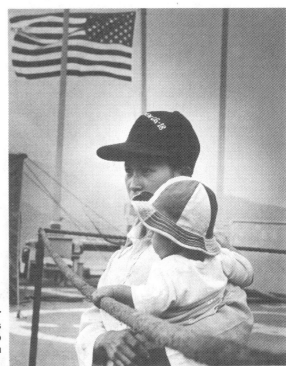

BENEATH THE FLAG they will adopt in a new land, this Vietnamese mother and her daughter look shoreward from the guided missile frigate Worden as they approach Subic Bay NB in the Philippines. While there, many clung to religion as a spiritual raft — knelt beneath the gentle and ominiscent Buddha and asked for solace and guidance in a troubled time.

PS&S photos, Bob Wickley

A FALSE DISASTER bring fledgling firefighters out to smother deliberately set flames at Yokosuka NB, Japan, where the Navy runs a school for smoke eaters. A fine, expertly spread spray forces the fire back, gradually reduces it to hissing steam. Petty Officer 1st Class John Koelon grimaces in a man-made downpour as he puts years of stressful experience to work to teach the students.

GROWING OLD but still agile on his feet and fast with a quip, Bob Hope cavorts with Raquel Welch before 9th Infantry Division troops at Bear Cat, 15 miles east of Saigon — one of the many away-from-home Christmases Hope spent with soldiers overseas. Three generations of Americans in three wars knew the comic who never wore a uniform but felt a kinship with those who did.

MOUNTED POLICE still ride at Clark AB, which is 50 miles north of Manila and was a cavalry post before rickety biplanes and supersonic jets came in. Watchful airmen ride over rugged miles and teach their mounts to jump and to "stand fire" — not to flinch at a sudden shot.

PS&S photos, Ken George

184

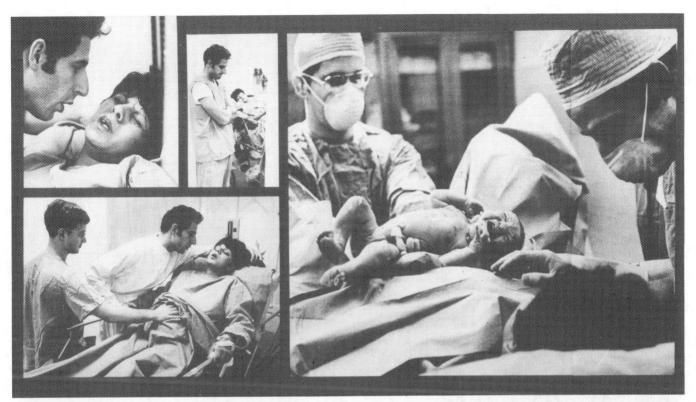

AGONY AND ECSTASY of birth was fully shown in a rare and dramatic picture series as photographer Bob Wickley stood by wife Sandy in the delivery room at Yokota AB, western Tokyo, watching as daughter Melanie Rose was born — healthy and in full cry. Also present was Chip Maury, Stripes photo chief — making his subtle and deliberate way around patient, doctor and husband as he recorded what Mrs. Wickley called "the most wonderful moment in a woman's life."

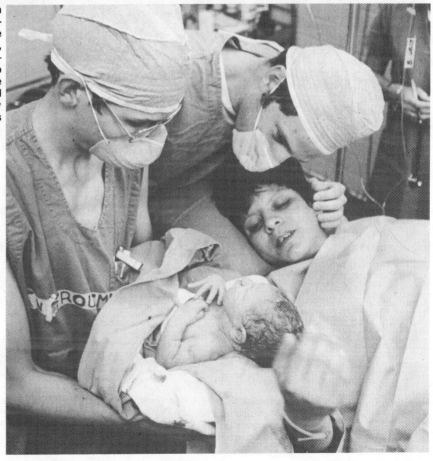

END OF THE WORLD — or at least of Tokyo — is shown as Tokyo Tower sinks like the mast of a derelict ship and the rest of the world's most populous city is engulfed by water and lava. The appalling disaster was all in the minds and hands of Japanese film technicians, whose expert use of miniatures and trick photography made it all come true on the wide screen. "Japan Sinks" was a huge success, but seismologists at Tokyo University warned that the capital sat stride deadly underground faults and might someday be shaken apart, sinking in a cloud of dust and rubble.

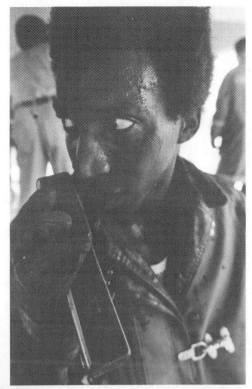

WEARY BUT SATISFIED, Sgt. Gerald Jones reports three lives saved at Yokota AB, where Japanese workmen were overcome by underground gas pockets and were close to suffocating when an Air Force rescue team — taking a long chance themselves — descended into a pit of fumes to bring them out. Bob Wickley, who made these pictures, was at the base on another story when he walked into a drama that no actor or director could have matched for reality.

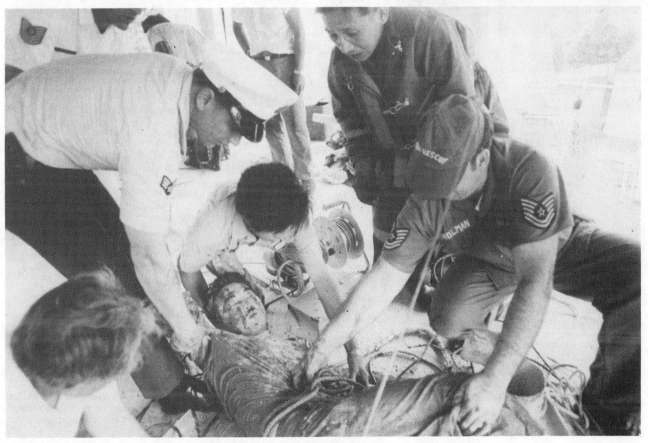

PS&S, Eikoh Goya

ANGRY STRIKERS look like soldiers assaulting a Roman phalanx as they charge the shields and clubs of Ryukyuan riot police outside Kadena AB, Okinawa — a clash that occurred as the All-Okinawa Military Employees Trade Union picketed to protest a layoff of workers on the base. The police said move, they didn't, and a violent scuffle followed. One of the best photographers the newspaper ever fielded closed in and took his chances to get this shot.

The bandit outlasted him. Hiratsuka passed the mandatory retirement age of 60 and had to step down. Kitano succeeded him.

"I am 62 now and my body would not cooperate with my brain," Hiratsuka sorrowfully said Tuesday during the last hours of the long investigation.

He was not at the station at midnight.

What now for the bandit? Authorities say he could be hauled into civil court if he showed himself and sued for recovery of the money. A spokesman for the Nippon Fire and Marine Insurance Co., which had to make good Toshiba's loss, said the firm would file suit against the bandit if he ever turns up. They have 11 more years under civil law to do that.

Many television commentators jabbed at the police with cruel jokes in the last hours and some, as midnight neared, took out stopwatches. One magazine showed the somber composite face of the bandit, in a police helmet, breaking into a wide grin.

But there were no smiling policemen in Tokyo as midnight tolled.

The term "generation gap" was undoubtedly lost on comedian Bob Hope. Seventy years old, he could step in front of an audience full of fans young enough to be his grandchildren and then some — and get the same roar of laugher and drumroll of applause. For 33 years and three wars, Hope gave up Christmas and traveled all over the world, saying "I never left home" because he was always among his own, the audience whose applause he appreciated far more than that of the cover-charge customers in Vegas — GIs. But time and age closed in on Hope, and he was sternly told by doctors that Christmas at home was best for a man of his years. This story was written as a tribute to what was billed as Bob Hope's last Christmas overseas.

THANKS FOR THE MEMORY, BOB

FEB. 4, 1973, BY HAL DRAKE

"Hey, fellas," said a young Marine as a stranger who was no stranger approached, "here comes Trader Corn."

Bob Hope laughed and later said he enjoyed jokes like that better than his own rapid-fire one-liners. He was an entertainer who didn't mind being entertained. He was in his element — among his own. For Bob Hope, the man who would perform before rulers and common citizens all over the world, always said that GIs were his favorite audience.

On that day, it would have been hard to separate performer from audience. Hope wore a steel helmet and camouflage-dappled fatigues that were limp with sweat. He performed gamely and tirelessly, wherever an audience of a few thousand, a few hundred or only a few could be found.

That could have been Da Nang in 1968. If Hope had been freezing instead of sweltering, it might have been Wonsan, North Korea — where Hope and his entourage, including Marilyn Maxwell and Les Brown and his Band of Renown, arrived in late 1950 to entertain American troops as some of them were still fighting to oust Communist forces from the city.

As it was, that exchange between Bob Hope and a group of young Marines occurred on one of the flyspeck South Pacific islands the Leathernecks took during World War II.

Trader Corn — it suggested a well-traveled peddler with a duffel bag full of stale gags. Hope did use one ageless joke — describing himself to three generations of American servicemen as a "chicken first class" — but most of his humor was hilariously topical. At Guantanamo, Cuba, just after Premier Fidel Castro severed relations with the United States and surrounded the politically besieged base with an armed frontier, Hope told a howling crowd of sailors and Marines that he was surprised by Castro's admission that he was a Communist.

"I thought he was an unemployed chicken plucker," quipped Hope.

And that "chicken" bit didn't go over with some of his young audiences — not those who recalled Hope performing within sound of rifle

189

shots in North Korea. Others would tell the story of how Hope, a show-must-go-on trouper, went on with a performance at Taegu after engineers cleared land mines from the site of his makeshift stage.

And there was Hope's self-inflicted close call — the time he was taken out of Yokota AB, Japan, on a jet ride and sleepily asked his pilot what lever he could pull to adjust his seat. The pilot told him — and a moment later screamed frantically as Hope reached for a lever that would have ejected him, sans parachute, at 18,000 feet.

A lot of people might have thought this a foolish and terrifying experience and done their best to keep it secret. Hope thought it a great joke on himself and told it freely — the same way GIs solaced themselves with jokes about misery and terror. This is perhaps the reason that no comic ever touched a responsive chord in GI audiences like Bob Hope.

And yet Hope himself has never worn a uniform except as a courtesy and a tribute. Born in England on May 26, 1903, he was brought by his family to America three years later and was too young for World War I, too old for the second. Safely out of the draft board's reach, Hope chose to travel more than a million miles to entertain young Americans who were displaced by destiny and politics. The airmen with the U.S. 8th Air Force in England knew him. So did the Marines on Bougainville and the infantrymen in Africa and Italy. Bob Hope could show up anywhere there was a hot and dangerous front or a maddeningly dull rear echelon.

"I'll go anywhere in the world," Hope once said — and he and his troupe, which often included songstress Frances Langford, did just that. Bandleader Kay Kyser cracked that Hope deliberately delayed the end of World War II because "there were five or six Army camps he hadn't played yet."

His patter was as familiar as his profile — the sloping nose that made Bing Crosby call him "droop snoot" and was the result of a youthful and unfortunate foray into amateur boxing.

"Were the boys at the last camp happy to see me," Hope might quip for openers. "They actually got down on their knees. What a spectacle! What a tribute! What a crap game!"

Or:

"Glad to be here, fellows. Really was a windy

ride. I won't say it was cold, but I haven't heard from my nose in three hours."

Once out of the war, Hope made some of his best film comedies and went on with a weekly radio show — the same show that had been played before thousands of servicemen during the war years.

When a new war came, Hope was ready. His first trip to Korea came only a few months after Communist troops moved across the 38th Parallel and President Truman ordered American forces to intervene. It was the first of 22 consecutive Christmases away from home — let alone the holidays he had willingly missed one war before.

In Korea, Hope flashed the same kind of "hot coffee" humor that was both warm and bitter. He joked about the things his audiences bitterly cursed but gamely accepted, the heat, the cold and the dust — once telling a group of combat engineers that their road was "the finest I've ever tasted."

And who else could have walked into a hospital ward full of limbless men and announce himself with, "Don't get up for me, fellows." No one but Bob Hope — our Bob Hope.

The 1953 Armistice came and the world took a breather between wars. But not Bob Hope. Servicemen along a silent battleline, or in Germany or Japan, knew him as well as those in Argentina, Keflavik, Baffin Island and Stephenville.

They knew him as a jaunty comic and a smiling, open-handed friend — even as he got older and his tireless manner was often a front. Those who knew Hope away from the stage describe him as a quiet and thoughtful man. "He is not one of those comics who is 'on' all the time," recalled Air Force Maj. Ed Swinney, one of Hope's escort officers.

In 1959, Hope collapsed with a blood clot in one eye — and blithely violated doctor's orders to slow down, working through dizzy spells and ignoring warnings that he could go partially blind. He took his troupe to Alaska that year.

Another war gradually embroiled young Americans — and Trader Corn couldn't slow down or stay home. There came another classic quip that could have only been spoken, without offense, by Bob Hope. Noting that Viet Cong saboteurs had blown up the Brinks Hotel in Saigon on Christmas Eve, Hope told troops at Vinh Long: "A funny thing happened to me when I was driving through downtown Saigon to my hotel last night. We met a hotel going the other way.

"I've never seen a house detective in full flight before . . . I was sent over here to give you live entertainment. Let's keep it that way."

With Hope was the usual entourage of beauty queens who were young enough to be his grandchildren. There was also Brown and old regulars like siren-voiced comic Jerry Colonna — another quiet man offstage.

Of all the entertainers who gave freely of their time and vigor to perform for servicemen, both youngster and elder would recall Hope as the first and the best. Just after the first draft number was drawn in 1940, Hope began playing Army camps — at a time servicemen were something less than first class citizens. More than that, he has always been a passionate advocate of any cause they fought for — the bond salesman and homefront spokesman during World War II, supporter of the controversial commitment in Korea, a hawkish conservative as far as Vietnam was concerned.

Hope's views were his to express, quietly and spiritedly, and to share with all who would listen. Yet he never took to the podium, threw tomatoes or spattered red paint on dissenters. When recently asked in Tokyo about Jane Fonda, the activist actress whose anti-war show FTA was touted as an answer to his own, Hope quietly expressed respect for her as an actress and also for her right to hold an opposite view.

Just as quietly, Hope announced he would "pull it all in" after his 1972 Christmas shows. When he went on from Japan and Korea to Vietnam, Hope added, he hoped to be performing for men at peace.

But hopes for peace had been all but atomized by the time Hope and his troupe arrived for his ninth Christmas in Vietnam. As usual, he had a bittersweet quip — the kind best understood by his favorite audience.

"We came out here prepared for peace . . . Not only did they fail to reach an agreement in Paris, but now they're fighting over the hotel bill."

As usual, as Hope performed at Tan Son Nhut AB, a baseball backstop was a loge seat and a tree served as a grandstand — the same as in 1950, when a soldier at Taejon laughed so hard he fell out of a tree.

Bob Hope's last Christmas with GIs? Hope said "let it be" in a way that touched all listeners. He wanted a peace that "lives and lasts for a long, long time."

What more could be said by a man who has spent more Christmases away from home than any of us?

On Christmas of 1983, Bob Hope — who had rounded 80 — spent his holiday with Marines holding a hostile spur of territory in Lebanon.

A tree grew in Panmunjom
It was a tall and thick Normandy poplar planted by Japanese colonizers 60 years before as a stalk of watershed and attempt to beautify a stubbornly rugged land. The poplar stood as one of the few beauty spots beside this Village of the Wooden Door Inn — this one-time way station for Chinese who stopped on their way to extract tribute from Korean rulers in Seoul. But Panmunjom's most important place in history had been as the site of the 1951-53 truce talks that brought uneasy peace to a troubled peninsula. Out of newsprint for years, Panmunjom made its dark way back into world headlines as blood flowed in what was supposed to be a sacrosant neutral zone. The tree was like a thing alive, a character in a dangerous drama that cost two lives and raised the threat of war.

REDS SLAY TWO U.S. OFFICERS

AUG. 20, 1976, BY GUNNERY SGT. MIKE RUSH AND TAE WON CHUNG

SEOUL — Two American Army officers were beaten and stabbed to death Wednesday at Panmunjom, 30 miles northwest of here, by about 30 North Korean guards wielding axes, metal pikes and ax handles and shouting, "Kill them!"

They were the first men ever to be killed in the Joint Security Area since the Military Armistice Commission began holding meetings there at the end of the Korean War 23 years ago, the United Nations Command (UNC) said. The Armistice Agreement guarantees free movement by both sides within the neutral area.

A South Korean officer and eight U.S. and ROK soldiers were injured in the clash which came as UNC guards were escorting tree trimmers in the area, a spokesman said.

Only one of the injured, a South Korean enlisted man, was hospitalized at the 121st Evac. Hospital in Seoul. His condition and the extent of his injuries were not immediately available.

The other men were treated for minor cuts and bruises and released.

UNC officials said the two American officers died from massive head injuries and stab wounds. Names of the casualties were being withheld pending notification of kin, the UNC said.

It was not certain whether or not military units in South Korea have been put on alert as a result of the attack.

A spokesman for the 2nd Inf. Div., the major U.S. combat unit in Korea which is stationed just south of the Demilitarized Zone, said he knew of no alert being called, but unofficial sources said at least five military camps not far from the DMZ were closed Wednesday and civilian employes were sent home. Such action normally is taken when an alert is called.

The UNC immediately called for a Military Armistice Commission meeting for 11 a.m. Thursday to protest the incident. The Communists often cancel such meetings simply by not showing up.

The attack took place at 10:45 a.m. Wednesday 35 to 40 yards from a UNC guard post at the south end of the "Bridge of No Return" which spans the military line of demarcation. The guard post reportedly was evacuated following the attack.

In a statement released Wednesday afternoon, the UNC termed the attack "unprovoked, brutal murder." A North Korean Central News Agency broadcast monitored by the Associated Press in Tokyo Wednesday evening, however, blamed the incident on the UNC, saying the Communist guards "acted in self-defense."

The UNC guards were escorting five Korea Service Corps — a civilian work force — tree trimmers. A spokesman said Wednesday night the trees are part of the UNC maintenance responsibility in the area and are trimmed whenever necessary.

Two North Korean officers and several guards approached the group and, during a discussion of the work, a North Korean officer expressed no objection to the tree trimming.

The North Koreans suddenly demanded the work be stopped, however, and a North Korean vehicle carrying more guards arrived. There are four Communist guard posts between the place where the attack occurred and the commission meeting rooms.

The North Korean officer who had been discussing the work reportedly told the Communist guards to "kill the UNC personnel" and the guards attacked.

A UNC quick reaction force sped to the scene and the North Koreans scattered.

The North Korean broadcast, however, said the "U.S. imperialist aggression troops with lethal weapons pounced on and beat North Korean guards who had gone to protest that the trees were in (an area) under North Korean control."

The UNC spokesman said he didn't know how the reaction force was armed Wednesday, but that such forces "normally respond to any alert with ax handles."

The news agency said the Communist guards "were compelled to take a step in self-defense," and called the incident "a provocation planned . . . to further aggravate the prevailing situation.

"This was proved also by the fact that the enemy side had kept ready some 100 armed personnel near the spot of the incident," the agency said.

It was not known how large the reaction force was or how many UNC and Communist troops were in the security area at the time of the attack. The UNC spokesman said, however, that "minimal numbers of UNC troops were on guard" since Wednesday was not a meeting day for the commission or its secretaries.

The incident was the second this month along the 151-mile DMZ. Gunfire was exchanged between North and South Korean troops in the central sector Aug. 5, but neither side reported any casualties and each accused the other of firing first.

There have been incidents in the past at the truce talk site but these were the first deaths recorded.

June 30, 1975, U.S. Army Maj. William D. Henderson, then acting commander of the Army Support Group at the Joint Security Area, was beaten and stomped by North Korean guards outside the commission meeting room while a meeting was in progress.

Wednesday's incident came amid a stepped-up propaganda attack against the United States and South Korea by North Korean delegates at the Nonaligned Nations Conference in Colombo, Sri Lanka.

North Korea has charged the United States is planning to invade the North and is "deploying 400,000 troops" along the DMZ.

"War could break out at any moment," North Korean Vice Premier and Foreign Minister Ho Dam has said.

South Korean officials have branded the charges "fabrications."

On Aug. 21, an American armored task force came in under a canopy of helicopters and that tall poplar no longer stood tall. They cut it down.

Fighting a wolf-at-the-door deadline, Jim Lea pounded out this account of how a Soviet Air Force pilot decided to change skylines and brought a valuable, top-secret package with him.

"PLEASE TAKE CARE OF MY PLANE"

SEPT. 8, 1976, BY JIM LEA

TOKYO — A Soviet Air Force lieutenant Monday dove his supersecret MIG25 "Foxbat" jet beneath the radar screen protecting Japan, landed at a tiny commercial airport on Hokkaido, fired a pistol shot into the air, then surrendered to police and demanded asylum in the United States.

Japanese police in Hakodate, on Hokkaido's southern tip, said the plane landed at Hakodate Airport at 1:57 p.m.

The jet, which flies at near 2,000 miles per hour, streaked down the 6,500-foot runway and into an 800-foot overrun, stopping just short of a barrier.

Police said the pilot opened his canopy as crash trucks sped toward the plane, fired a single shot into the air and shouted, "I am a lieutenant in the Soviet Air Force. I want to go to the United States. The plane is a MIG25. Please cover it up and take good care of it."

A police spokesman said the pilot surrendered with no further incident. Police would not say Tuesday, however, where the pilot is being held.

Japanese Foreign Ministry officials here have not yet identified him. However, a United Press International report from Moscow said the foreign ministry has identified him in an official report as 1st Lt. Victor Ivanovitch Valenkov, 29.

There were reports that the Soviet Embassy in Tokyo has asked to talk to the pilot but that the foreign ministry has not allowed him to be questioned by the Russians.

Other reports say the Russians have demanded return of the plane, which U.S. officials called "probably the best interceptor in production in the world today."

The foreign ministry refused to comment on any of those reports, however.

In Washington, State Department officials confirmed that the pilot has requested asylum in the United States and that the request is under consideration.

"We are in contact with the government of Japan," a spokesman said.

Japan does not grant political asylum but has, in the past, allowed persons requesting it to remain in the country until another country accepts them.

The Foxbat reportedly is one of the most advanced aircraft in the world. It has a speed estimated by Western officials at 3.2 times the speed of sound and set an altitude record of nearly 119,000 feet three years ago.

The intelligence-gathering model of the plane reportedly flies reconnaissance missions over U.S. bases in Europe from East Germany.

The Hakodate Airport spokesman said the plane landed on a runway used normally by Boeing 727 passenger jets.

"We normally have 14 flights a day and had to cancel eight Monday after the plane landed," he said.

He said 60 Hokkaido police who were rushed to the airport covered the jet with canvas shortly after it landed.

The landing left Japan Defense Agency officials redfaced.

Agency Director General Michita Sakata reportedly termed it an indication that the nation's "present air defense system is insufficient for planes coming in at low altitudes," and called for a study of the radar net protecting the country.

Agency sources said the plane first was detected on radar about 190 miles northwest of Hakodate at 1:19 p.m., headed toward Japan at more than 500 m.p.h. at an altitude of 21,000 feet.

Two Phantom jets were scrambled by the Air Self-Defense Force from Chitose AB, north of Hakodate, at 1:20 p.m. to intercept the plane. They reportedly warned the pilot he was about to enter Japanese air space but received no reply.

Four minutes later the plane entered Japanese air space and dropped beneath the radar screen. It was picked up once more on radar, but reportedly disappeared from the screens in seconds.

Japanese officials reportedly said after the landing that the nation's radar system is "ineffective for aircraft approaching at less than 300 meters (about 1,000 feet)."

The defector's name was later corrected to Viktor Belenko and Japanese police briefly charged him with illegal possession of a handgun, ownership of which is forbidden in Japan. His aircraft was well taken care of — disassembled and minutely examined before it was returned to the Soviets, who responded by boycotting a Japanese air show. Belenko lives under constant guard in the United States and is said to like the American lifestyle.

This story, from the U.S. Army Garrison-Okinawa Public Affairs Office, provided a comprehensive and readable wrapup of a crisis that lasted weeks into months.

SANTA CLAUS WAS STEVEDORE

FEB. 28, 1977

MAKIMINATO, Japan — It isn't Galveston or Gulfport, but a dock strike at Naha Military Port tied up thousands of tons of cargo and the inexperienced hands of servicemen kept it moving.

About 50 soldiers at a time, along with members of other services, worked 10-hour shifts — hard, all-hours labor without any of the overtime that cushions a tough job for civilian workers.

Near them as they worked were civilian dock workers who set up picket lines outside the gate after negotiations for a new contract broke down in late November.

Servicemen became novice stevedores, not knowing when they would go back to being clerks, mechanics, riflemen or cannoneers.

They lifted and hauled with the best of them, but their biggest burden was inexperience. Stevedoring, they found, was not just a muscle job and required seasoning and skill.

Yet, officials say, 710,000 measurement tons of cargo go in and out of Naha every year — it is the "main valve" for the flow of goods up and down the island.

Going out are things like privately owned vehicles and household goods. Goods coming in include items for unit supply rooms or post exchange shelves. All of that, and a lot of other stuff.

It must all be moved — by amateur hands if professional ones refuse to pick up cargo hooks or pull at winches.

It all started when the civilian stevedores, with negotiations for a new contract underway, prodded management by staging a work slow-down Nov. 20-25.

Brig. Gen. Warner S. Goodwin Jr., Army Garrison commander, knew it would mean a square knot in the movement of cargo. He asked for and got 174 workmen from all four services. By Nov. 26, with tons of goods piled up, they were at work, clearing a lot of it before the port workers began laboring at their normal pace.

But negotiations were on their last legs and the hard-working neophytes were housed in the Makiminato Service Area close to the docks. The picket lines went out and the strike began.

Some jobs couldn't be handed to non-professionals, so the Army imported four crane operators from the 119th Trans. Co. at Fort Eustis, Va. They got here Dec. 10, just in time to join a strange kind of Christmas rush.

One vessel, a container ship, bulged with things like turkeys and Christmas trees. It would be a barren Yule for a lot of families if the cargo didn't come off fast.

Seeing themselves as Santa Claus for the whole island, the amateurs went in with spirit and effort and got it done.

Up to three ships at a time were docked and sometimes 700 tons a day were unloaded — a total of 85,000 measurement tons in their month and a half as dock workers.

After a time, professional help arrived — the 155th Trans. Co., 188 men and women, flew from Ft. Eustis and landed at Kadena AB Jan. 9. They were rushed into the effort to keep Okinawa supplied.

Learning long before that the Army is full of surprises, the pros had been pulled out of their homes and flown thousands of miles to a cultural third dimension. They responded, their commander said, with a shoulder-to-the-wheel eagerness because this was for real, not just handling dummy cargo in dull training exercises.

"It's the best thing that could have happened to the 155th," said Capt. William Sawyers.

The cargo was moving, smoothly and well — those crane operators, Sgt. William Tolbert, Spec. 5 Wayne Johnson, Spec. 4 Richard Bettencourt and Spec. 4 Robert Graham, had been followed by many others.

One last time, Jan. 17, the amateurs were told to report again — to hear words of thanks and tribute from Goodwin and senior commanders from other services.

The story isn't over yet.

Three of the crane operators are still working and the 155th is hauling cargo 7,000 miles away from home.

And it's still moving.

The strike was inevitably settled. The professionals went home and sore-muscled amateurs filed back into offices — to catch up on weeks of laid-aside paperwork.

As neatly written as a detective thriller, this crime story from the 8th Army Public Affairs Office in Seoul was one of the best seen in years — all fast action and factual movement, with a satisfying, good-guys-win ending.

"THAT BLACK MARKETEER MADE ME MAD"

JUNE 5, 1978 BY LOUIE JONES

SEOUL — An Army sergeant turned under-cover detective to smash a black market ring dealing in medical supplies — with the help of his noisy mother-in-law.

Staff Sgt. Bobbie Hutson is wearing the

Meritorious Service Medal for his work and a black marketeer identified only as Mr. Kim is wearing the drab clothes the Republic of Korea issues to unwilling guests of the state — all because he made Hutson mad.

Hutson, NCO in charge of the Receiving Section of the 6th Medical Supply Optical and Maintenance Supply Unit on Yongsan South Post, told of how Mr. Kim approached him at his offbase home with a long "shopping list" and what Kim thought was an attractive bargain. If Hutson would steal a whole bunch of medical supplies, including albumin serum that cost the Army $27 but retailed in Korea for $300 a bottle, they could split some lucrative profits.

It was Mr. Kim's glib approach that tripped him up. He told Hutson that all GIs were cynical money grubbers who would dump their ethics for a dollar.

"That really made me see red," Hutson related. He went to his boss, who called the CID. Investigators told Hutson to play along with Mr. Kim and get the goods on him.

That wasn't easy. Hutson at first couldn't get Kim to come into the house — only the back porch steps, where he was hidden from view and CID agents couldn't get a picture of the two talking together. So Hutson got his whole family of noisy females into the act.

"I had the girls constantly interrupt us and make so much noise it was impossible to talk," Hutson grinned. His wife's mother, Mrs. Alvina Fiechtner, was visiting the family and added her voice to a distracting chorale of noise.

Hutson and Mr. Kim finally fled to the roof of the house, where hidden agents easily got their pictures. Hutson had already nodded along with Mr. Kim's deal.

"There was a shipment coming in at Osan Air Base," he said. "I normally don't personally pick up deliveries. I had to get a license to drive the truck down to Osan to pick up that one."

Hutson picked up the supplies and then Kim, who was glibly confident as the truck was heading for his brother-in-law's place in nearby Suwon. But he got nervous as two ROK Army jeeps and a green sedan began trailing them.

"Of course," Hutson related, "he didn't know about the agents hiding in cardboard boxes in back of the truck."

The next thing Kim and Hutson knew, they were staring at pistols and both were brusquely hauled away, along with a confederate who had been waiting for Kim.

"Kim didn't know, until I went down to the office where he was held the next day, that I was one of the good guys," Hutson said.

He's proud of the medal, but insists that wasn't why he did it.

"He made me angry by stereotyping U.S. soldiers," Hutson said of Mr. Kim. "Only a handful of GIs actually get involved in the black market."

Tech. Sgt. Butch Wehry, one of the most capable Army journalists in the trade, has served in both public affairs offices and as anchor man of the Stripes bureau in Seoul. His fine hand is evident in this story of a television commentator who used a bizarre but commendable approach to get the attention of his audience.

RUSSIAN ROULETTE — LIVE, IN FULL COLOR

JULY 3, 1978 BY BUTCH WEHRY

SEOUL — An Air Force technical sergeant has been commended by the U.S. Forces Korea Safety Office for doing something that ordinarily would have landed him in front of a psychiatrist — playing a kind of Russian roulette.

What's more, Don Novak did it before thousands of witnesses, getting nothing but the grateful thanks of safety officials who think he may have saved a few lives.

Americans in South Korea know Novak as the personable forecaster who comes on American Forces Korea Network (AFKN) every night with the "Weather or Not" show. On one of those, Novak wanted to make a dramatic presentation of the dangers of ondol — the under-the-floor charcoal heating system that is found in many offbase homes and has killed a large number of people, Korean and American, with deadly carbon monoxide fumes.

A tragedy had touched Novak's own life, and he wanted to give viewers something to remember.

He did.

Novak told of how he sat up into the early morning hours trying to come up with something that would carry sharp and telling shock value. Over "wake up" coffee, a flash of inspiration hit him.

It was like something out of the film "Network."

"I called the safety office," Novak said, "and asked them to get me a gun."

As the show started that evening, Novak sat with a .38-caliber revolver in front of him. He picked it up, swung the cylinder out and chambered a round.

That, Novak said, was like closing a window in an ondol-heated home and giving fumes no place to drain.

Another round clicked in as Novak told of how carbon monoxide, which shuts off oxygen to the brain and kills most ondol victims while they're asleep, seeps through a leaky floor.

Playing it like Peter Finch, Novak put five bullets in a six-shot revolver, thumbing in a round every time he made a point — and then spun the cylinder. But he didn't play it out to a gruesome finale by putting the pistol to his temple and squeezing the trigger.

"This is what happens when you use ondol," Novak told his viewers. "It's like playing Russian roulette."

That was during the winter months. While 90 GIs were treated for monoxide poisoning, there were no deaths. Safety officials believe Novak's chilling performance might have had something to do with that. He got a special award in a ceremony at Yongsan.

Novak said his heart was in that particular show.

"I had a very close Korean friend who died from carbon monoxide poisoning."

In his spare time, Wehry is a novelist and student of Korean history — parlaying both into "The Yobo," which was recently published and is enjoying a brisk sale.

The out-of-nowhere hero, it seems, is never out of fashion — the guy who happens along, saves a life, shrugs it off and rides away like the Lone Ranger. Jim Davis, a public affairs office reporter, treated this one just right.

NO BIG THING, CAPTAIN — JUST A LIFE

AUG. 18, 1979, BY JIM DAVIS

SEOUL — An Army captain who saved the life of an apparently drowned Korean woman, then went to lunch in his wet fatigues, simply can't figure out why everybody is making such a big thing out of it.

"I just did what I thought needed to be done," said newly-arrived Capt. Paul A. Baldy, who heads the United Nations Command Honor Guard. "Frankly, I'm a little puzzled about all the fuss being made over this."

But a very impressed Gen. John A. Wickham Jr., UNC Commander, gave Baldy an Army Commendation Medal and Kim Yeon Hee, whose life he saved, likely thinks he's the greatest.

Baldy was on his way to a luncheon at the 8th Army Religious Retreat Center when, 100 yards from the gate of the center, he was flagged down by a frantic soldier he described as a ". . . visibly upset GI."

"All I could understand from the soldier was that a girl was drowning and nobody was helping," explained Baldy, "and when the GI

197

pointed in a general direction, I hopped out of the car and started running. Not really knowing where I was going, I asked the soldier if the pool was to the right. He nodded, so I just bore right."

Baldy scrambled over a 20-foot embankment, climbed through a hedgerow, scaled a cyclone fence and landed in the parking lot of an apartment complex below the retreat center. "When I looked up," recalled the captain, "I could see what looked like 50 people pressed against the fence up the hill at the retreat center, all looking down. Closer to me, were about 26 Koreans gathered around a swimming pool, staring into it. When I reached the pool, I could see the body of a Korean girl lying on the bottom in about 10 feet of water."

Realizing no one was doing anything to help the girl and that she obviously had been underwater for several minutes, the 28-year-old West Point graduate went straight into the pool — still wearing his fatigues, boots and hat. "She'd already taken in a lot of water and was very heavy," he said. "I couldn't bring her up on my first try so I came up for air and went back down."

The Honor Guard Commander brought her up on his second try and had to get her out of the pool single-handedly. Baldy then searched for signs of life. "I couldn't find any vitals at all," said the captain, shaking his head, "no heartbeat, no pulse, no respiration . . . even her pupils were dilated. I remember thinking, 'Dear God, I hope she's not dead.' But, at the same time, considering how long she'd been under, I suppose I felt she really was."

Nevertheless, Baldy went quickly to work applying closed heart massage, a technique he'd learned during Special Forces training. "After about a minute, I began getting a faint pulse," he said. "So I switched over and began giving mouth-to-mouth resuscitaton." For the better part of half an hour, the captain alternated between mouth-to-mouth resuscitation and closed heart massage until an ambulance that someone had called arrived.

"Her vital signs were getting stronger and she seemed nearly conscious a couple of times," reported Baldy, "but the last I saw of her was when I helped them put her in the ambulance. I just hope she's OK."

Miss Kim is alive and back home now.

Baldy went to the luncheon in his wet fatigues.

He arrived in South Korea three weeks ago and calls Pensacola, Fla., home.

Chet King, a Navy journalist with a send-me-in-coach spirit, came to Pacific Stars and Stripes with impressive credentials — a photojournalist trained at Syracuse University, which turns out the best. King quickly showed he had ability to back his diploma, turning out this poignant gem about an abandoned pet and the man everybody hates.

PITY THE POOR DOGCATCHER

JUNE 23, 1979, BY CHET KING

My name is Horosha.

That means tramp, drifter, hobo, bum.

I had a home once — loving hands, regular meals, even a place to sleep.

Now, whenever I see people, I have to cut and run.

Like that Japanese lady the other day. There was nothing to eat on base, so I trotted off to pick up whatever I could find. There, in an open garbage can, were the appetizing remains of somebody's feast — bones with a few nibbles of pork on them.

They were delicious while they lasted — until the lady came out, hurled a rock and called me "gomi hiroi."

That's the lowest kind of scavanger.

I really don't deserve all this. A fellow has to eat.

I haven't known where my next bite was coming from since the family left — the people who picked me up from their neighbors, gave me to their kids, friendly little people who were nice, even though they did twist ears and pull fur.

Well, I got older and bigger, and it was time for them to go home. It would have cost a bundle for them to take me along, almost as much as they'd have to pay for one of the high and snooty breeds in a swank pet shop. I wasn't lucky enough to be born valuable.

So they turned me loose. Just like that — left me nothing but an empty dish on the back porch.

It's a hard way to go.

I have to stay out of everybody's way — even a nice guy like Hajime Masumi . . .

Masumi is 56, the first and perhaps the last man to be hired by Americans in postwar years and given a distinction he has often thought he could do without — the job title of dogcatcher.

It cost him something.

He's disliked, and doesn't like being disliked.

Japanese call him inu koroshi — dog killer.

But work was work back in 1949, when Americans enforced the law on and off base and had understandably narrow attitudes about a lot of stray dogs running around.

Masumi got a net that was bigger than he was, and was the only dogcatcher who could go into places like Yokohama's rowdy Chinatown, where he was as welcome as a storm cloud over a barbecue. He was often chased by angry citizens, sometimes forced to run into doorways and barricade himself.

Still, life was pretty good. His pound and his home were near an area that would later be called Yamashita Park. American officers lived there, and he got generous payments of sugar, coffee and cigarettes for taking care of people's pets. He tasted Coke for the first time there, and gave the dogs conscientious care — fed them C rations.

Those, he reflected, at least had homes — not like the 20,000 strays he would send to be gassed, electrocuted or put away with lethal injections.

Masumi feels badly about that.

Every year, he finds time to go to a local shrine, where combined Shinto-Buddhist ceremonies are held in remembrance of dead animals.

Then it's back to work he still doesn't care much for, but performs with proficiency and competence. He introduced use of a wire lariat to snare strays, flipping it from the cab of a truck and bringing them down with the flair of a rodeo star.

People started calling him "Cowboy." Kids usually like cowboys. They don't like Masumi. Nor do housewives who rail angrily as he takes some whimpering orphan off to certain death.

"I'm just doing my job," he protests. But nobody sympathizes with a dogcatcher.

Masumi has been bitten many times, often with onlookers cheering for the dog. He threatened to quit, but never did. This is a job somebody has to do in a place like the Yokohama Navy Housing area, where strays are bad news.

A man he knows well, Chief of Security Yoshio Takita, insists dogcatchers mean well and has a nod of sympathy for Masumi.

"Our number one priority," Takita insists, "is to find homes for the puppies we pick up. We're not evil. We just do our job."

That's what all the dogcatchers say — guys like Takashi Ozawa, who worked for the Navy as a forklift operator until an economy cut left him jobless. He wanted to be a security guard, and got a crafty nod from an interviewer. Yes, there was such a job open, but it involved work as a dogcatcher — only part-time, of course.

It didn't work out that way. Sweeping up strays is all Ozawa does now, around the Yokohama, Yokosuka and Nagai housing areas.

He hates to ride or walk around his own neighborhood.

People still shun and whisper about an inu koroshi.

But, as both dogcatchers see it, they wouldn't have a job if people would only do right. Instead of dumping their pets into a wilderness of lawns and trash dumps, they ask, why don't they bring them over to the pound at Bayside Courts? That way, they'd at least have a game chance of winding up with loving owners again . . .

This is Horosha again. Listen to them, will you? For as long as it's going to last, this is an awful way to live.

Masumi retired in 1982, not at all unhappy to leave his hated trade. King left Pacific Stars and Stripes to become one of the Navy's most noted and accomplished photogaphers, digging his own bunker-photo lab with the Marines in Lebanon.

From time to time, rank amateurs send in wonderful, first-rank stories — such as this Navy wife's Kipling-like account of how she conquered a formidable mountain and muzzled a mythical dog.

THE FANGS OF THE FIERY DOG

JULY 7, 1979, BY PATRICIA J. REILY

Deploring the day a scrap of paper told me I would reach great heights, I paused and gasped. The fiery dog was nipping at my haunches, threatening to sink his teeth and drag me back down the tallest mountain in Southeast Asia.

I would never, I told myself, open another fortune cookie.

The purple, cloud-webbed crest of 13,455 foot Mt. Kinabalu, the granite crown of Kinabalu National Park in Sabah, Malaysia, was still far ahead. The steep trail grew sharp rocks and a thick tangle of bushes and vines.

I recalled what I had read in a book that quoted Alexander Dalrymple, one of the first Englishmen to write about this mountain in the days another flag flew over Malaysia. He came on like Kipling as he told about the natives and a height that was supposed to be a locked vault against women, with the spirits keeping a watchdog on leash to drive them away.

"The Kadazans have very many whimsical religious tenents; paradise is generally supposed to be atop of Keeney-Balloo . . . guarded by a fiery dog who is a formidable opponent of the female sex."

I silently cursed that fiery dog.

But I couldn't dissolve in tears of exhaustion and turn back. Not in front of three Kadazans, one of whom was our guide. Not before my husband and two other men, one of them an admiral.

If I dropped out now, after only three hours, those porters might wisely smile and nod to legend. I would be woman weak, demeaned forever to the flatlands.

I had to make it, for myself and someone else who had climbed above those clouds long before . . .

There were four people in our party as we left Subic Bay NB in the Philippines and caught a plane out of Manila, bound for Kota Kinabalu and that mountain that was the summit of Borneo, the highest between the Himalayas and Wilhelmina in Irian.

I had no feelings this would be a larkish jaunt, even though that fortune cookie had vaguely told me I would reach some kind of summit. When we got off at the small airport, I was tempted to keep my comfortable seat and go on to Kuala Lumpur, where shoppers had more fun.

But there we were; myself and my husband, Lt. James D. Reily, along with Lt. Cmdr. Craig Vanderhoef and Rear Adm. Robert B. McClinton, who commands Surface Group Western Pacific at Subic, where my husband and I were rounding out a tour.

Our airport limousine was waiting — a game and scrappy Land Rover that would take us to the park and the great mountain that was like a rugged altar. I had that usual postflight urge for a shower and dinner, deferred for three stressful hours as the Rover slammed over dusty miles of corrugated road.

As we got out, finally, my husband moaned that he felt as if he had been massaged by a drunk, 300-pound sumo wrestler. I was thankful my teeth had stopped rattling.

But I was suddenly glad I had come. This park was prehistorically beautiful, even in the dark. A comfortable cabin and a delicious curry dinner awaited us, along with a shower and comfortable beds.

The sight we awoke to was awesome. The mountain was the color of blue steel, the summit cowled by fleecy clouds. It rolled up abruptly from the hills of Sabah, those kneeling vassals that were far below the spearpoint peaks that gave beings on the flatlands an exaggerated sense of its height.

My legs suddenly felt rather frail.

Our three porters met us at the lodge, all of them rugged and wiry Kadazans who live around the mountain. We each donned three small packs and the porters pulled on larger ones as lightly as bundles of feathers.

The trail was an open air hallway through a confetti-like multitude of flowers on hanging draperies of exotic green, with delicately-spun spiderwebs hung with droplets of dew that glittered like jewels. It was only scenic, not at all stressful — yet.

My legs shook and the fangs of the fiery dog

nipped at muscle and tendon. I didn't dare complain, haunted by that Englishman's telling passage. I trudged along, without a bleat of pain, resolving to carry a torch for womanhood up that summit.

I had to, finally, keeping that faro dealer's face as I casually mentioned that my legs hurt.

He didn't wonder, the admiral said, suggesting with a helpful chuckle that my size 8 paratrooper boots might be too heavy. I took them off and switched to tennis shoes. My bootless feet felt like wings. The porters, a silent lot, nodded their approval.

By midday, the trail wound through a ghostly, twisted woodland and we were engulfed in clouds, surrounded by dead scenery that looked like the setting for a Frankenstein movie. I could see why the Kadazans regarded the mountain as a fearful and spooky place inhabited by dragons and the spirits of the dead, along with that pesky dog. I was climbing, climbing, lightly borne by the realization that I was passing through clouds, leaving them behind.

But that watchdog was still on the job.

He made repeated lunges, tearing at leg and shoulder and back. It got harder to breath in thinning air and we frequently stopped to let our hearts slow down. We took desperate gulps of water and I flopped down to rest, if only for a few minutes.

The steepness, at first insidious, was now sharp and obvious. We were out of the ghostly forest now, struggling over barren fields of granite that had pygmy shrubs and dwarf trees struggling through the rocky flesh of the mountain. In the distance, there was a speck of life — Sayut Hut, shelter and landmark, the doorway to the grail. It told us we had come 12,500 ft.

We would spend the night there and assault the crest in the morning. In an hour, the mountains would lock away the sun. The porters lit a fire to cook their rice. Vanderhoef gave them a cigar and some chewing tobacco and their faces, before as expressionless as profiles on mahogany figurines, lit up with grateful smiles.

They pondered over these rare and puzzling delicacies, then ate the cigar.

We were up before dawn the next morning, lightly bolstering ourselves with tea and nothing else. We set out in the dark and the trail was bald granite, occasionally webbed with lengths of climbing rope. The thin air made me gasp and halt every 15 steps, until my heart stopped its labored thumping.

As the dawn broke, we were picking our way over jagged rock and daylight was slowly rolling over the South China Sea and the Malaysian plains. A flag fluttered on a peak about 40 feet away.

Breathing was painful, taken in hoarse and labored wheezes. The last gasp was joyous. We did it — stood with McClinton as he planted his flag with the flourish of a great explorer.

The sherry came out again. We made a toast to Sir Hugh Low, who first stood where we did in 1851. I raised my glass to Miss L. Gibbs, the British Museum botanist who in 1910 became the first woman to outdistance the fiery dog.

She wasn't denied, and neither was I. That beast was somewhere down on the lower heights, yipping furiously.

Coming down, I was to discover, was worse than going up. I wasn't driven by a challenge, but a vision — a tall cold drink and the comfortable chair on the porch of the park cabin. But that had to wait until I put away 12 hours of blissful sleep.

Since the longtime American presence in the Far East began, U.S. military authorities have had a woeful time convincing some young troops that they are accountable to foreign laws that mirror none of the rarefied liberalism of Berkeley or Los Angeles, particularly those laws that forbid the use of illegal dream-makers — drugs. This story, one of many, was aimed at driving this point home.

IN JAPAN, KEEP OFF THE GRASS

OCT. 9, 1979, BY HAL DRAKE

TOKYO — Cornered by a palm tree, surrounded by the restful shade of a ginkgo grove, the plain building looks like a small factory or a temple whose believers disdain finery and comfort.

Inside, a policeman talks like a priest.

"You should not seek happy feelings in drugs," says Eiichi Nakazawa, softly and thoughtfully, "but happiness in yourself, your work, your family, your life."

Nakazawa not only practices his philosophy. He enforces it.

Thirty-four Americans, trading uniforms for jail garb, are doing time in Japanese prisons for trampling Nakazawa's beliefs — solidly backed by laws that mirror none of the tolerant Western thinking about some drugs.

As chief of the Kanto-Shinetsu District Narcotics Control Office, his quiet manner never changes as he moves in on malefactors — often for misuse of a pungent herb the president of the United States has asked Congress to legalize.

Arguments that marijuana isn't harmful and should be legalized are lost on Nakazawa.

And the Japanese National Diet, which passed the harshly strict Cannibis Control Law in 1948, hasn't budged an inch toward liberalizing it.

Not in Japan. Not at all.

An American on Okinawa, jailed for trafficking in long-stemmed leaf, put it this way: "The Japanese think that if you use a drug, any kind of drug, you're some kind of criminally insane. They really mash it on you."

A recent American visitor to Nakazawa's office, listening to his priestly talk, recalled what an Air Force legal officer had said to him a few years before.

"No there's nothing wrong with the way they look at grass. It's their way — a different attitude, a different philosophy, a different way of looking at things. We have too many long-haired laddie bucks who come in here thinking, when they (unprintable) up, Japan should magically transform into America, just for them. Well, I'm here to tell you it doesn't work that way, not in this country."

A U.S. Forces Japan legal official at Yokota AB points out that, under the U.S.-Japan Status of Forces Agreement, the Japanese have first call on any offender arrested on or off base — and may very well elect to prosecute him, like a Japanese, in a Japanese court.

Nakazawa nods along with that.

His business, he says, is slow.

Some 1,200 people are imprisoned in Japan for drug violations. Nakazawa says 408 of these are foreigners. Not a few are GIs, one doing a total of seven years on two convictions.

While that's fractional compared with other countries, Nakazawa feels it's still too much. He thinks Americans, in particular, should launder their attitudes about grass, hash and a lot of other things before they step off a MAC plane or go through a customs turnstile.

"They do have this loose attitude," he said, his voice still as soft as poured sand. "It's big trouble for us. Americans are not exceptional — nor are Frenchmen, Englishmen, Africans, Australians or any of the others.

"It's very annoying when they break our laws."

Now the priestly policeman takes out the exact text of the law that has remained unchanged for 34 years.

Anyone who uses, transfers or possesses marijuana, which in Japan goes by its botanical alias, cannibis — up to five years.

Anybody who imports, exports or cultivates same — up to seven.

Nakazawa allows that, in Japan, there is some minority dissent of the Cannibis Control Law, adding with a wry grimace that much of it comes from offenders — artists, models, stage and film stars, other critics who frequently get bad reviews in court.

"In America," Nakazawa says, "drugs are rampant. Here, not so much. But what you would call minor, we call major. I know, in America, that prisons would bulge if you arrested everybody caught with drugs. Here, no such drugs are grown or produced. And our prisons are not so full. We have plenty of room."

Nakazawa becomes quiet and thoughtful again.

"Why can't people find happiness in themselves? Work hard, live well and don't expect heaven to come down to you."

But, his visitor offered briefly, Japan will certainly modernize that old law in some way. Why, in Oregon, marijuana is legal and in California, those who want it are allowed a small quantity for their own use.

Nakazawa seizes the point triumphantly.

"There you are. If it's completely harmless, why have only two states legalized it? We know it's harmful, we're sure of it."

Reporter Ron Hatcher wasn't an easy man to tell no. Tipped off on a terrible happening, he talked his way aboard a helicopter, made his diplomatic way around pushy and irritable guards and wrote a first-hand horror story about an awful event.

"PEOPLE WERE SCREAMING ALL AROUND ME"

OCT. 21, 1979 BY SSGT. RON HATCHER

CAMP FUJI, Japan — Typhoon Tip triggered a freak fire here Friday that killed a Marine and injured at least 41 other persons, according to Marine officials.

The dead man's name is being withheld pending notification of his relatives.

At least seven Marines are listed in serious condition at Yokota AB, said a U.S. Forces Japan spokesman.

The dead man was to have returned to the United States Wednesday, according to one of his friends.

Lt. Col. John Redgate, commander of a battalion landing team at Camp Fuji, said about 5,000 gallons of gasoline burst free from a rubber storage bladder and ran through the camp before being ignited by a stove.

Redgate said the bladder was secured behind a retaining wall, but rains from the storm eroded the wall and allowed the bladder to slip. As it slipped, he said, hoses were torn free, spilling the gasoline.

The "fuel farm" is uphill from the Quonset huts where more than 1,200 Marines were huddled against the raging typhoon.

"I've been in this business 23 years and have never seen anything like this," said a Navy medical officer from Atsugi NAF.

Navy Hospitalman Fred Odom barely escaped the fire to assist in treating the injured. He said he was lying on his bunk writing a letter when he heard an explosion and saw the bunk across from him burst into flames. He said he jumped out of bed and saw flames spreading over the floor. "I looked back and my bunk was on fire," he said. "I made it out the door by running across the tops of bunks."

Odom said many of the Marines had barricaded doors and even nailed some shut because of the typhoon's winds. He said many of the men crawled out windows to escape.

"People were screaming all around men," he said, "and when I got outside there were guys wrapped in blankets rolling in the mud."

Hospitalman Timothy Terrell said fire was shooting out the windows of the huts "like torches." He said he saw naked men outside, crying, their bodies smoking and skin falling off. "When we tried to get them inside the aid station," he said, "many refused to come in out of the rain. I guess the rain felt soothing to them."

Terrell said one of the injured men pleaded with him, "Please, Doc, take care of me, take care of me. Don't let me die."

Redgate said 14 Quonset huts were destroyed and several damaged in the fire. He said the camp laundry was destroyed and the camp exchange and gift shop were damaged. Damage estimates were not available.

Redgate said 39 Marines were injured in the fire along with two Japanese employees. A United Press International report said three Japanese were injured in the fire.

One of them, Sumiko Yuasa, told UPI, "I would have been killed if a U.S. Marine did not rescue me."

All of the injured were taken to hospitals in Gotemba, a city near the camp, for initial treatment. They were ferried overnight to Yokota AB aboard Navy, Army and Air Force helicopters.

Medical supplies and personnel were flown in to Yokota and Fuji from several U.S. bases in Japan, said Redgate.

He said a burn treatment team was on its way from Brooke Army Medical Center in San Antonio, Tex. Redgate said the team would determine which patients would return with them for treatment in San Antonio. Brooke is the military's major burn center.

Japanese firemen fought the blaze in the rain and 50 mph winds for more than two hours, said Redgate, before it was brought under control. "It was under control," he said, "but it wasn't put out. It just had to burn itself out."

The buildings were still smoldering at daybreak Saturday.

Tip, the strongest typhoon to hit Japan in 13 years, left 25 persons dead as it swept Japan. Among the dead was a Marine swept to sea when Tip brushed Okinawa. Typhoon Tip had winds gusting to 115 mph.

The rains destroyed at least 138 houses and flooded 20,000 others. In the metropolitan Tokyo area train service came to a virtual halt, affecting some 4 million commuters. Tokyo's largest buildings swayed in the gusts.

Tip knocked out 550 roads throughout Japan and ruined 45 bridges. Five ships sank in heavy seas off the coast.

The final death toll was 14. Staying on the story, Hatcher told of how hours of sleepless, dedicated work at the Air Force hospital saved many lives.

Diego Garcia, British-owned and American-occupied, is another one of those faraway sandtraps valuable only because it became "strategic" — an outpost in the Indian Ocean, a chesspiece against hostile presence in the Arabian Sea and the Persian Gulf. It's a lonely, not-much-to-do place — unless you're a game sort who can make his own kind of music. Navy public affairs journalist Jeff Powers told of one unique way sailors on Diego Garcia banished seven-shades-of-grey boredom.

HERMITS AWAY!

MAY 27, 1980, BY PETTY OFFICER 3RD CLASS JEFF POWERS

DIEGO GARCIA — Every day is sunny and the track is always fast here as they claw their way to the finish line — and no slow or timid hermits need apply.

Seabees race hermit crabs — the small, snail-shelled crabs that might have been kicked aside or stepped on in another time. It's another way for people here, in the middle of the Indian Ocean, to keep from feeling like the Ancient Mariner on a raft of sand.

The idea was the brainstorm of Seaman Thomas Dougherty and Petty Officer 2nd Class Larry McCroy, Naval Mobile Construction Battalion 133, who were stationed together earlier in Alaska.

"It was too cold for crabs up there," said Dougherty, "but to relieve Alaska boredom we used to train mice and race them. It's no different here, so we decided to do something and began using hermit crabs.

"They're fascinating little beasts.

So far Dougherty's little beasts have won him five out of nine matches.

Dougherty claims to have found a herd or flock of the crabs. "Over 150 of them in the woods just off the shoreline, all bunched together, and big, too," he said.

Crabs, in a way are like people. They are not all born racers.

"It begins with a selection process," said Dougherty. "First you pick out about 20 promising candidates."

Next the trainers try to weed out the timid and slow hermits with trial runs. They look for fast and consistent crabs.

Once the field is narrowed down to three or four potential champs, the training begins.

The experienced crab trainers on the island tie strings to the crabs and take them on long daily walks.

According to Dougherty, the right food is a very important part of the crab's training.

"While in training they are restricted to eating only coconut and chicken meat. A few trial runs, then at last they are ready for the big race."

An eight-foot circle is drawn in the coral sand. The crabs are placed under the official coffee can in the center of the circle. For the next 90 seconds the Seabees gather around in absolute silence as the crabs calm down and come out of their shells.

The can is raised and the race begins.

"The interesting part," said Dougherty, is watching 45 guys holding back the noise for the length of the race, even though they want to scream. Noise will make a crab go back into its shell, and it might be the one they are riding on.

"It's a good sport," said Dougherty, "because they are very unpredictable and size doesn't determine the winner.

"More than one race has been decided by a crab that made his break a minute before show time."

Once the winner crosses the finish line, all the crabs are released and the process begins again.

For generations, editors have persistently drilled novice reporters on one hard-driven point — tell the story straight, without getting flowery or emotional. A simple recital of the facts can hit with tremendous impact. This 8th Army Public Affairs Office story — telling of how two lives were shattered by a small-profit robbery — upholds that old lesson beautifully.

LESS THAN A DOLLAR

MAY 4, 1980

SEOUL — Two soldiers will be imprisoned and thrown out of the Army for robbing a Korean taxi driver of less than $1, military courts have ruled.

Spec. 4 Matthew W. Brown and Spec. 4 Charles F. Prather were found guilty by separate general courts-martial of conspiracy and robbery, charges brought after both confessed to taking a taxi driver to an alley and robbing him.

The courts found that the soldiers, both from B Company, 304th Signal Battalion, caught the taxi at Wonju Train Station and told the elderly driver to take them to a residential area in that city. They turned him down an alley, the court found, and he saw it was a dead end.

Prather held the taxi door shut while Brown hit the driver on the head with a rock. The cabbie got away, and the two got his coin purse, which contained less than $1 in won, the courts found.

Brown got 20 month's hard labor, plus a dishonorable discharge, and Prather was sentenced to 10 months and a bad conduct discharge. Both lost all pay and allowances and were broken to private.

Stories like this lie dead in the dust of history — until persistent and tireless reporters get the dust of research on their hands to dig them out. This story, written by Sunday Magazine Editor Frank Sugano, involved his search-and-probe eyestrain — and the piece-by-piece digging of Hiroshi Chida in Tokyo, Staff Sgt. Steve Davis in Seoul and Master Sgt. Dwight Trimmer in Washington.

THE GHOST BATTALION

NOV. 8, 1981

More than 600 Korean residents of Japan fought with U.S. forces in the Korean War, but their contribution has been ignored because they were part of a "ghost battalion," says the former officer who commanded the battalion.

Surviving Koreans say that out of 644 volunteers, 159 were killed. The names of the dead are not officially listed anywhere, they say, and because the men were never recognized as authorized personnel, they have never been credited with serving in the war.

"We joined U.S. forces in Japan and landed in Inchon on Sept. 15, 1950. Yet after our time in

205

the war was over, the Americans said no relationship exists," said Bae Kwang Do, one of the volunteers who went to fight after North Korea invaded the South on June 25, 1950.

About 40 volunteers later joined the Republic of Korea (ROK) army, Bae said, but the rest were absorbed into U.S. units. Length of service ranged from four months to 2½ years.

Jimmy Gozawa, who retired from the U.S. Army's reserves as a lieutenant colonel, said he was a first lieutenant in October of 1950, when he was assigned to command the Koreans. He said he led the "ghost battalion" for less than a month, after which it was ordered disbanded.

"They were put in American uniforms and trained by American officers at a camp near Tokyo (Camp Drake)," Gozawa said. "Then they landed at Inchon, where the American officers left them, explaining that someone else would take care of them. That's where the foulup happened. Nobody did.

"So there were these Koreans in American uniforms, with American-style dog tags — but tags without numerical designation, only names.

"There was talk of sending these people back to Japan because they made a nuisance of themselves. But what the heck! They had no unit designation, no officers, no pay — nothing!"

Gozawa said it was by chance that he was in the chief of staff's office when the subject of the Koreans was being discussed.

"Some officer said, 'Send the bastards home,' and that's when I stepped in," Gozawa said. "I said, 'Send them to the front and let them fight like hell. And then parade them up and down Tokyo and Osaka and everybody will be happy.'

"The general said, 'OK, you're the unit commander.' "

Although "never dreaming that I'd end up with them," Gozawa — a Japanese-American who spoke Japanese, the adopted language of the volunteers — took the men and began training them.

The commander of the 3rd Logistical Command, Brig. Gen. George Stewart, was desperate for a solution, Gozawa said, because he had never been able to find out who these men were or who had sent them to Korea.

"The general got in touch with the Korean government, and it had no information on the men," said Gozawa, 65. "And of course they had

nothing to do with the Japanese (who were still under U.S. rule). When the general got in touch with GHQ (Occupation Army headquarters in Tokyo), nobody wanted to talk about it.

"Where did the authority (for these men) come from? Certainly not from Gen. (Douglas) MacArthur's headquarters. That's my personal feeling, because if this had been the case, these men would have been given a unit designation.

"Obviously they came by military order, because they landed in ships officered by Americans. But who authorized them?"

The Department of Army confirmed that a group of Koreans residing in Japan was recruited by American forces and transported to Inchon in mid-September. The Army also confirmed that the group trained for a brief period under Lt. Gozawa, 3rd Logistical G-2 staff.

The Army, however, said the Koreans were recruited for the ROK Army, with consent of the ROK government given through representatives in Japan. But when the men arrived in Korea, the ROK army would not accept them, the Army said.

"That explanation utterly stinks," Gozawa said. "That may have been the purpose, but these men never were told that."

Bae said that more than a month after their arrival in Korea, the volunteers at Inchon — about 400 of them — were asked if any wished to join the ROK army.

"About 40 of them said yes, and they were transferred to ROK units," Bae said. "But the rest of us wanted to stay with U.S. forces and fight together like the 442." (The 442 was the much-decorated Japanese-American unit that fought in Italy during World War II.)

Bae, vice-chairman of the Korean Veterans Association of Japan, said he assumed that the men were not recruited for the ROK army. If that were the case, he said, why did the U.S. give them the option of serving in the Korean army, and why did ROK then accept the men who wanted to transfer?

"On June 27 (two days after the invasion), nine of us in our group went to volunteer at GHQ," Bae said. "I cut my finger and signed a letter in blood. The others did, too. It was just a letter saying that we wanted to fight in Korea. They (U.S. military officials) didn't accept it."

Later, GHQ and authorities representing South Korea authorized the Korean Residents'

PS&S photos, Don Gunn

WAKE OF A RIOT is shown in the flotsam of helmets dropped by demonstrators as police at the depot cleared the way for the trucks that carried the tanks. The snake-dancing "demos" got a riot-act warning, ignored it and came apart as a storm wave of *kidotai* crashed in and broke their line.

TWISTING AND WEAVING like a break dancer, a student demonstrator heckles Japanese riot police in front of the gate of the U.S. Army's Sagami Depot outside Tokyo, where leftist students and Japan Socialist Party members demonstrated against the movement of tanks — bound for Vietnam — to Yokohama Port. The tanks moved and so did the protesters.

A SELF-DECLARED HERO in his own country, North Korean President Kim Il Sung gets short shrift from more than 300,000 South Koreans in Seoul Stadium. They burned Kim's effigy to protest an unsuccessful attempt by a communist assassin to kill President Park Chung Hee. He missed the president but killed First Lady Maria Park. Park was later slain by his own intelligence chief.

JAPANESE WACS stand tall after marching with the precision of Rockette dancers in the Japan Self-Defense Force parade in downtown Tokyo. A tank commander snaps off a salute to his prime minister as citizens of all classes watch a procession of firepower roll by.

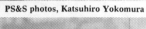

PS&S photos, Katsuhiro Yokomura

209

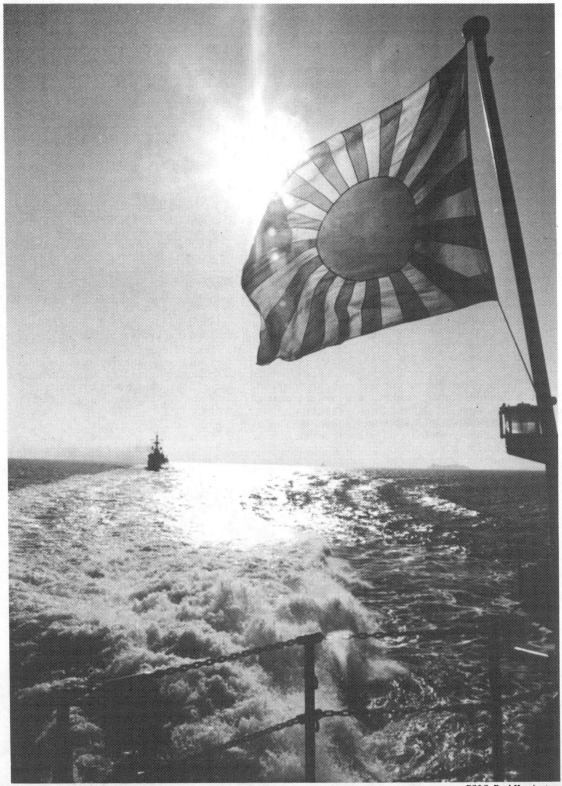

PS&S, Paul Harrington

RISING SUN FLAG, once an instant target of American guns, flies from the stern of a Japan Maritime Self-Defense Force ship, years after the JMSDF was started with castoff American warships. The Japanese build their own now, and deploy them with impressive grace in naval reviews, such as this one in which the flag meets the sun near Sasebo NB in southern Japan.

PS&S, Ken George

BROKEN AIRLINER is surrounded by rescue craft and a floating ramp for workmen after the Japan Air Lines DC8 fell short of the runway at Tokyo International Airport and crashed into Tokyo Bay, killing 24 passengers in one of Japan's worst domestic air disasters. Investigators said that an emotionally disturbed pilot reversed engines while making an approach to land.

THICK SNOWFALL in Tokyo gives a temple roof a white cowl and dresses the barren branches of a birch grove, giving the city a fragile scenic touch that was gone as the sun broke through. Evergreens stand like umbrellas with bent stems, making the picturesque best of a rare event in the Japanese capital.

AN EMBASSY SEIZURE in Iran meant hard work for 7th Fleet sailors in the Indian Ocean — the Gonzo Station that meant weeks away from home and a deferred Christmas for thousands of sailors who launched warplanes and were a meaningful presence in an important area. Warplanes stood like sheathed daggers on the carrier Midway — ready to be drawn if the worst thing happened.

PS&S photos, Ken George

213

LITTLE SAILOR waves anxiously to daddy from dockside as the Midway returns from a long cruise — a scene that will be repeated often because the Midway is the John Henry of the 7th Fleet, the steeldriver that is constantly at sea and always at work. One home-from-the-sea sailor lifts an infant daughter who is timid about the abrasive bush on his lower jaw.

PS&S, Chip Maury

PS&S, Ken George

214

SOLEMN FACE of former Prime Minister Eisaku Sato, who governed Japan during the difficult Indochina War years and concluded with the United States the agreement that returned Okinawa to Japanese control, is banked by mournful black bunting as an honor guard and thousands of citizens gather in the Budokan, an indoor stadium, to pay their last respects at his funeral. The face of rage shows outside the stadium as police grapple with a man who attacked Prime Minister Takeo Miki, jarring a dignified ceremony.

PS&S photos, Hideyuki Mihashi

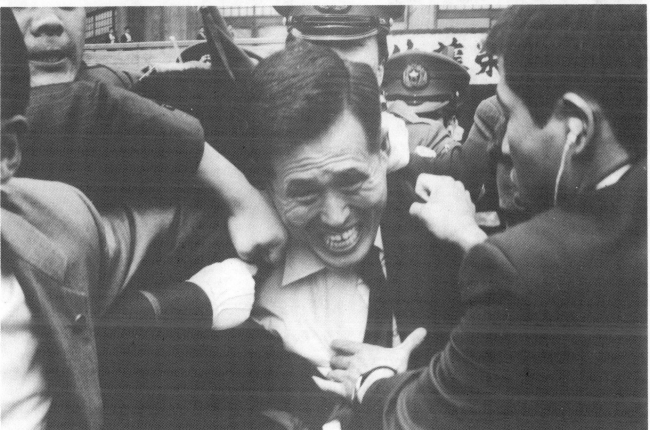

STREETS BECOME RIVERS full of fast and deadly current as a typhoon smashes the central Philippines and raises roof-level flood waters. Old and useful friends in need — the U.S. Navy's Beach Master Unit at Subic Bay NB — came out with barge and gear, ready to give swimming refugees a handhold and pull them aboard. Hundreds of lives were saved.

216

Union of Japan (Mindan) to serve as a recruitment center, Bae said. On Aug. 7, he signed up and went to Camp Drake for several weeks of training. He said he and the other volunteers were told that they "were entrusted to U.S. forces."

Many of the men had had previous military training as members of the Japanese military. (Korea was under Japanese rule from 1910 to 1945.) Bae was conscripted in 1943, as were three other Koreans interviewed.

Their military experience was a big reason why U.S. forces accepted them, said Bae, 57. "I met some GIs at a bar in Kobe," he said. "They said they'd defeat the North Koreans and be back drinking at the bar in a week. They never came back.

"That's why I think the Americans took us into the Army. The situation was very bad early in the war. The situation also was very confused, and that could be why our status was confused.

"At the time we asked for clarification of our status, but the commanding officer (of each unit) would always say, 'I'm sorry. It's up to the Pentagon.'"

The invasion had taken the United States and the ROK government completely by surprise. By Sept. 15, the day of the landing at Inchon, the communists were in control of Seoul and had moved south. By Oct. 13, when Gozawa arrived at Inchon, Seoul was again Southern territory and the United Nations forces were crossing the 38th parallel.

Gen. Stewart, meanwhile, was wondering what to do with the Korean volunteers, Gozawa said.

"When I was given command of the unit," Gozawa said, "I gathered the men together and said, 'Hey, we've got to call ourselves something. What'll it be?'

"They said, '3-1,' because to a Korean March the 1st is a great day for them. (On March 1, 1919, millions of Koreans in Korea and Japan rebelled against Japanese rule. The uprising was put down at a cost of 28,000 lives.)

" 'All right,' I said, 'we'll call ourselves the 31st Independent Combat Battalion — until such time we are told we cannot use that designation.'"

According to Army records, that time came on Nov. 2, when the battalion was ordered disbanded.

"My men formed in front of headquartes at 8 o'clock, as they did every morning for training," Gozawa said. "But when they heard the news that the unit was disbanded, they refused to move. They stood at parade rest until 11."

"We waited to hear the order directly from the general," Bae said.

"I guess the Army finally realized it couldn't have an 'independent' battalion among its units," said Chung Chun Moon, who was the liaison between Gozawa and the volunteers.

"They wept," Gozawa said. "They just couldn't understand why they had to disband. They had been training and wanted to go the front. Their frustration was something so beautiful you just can't imagine."

Army records do not refer to them as members of the 31st Battalion. Instead, they are variously known as ROK Volunteer Group, Korean Training Group and Provisional Training Group. Nor do records state why the battalion was disbanded, only that members were subsequently attached to various units of the 3rd Logistical Command, including quartermaster and ordnance units.

Bae went to Byupung, near Inchon. Chung and Chi Suk Chin went north to Pyongyang.

Another veteran, Im Sung Sop, was never attached to the 31st Battalion. He was one of 200 Korean volunteers who, in mid-October, boarded ships for a second landing at Wonsan.

Im, 59, pulled two photographs from a scrapbook. They were of himself as he was 31 years ago. In one, he is standing with a GI in front of snow-covered trees. In the other, he is with another Korean volunteer.

"We were encircled by Chinese, but we broke out," Im said. "He (the other Korean) was killed. His name is Kim."

Volunteers who served with Kim later informed the man's family and helped pay for the funeral. As "unauthorized" personnel, Kim merited no acknowledgement from U.S. forces, the Koreans said.

"We feel like ghosts," Bae said, "because our names aren't registered anywhere."

He referred not only to the volunteers who served and died in the Korean War, but also to those 170,000 Koreans who served as members of the Japanese military in World War II.

Bae said that at Yasukuni Shrine, in Tokyo, 2.5 million names — of those soldiers who died serving Japan — are written in stone. The list includes 20,000 Koreans, but their names are not recognizable as Korean because, in 1935, Japan ordered that all Koreans adopt names that can be read in a Japanese way.

"I've been in two wars," said the 54-year-old Chi, who was in the Imperial navy at age 17. "And I never got paid for fighting in either."

But Chi's bitterness is not directed at the United States. "The GIs were nice. They knew we didn't have any money," Chi said. "At Thanksgiving and Christmas, they would always come around and give us beer and we'd celebrate."

"I love the Americans. Many of them died to save our country," said Chung, 57, a writer who has had 10 novels published.

But he added, "All I want is a ribbon showing that I served. I want the U.S. military people to share the feeling that we fought together."

Like the others, Chung keeps papers that document events elsewhere denied. The white bond has yellowed, and creases obliterate words here and there. "This is my history," Chung said.

One of his papers reads:
"SUBJECT: Commendation

"To 1st Lieutenant Chung, Chun Moon

"Upon your departure from this unit for return to Japan, it is my desire to commend you for your excellent performance of duty while a member of this unit . . .

"(Signed) William T. Carney
"Captain
"Commanding"

Bae said none of them seeks compensation or benefits — only recognition. They want their names in U.S. Army records, he said. "It's a matter of roots," he said. "We fought to save our country. It is a fact that we fought — wherever we belonged. It should not be neglected or ignored."

The Army said: "Army officials have verified through a research of the National Archives that a group of Koreans commanded by then Lt. Gozawa trained for a short time with the 3rd Logistical Command and were then disbanded.

"Names of these individuals are unavailable."

"We didn't do a damn thing as a battalion," Gozawa said. "We didn't shoot at anybody. We didn't get a chance.

"But these people were all heroes because they were ready to die."

By the early 1980s, the military services had cracked down on all traces of the permissive, free-wheeling 1960s, bringing illegal drug use under heavy and constant fire. But some residue of a dangerous problem still remained, as shown by this short and frightening story.

LSD STAMPS HIT KOREA

MARCH 21, 1982 BY HELEN WEBB

TOKYO — Postage stamp-like children's stick-ons laced with LSD have been found in Korea, according to U.S. Forces Korea public affairs officials.

The stick-ons are approximately one-half-inch square and come in strips of 100. They have a white background with a red picture of the cartoon character Snoopy, but there may be other designs, officials say.

Military officials elsewhere in the Pacific were checking to see whether the stick-ons had appeared in their areas.

The stamps are used to camouflage drug contraband. However, they could possibly fall into the hands of unsuspecting victims, so the officials are urging caution.

"The stamps are the type of novelty item a child might lick and stick on a notebook," the Seal Beach, Calif., Weaponeer newspaper said in an article earlier this year. "They are about half the size of a postage stamp" and sometimes come in 1-by-2-inch strips.

The officials in Korea warned that even handling the stick-ons could be dangerous, since the drug can be absorbed through the skin.

Pictures on the stickers found in California include Mickey Mouse, Goofy, a red Oriental dragon and a golden spade.

Stickers with Mickey Mouse cartoon drawings were discovered on Okinawa in November 1980.

"The LSD does not have to be eaten to have an effect," the California newspaper said. "Licking can cause severe brain damage or even death, depending on the size of the individual."

Anyone finding stick-ons resembling those described is urged to contact the nearest Criminal Investigation Division, military officials said.

The Navy stressed that drugs were out and so were sailors and Marines who ignored no-trespassing signs, sternly posted at the limits of the law. To nail offenders, they put drug enforcement on rotors and wings. This account of a raid that fell like an avalanche came from a Marine public affairs office, and was remindful of a scene out of "Blue Thunder" or "Apoc-alypse Now."

"WE'RE NOT EVEN SAFE AT SEA!"

MARCH 25, 1982, BY STAFF SGT. RALPH ROSE

CAMP S.D. BUTLER, Japan — Twenty-six arrests were made when a Navy anti-drug team that included three drug-sniffing dogs swooped down by helicopter onto the amphibious transport dock Duluth and the amphibious assault ship Tripoli while the two ships were at sea, military officials said.

Ken Anthony, special agent in charge of the anti-drug team — a unit of the Naval Investigative Service's Criminal Investigation Division — said he overheard one sailor exclaim: "Holy cow, we're not even safe at sea!"

Those arrested included Navy men and Marines. One hundred twenty grams of marijuana, with a street value of $3,600, were confiscated, officials said.

Maj. Gen. Stephen Olmstead, commanding general of the Third Marine Amphibious Force, and Rear Adm. George Schick, Seventh Fleet Amphibious Force commander, invited the anti-drug team aboard the two ships to help shipborne commanders make drug inspections.

They did so to help dramatize the chief of naval operations' and the commandant of the Marine Corps' push for the elimination of illegal drug use in the two services, officials said.

The drug inspections affected an equal number of sailors and Marines who were part of an amphibious task force that steamed into White Beach Saturday to pick up more Marines and gear bound for Team Spirit '82 in Korea.

The anti-drug teams and dogs searched work and berthing spaces of the ships during an inspection which lasted nearly eight hours.

Twelve persons on one of the ships were tested with a urinalysis kit after preliminary evidence indicated the 12 were possible drug users, officials said. Testing indicated that nine of the 12 had used drugs.

The urinalysis tests were conducted by a urinalysis testing expert who was part of the anti-drug team.

"We like to think that our team operates under the old motto 'Hit 'em where they ain't,' " provost marshal Lt. Col. Herbert Winston said of the anti-drug team's role in the drug inspections. "And we're going to do everything we can to let drug users know that we're serious about enforcing the commandant's (and chief of naval operations') new drug policy."

Drug stories, once so plentiful that all but the most important were discarded, became rare in Stripes pages, and not only because of a "tighten-up" policy by the military. GIs were subject to local laws in foreign ports. In Japan, possession of marijuana meant a prision sentence and in Singapore, drug offenders faced penalties that ranged from flogging to the death sentence.

Korea, the Land of the Standdown War, is still ruggedly demanding and meanly cold — a crucible in which thousands of American troops, some of them from the warmly reasonable climate in Hawaii, face an annual ordeal called Team Spirit. It's all there, the feeling of slogging through the thaw or battling through a blizzard — everything short of being shot at. Don Tate, who had covered the Indochina War as a Scripps-Howard newsman, was no command-post reporter as he took on Team Spirit — which he saw as a tribute to the fortitude and expertise of professionals who soldiered for a living.

AMERICAN GRUNT '83

APRIL 15, 1983 BY DON TATE

Bugles, the sound of crazy bugles from the hills ahead . . . smoke, gunshots, fires burning. Bravo is all spread out leading the advance across the rice paddies, firing as they go . . .

They were up at 3 a.m. Hasty breakfast, gummy swallows in the dark, gulp, gulp. What was it? Who knows. Soon the enemy is firing from the hills across the paddies . . . and as light breaks, Bravo is firing back . . . sweeping forward . . .

They are practicing the art of advancing by fire and maneuver . . . of squads leapfrogging squads, platoons protecting platoons, of not wandering around and getting lost, or not shooting each other in the back in the heat of battle, of maintaining the momentum of the attack. . . .

They come trudging under heavy packs into the paddies. Here comes one in his eager dogtrot. Here comes another far from eager, stepping gingerly on the ice that cracks and plunges his boot into ice water. Another stumbles over the stump that everyone else has avoided, losing his helmet . . .

It's hard-going across the terraced paddies. Icy, slippery dikes high as your chest or head have to be gotten over by men carrying weapons and big loads on their backs . . . then, over one dike, it's down into a frozen or half-frozen paddy . . . then up and over again. . . .

Men falling, getting up . . . all the time firing and listening to shouted orders by Captain MacDonald and his sergeants. . . .

"From a wedge . . . Move toward the objective . . . Second, dammit, where are those machine guns? Jammed? Jammed, hell! Do any of those 60s work? Fire those 60s! Fire those weapons!

Suddenly, the machine guns on his right flank start clattering and MacDonald cheers.

"Straighten up those flanks!" a sergeant bawls over the hopping of the guns.

"Second platoon drive on!" MacDonald yells, waving them forward.

Then he's on the radio. "Fitch . . . Fitch . . . this is Big Mac. What kind of enemy sitrep have you got? Over . . . Say again . . . again . . . That's a roger. That's a good copy. Over."

Incessant bugling ahead from the enemy's hills . . . bunch of bugle freaks up there . . . little blips of light flickering as they fire . . . all kinds of estimates of enemy strength coming, but basically the Blue is fighting delaying actions with small units while its main body retreats toward the Han . . . this is one battle of many, involving thousands of troops on both sides.

"I need one element to drop rucks and go forward . . . the other clears the low area."

Troops crunch ahead through the snow and ice, up hill, down hill, on the road, off the road, then back into the paddies, jug, jug, slop, slop across a stream, boots breaking through ice into running water. . . .

Out front, walking point, leading the whole show, is Cpl. Wes Goldman of the Do-it-Again Squad. Carrying so much gear — chemical suit, ammo, poncho, entrenching tool, shelter half, tent poles, sandbags, chow, canteens, etc. — and studded with weapons, he looks like a walking armaments factory.

"I'm tired," he says. "I'm tired and cold. But it's OK. I'll make it. Cause we're kickin' ass and takin' names and that's it . . . Only thing I don't like about it so far is a lot of people getting cold. I lost one man last night. Last night was cold, man, cold.

"But the worst thing . . ." Goldman says, breathing hard, half tripping forward, ". . . is that we didn't get attacked last night. I was really irritated about that. . . ."

The bugling has stopped. The shooting has stopped. The Blue is again retreating into the endless hills, with Bravo and the battalion pursuing on foot.

Manny Sanchez, 20, of Tucson, Ariz., feet soaked, hunkers down to change socks.

Tim Creighton, the machinegunner, crouches by a dike cradling his M-60. He says he knows he got about nine or ten of the enemy.

"I got 'um for sure. Right now, I don't feel cold. It was real cold this morning. But this is great. Once I start moving and get into action, I forget about the cold."

Nearby, another young troop can't say the same. He lays back, wet-dog shivering, boots off, bluish feet up in the air, while men try to warm them up.

"You don't have any feeling in them at all?" they ask assistant machinegunner Alton Sanders, 18, of Hornwall, Tenn.

"Not much, not much. . . ."

Sanders will be going to the rear, at least for a while.

"Graham is down!" comes the shout.

Another man down to the cold out in the paddies, and medics rush to his aid. Most of these casualties, after a warm-up in the rear, will be back out here humping.

And that's what it's going to be this day . . . hard humping . . . intermittent battles . . . then more bull labor . . . hardly time to get cold . . . dreamers of pushbutton warfare pushing one leg after the other . . . legs and backs challenging big snow and mud-sloppy hills. . . .

At 2:30 p.m. an enemy chopper rips by overhead. Everybody peels off the road and hits the ditches . . . the chopper keeps going and disappears over a ridge.

At 2:45 p.m. Bravo's on a snowy road between two hills when the cry of 'Gunship! Gunship!" goes up "Here it comes! Here it comes!"

A Blue gunship, nose down, comes blowing out of the sun blur, whap-whap-whapping down the road, low-leveling straight down the road toward men sprinting off left and right. . . .

"Fire team leaders take charge!" MacDonald yells . . . as the gunship strafes the road, and Bad Company is handing it back in a terrific racket of muzzle flashes, guns jumping all over their shoulders . . . as the gunship bellies upward ("that's the time to get them," someone is saying, "when they're low and slow") and disappears into afternoon sun speckles. . . .

Bad news for Bad Company . . . the gunship knocked off eight — seven wounded and one zapped (according to the controllers, they didn't disperse fast enough) . . . and got away clean.

Four of the eight are from the Do-it-Again Squad, which, says Goldman, will just have to get more men and do it again.

On the march again . . . going up a big one, 1,700 feet to the top, up a narrow, winding dirt road all turned to slush and mud . . . deep ruts and gashes where wheels have been . . . Not much wisecracking now . . . all your breath is for breathing. . . .

This is infantry . . . the marching becomes hypnotic, boot following boot, each man looking for a firm spot to step, ankles twist, men stagger, lose their footing, going up, up, a couple of grunts slips a 100 feet down an incline and are helped back up in one piece. . . .

Others wobble from fatigue . . . radiomen with their heavy equipment go down and are helped up . . . but they're all back up and still humping . . . this is what they came for . . . the testing . . . and they are getting it. . . .

At the top . . . they have defeated the hill . . . one grunt comes staggering up, eyes rolled back in his head, weaves around and is caught by someone as he starts to fall . . . But he's soon back up, taking in the great scenery all around. It's white on white, little humps of hills growing into bigger hills swelling into mountains . . . beautiful . . tell that to your feet . . . "Let's go, Bravo . . . saddle up . . ." And it's down the other side. . . .

At 5 p.m. still going . . . another long march . . . men exchanging glazed looks, but still striding out through the snow and mud mushing underneath, which will soon be frozen solid. . . .

Again the sound of many boots moving, almost hypnotic in their rhythm . . . climbing into the high country again, the cold air hitting harder, the sun has melted behind a mountain and now the boots are moving like a locomotive in the dark, through snowy slop so deep it's like wading in a swamp, every step now loaded with menace, grunts stumbling and cursing softly, equipment, rattling, a rifle banging against a tree, men blowing hard, taking big, sucking breaths under their rucksacks cut into shoulder . . . this is what they came for . . . and they are finding it. . . .

After their little hike in the mountains, with the temperature plunging, Bad Company finds at the end of the trail a shortage of C rations and sleeping bags ... a man pulling a rolled-up shirt from his pack finds it frozen stiff and bangs it across his boot like a pipe to loosen it up ...

Grunts knock away the snow and rocks in the dark, and huddle close together under ponchos, mustering up all their body heat and survival instincts ... somebody jams a boot in somebody's gut ... and that's OK ... it's all Ok ... it's another golden opportunity for the bad ones to see how bad they really are ...

Morning breaks out with thunder on the left ... gun flashes ... many smoke puffs rising ... the hammering of automatic weapons from the ridgeline to the northwest ... they're shooting down Bravo's throat ... Bravo is scattering and scrambling ... that's the trouble with making war in the high country, whoever gets the highest spot wins ...

Or do they? There's confusion ... it's a Korean Blue Force firing at Bravo, and the Blues are not sure whether they have Bravo trapped, or should they — the attackers — retreat? Bravo is not sure who's dead and who's alive ...

The Blue controller speaks no English and Bravo's speaks no Korean, so the outcome of this battle remains in doubt while language barriers are overcome ... It is finally determined that the Blues were in error for trying to slay Bravo, that they must retreat and Bravo will continue its advance ...

While the general scenario of these military exercises is known, the specific events, battles, and so forth are not usually known down at the grunt level until they happen ... and sometimes problems of timing, language mixups, un-cooperative weather, uncoordinated grid coordinates, mechanical breakdowns, bad roads, occupying the wrong hill in the dark, and other small confusions get things to happening on their own ...

There's another real casualty ... a Korean soldier attached to First Battalion is so cold he can't wake up ... hypothermia ... even after a big fire has been going near him for an hour, and medics working over him, he's still terribly groggy and just wants to sleep ... and stays behind as Bravo moves forward ...

Slowing through the goulash ... up another slope ... maybe the meanest in the mountains ... but it's no sweat ... because something's happening to Bad Company ... and the captain puts it into words, "We're getting stronger and stronger ..."

You can see it in the faces and the way the legs move ... Maybe it's the weather, it's not warm, but it's warmer ... and that's a sun up there ... not just a littly runny-egg sun, but true sun ... there are even beginning to appear patches of earth and grass where a man can sit and not get his pants soaked through ...

Or maybe it's a little something more than the weather . . . On top of the hill, taking up hasty defensive positions, watching an enemy battalion winding down the road far below, MacDonald says it again . . . "Everyday we go, we get stronger . . . Now I know we can do whatever we gotta do . . ."

What Darwin Dinkins from Brooklyn is doing is sitting beside a deep-dug ex-enemy fighting hole and struggling to get his boots off . . . What Randy LaBelle of Massena, N.Y., is doing is just sinking down into that hole and falling instantly asleep . . . he's been getting about three hours a night . . .

Overhead, somebody's jets circle and dippety-dooda around . . . suddenly, there's this quick silver streaking from behind, swept-back wings going over, banshee howling through your head and down your spine . . . but it's unclear whether he's friend or foe . . .

Down here, Dinkins sings softly as he gets those grungy boots and sodden, miserable socks off (out here brains are fine, but feet are beyond compare) . . . a look of ahhh . . . near ecstasy floats over his face as he pulls on dry ones . . . then he smiles and leans back . . . Dinkins knows how to live . . .

Then, humming pleasantly . . . "Nobody knows the trouble I've seen . . ." he heats up some C-ration spaghetti, which is "terrible" when eaten cold, but "devastatingly fine" when hot, much to be preferred over common "grenades and rocks (meatballs and beans)," which are for "peasants . . ."

A peasant nearby is looking oddly down at his own hands, strange, dirty things, all nicked and taped with about a pound of Band-aids, and laughs . . . as he tosses away an empty tin of grenades and rocks, and seizes hold of his favorite field dish, the irresistible sliced peaches . . . holds the can up like a glass of beer . . . and slurps it all down hardly stopping to breathe . . .

Half down in another hole a couple of grunts can't help laughing . . . "Year," says one, banging crud off his boots, "before I got in, I kept hearin' all 'bout this push-button war . . . like all we have to do is sit around pushing on these little buttons, heh, heh . . . but, Jack, *where* are the buttons?''

No time to look for them now . . . Bad Company's on the march again . . . then, rounding a bend at the top, there's a brief halt . . . and men stare down what they have come up through . . . they're bone- and muscle-tired, but they know they're kings of these hills . . .

Strange sounds start coming from throats, get louder as unit passes unit . . . "Uhhh . . . uhhhh . . ." one unit challenges . . . "Ahoooa . . . ahoooa . . ." responds another . . . whoops, grunts, growls maybe never before recorded, not for tender ears . . . Someone starts to sing . . . "I may hurt and I may cry, but I know damn well I won't die . . . Cause Bravo leads the way . . ."

Down the long mountain road they go, Bravo leading the way . . .

They are down in the river valley now, a few miles from the Han . . . it's drier, warmer, the snow's mostly gone, the humping is a piece of cake, and there's only one problem . . . Today Bad Company dies . . .

Or at least a bunch of them . . . because it's in the plan, the scenario. Bravo is to be airmobiled across the river, inserted behind enemy lines, virtually surrounded, then forced to retreat . . .

Ugly retreat . . . back across the Han. For proud Bravo it's all backward from here on . . . because they've got to lose, it's in the plan. They, after all, are the Orange . . . the aggressors. As a controller says, "It's too bad, but they're on the wrong side, we're going to have to attrit the hell out of them. . . ."

Many in Bravo will fall . . . but paper losses are not blood losses. Taking the zapping out of war is like taking the burn out of fire, the cutting out of a knife. There's a certain lack of adrenaline rush, the heart doesn't pound as hard . . . when you know those muzzle flashes can't really do it to you . . .

Three decades after a brusque exchange of signatures stopped the shooting along a spur-shaped wedge that would become known as the Demilitarized Zone between North and South Korea, the face of the truce village at Panmunjom had changed — but too little else. A Navy admiral gamely tried to negotiate with a fugitive killer. United Nations and Communist guards still exchanged looks of hostility and suspicion over the border between two worlds. Yet it all had to be recalled and told . . .

TRUCE WITHOUT END

JULY 27, 1983, BY HAL DRAKE

After 30 years, what hath peace wrought at Panmunjom?

There is, still and always, the Joint Security Area, the settlement atop a plateau and between two worlds. The shabby little tent town was not supposed to last beyond six months after the Korean War Armistice was signed on July 27, 1953.

That was three decades ago Wednesday, and Panmunjom — the Village of the Wooden Door Inn — has never gone back to being the peaceful farm hamlet that fell in the first minutes of the Korean War. The tents are gone; Panmunjom has been paved over and prettied up, with pond and pagoda. It is attractive — and tragic, because it's permanent.

Pablo Picasso's Peace Pagoda — where an American general named William Harrison and a North Korean field marshal, Nam Il, exchanged signatures in a ceremony that lacked the dignity and permanence of Appomattox or Reims — is long gone. A taller one towers above the bayonet-wound boundary between North and South Korea.

The Military Demarcation Line. Outside, it is a concrete curb crossing the ground and running into the stucco wall of the Armistice building.

Inside, it is a microphone cord strung across the exact center of a green felt-covered table.

It slashes through the Joint Security Area where representatives of the United Nations Command, the Korean People's Army and the Chinese People's Volunteers still thrust and parry over the longest unresolved armistice in history.

Violations are frequent. Words and charges, however, have replaced bullets as ammunition fired at the Military Armistice commission meetings.

So it was one recent day, when an American with the seafaring name of Rear Adm. James G. Storms III left Seoul, the world of comfort and reason. His spotless Navy whites, to be worn for the last time at Panmunjom — he has since been relieved by Rear Admiral F. Warren Kelley — would look out of place on that northward plateau, where truth was smudged and reason was stained.

The old command headquarters at Yongsan has a changeless facade of brick raised during Japanese colonial days. It is short-haircut, flawless-crease country.

Under five flags, honor guard troops, some of them Gurkhas who carry the deadly and distinctive kukri knives, drill on the gritty parade ground before the newest and most handsome building — the refrigerator-white United Nations Command ROK/U.S. Combined Forces Command Headquarters.

Afternoon crowds will pour into the Moyer Recreation Center to take theater-in-the-round cushion seats and watch a soapy serial called "Ryan's Hope," piped onto the wide screen by American Forces Korea Network.

White-haired, well-cast in his role, Storms is empowered to sit flush against North Korea and argue face-to-face with an enemy who despises him.

On the way to Panmunjom, Storms has time to reflect on a career that is a year younger than this truce without end.

Before he first put on a uniform in 1954, Storms was an NROTC student at Rensselaer Polytechnic Institute in Troy, N.Y.

"As a matter of fact, I worried . . . whether I was going to get to finish or not. There was a thought, when I was a junior, of commissioning everybody and sending them off. I was looking for a commission, but I also wanted to finish my college education . . ."

Now, after years of staff job and ship command, he finds himself in the breech at Panmunjom, which was supposed to fall rooftop by tentpole so long before.

In his job for two years, Storms will mark his last time here today before moving on to Pearl Harbor.

Will this last meeting be a double echo of his first? Will he be compared to the thief who denies he steals chickens and holds up a duck's foot for proof? Or will he be the "thief who calls stop thief," the imperialist harbinger of the war plague?

The Communists called for this meeting, and it promises to be nothing more than the usual hollow drone of Hate America. Any day between the 33rd anniversary of the beginning of the war and the 30th marker of the truce is an important square on the Communists' propaganda calendar. Each is penciled off for purposeful invective.

Panmunjom does not look like a crucible. Located dead center in the Demilitarized Zone, a 4,000-meter buffer that separates the two Koreas, Panmunjom rises gracefully above a gone-to-seed wilderness. Beauty marks installed by both sides dot the site.

At the southern approach is a large pond the shape of a trampled Valentine, spanned by a stone bridge beneath the Freedom House complex — a tile-topped pavilion of many colors. It is the head above one shoulder that is the Korean Red Cross Liaison Office and another used as a lounge for the joint duty officer who daily exchanges documents on truce matters with the North Koreans.

On the northern side, a two-story building that is a formidable and ponderous piece of political architecture takes up most of an evenly planned rise, overlooking a guard tower-pavilion that is of berserk color. Americans call that one the Ice Cream Parlor.

The meeting place, a house-divided split by that line, is as plain as a Wisconsin Grange Hall, with gable-like doorways north and south.

The concrete and speaker-cord boundary might as well be a 14-foot wall because Panmunjom is no longer truly neutral. Officials and visitors are not allowed to freely wander north or south — not since Aug. 18, 1976, when two American officers supervising the pruning of a poplar were assaulted by North Korean guards and axed to death.

Storms seats himself at the long plank between two political planets, flanked by two South Koreans, an Englishman and a Filipino — a representative sampling of the powers beneath the blue and white United Nations flag. Across from Storms is North Korean Maj. Gen. Han Ju Kyong, a lean and angular man whose sharp profile is like the edge of a halberd.

The only sounds are those of chairs scraping and feet shifting — the hissing-fuse calm before the political storm.

Han sits only a few centimeters from the country he fled as a fugitive.

Outside, as U.N. soldiers are stiffly mute at parade rest, those on the other side of the border curb are changing the guard. In uniforms that are of Wehrmacht tan with red armbands and lapels, they march in a Red-Square-on-May-Day step that is a long, flat stride and pompous stomp.

"Some of them try so hard to look mean," a bystander chuckles.

Always, they wear the same glum grimace, sometimes with an unconscious flexing of calloused, ox-goad fists, honed into weapons that could make bonemeal of a human frame. On the chest of the closest one — a large man with a rifle-bore stare — there is a small badge, a Mao-cult cameo of North Korean President Kim Il-sung.

Inside, Han leads off with charges that have no crisp stride at all. The elephant-walk aria moves at a tiresome drone, first in Korean, then English and finally Chinese. Not a day or minute of "Anti-U.S. Struggle Month" is to be wasted as Han fires off familiar charges — the UNC makes a frequent and dangerous habit of violating North Korean sea and air space and the United States is stockpiling illegal firepower in South Korea, "increasing by several times" the armament of "the South Korean puppets."

All of this, Han charges, ignores and violates an Armistice provision that petrified weaponry at the 1953 level and forbade anything new.

Storms hears it out as he'll tell an interviewer he always does — "with a clenched jaw." The game is to look patient and dignified in the face of falsehood — listen as Han misses not a note in the play-it-again propaganda concerto, "military provocation" followed by "criminal acts" and all the rest.

The admiral replies no and takes the cover off his counterfire, calling any buildup south of the line a measure-for-measure response to the arms North Korea began acquiring "before the ink was dry on the Armistice Agreement." In the face of this, the UNC long before suspended that status quo.

There is no emotion on Han's Rushmore face as Storms goes on, accusing the man who has just accused him. As a white-tuniced Marine aide steps up to an easel, the admiral tells of a UNC guardpost raked by Communist fire and the first signboard-sized panel falls away. A crew-served multi-bore weapon of the sort that delivered the fire is revealed. The aide's pointer, the tip a tracer-bullet red, slaps the picture, which falls away to reveal a color photograph of four pieces of impact-flattened iron, still clearly identifiable as 14.5mm-caliber.

As the pointer hits the board four more times, each piece of shrapnel comes out of Storms' hand, onto a piece of line-ruled paper in front of Han.

Han turns to whisper and smile to an aide — a brittle, mirthless grin.

Does nothing move this nerveless man with the mummified feelings? Certainly not Storms' next charge, illustrated by the grisly color mural of three corpses in flipper and wet suit.

"I will now report to this commission the details of your side's armed infiltration into Republic of Korea territory on 19 June 1983 . . ."

Storms tells it all, how two South Korean guards, patrolling a bridge, intercepted a trio of infiltrators some 12 kilometers south of the zone. Two died outright in an exchange of gunfire and grenades. The third, cutting himself from the cable that bound all three, was hunted down and slain.

"How do you answer this charge?"
Han is predictably rigid.

Storms next finds himself saying: "Your refusal to address the United Nations Command charge of an armed infiltration, without the slightest attempt to investigate, is characteristic of your side's irresponsible approach to these meetings."

Storms is always factual and never flamboyant, next laying out a piece-by-piece display of evidence, pictures in hand, weapons cache and captured equipment on an outside table.

"This is one of three lightweight 7.65mm machine pistols carried by your side's infiltrators. This weapon, manufactured in Czechoslovakia, is a Model VZ-61 Skorpion. . . ."

It could be a toy or a piece of scrap for all the attention Han gives it. Nor does he consent to step outside and examine it all — the three dented scuba tanks, flippers, utility knives, counterfeit South Korean uniforms, machine pistols, code sheets, sophisticated Japanese cameras and lenses, medical supplies and powerful, hand-held radio transmitters. The three carried a portable depot of espionage gear.

"Your assertion that the dead infiltrators are fabrications is ridiculous . . ."

The meeting is moving toward its own kind of nothing-done truce — adjournment.

Bravely factual, Storms is answered only by baseless abuse. Yet the admiral has had it easier than many of his predecessors. Nobody on the north side of the table has called him insane, urged him to check into an asylum or waved a pistol at him. He even has something close to compassionate understanding of Han.

"I really don't get upset with General Han because I think I know where he's coming from. I think he delivers his message with a great deal of aplomb . . . he does well in his job, given that which he has to work with. I don't know if he is personally inflexible, but I think he is made inflexible by his system."

He very probably believes every one of his illogical responses and dogged denials, Storms feels.

"And that's after thirty years of indoctrination in their system. Any human being having that kind of . . . indoctrination over that period of time, and you have no other relative fact or piece of information to judge it against, it's going to affect your reasoning capability."

None of this would be lost on Horace and Richard Underwood, lifetime educators and missionaries in Seoul — grandsons of a man who disdained a family fortune in typewriters and business machines, turning instead to religious work and singling out Korea because it was a remote and despised place that no other missionary wanted.

Expelled by Japanese occupiers just before the Pacific War, ousted again by the North Korean invasion, the Underwoods returned in the uniforms they first wore during World War II — Richard an Army lieutenant, Horace a Navy commander. Horace came ashore with MacArthur at Inchon and, as the Marines took

Seoul, followed painful orders to call artillery fire on his own family home.

When Soviet U.N. Delegate Yakov Malik proposed Korean truce talks in 1951, the UNC choice of interpreters could have only been the Underwoods, among the very few foreigners who spoke a tongue that baffled scholar and linguist.

Both walked the acres of Panmunjom as Storms still walked a campus and worried about nothing more stressful than next week's physics test.

They got a cold baptism at Kaesong, which came before Panmunjom as a truce site and was supposed to be disarmed and neutral. The night before the "very, very first" preliminary meeting between the two sides, Richard scouted the city and found it "empty, lifeless." Hearing that, Gen. Matthew Ridgway nodded his delegates aboard helicopters — and they landed to find "at least two divisions of North Korean and Chinese forces."

They weren't openly hostile, Richard recalls, but "definitely the people who were armed welcoming the people who weren't armed."

Vice Adm. C. Turner Joy gamely ventured into the talks, where the sullen and imposing Nam Il presented an agenda that Horace relates was full of "conclusions" that amounted to take-it-or-leave-it demands — among these that the truce line be set up along the 38th Parallel and the UNC give up a jagged spur of territory it had taken above the old prewar marker.

Nam also wanted to discuss the withdrawal of all foreign troops, which the UNC, then as now, regarded as a political issue to be settled at a post-truce peace conference.

American delegates naively went along with requirements to hang jeeps with fender pennants that looked like white flags, helping along the illusion that the UNC was coming in for a tail-between-the-legs surrender.

Richard was chagrined that Kaesong, bypassed and unoccupied during an Allied counterattack, was within the Red orbit when the talks began. It was the first hard-learned lesson.

"It would have been better if . . . we had left, we had said no, we are not going to meet in your city. Eventually, we had to do that anyway . . ."

The Communists would charge the UNC with bombing reputedly demilitarized Kaesong. Ridgway countered by breaking off the talks, which reconvened in what Richard recalls as "truly neutral" Panmunjom — a drowsy village that had an obscure but significant niche in Korea's sad history. Emissaries of Chinese kings, on their way to squeeze tribute out of Korean royalty in Seoul, tied sweaty horses outside a luxury pavilion built for them — the Wooden Door Inn.

Centuries later, Chinese and North Koreans wanted a harsher tribute — the no-questions-asked exchange of all prisoners of war, despite the fact that many in UNC hands made it clear they didn't want to go back.

"It would have been terrible, absolutely immoral to just hand them back," Richard says, crediting his country with two moral milestones in the Korean War — the contained and limited war and an unyielding stand that a prisoner was a creature of decision and not a bargaining pawn.

For a year, Horace says in chorus with Richard, the UNC fought only for the principle of no forced repatriation — sacrificed lives for the rights of former enemies.

"We had agreed to everything by May of 1952 — except the prisoner of war issue," Horace relates, telling of how he sat at the elbow of Joy and then Harrison — whispered what Nam Il rumbled at them, then relayed his superior's reply.

"We didn't have (voluntary repatriation) at the end of World War II and we sent thousands of people back to their deaths in Russia, forcibly." Horace smiles. "I don't think that's likely to happen now."

As the UNC successfully insisted, prisoners were brought to Panmunjom and given an either-door, north-or-south choice.

Neither Richard nor Horace was at Panmunjom for the signing. With negotiations finished, Horace dashed back to Japan for the birth of a son. Richard was already out of uniform, finishing college in America.

Both still live in a homeland away from their homeland. Horace is an assistant to the president of Yonsei University, founded by his grandfather. Richard is the headmaster of prestigious Seoul Foreign School.

One other cast member of the Panmunjom drama is displaced by choice.

On March 17, 1949, a year before the war storm rolled over Korea, five young leftists broke into the Underwood home.

"Part of their thing was to terrorize educators," Horace recalls. "My mother tried to stop them and they shot her."

Horace doesn't know which of the group fired the carbine burst that killed 60-year-old Ethel Underwood. One was apprehended and hanged. Another fled his birthplace to save his life.

Han Ju Kyong.

"This was 35 years ago, and I can't build up hate for some individual I've never even seen. That's not my nature, that's all." Horace shrugs helplessly. "What am I to do, go out and shoot him?"

Storms would later note with satisfaction that he once cracked the waxen gloom on Han's face, ending a holiday season meeting by wishing him a Merry Christmas and a Happy New Year.

"His eyes got large, he sort of laughed."

Wherever they go, Americans carry luggage unseen by inspectors as they clear customs wickets — the American lifestyle, a love for the rowdy strains of country music and the noisy stomp of the breakdance. Here it is, in full sound and color, howling to life in a place that could be called the Gilley's of the East.

SPIRIT OF THE ALAMO

MAY 8, 1983 BY BILL CRAIG

The place is up at the top of the hill, in the middle of the area's hottest bar district. The street teems with night people. During the day, the doors are shuttered and the street deserted — except perhaps for a little dog picking through a trash pile. But at night . . .

Vendors hawk shrimp dead-swimming in big

vats of oil, ladies peddle custom-made combat boots, rock 'n' roll music slams into the street like cops on a raid. Everything comes to life after dark . . . bars . . . bars . . . and these no-tell motel joints — the types with no front desks.

The area crawls with GIs, and has since the Korean War. Itaewon, they call it, a section just outside Yongsan Garrison in Seoul. Saigon had a neighborhood like it. Cities like San Francisco still do. The similarities with Itaewon end right there.

Itaewon has Sam's Place.

The river of street life crests about 9 every night, but little of it spills into Sam's Place. The cultural sandbags are too high. After all, how many people understand Texas?

"It's the Gilley's of the Far East," says one customer.

Sam's Place is pure country — Texas-style.

A bucking bronco arches over the doorway to Sam's Place. Inside, John Wayne stares down from the wall. The Duke looks like most of the guys in Sam's Place.

Across the room from the Duke is a picture of a buxom country princess. She's just lying there, smiling come-hither, y'all.

The decor of Sam's Place is Early Pioneer. Cowhides and bullhorns decorate the walls, which are thick logs, stripped and varnish-coated. Overhead, chandelier lights cascade from an authentic Texas wagon wheel.

The ambience of Sam's Place is Alamo. "Every now and then," says one regular, "some fool makes an insult or something when they're playing 'Texas' and fists bust out."

Sam's Place's comfort range is 50 customers, but country lovers seem to prefer it cozy. On a typical night about 100 Texans (some natural-ized) gather at Sam's to listen and dance to country music — "Running Bear," "Rocky Top," "The Red Neck National Anthem." Good hard country music.

"Every once in a while some newcomer has to learn that lesson the hard way," says Beau Hornig, a civilian English teacher. "Just the other night some guy walked in here and gave the DJ a record to play. Turned out to be a rock and roll song and that don't go over so good around here. The song wasn't on for 30 seconds before the manager grabbed that record and broke it in a thousand pieces."

Sam's patrons gather to listen and dance and, of course, drink. At one table four guys work on three cases of beer. That's 72 bottles. Finished, they order another case. After that, they order another. That's the way they drink at Sam's. All the real cowboys seem to drink beer.

Sam's customers are always the same people. Or at least the same kind of people. There is the regular crowd, of course, but sprinkled among them are patrons that show up courtesy of Space-A from the Philippines, Japan and back home. There's even one embassy Marine guard who makes regular trips from Saudi Arabia.

Sgt. Jim Reid says he makes frequent trips to Korea and, when he's here, he spend most of his evenings at Sam's. A native of San Antonio, Reid met his fiancee, Jeanette Riebe, at Sam's a few years ago while he was stationed at the U.S. Embassy in Seoul.

"I been stationed all over the Far East and I can tell you there just aren't any other places like this," Reid says. "A lot of places have tried to cash in on the popularity of country music, but somehow they just don't measure up to Sam's, the place is one of a kind."

GIs, though, can't stake an exclusive claim to Texas-in-Itaewon.

"This place is not a GI bar," says Hornig. "I've been coming in here for years and I think it's the only place I've ever seen where you'll meet military people, officer and enlisted, corporate executives, embassy people, even Korean farmers.

"Everyone has something in common — they love country music. And they know that Sam's is the best place in this part of the world to listen to it."

Nobody seemed to know how long the place has been there. Like legend, its origins are lost in antiquity — or at least as far back as 11 years. One old-timer says that that's how long he's been going to Sam's Place.

"In all that time," he says admiringly, "they never have tried to change the image of the place. No rock, no disco, it's always been just what it is now. I guess that's why the folks who come here are so loyal."

Loyal not only to Sam's Place, but to country music and Texas. The flag of the Lone Star State dwarfs the Old Glory, which along with the Confederate flag and the banner of the Confederate Air Force, hangs over the dance floor. The flags are saluted every night in a musical tribute.

The song is "Texas." Everyone stands with

their cowboy hats over their hearts. Except for the strains of "Texas," the room is silent — as silent as the moments following a shootout. They're dead serious about Texas at Sam's.

And they haven't forgotten about the Ayatollah. He frequently gets his own musical tribute. A cowboy-chorus line forms to the first strains of Charlie Daniels' "In America."

The chorus line picks up steam as the next song comes on, a parody of the old Beach Boys' hit "Barbara Ann." This one's called "Bomb Iran" and, as it winds up, the dancers turn and face away from the crowd. On the last note the audience yells, "Here's to you, Khomeini," and the dancers half-moon the ayatollah.

"It's like being back home in Texas," says Hornig, referring to atmosphere of shared feelings about music, good times and country. "You find out that there's a place where you can meet people who like the same music and lifestyle you do, it's only natural to check it out. And if you like it, you tell your friends.

"I first heard about it from a buddy of mine back in Texas. He told me, 'If you ever get to Korea check out Sam's.' At that time I was a security policeman in the Air Force.

"My daddy always said he had the only kid in town who was dumb enough to join the Air Force and wind up in the infantry . . . but that's another story.

"Anyway, I got orders to come over here to Osan AB and took my friend up on his suggestion. Since then I been a regular. This is where I've met all the people I associate with. It's really the only place in Korea I really feel comfortable in."

Spec. 5 Sharon Roman knows the feeling.

"After being in a few of these other places around here," she says, "I was desperate to find some decent atmosphere, you know, for a female. At Sam's we're like a big family. We drink, we dance and have a good time.

"These are the kind of people I like to be with."

This was one of the best maritime stories that ever saw print in Pacific Stars and Stripes, worthy of C.S. Forester in the way it gave a dying ship soul and feeling — made the crewmen seem like mourners at the deathbed of a close friend as they heard an outdated diesel heartbeat falter and stop.

GOODBYE TO THE GRAYBACK

JAN. 8, 1984 BY PETTY OFFICER 1ST CLASS GLENN JOCHUM

The early morning Philippines sun strikes the Grayback at a low angle, giving the gleaming, jet-black submarine a look of malevolence. Its fluted, bulbous prow seems socketed with sinister intent. Awesome and ancient, it is a dinosaur from the depths, looming large at pierside.

In sad fact, the Grayback is a dinosaur — a 26-year-old diesel submarine that, in this age of nuclear power, belongs to the past.

And on this particular morning — there will be none like it again — the Grayback crew is waiting topside. Some read papers, others stare into the water, lost in thought. The Grayback's fringe of seaweed dances below the water line.

Soon, men in camouflage uniforms arrive, carrying equipment. They are members of a special warfare team that will be conducting diving operations with the 7th Fleet submarine.

When the chief of the boat, Master Chief Jack Cromer, boards, the men automatically gather around him.

"Let me remind you how important it is to be particularly careful on this cruise," Cromer says. "Now, let's do it."

The crew knows exactly what to do and what to expect. But the men are tense. Their work has taken on an added importance: This will be their last mission aboard the Grayback, which is set for decommissioning Jan. 15.

The mooring lines are hauled in and slowly, noiselessly, the 334-foot Grayback — the largest diesel-powered submarine in the world — begins its final operational transit out of Subic Bay's naval facility.

High atop the Grayback's sail stands Cmdr. Peter B. Smith, the skipper, a three-time Grayback veteran, busily briefing the executive officer, Lt. Cmdr. Bob Sands.

Not far away are two petty officers, searching the horizon through field binoculars while an enlisted phone-talker relays information supplied by Lt. Jack Spiller, officer of the deck, to the control room below.

Spiller, like his father and grandfather before him, is a Naval Academy graduate and submariner. Unlike the Grayback, his career stretches before him like the calm, sun-studded waters of the South China Sea he is sailing.

As the boat noses past Grande Island, where bathers ogle Grayback's distinctive outline, Spiller passes the word to secure the maneuvering watch. Several minutes later, the order is given to rig the boat for diving.

"Lay below and submerge ship," comes the command.

The men topside descend the 30-foot shaft that joins daylight and the netherworld. The hatches close and, for a new submariner, small eternities pass. For this, an E-4, say, receives $125 a month in extra pay. Some might think it small recompense. The claustrophobic conditions, for one thing, and then there's the smell, which clings to clothes even after several washings. Diesel fumes permeate the ship. It is like riding behind a bus in city traffic.

The klaxon sounds the order to dive and — whooooosh— the ballast tanks fill with water.

This is the Grayback's 1,618th dive and for most, more or less routine. But for Senior Chief Phillip "Pinky" Morgan, the Grayback's oldest sailor, these last three days of operations have special significance: They will end a 30-year Navy career, nearly half of which has been spent on submarines. The Grayback is his 16th.

A smile crosses Morgan's weathered face, and he says, "I hope my dives and my surfacing come out even."

Morgan's career neatly parallels the demise of the diesel submarine. Younger men like engineman Larry Chrisman could find themselves out of a job before their naval careers are through.

The diesel submariner, says Senior Chief S.A. Worthley, "is a dying breed. There's no place for a non-nuclear-trained engineman in the submarine Navy. Eventually he'll have to go surface."

As a result, most enginemen on diesel submarines convert to the nuclear ratings, such as machinist's mate or interior communications electrician. Chrisman, a chief petty officer, is reluctant to make the move.

"I just may stick it out," he says. "I've always been on a sub and it's kind of scary, thinking of going to a surface ship. I'm used to a small community where everybody knows everyone else."

Chrisman has few chances left to serve his eight remaining years aboard a diesel sub. When the Grayback's flag is hauled down for the last time, there will only be five left in the entire U.S. fleet: Barbel, Bonefish, Blueback, Darter and the search-submarine Dolphin.

Some of the younger sailors look at diesel submarines as a dead end. At 30, David Rossell is a shade older than the electronics systems he maintains aboard the Grayback. "Working on these systems isn't helping my future," he says. "I'm ready to do something different."

Hospital Corpsman Dale Johnson says he volunteered for Grayback for nostalgic reasons. "Back then the Navy had trouble finding people to serve on Grayback," he says. "While I'm glad I served aboard her, I feel as if I've been out of the mainstream of the submarine world. It's not the way the Navy's going."

All the same, the Grayback is one of a kind. Its appearance, mission and personality make it unique in the submarine community.

The Grayback was built to carry Regulus missiles, and the hangars that once held them were later used solely as transition chambers for the Grayback's special warfare divers. Here, divers became acclimated to the water pressure outside the submarine's hull, or following dives, could prepare for re-entry to the boat.

The Grayback's darkest hour occurred there on Jan. 16, 1982, when five swimmers died in a diving accident. According to crew members, the Grayback's recovery was slow and painful in the wake of the tragedy.

"There was a time we couldn't even do preventive maintenance without being observed by a chief petty officer," recalls a petty officer first class.

Sands, the executive officer, says a drastic turnover in personnel since the accident has relegated the incident to the status of second-hand news. He estimates that about 12 of the crew members who were aboard that time are still on board. "The Grayback that was then is not the same," he says. "Since then, the systems have been re-designed to make them nearly foolproof."

The Navy is also losing its only submarine specially configured for operations on the ocean floor.

"Our reinforced keel allows us to conduct bottoming operations for diving," Lt. Malcolm Baird says. "Nuclear subs can't because their sonar bows would get damaged."

Chief of the boat, Cromer, says with a smile, "Our navigators don't like to go aground, but the Grayback does it on purpose."

Its size — about as long as a football field, plus an end zone — makes the Grayback a luxury liner among diesel boats. The Darter, the second largest in the U.S. diesel fleet, is 284 feet long. The Grayback's additional space is the result of a forward crew's berthing area and the diving hangars.

But bigger is not always better for some Grayback sailors who have gotten lost when temporarily assigned to nuclear-powered submarines such as the 560-foot-long Trident.

"These (diesel) boats are smaller, more cramped, but that's the price you pay," says Petty Officer 1st Class Winton Worth, who served on six different submarines and a tender before coming to the Grayback. "I don't think I'd want to serve on a Trident. They're too awesome for me."

Diesel submarines are known to spend a fair amount of time recharging their batteries on the ocean surface, but Grayback's special warfare mission keeps her on top of the situation more than most.

And occasionally, in between diving operations, "steel beach liberty" is announced over the boat's intercom. Crew members grab fishing poles, suntan lotion and guitars and scramble topside. "We're the only submariners with tans," said the ship's public affairs officer.

Events shape a ship's personality as much as does its mission. Most of the decommissioning crew rank two events, both occurring in 1983, as their highlights aboard the Grayback: Thai Princess Chulabhorn Valayalaksana's visit to the submarine and the rescue of 29 Vietnamese refugees.

Refugee rescues are hardly news to the 7th Fleet any more, but for submarines, they remain a novelty. "It affected the whole crew," says Sands. "They would have died if we hadn't discovered them."

The Navy has no current plans to replace the Grayback. There is, however, a possibility that designated nuclear-powered submarines may be outfitted to perform some of Grayback's chores.

"It would be nice if they'd put her in my backyard," says Petty Officer 1st Class Bonifacio Cleto.

The boat could be scrapped and reused for steel products. "I wouldn't mind shaving with her," says Petty Officer 2nd Class Michael Dixon.

"I think every one of us hates to see her go," says Cromer. "In the best case, she could be used by the reserves (to train divers), but in the worst case could be used as a target."

Her sister guided-missile submarine, Growler, which was decommissioned in 1964, was used as a source of spare parts for Grayback for 16 years before being stricken in 1980 for use as a target.

"When Grayback is gone they ought to bring back another that can do the same things," says Winton Worth, a diesel submariner for more than two decades. "If someone asks me to serve on it, I will. And if no one asks me, I'll ask them."

The nearest thing to a eulogy lingers behind in the form of an official message dispatched by the Grayback's commanding officer on the day after the last operational deployment. It gave the time, the day and the year, and closed:

"The Gray Ghost of the China Coast surfaced for the last time . . . we wish we could do more."

The profiles of many old seahorses disappeared from the Western Pacific skyline, and both young sailors and old salts took it with a death-in-the-family sting. The surest sign of changing times came in late 1979, when the venerable Oklahoma City — launched in 1944, mothballed between wars and recommissioned as the 7th Fleet flagship in 1964 — left Yokosuka NB for the last time. Pacific Stars and Stripes paid proper tribute to one of the last of the big-gun cruisers, recalling her glory days as "king on the Pacific chessboard."

It was, said somebody who flew over an expanse of ocean that was tombstone grey, a terrible place to die. But 269 passengers and crew that had traveled aboard Korean Air Lines Flight 7 were locked beneath the North Pacific. The Soviets were still blandly justifying the shootdown of a jetliner they claimed was a spy plane. The victims could not speak — only the searchers.

A FEW FLOWERS FOR 269 LIVES

SEPT. 24, 1983, BY HAL DRAKE

WAKKANAI, Japan — The Japanese woman journalist threw a bouquet from a Navy helicopter and the rotor wind whipped it past the tail and scattered the flowers, somber confetti over a scene of sadness.

The floral offering fluttered down to float with other wilted petals, dropped earlier over the scattered remains of KAL Flight 7, shot down Sept. 1 by the Soviets with loss of 269 lives.

"I just wanted to do it on behalf of myself and others," said Fuji TV reporter Yoko Nakamura, traveling with other journalists in a CH-54 Sea Knight that flew within the 350-square-mile grid that American ships plumbed for remains of the Boeing 747 and its passengers.

For days, they had turned up nothing — not a scrap of wreckage or a human husk hulled of life. Most sought after was the black box that, through instrument readings and cockpit voices, could tell of what happened aboard the doomed jetliner that strayed over Russian territory.

The box had yet to be found and raised, but the searchers were down there, moving at purposeful pace — the Coast Guard cutter Munro, the frigate Badger, the guided missile destroyer Callaghan, the search and recovery ship Conserver, and the fleet tug Narragansett.

Theirs was not the only flag in these waters. A Soviet Riga-class frigate and two other warships cruised watchfully by, over waters that had been traversed before by Russian fishing boats of suspicious motive — trawling with gear that could perhaps snare wreckage rather than sea life.

It was as Rear Adm. William A. Cockell Jr. had said — there was nothing meaningful to see, only a white basin and a remote wriggle of ships crewed by men at work.

Off the line, in sight of a bald Russian rock called Moneron and close to the crooked leg and cloven hoof of Soviet Sakhalin Island, the guided missile cruiser Sterett stood down for a day, taking aboard "fuel and toothpaste" from the replenishment oiler Wichita, a kind of floating supermarket that lavished supplies on all friendly comers.

They were full of sailors dispatched on sudden mission — and it was cause for bewildered anger.

On the Sterett, Petty Officer 3rd Class Ronald L. Sparkman refused to speak only of the 61 Americans aboard the KAL flight, feeling that nationality was obliterated by the dismal death toll.

"To clean up my language, I didn't like it too much," Sparkman said. "It was totally uncalled for. All those people, no matter what their nationality, they still were innocent people."

For Seaman Steven Kribstock, a 19-year-old from Detroit, it was the first taste of the unexpected he now accepts as part of a sailor's life. The Sterett was docked at Subic Bay NB, in the Philippines, when the Soviet Su-15 fired on KAL 7. Kribstock told of it with the flair of an old salt.

"The day before, they had some Senator (Henry "Scoop") Jackson die, and I came back off liberty and the flag was down, and then at half mast again. I said, 'What's the matter?' They said, 'the Russians shot down a jetliner.' Next thing you know, we had an emergency recall (of sailors off the beach) and we're sitting up here."

Pulling hawsers and laying willing hands to whatever else had to be done, Kribstock also learned that isolated and overworked sailors made their own light moments — such as the cookout on Sterett's fantail, performed while a Soviet frigate cruised by.

Lt. Cmdr. Robert Reilly, the engineering officer, recalls with great relish the moment hamburgers sizzled on the grill and a smoky aroma rose, perhaps wafting over to Russians who lined the rail of the frigate.

"We all wondered what they were after," Reilly said. "I wonder how well the political officers explained the smell of what was happening on our fantail. I don't know if any of

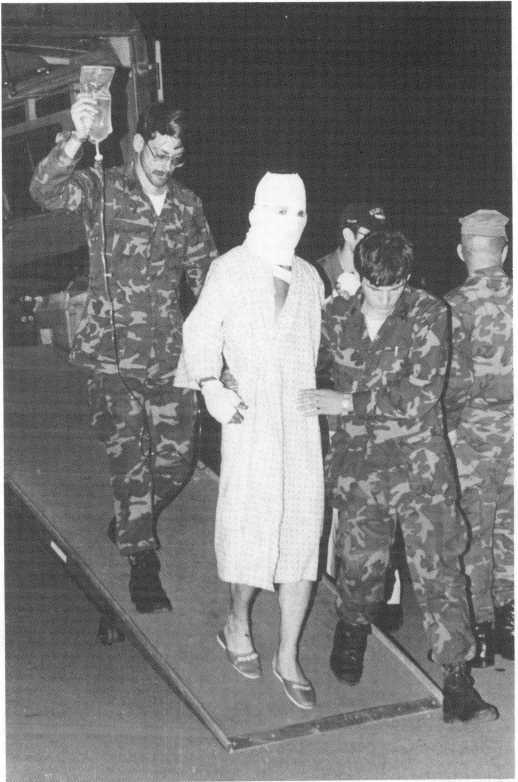

CRITICALLY BURNED, a young Marine is gamely on his feet as medics walk him to an emergency room. He was one of the victims of blaze that broke out when a typhoon ripped a rubber fuel bladder apart, spilling 5,000 gallons that caught fire and made a Marine encampment below Mount Fuji a lake of flames. Fourteen Marines were killed outright or died in hospitals in the United States and Japan.

PS&S, Ken George

FLOATING PICKET LINE sails past the carrier Enterprise as it heads for a berth at Sasebo NB — a sight seen more than once as the base, all but abandoned by the United States after the Indochina War, was again full of 7th Fleet warships. Leftist demonstrators didn't care for them, but beyond the picket boats and the base gate was a town that lavishly welcomed free-spending sailors. First a Japanese Imperial Navy settlement and then a port for Americans during occupation and treaty days, it needed somebody's Navy to prosper — and was never sorry to see white hats in the streets.

PS&S, Ken George

BEAMING BENEATH HER PORTRAIT, actress-singer Liza Minnelli basks in a superstar glow at the Shinagawa Prince Hotel, where she performed at banquet-sized prices and declared that she wanted to forget singing and do Shakespeare.

REAL NAILS pierce the hands of a penitent flagellante, a sect that reenacts the agony of Golgotha during Easter Week in the Philippines. Believers carry heavy crosses for miles and cut themselves with glass during devotions that are an annual ordeal. The Catholic Church has condemned the practice, which dates back to medieval times in Europe, but it still goes on.

PS&S, Ken George

DISNEYLAND reaches from California to Florida and made its initial Far East thrust into Tokyo, where an honor guard of Marines who had seen many skylines marched in precision step beneath Sleeping Beauty's Castle. Mickey and Minnie rubbed noses for happy youngsters who wouldn't believe there were real people under those big masks.

EYE OF THE TIGER glares balefully over an M16 in a frontline guardpost at the edge of the Demilitarized Zone — 4,000 meters of dead land marked off by the 1953 Korean War Armistice as a peace preserve between the two Koreas. This toughly-primed 2nd Infantry Division trooper has his work cut out for him — a ready but disciplined finger on the trigger as he keeps watch on a standdown war that has never been ended by peace treaty or political settlement. It is the longest armed truce in history.

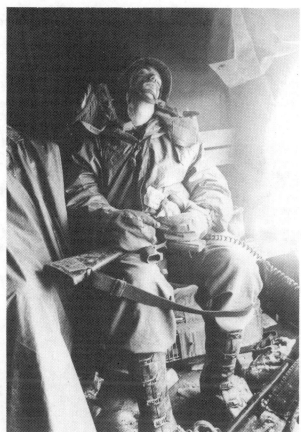

PS&S, Harold China

TIRED SOLDIER learns the first rule of mock combat or real warfare as he gets a few golden minutes of sleep on a helicopter lifting him to his next objective during the yearly Team Spirit maneuvers in South Korea. The shot below, seized by the quick eye and fast lens of Chet King, could have been taken as Marines stormed Tarawa or cleared Happy Valley close to Da Nang. It was a realistic beach maneuver on Okinawa.

PS&S, Masahiko Nakamura

DANCING OUT of Japan's past, the daimyo procession — a pageant that recreates the procession of a feudal lord — streams out of historic Odawara Castle, which was disassembled during the Meiji Reformation that restored Imperial rule and rebuilt as a cultural treasure decades later. The long arm of a gloomy green giant — the massive statue that is the centerpiece of the Peace Park atomic bomb memorial in Nagasaki — is a roost for pidgeons that are fed and fattened by daily crowds.

PS&S, Ken George

240

A LOST HORIZON is unseen by any except those who go through the strenuous but rewarding ordeal of climbing 12,392 foot Mount Fuji. This stretch of sharp lava rock, surrounded by mist-caped mountains, is close to the summit and has a magnificence that no mortal hand could conceive or fashion.

them ever had baked chicken or hamburger . . . I think if, they'd come close enough, they'd have lost them — commissars shooting people, just to keep them from going over the side to get some chow."

On the Wichita, one sailor saw no light or laughable side of the Russians at all.

"Hey, you guys know all the answers," he told one reporter facetiously. "So tell me. What's my mission? Why am I out here?"

Well, the reporter fumbled back uncertainly, he was on a mission of compassion and humanity, to . . . "Yea," the sailor cut him off. "I sure as hell am mad at the Russians. Nuke 'em off the map. Make a Sears parking lot out of the whole damn place."

Not too many years before, an American who traveled through mainland China did it at the displeasure of the State Department and imperiled his or her passport. China was tainted by political pox and rigidly quarantined. American journalists could do little more than glance across the frontier at Hong Kong and question Swiss or English travelers as they came out. That all changed in 1980, when the United States at last recognized the Peoples' Republic of China — by that name — and gave unrestricted travel an approving nod. Julie Jacobs, a Stanford undergraduate who came to Stripes as a student intern, didn't travel to the PRC to buy plaster dragons or get snapshots of the Great Wall. A beginner who wrote like a professionally seasoned reporter, she gave a long-shuttered monolith a fair and observant eye.

"PRACTICE THRIFT, FRUGALITY AND BIRTH CONTROL"

MARCH 11, 1984 BY JULIE JACOBS

The train into China from Hong Kong quickly leaves behind skyscrapers, traffic, urban sprawl. Acre after acre of farmland are worked without visible machinery or motor-driven transport. Among narrow rectangular fields are occasional oxen and clumps of peasants, stooped under the sloping-brimmed "coolie" hats we thought were just a stereotype.

Our stop: Guangzhou, or Canton in English. The station and main streets are lined with billboards. Some are the expected political posters filled with smiling workers, but most are advertisements, styled in international garish, for Chinese movies, medicinal toothpaste, washing machines, Nikon cameras.

Our guide explains that the people of Canton will eat anything. The city's most famous dish, called "phoenix, serpent and dragon," is made from chicken, snake and dog, he says. He gets the anticipated, horrified response from our tour.

The government-sponsored guides are stocked with plenty to shock and impress us. We're whisked from one high point of the city to another; at every stop is some version of the Friendship Store, where we snap up goods made specially for foreigners and high-ranking Chinese. We eat too much and spend too much. There's little time to wander from the packaged China we're presented.

But the tour guides can't hide the dirty, unlit workrooms; the carcasses hanging in the open or stacked on the ground to be sold; the waiter who dropped a chicken, then picked it back up and replaced it on the serving plate.

China wants to sell herself to us, but she can't always control what we see.

Three cultures are represented in Canton, with two sequestered on the Island of the Former Concessions where our hotel is located. The buildings around us are European, all balconies, pillars and stone curlicues, built to house European ambassadors and missionaries of the last century.

Now the buildings and churches are crumbling, many supported by bamboo scaffoldings. They seem to house kindergartens and lunch halls.

The decaying European buildings remind me of the temples I've read about in overgrown jungles, overtaken by vines and baboons. They are as startling as the deserted tenements in New York City — they seem to represent a

242

civilization expiring, leaving rotting buildings behind like a discarded skin as it slinks away to die.

Our hotel is by far the tallest building on the horizon, and most likely the most luxurious, complete with a waterfall and terraces in a dramatic atrium. There's quite a contrast between the plush hotel and the teeming neighborhoods around it. Those of us who stray from the happy-talk tour see Third World conditions, dogs butchered for food, dim rooms housing what seem to be family factories. I'm conscious that I'm already judging China by my Western standards.

The busy storefronts, large trade centers, billboards and other signs of prosperity are built on money brought in from courting capitalists. Our guide says the people of Canton are in fact spoiled by the relative luxury they enjoy as caterers to Western trade.

I imagine tension building as American wealth enters the city. I imagine conflict among new social classes. One of our professors tells me I don't understand the Chinese, that they call Western greed disgusting and beneath them. I try to look at China with ungreedy eyes, but my time here isn't long enough to change the way I look at the world.

I'm here with the University of Maryland's study tour, speeding through China in two weeks. The trip is like a waterslide; exciting, expensive, over too soon.

In a country of a billion people, no stereotype holds; we are finding contrasts and contradictions when we hope to find simple packages of insight to carry home with our other souvenirs.

Down the road and across the river from our hotel is Canton's lovers' lane. One side of the river is lit brightly with streetlights. The opposite bank, dim and shady, swarms with couples — embracing every six feet or so against the riverbank railing, folded around each other on the couple-sized benchettes spaced modestly under protecting trees. This must be the acceptable place for public affection for young Cantonese, because there's at least a mile of couples.

On the way back to the hotel, a man in his 30s wheels his bike over the pedestrian bridge next to us. We nod, compliment him on his spiffy black, thick-stemmed bike, similar if not identical to zillions of other black bikes in Canton. China has 154 million bikes, and they all seem to be here, whizzing past us under the mild evening's moonlight.

Our cyclist friend speaks no English, so we continue talking anyway, smiling back and forth as we cross the bridge. We're relaxing; this Communism stuff isn't so weird, people smile and kiss on shady riverbanks like anyplace else. We're separated from our biker as we pass two guards, whose uniforms are already beginning to be familiar.

Then a chill passes through the springlike evening — these men are carrying machine guns, casually, although to protect whom from whom we don't know.

The machine guns signal a part of China we're not allowed to see. There's no time on the tour, between lavish meals and glorious temples, for the guides to explain the tight control the state holds over every part of society.

Couples are only allowed to have one child each, for example — and the rule is made to stick.

If a woman already has a child, or if she hasn't asked permission to bear a child, she can be forced to have an abortion as late as the second trimester. Each woman must report her monthly period to a central authority, so that pregnancies may be detected.

Since boy babies are considered more valuable than girls, one method of population control even now, even in the cities, is infanticide. One source estimates that more than 200 babies were killed in Canton alone last year; most were girls.

In rural areas, one report says up to 80 percent of the surviving babies are male. This means that when it's time for these children to marry, there will be one woman for every four men.

Yet the state realizes something drastic must be done. Currently, 25 babies are born in China every minute. This tremendous birth rate means any advances China makes in production will be swallowed by the swelling population.

To stop the trend, Chinese marriage certificates remind the newlyweds from the beginning of the state's priorities. They are stamped with this slogan:

"Practice thrift, frugality and birth control."

We soak up the sparkle of the children, this afternoon in Shanghai. We're touring an afterschool center for kids called a children's palace. About 300 kids come to this tall old house each day, to play on the carnival rides in the yard, study bugs under a microscope, play Ping-Pong, program an Apple computer in BASIC.

Most of the children here are the kids of party members, one of our professors says. Some of us walking among the happy children murmur to each other that it seems unfair, only 300 in a city of 14 million enjoying this castle. Just outside the palace gates, another group of kids kicks a soccer ball in an alley. Born to the wrong parents, like in any other country.

Our tour group is crammed into the practice room for traditional Chinese music, as the afternoon sun slants a blue light through the window. Two almost-teens play what look like xylophones but aren't; kids who don't look more than 5 race their fingers over the strings of skinny violin-like instruments. Each instrument is new to us.

The scratchy music is new to us too, but the children seem to be carrying off the tunes like professionals. One girl stares sweetly over our heads, her head swinging gracefully as she listens to the music in her fingers. A boy, his eyes closed, bounces his head from side to side, knocking the beat against his shoulders.

The concert ends, and the two groups, musicians and audience, mingle as they move toward the door. I kneel before one of the first row's players, and ask her in English to show me how to play her er-hoo, a long, two-stringed instrument. I wonder what she thinks of this stranger on the floor before her. She eventually understands what I'm after and politely plays a pebbly, minor scale.

She switches to melody, one I'm surprised to recognize — "Twinkle, Twinkle Little Star." The scratchy, drawn-out notes no longer sound like those of a child prodigy, but like any American child's first painful violin lessons.

Thin children's voices spontaneously take up the song in Chinese. I look up to see the singers, and the afternoon sun catches me full in the face, blinding me. We Americans begin singing the song as we know it, and for a second the two groups become one, singing the same song amid differences.

I break my gaze from the sun's grasp, our tour group streams toward the door, the song ends. We are once again tourists.

One little Chinese girl in long, high pigtails drags a grandmotherly woman from our group toward the door, to show her some other treat down the hall. The woman talks to her as if she could understand, as if the girl were her granddaughter: "Just a minute, I'm coming, slow down, dear."

We are once again the same.

The Chinese don't share our sense of personal distance, one of our professors says. People will mob you out of curiosity and will seem to get too close, by American standards.

The children everywhere bear this out, crowding around to play the "hammer-scissors-rock" hand game or to accept our hugs and candy after they sing the ubiquitous "Jingle Bells."

The adults, too, are chummy in their stares or physical crowding. I try on a series of jackets at the "Shanghai No. 1 Department Store," and am immediately surrounded by 25 or so people.

"What do you think, gang?" I ask the sea of blank faces. "Should I get this jacket, or the plum-colored one?" No one in the crowd answers.

I hand out my card to random members of the audience, and thank everybody for their guidance and support.

A crowd forms again when I stop at the musical instruments counter, and again at the department to buy office equipment (abacuses and chops, or carved stamps to sign documents).

There's no shame in these stares, just as we have no shame at snatching photos of the private lives we pass.

On the public bus in Shanghai, one passenger is able to explain in English how to get back to the hotel. We ask him to ask two other passengers, egg saleswomen, how much the fresh eggs in their baskets cost.

About 2 cents each, he says. Then he confers again. No, 50 cents each.

I ask if this means 2 cents for locals and 50 cents for us. Yes, he says.

We Americans do the same thing — that's capitalist accounting, and it's something I can understand.

He returns my smile, but our conversation is over. Someone might hear.

Zhou Min-wei's family owns a refrigerator, washing machine and television, unlike most of their 14 million neighbors in Shanghai.

His father has been a member of the Communist Party for 36 years. His mother joined 16 years ago. Zhou, 28-year-old international relations student, has been a member himself for a year.

Zhou's father earns $113 per month, almost four times the salary of the average Chinese worker. He even has access to a car, owned by the utility company where he is a chief engineer. Few cars are privately owned in China.

Zhou estimates that most Shanghai families can afford to rent two rooms, totaling about 16 by 16 feet, for a family of five. Zhou and his parents rent the top floor of a three-story building, with four rooms, a kitchen, bath and two balconies. The family even owns a hot-water heater. Most families in southern China have no heat in their homes.

Here at Fudan University, in Shanghai, many of the students meeting with us are shy; the women sit in the second row, giggling.

Zhou is the oldest student in the international relations department because during the Cultural Revolution he was assigned to a coal mine for eight years instead of to a university.

"My family suffered a lot during the Cultural Revolution," Zhou says. Hunched in his coat in the unheated meeting room, he speaks with disarming openness, as if to bridge the language gap with sincerity and humor when we can't cross it verbally.

"My father was beaten a lot. He had to stop work, and was sent to a farm in Anhain province. It's a very poor province, and far away. He was there four years."

Zhou's mother teaches Chinese and history to middle school children. "The Gang of Four (Mao Tse-tung's wife and her cohorts) thought the teachers were teaching Western cultural pollution, so they punished them," Zhou says.

"My mother wasn't teaching about the West, but she and most of the other teachers suffered."

Zhou warms his hands around his tea mug. Fragrant steam drifts around his head as he tilts the lid up to slurp jasmine tea.

Zhou's mother was sent to work on a farm in Jiangzhou province from 1967 to 1969. The four children in Zhou's family lived on about 20 yuan per months, or $10.

In 1969, his oldest sister was sent to work in a chemical factory. His brother was assigned to a farm in 1970, and his second sister was shipped to another distant farm in 1971.

Now, the "moral confusion" of the Cultural Revolution is ending, Zhou says. Then, the traditional stabilizers of Chinese society, such as condemning criminals and respecting hard work, were forgotten. The uneducated received the same benefits as the educated, he says; lawbreakers were treated the same as traditional Chinese who treated others with respect.

"But that's now changing. I think (social standards) will go back to the way they were before the Cultural Revolution," Zhou said.

"During these years, whether you worked or not, you got money. Now good workers are respected again."

These old-time Chinese values, I tell him, sound similar to capitalist law-of-the-jungle standards.

"All the people in our country have the same benefits. They have no social controversy, and no fear of hunger," he says. "Under Marxism, everyone gets an equal chance at jobs. Our country hasn't reached that level yet, but we no longer have class privileges."

Yet, don't the benefits his family enjoys create a new class system?

"In recent years, our country is taking good care of its intellectuals, because the party leader now considers them important to our country," Zhou says. "So it's not a privilege for our family (to own these luxuries). It just gives us much more convenience.

"Foreigners consider it a privilege, and some Chinese consider it a privilege. We consider it recognition for intellectuals."

We visit Xian University, a dusty, eroding engineering school in a dusty, provincial town. Ma Li, a 22-year-old senior specializing in missile design, talks at length about her boyfriend. He's also an engineer, a year older, sent to work in Beijing (Peking).

It's very unlikely that she will also be assigned to Beijing, she says, and so it's unlikely she will be able to marry her boyfriend. Would she want to marry him? Yes, of course. Do her parents approve? Yes, even her grandmother who raised her approves. Can nothing be done? No, nothing can be done.

We walk around the campus on an official tour. We're shown video equipment, shiny wind tunnels, more preschoolers singing — every toy available at the school is brought out for us to play with.

I ask if we may visit her dorm room instead of playing volleyball as her school has organized. She asks her professor; I ask mine. Mine says sure, go ahead, and continues to kick a soccer ball.

Hers asks me, "Wouldn't you like to play volleyball?"

"No, thank you, I'm not very athletic."

"But we don't have time to show you a dorm room."

"My professor says we have nearly an hour. Is that long enough?

"Let me see."

Three authorities later, it becomes clear I may not visit Ma Li's dorm room. I ask her if she'd like to show me around, even though we know she can't.

"We shouldn't," she says.

"But would you like to?"

"I want to, but we shouldn't," she replies.

The women in the tour are scheduled to take on the Xian University third-string women's volleyball team, a group that had once held back 15 sabre-toothed Huns or something equally remarkable.

We were slaughtered. And every missed serve, every ball bumped by a high-heeled tourist over a fence, every collision between our players was met with such hysterics from the audience that we were sure that our tour could help better relations with any foreign country, if only by convincing them they were superior.

The whole afternoon, I had tried to explain to Ma Li that I wanted to hear about her life as a student, not see wind tunnels or video equipment, shiny as they may have been.

She described some parts of her life — hours of studying each day, a visit next year from her boyfriend, her grandmother's love for her, her daily running.

We had more trouble with my other questions. What does she want to do? It's up to the state. But what does she dream of doing?

Could I understand her inner world, since her outer world is so foreign to me? Of course I can't explain even to myself what I'd like to know, and I'm sure it's none of my business.

We're getting back on the bus. Ma Li and I exchange pins for our jackets; she gives me one saying Xian University in Chinese, and I give her crossed American and Chinese flags. She'll never leave China, and I'll never be back, even though others on my tour plan to come back that evening for a party.

As I'm about to step on the bus, she squeezes my arm. "When you come back, I'll tell you about my daily life here," she whispers. I look at her trusting face without knowing what to say.

Most young Chinese aren't as lucky as Ma Li. According to an article in the English-language newspaper, the problem most often addressed in a Shanghai advice column for young people is the role parents play in choosing their child's partner.

The Chinese Dear Abby sometimes "gets in touch with authorities" to help arrange the marriage, the China Daily article said.

The columnist addresses other problems, too. One young man wrote that he liked to joke during breaks or slack time, but his boss "didn't like his apprentice to be running around making jokes."

The columnist replied, "It is only natural for young people to be vivacious. But you should never break work rules, let alone make jokes during work time."

A young woman who wanted to know if it was "all right for her to have dresses made according to the latest fashions advertised in magazines" was told not to spend time on fashion, because "young people should concentrate their energies on work and study."

And a high-school boy in Shandong Province wrote in to ask if he were allowed to read love stories, since "high school students are discouraged to date and form boy-and-girlfriend relationships."

One should read as much as possible, the columnist wrote, but "an early interest in reading love stories might distract students from their normal studies."

Our Chinese guide likes to sing. She and I sit at the front of the bus, singing "Edelweiss" from "The Sound of Music."

"Edelweiss, edelweiss . . ." We pass tall carts filled with straw, the driver asleep up top and the horse plodding along on cruise control.

"Bless my homeland forever . . ." We jostle past fields where winter crops are covered with plastic tents and banked with straw; past boxy apartment buildings under construction; past Maxim's of Beijing.

She's seen the "The Sound of Music," along with "Singing in the Rain," "Guess Who's Coming to Dinner" and "Black Stallion." She missed "Snow White" and the few other American films to make it to her neck of the Republic.

I ask her if she'll ever visit the States. She probably won't be allowed. If she were allowed, I ask, would she consider living in the States.

A pause.

"China needs me more," she says, jaw firm, staring straight ahead down the road.

Change is the history of everything — and this is why Pacific Stars and Stripes has been and will continue to be like a daily-installment history book.

SPORTS

10,000-Meter Thriller
MILLS SCORES UPSET

PACIFIC
STARS AND STRIPES

AN AUTHORIZED PUBLICATION OF
THE ARMED FORCES FAR EAST

10¢ DAILY
15¢ WITH SUPPLEMENTS

Vol. 20, No. 289   FIVE-STAR EDITION   Friday, Oct. 16, 1964

TOKYO (AP) — Gritty Billy Mills, a marine from Coffeyville, Kan., won the 10,000-meter run Wednesday in one of the greatest upsets in Olympic history while American swimmers and divers continued to dominate their sport and pushed the leading U.S. medal harvest to 20.

Mills, a 26-year-old crew-cut Marine lieutenant, was timed in an Olympic record 28:24.4 after pulling away from world record-holder Ron Clarke and one of the finest 10,000-meter fields ever assembled.

His victory was the first ever at that distance for the United States. The first over 3,000 meters since 1908 and one of the biggest shocks ever. It helped build the U.S. medal count to seven gold, seven silver and six bronze. Russia has 12 - four gold, three silver and five bronze.

Other U.S. gold medal winners on this fourth day of the 18th Olympiad were:

1. Ken Sitzberger, River Forest, Ill., who won the springboard diving with a total 159.9 points and led a 1-2-3 American medal sweep. Frank Gorman, New York City, was second with 157.63 and Larry Andreason, Los Alamitos, Cal., third in 148.77.

2. Cathy Ferguson, Burbank, Cal., who took the women's 100-meter backstroke in world record time of 1.07.7.

3. Dick Roth, Atherton, Cal., who won the men's 400-meter individual medley in world record time of 4:46.4.

4. The U.S. 400-meter freestyle relay team, also in world record time of 3.33.2. The team was made up of Steve Clark, Los Altos, Cal., Mike Austin, Rochester, N.Y., Gary Ilman, San Jose, Cal., and Don Schollander, Lake Oswego, Ore.

Mills considered far out of his class against one of the finest 10,000-meter fields ever assembled, stayed with the leaders all the way. He took the lead on the 20th lap, was involved in a brief elbow skirm-
(Continued on Page 8, Col. 4)

Johnson Aide Arrested on Morals Count

NEW YORK (UPI) — Walter Jenkins resigned Wednesday as special assistant to President Johnson, the White House announced. Johnson accepted the resignation and appointed Bill D. Moyers to succeed Jenkins.

WASHINGTON (UPI) — Walter W. Jenkins, a special assistant to President Johnson, was arrested Oct. 7 on a disorderly charge involving "indecent gestures" and forfeited $50 collateral.

A check of District of Columbia police records disclosed the incident Wednesday after rumors swept Washington political circles that Jenkins had been arrested by officers of the D.C. Morals Division.

The record showed that Jenkins, 46, was picked up at the YMCA by two plainclothesmen of the Morals Division at 8:35 p.m. Wednesday, Oct. 7, on a charge of "disorderly (indecent) gestures." It said he "elected to forfeit."
(Continued on Back Page, Col. 2)

Nobel Prize to Dr. King

Compiled From AP and UPI

OSLO, Norway — Civil rights leader Dr. Martin Luther King Jr. was awarded the 1964 Nobel Peace Prize Wednesday.

The prize this year will amount to $53,123.

In Atlanta, Ga., King said he intends to spend every dollar of the prize money on the civil rights movement.

The Southern Christian Leadership Conference, of which King is president, will get most of the money, he said.

King said the award brings with it "a demand for deepening one's commitment to nonviolence as a philosophy of life . . . .

"It is also gratifying to know that the nations of the world recognize the civil rights movement in this country as so significant a moral force as to merit
(continued on Back Page, Col. 1)

'Arsenal' Seized in LBJ Threat

CORPUS CHRISTI, Tex. (UPI)
A reported threat to assassinate President Johnson led sheriff's deputies Tuesday night and Wednesday to an arsenal including weapons as big as a field mortar and a collection of Nazi relics.

Deputies arrested Julius Schmidt, 29, a plumber and gun trader, and another unidentified man who worked on guns. Still sought was the man who reportedly made the threat — a former mental patient believed to be in the Corpus Christi area.

"I do not believe there was a plot to kill the President, but I do think that one individual made such a statement (to kill the President) to an informant
(Continued on Back Page, Col. 3)

U.S. Marine Lt. Billy Mills is shoved by Tunisia's Mohamed Gamoudi near the end of the 10,000-meter run in the Olympics Wednesday. Mills held on to become the first American ever to win the event.   (AP Photo)

HST Better; Barry Sends Flowers

Compiled From AP and UPI

KANSAS CITY, Mo. Harry S. Truman, recovering satisfactorily from injuries suffered in a fall Tuesday, awoke Wednesday in a jovial mood in his hospital bed and quickly received his first flowers—from Sen. Barry Goldwater.

Along with the dozen red carnations was a card that said: "Get well. No campaign is worth the name without you." It was signed Barry Goldwater.

Commented Truman:

"That's one for the books."

Truman suffered two cracked ribs and a forehead gash in a fall in the bathroom of his ho...

A Research Hospital spokesman said Truman read the morning
(Continued on Back Page, Col. 4)

Yanks Rip Cards, Tie Series at 3-All—P. 9

YOU'RE OUT!

OCT. 5, 1950

2D DIV. IN KOREA — "Don't! Don't throw it!"

The screams rang through an area occupied by a 2nd Inf. Div. collecting company in Korea. Men looked up to see Sgt. Lewis Sowles sitting bolt upright in his foxhole, screaming.

Everybody hit for cover, thinking Sowles was shouting at a North Korean grenade thrower.

Then he subsided.

It developed the sergeant was having a nightmare. The Yankees were beating the Dodgers, and the third baseman was about to heave the ball to first while the runner was sneaking home. Sowles, whose home is in Saratoga, Calif., explained that he was just a rabid baseball fan.

1,275 STROKES — PAR FOR MOUNT FUJI

JULY 19, 1956 BY DON SCHUCK

TOKYO — Painfully, I lined up the putt.

I dared not rim the cup or overshoot.

Some stones in the way . . . I brushed them aside. My guide motioned other climbers into silence.

I settled myself, placed the club, a pitching iron, wiggled, then slammed the ball 2,000 yards into the crater of Mt. Fuji.

Dreaming?

No, sir!

Tuesday I became the first man in history to drive a golf ball up Mt. Fuji.

And I did it in 1,275 strokes plus 27 lost balls and a charley horse. What's more, I dropped eight pounds.

It all started when I made a few rash statements that American League sluggers would blast the National Leaguers right out of Griffith Stadium in the recent All-Star game. I had more takers than there are getas in Japan. I accepted a bet from co-worker George Payette.

The stakes: Loser drives a golf ball up Mt. Fuji. The loser: Me. Nationals won 7-3.

Armed with permission from local police, prefectural authorities and Ikou Fujimura, chief of the Mt. Fuji Observatory, a fellow worker, Lee Torliatt, and I left Monday after work.

We spent the night at the base of Mt. Fuji, then began the climb early Tuesday.

At 5:30 a.m. Tuesday I teed off.

What a fairway! A 12,395-foot sand trap full of rocks, climbers and horses . . . and uphill all the way.

Our pre-climbing exercises — swimming, walking, riding streetcars — began to pay off.

Some of those slopes were so bad I played polo trying to keep up with the roll-backs. Once the ball hit a rock and bounced halfway back down the mountain.

We had expected some reaction from the other climbers . . . but not a single double take. They apparently expected to see an American hitting a golf ball up Fuji.

The only exceptions were caretakers at rest stations. They always came out to take a few swings. One caretaker slammed a ball into a rock and it ricocheted off and hit me.

He "gomened" all over the place until I hit a ball and ricocheted it into myself.

Satisfied it was all part of the game, he went back inside.

By 4:20 p.m. we had reached the top and I sank my putt to hole out in 1,275 strokes.

Then I racked up another record for myself. The longest drive in golf history . . . 12,395 feet . . . straight down Fuji.

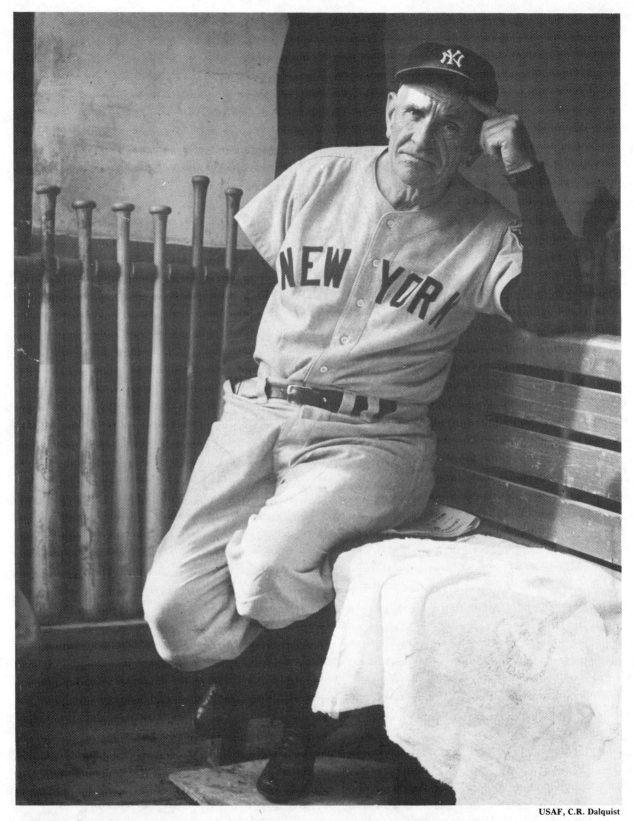

GRAND OLD MAN of the grand old game, Casey Stengel, looks moody and pensive in a Japanese dugout during a 1955 tour by the New York Yankees — perhaps because of his strained ties with second baseman Billy Martin, a hard-to-handle handful even back then.

PS&S, Ken George

HIS EYE ON THE BALL, Hank Aaron sends an out-of-sight drive soaring over the head of the crowd at Korakuen Stadium in Tokyo, giving fans all the powerhouse performance they paid to see. Not bad, they allowed, for a man who had passed 50 and was as old as professional baseball in Japan. Aaron came to mark the anniversary with thousands who still remembered his 1974 batting duel with Japanese ace Sadaharu Oh (inset), who had an alltime homer record of 868 to Aaron's 715.

JOLTIN' JOE DiMaggio shows a Japanese player how to put shoulder and torso behind a home-run drive during a 1950 exhibition game at Korakuen Stadium, Tokyo. Lefty O' Doul, San Francisco Seals manager, gives the master's lesson a critical eye.

LOSING GAMES BUT WINNING FRIENDS, Brooklyn Dodger batting ace Duke Snider greets a young fan who came to cheer him up as the Dodgers marked up their second loss in three games during a disastrous 1956 junket around Japan. "Dem bums" looked and played that way the entire tour.

We spent the night there, then returned Wednesday to Tokyo. The cheers and acclamation of my wife greeted me.

"I was so worried," she sobbed. "You had the car keys with you."

Hillary and Tensing, I'm ready when you are.

A profile on former boxing great Barney Ross, who died of throat cancer at the age of 57 in Chicago Wednesday.

THE CHAMP'S LAST FIGHT

JAN. 22, 1967 BY KENT NIXON

A few drinks and some men are what they once dreamed of being — but Barney Ross was what he once had been.

"Hit me," he commanded.

"Barney!"

"I mean it. Throw a punch" His voice was calm. He stood straight, all 5-feet-7 inches of him.

I had had a few, also. But he was 25 years older and nine inches shorter. More than that, I idolized him. In a case like this, you do what you are told. I swung at him — but with his open hand he blocked my effort before it had gone six inches.

I tried a left, only this time he was faster and he seemed like a scoutmaster reproaching me for dirty fingernails as he looked disdainfully at my hand.

"See what I mean? The moment I saw your shoulder twitch, I knew you were going to punch. Now, notice how I plant my feet. I'm not going to move them but watch the rest of me."

He dodged, feinted, bucked, bobbed his head, rolled his eyes implying he would hit my left side and then shot a jab toward my right shoulder — a jab he kept from landing.

"See?"

I said I did and, to change the subject, quickly turned to order another round.

This happened in 1960 at Grossinger, N.Y., the lush Catskills resort where then heavyweight champ Ingemar Johansson was training for his first defense against Floyd Patterson.

I was there to get the usual pre-fight stories on Ingo, yet it was Barney, vacationing there, who left the more vivid impression.

Let's go back to Yankee Stadium, which can be the most beautiful place in the world on a bright sunny day in June. It was just that on a day in 1946 when thousands of fans in the seats behind and around home plate jumped up to yell:

"Yaaay, champ!" "Way to go Barney!" as a paunchy beefy-faced grey-haired little guy stepped jauntily to his seat.

Some theater people have been known to make a work of art of a short walk across a stage. Barney's walk was his own Declaration of Independence. Chin up, shoulders back, head high and from somewhere in his ankles to his calves those springs that gave him that bounce. Not the "dream street dance" of ex-fighters who have been hit on the head too much. Those guys are on their heels. Barney bounced up and forward. Always.

Unknown to most of those who cheered him, it was a moment of triumph for Barney. He had just won his biggest battle over his toughest foe. He had just defeated drug addiction. After several months in the U.S. Public Service Hospital at Lexington, Ky.

The look on his face? It was an ear-to-ear smile of wonder tinged with disbelief that this spontaneous accolade was for him, that the Big Town still remembered him, and cared, though he had fought his last fight near there eight years before.

But why not? Ross, a hero in the ring as lightweight, junior welterweight and welterweight champ in a city that takes its heroes to heart, joined the Marine Corps when he was 32 and won the Silver Star on Guadalcanal.

It was because of wounds he received there that he was injected with morphine, setting him up for the addiction and, ultimately, his biggest victory.

But the words "drug addiction" until recent-

PAST HIS PRIME but still fit, former Heavyweight Champion Joe Louis wears the glum deadpan of his glory days as he steps through a lively round with Navy Petty Officer 3rd Class Lee Giles before Japanese and American fans at Korakuen Stadium in Tokyo. Giles was picked as the best of the local service boxers for the 1951 one-rounder, a benefit exhibition for underprivileged kids.

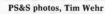

BIZARRE MATCH between Heavyweight Boxing Champion Muhammad Ali and alleged world wrestling titlist Antonio Inoki was supposed to resolve a profound question that had moved generations of barflies to spirited debate: which of the two skills would beat the other in a mixed bout? What fans at the Tokyo Budokan saw was a boxer who, instead of knocking his man down, spent the whole miscalled fight trying to get him on his feet. Inoki stayed on his back and kicked at the back of Ali's legs, trying to pull him down for a killing hold. The two combatants looked like nursery brawlers and the farcical 15-rounder, ruled a draw, finished with a shower of debris from outraged fans — particularly those who had paid $1,000 for ringside seats.

PS&S photos, Tim Wehr

THUMPING LEFT from American bantamweight Louis Henry Johnson throws grimacing Dutchman Jan Huppen against the ropes in a flash of action during the 1964 Olympic boxing tournament at Korakuen Ice Palace. Johnson won that fight but no Gold Medal.

PS&S, Hideyuki Mihashi

ON HIS WAY TO A WORLD TITLE, via the 1964 Tokyo Olympics, American heavyweight Joe Frazier ruins the whole evening of Soviet semifinalist Vadim Yemelyanov by dumping him in the second round. Frazier, who won the Gold Medal, was a last-minute team substitute for a fighter who had broken his hand.

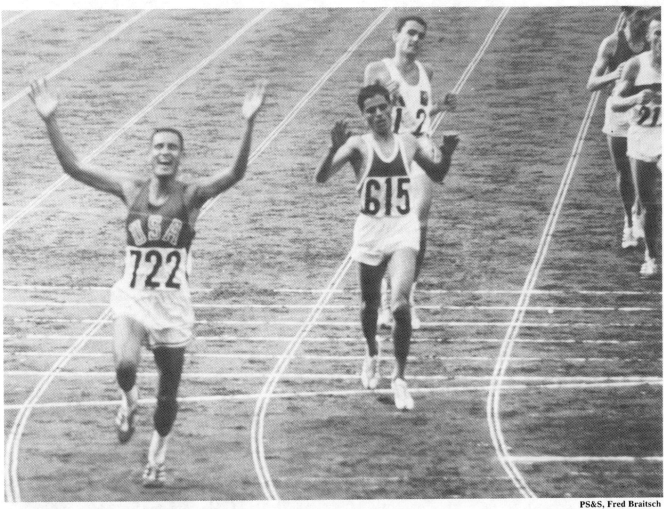

PS&S, Fred Braitsch

A JOYFUL WINNER, U.S. Marine Lt. Billy Mills snaps the tape at National Stadium in Tokyo to finish first in the 10,000 meter run at the 1964 Olympics — the first American to win that event in the history of the games. Mills recovered from being knocked off stride by Tunisian Mohamed Gammoudi (615), who is just ahead of Australian Ron Clarke. Clarke, heavily favored to win the race, was asked if he'd worried about Mills. "Worried about him?" Clarke said of the unknown and little-rated Mills. "I never even heard of him."

IN ATONEMENT for a poor showing during a tournament in Tokyo, Barbara Potter clamps her racket between her teeth as she walks off the court at National Gymnasium — the scene of many important tournaments as Japan, still young in tennis, moves toward becoming a major force in the game. Jimmy Connors, another frequently seen star on Japanese courts, shows graceful form and two-handed power as he smashes back an opponent's drive.

PS&S photos, Ken George

EAST AND WEST MEET — literally and violently — in the Far East, as a collegiate East-West All-Star team from the United States clash in the annual Japan Bowl game before 26,000 Japanese and American fans in Yokohama. American football, played by Americans, has made a slow but meaningful start in Japan, where it has to compete with a longstanding rival — European soccer. This close and thrilling game, in early 1984, ended 26-21 and probably did a lot to win Japanese fans over to classic, crash-and-maul American football, a game that followed the first occupation troops ashore in 1945. One other sport played by military teams in those years — volleyball — was proficiently adopted by the Japanese, who fielded a Gold Medal women's team in the 1964 Tokyo Olympics and have impressed fans all over the world since then.

ly, were as savory as leprosy and for years Ross had to keep his chin high against slow-dying gossip. "Once a junkie, always a junkie," was the rumble behind his back.

On a plane ride to Indianapolis in 1955, I sat next to Jack Dempsey.

"Barney Ross is on the plane up front," Dempsey said proudly. He was quick to read the question, no, the accusation my frown formed. "Oh, no," he rallied to Ross's aid, "he's off the stuff. Has been since '46."

Back to Grossinger's in 1960. "Barney, what about Henry Armstrong, the man who beat you and took your title away from you in your last fight in 1938?"

"He was ordained a Baptist minister in 1951," he answered in his way of just saying the words, letting their value add up.

The fight Ross and Armstrong had May 31, 1938, in Long Island City Bowl, N.Y., was one of boxing's classics. Actually there were two champions in the ring at the same time. Armstrong, who pummelled Ross almost at will in the later rounds, was the emerging champ. Ross, proud, gutsy, calling on skills he no longer possessed, went the full 15 rounds and lost the way a champ should — giving it all he had.

Nobody knows people in the way a fighter does. You stand and slug it out toe-to-toe with another guy and you know when he's hurt, and he knows when you're in pain, but the name of the game is do your best, beat the other guy, yet in a sense you and the other guy are partners in something that is the essence of life: The quest for perfection.

The purity of that search may have been forged into the lives of these two men as they did their best to annihilate each other that night.

Armstrong became a fighter for people's souls.

"And you, Barney — what about you?"

"Aw, I make a buck here and there reffing fights. Sometimes a little PR work."

Let Whitey Binstein, the veteran trainer, at the resort on Johansson's behalf, tell it:

"Barney Ross belongs to the public and the public never had it so good," he said when Ross wasn't around. "Benefits, veterans' hospitals, people with the (drug) habit. He's on call 24 hours a day. He doesn't really belong to himself."

Five years later, I saw Barney in Tokyo. He was here to be the third man in the ring for the bantamweight title fight between then champion Eder Jofre of Brazil and Masahiko (Fighting) Harada of Japan.

Those who saw the fight on TV or at Nagoya will recall that when Ross was introduced he danced, shuffled and threw a few fast shadow-boxing punches.

Two days before the fight he opened up, told about "my real interest," a Harlem clinic (The Haven) where he had been helping youths shake drug addiction. "A shocking number of our kids have become addicted. But I know boxing is a key to the development of kids with narcotics and other problems. It's how I got my start through the Catholic Youth Organization in Chicago."

When Barney looked at you and talked to you the walls could be falling around him and he wouldn't stop. He was like this when I asked if he might visit U.S. troops in Vietnam.

"I want to but I've had 31 malarial attacks and the doctors won't let me."

Did he have any message for the boys down there?

When Barney smiles it's like a reward for something you don't deserve.

"For the boys? Tell 'em I'm with 'em the only way I can be — here." He thumped his fist against his chest.

He said good-bye in the dimly lighted (for artistic reason, perhaps) lobby of a downtown Tokyo hotel. "Take care, huh?" he said, turned and — with that jaunty bounce — went to the elevator.

I like to think there was something prophetic about it. There he stood in the shadows with several other persons. You couldn't recognize faces, just their silhouettes, in the faint light.

The elevator door opened, he and the others stepped in, the door closed and they went up.

How do I know he went up? I knew Barney.

SUMO WRESTLING, in feudal Japan a stressful offering to gods who might otherwise deliver a poor harvest or unleash a destructive typhoon, is today a ceremonial sport followed by millions — including Americans who have chapter-and-verse knowledge of wrestlers and ratings. One of the most popular and well followed is Hawaiian-born Jesse Kuhaulua (above), the first foreigner to crash into top ratings. The sport is colorful ritual and a brief flash of action, with matches often lasting a few seconds and seldom going beyond a few minutes — until one contestant is forced off his feet or pushed beyond a circular barrier atop an earthen mound. An important part of the warmup is the stomping of bare feet to trample evil spirits, purifying the ring for lively action and fair play.

PS&S, Bob Wickley

265

LOOKING PRAYERFUL, a young sumo novice limbers up before a hard day of drills and workouts, supervised by seniors in the Takasago Sumo Stable. He was up before sunrise and will be pushed through brutal labor past dusk — to see if he has that spark of *yamatodamashi* fighting spirit that makes a champion.

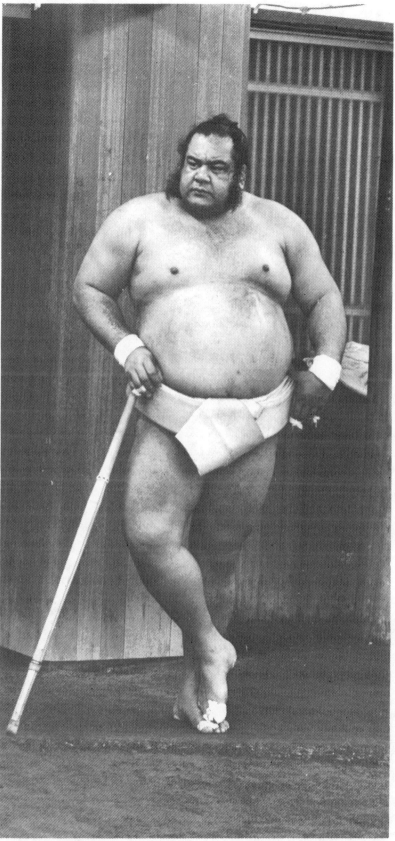

TAKAMIYAMA — the ring name Jesse took for himself in Japan — little resembles the lean, fit high school football star who first came to Tokyo in the 1960s. He put on the traditional bulk of most sumoists, the kind that would be the despair of trainers and coaches in another part of the world. In his later wrestling years — before a disabled elbow forced his retirement — Jesse was a frowning taskmaster, standing by with a bamboo rod, ready to swing it on any novice who wasn't showing that combative spark or putting forth his best.Takamiyama took Japanese citizenship, today runs his own stable of ambitious beginners.

INDEX